Detecting Deception

Wiley Series in

the Psychology of Crime, Policing and Law

Series Editors
Graham M. Davies and Ray Bull
University of Leicester, UK

The Wiley Series in the Psychology of Crime, Policing and Law publishes concise and integrative reviews on important emerging areas of contemporary research. The purpose of the series is not merely to present research findings in a clear and readable form, but also to bring out their implications for both practice and policy. In this way, it is hoped the series will not only be useful to psychologists but also to all those concerned with crime detection and prevention, policing, and the judicial process.

For other titles in this series please see www.wiley.com/go/pcpl

Detecting Deception

Current Challenges and Cognitive Approaches

Edited by

**Pär Anders Granhag, Aldert Vrij
and Bruno Verschuere**

WILEY Blackwell

This edition first published 2015
© 2015 John Wiley & Sons, Ltd.

Registered Office
John Wiley & Sons, Ltd, The Atrium, Southern Gate, Chichester, West Sussex,
PO19 8SQ, UK

Editorial Offices
350 Main Street, Malden, MA 02148-5020, USA
9600 Garsington Road, Oxford, OX4 2DQ, UK
The Atrium, Southern Gate, Chichester, West Sussex, PO19 8SQ, UK

For details of our global editorial offices, for customer services, and for information
about how to apply for permission to reuse the copyright material in this book please
see our website at www.wiley.com/wiley-blackwell.

Library of Congress Cataloging-in-Publication Data

Detecting deception : current challenges and cognitive approaches / edited by
Pär Anders Granhag, Aldert Vrij, and Bruno Verschuere.
      pages cm
  Includes bibliographical references and index.
  ISBN 978-1-118-50966-1 (cloth) – ISBN 978-1-118-50975-3 (pbk.)
1. Lie detectors and detection.   2. Forensic psychology.   3. Deception.
I. Granhag, Pär Anders, editor.   II. Vrij, Aldert, editor.   III. Verschuere,
Bruno, editor.
  HV8078.D463 2015
  614'.15–dc23

                                                                2014020572

A catalogue record for this book is available from the British Library.

Cover image: Women behind mask © selimaksan/iStock
Set in 10/12pt NewCenturySchlbk by SPi Publisher Services, Pondicherry, India
Printed and bound in Malaysia by Vivar Printing Sdn Bhd

1   2015

Contents

Contributors

Charles F. Bond

Texas Christian University, Fort Worth, TX, USA

Franziska Clemens

Department of Psychology, University of Gothenburg, Gothenburg, Sweden

Stacey M. Conchie

Department of Psychology, Lancaster University, Lancaster, UK

Evelyne Debey

Department of Experimental-Clinical and Health Psychology, Ghent University, Ghent, Belgium

Eitan Elaad

Department of Behavioral Sciences, Ariel University, Ariel, Israel

Giorgio Ganis

School of Psychology, University of Plymouth, Plymouth, UK
Department of Radiology, Harvard Medical School,
Boston, MA, USA
Massachusetts General Hospital, Athinoula A. Martinos Center for Biomedical Imaging, Charlestown, MA, USA

Pär Anders Granhag

Department of Psychology, University of Gothenburg,
Gothenburg, Sweden
Norwegian Police University College, Oslo, Norway

Maria Hartwig

Department of Psychology, John Jay College of Criminal Justice, City
University of New York, New York, NY, USA

William G. Iacono

Department of Psychology,
University of Minnesota, Minneapolis, MN, USA

Samuel Larner

School of Language Literature and International Studies, University
of Central Lancashire, Lancashire, UK

Timothy R. Levine

Media School, Korea University, Seoul, South Korea

Erik Mac Giolla

Department of Psychology, University of Gothenburg, Gothenburg,
Sweden

Ewout H. Meijer

Department of Clinical Psychological Science,
Maastricht University,
Maastricht, the Netherlands

Kristina Suchotzki

Department of Experimental-Clinical and Health Psychology, Ghent
University, Ghent, Belgium

Paul J. Taylor

Department of Psychology, Lancaster University, Lancaster, UK
Department of Psychology of Conflict, Risk and Safety, Twente
University, Enschede, the Netherlands

Bruno Verschuere

Department of Clinical Psychology, University of Amsterdam,
Amsterdam, the Netherlands
Department of Clinical Psychological Science, Maastricht University,
Maastricht, The Netherlands
Department of Experimental Clinical and Health Psychology, Ghent
University, Ghent, Belgium

Aldert Vrij

Psychology Department, University of Portsmouth, Portsmouth, UK

Sophie van der Zee

Department of Psychology, Lancaster University, Lancaster, UK

Series Preface

The Wiley Series on the Psychology of Crime, Policing and the Law publishes reviews of important areas of contemporary research. Books in the series not only present research findings in a clear and readable form, they also bring out their implications for both practice and policy. Thus, books in the series are not only of use to psychologists but also to all those concerned with policing, crime investigation and prevention, and judicial processes.

The current volume has a focus on the detection of deception and of truthfulness. Each chapter commendably commences with a clear statement of the main issues to be addressed. Chapter 1 overviews three techniques for assessing the veracity of verbal accounts and importantly it then compares these with United States Supreme Court guidelines regarding the admittance of expert evidence. Chapter 2 has a complementary focus on the possible use of non-verbal techniques and innovatively contends that those cues which might be the most useful are those that have relatively rarely been researched. It also mentions some crucial research on the effects of people having the appearance of being honest/deceptive. Chapter 3 interestingly highlights the promises and pitfalls of the use of polygraph procedures for the detection of truthfulness/deception, and it also presents new research on trying to extract/determine information not yet known to the investigator. Although this chapter does not review 'countermeasures', this is done in Chapter 4 on the use of event-related brain potentials. That chapter also importantly mentions procedures that should prevent participants trying not to attend to the stimuli being presented, though more work is needed on how best to try to detect those who have 'guilty knowledge' because they are falsely 'confessing' on behalf of someone else who has passed on that 'knowledge' to them.

Chapter 5 is on the possible role of brain imaging (i.e. functional magnetic resonance imaging, fMRI) which focuses on the 'mental states' that may be associated with lying/truth-telling, rather than on other detection phenomena (such as contradictions in what a person says). It offers some optimism that when further research has been conducted, such a procedure may turn out to be of some use in certain situations (e.g. when the person being tested agrees to have their brain activity monitored). Chapter 6 examines the beliefs that most people have about the behaviours associated with lying, which seem to be rather similar across the cultures studied to date. A limited number of such beliefs are supported from research on actual cues, such as plausibility/coherence/inconsistency and amount of details. Interestingly, prison inmates' views seem to be more valid than other people's. Lying about intentions is the focus of the following, innovative chapter, Chapter 7, which addresses the crucial question of whether what we know concerning lying about the past can fully generalize to lying about the future. However, lying about intentions may sometimes involve lying about past thoughts (of not yet conducted actions).

Chapter 8 importantly demonstrates that the accuracy of truth/deception detection can be poorer when made cross culturally and reminds us that cultural differences exist in the acceptability of deception. Chapter 9 adopts a 'cognitive load' approach, looking at interventions rather recently developed to try to enhance the difference in such load between truth-tellers and liars that may result in less plausible accounts/answers or fewer details being produced by liars (if people are interviewed/interrogated in ways that allow them to provide as much information as possible). The strategic use of evidence is the focus of Chapter 10 which meaningfully presents detailed explanations and examples of ways in which interviewers can reveal information to suspects not only in terms of the timing of such disclosures but also in the 'framing' of the information.

Chapter 11 examines the relatively new topic of what stimulating certain parts of the brain could tell us about deception processes. The few studies available to date have not produced consistent results. Whether it takes deceivers longer to react to certain items is covered in Chapter 12, which suggests that it might – though research on real life conditions is needed. Chapter 13 addresses the crucial topic of suspects' counter-interrogation/interview strategies on which little research has to date been published. Such strategies include those who are being deceptive saying as little as possible, thus it is important to interview these in ways that encourage them to speak/converse (as advocated for over 20 years now by the British PEACE approach). The final chapter, Chapter 14, focuses on 'covert' methods such as micro expressions, voice stress, eye tracking, and facial thermal imaging, noting that these raise issues of ethics/consent/privacy. In addition, research on these topics has not produced consistent findings on possible efficacy.

One of the many strengths of this book is that its chapter authors appropriately mention the limitations of the available research, including their own work. Thus, the contents of this excellent book are believable.

Ray Bull, April 2014

Introduction

Deception, a deliberate attempt to convince someone of something the liar believes is untrue, is a fact of everyday life. DePaulo and her colleagues (1996) asked participants to keep a diary for a week of all their social interactions that lasted more than 10 min and to note how often they lied during these interactions. Almost all participants admitted that they had lied during the week they kept a diary. They lied in one out of every four social interactions and to more than 30% of all the people they interacted with.

The overwhelming majority of lies people tell are not serious, and many lies told in daily life are social lies (e.g. 'I like your hair cut'). Conversations could become awkward and unnecessarily rude, and social interactions, including friendships and romantic relationships, could easily turn sour if people were to tell each other the truth all the time. In order to maintain a good working relationship with colleagues, it is better to pretend to be busy when invited for lunch than to admit that you find their company boring and would rather avoid them. Similarly, it may be kinder to respond with enthusiasm when receiving an expensive present from a friend even when you don't like the gift. Social relationships benefit from people making each other compliments now and again because people like to be liked and like to receive compliments (Aron, Dutton, Aron, & Iverson, 1989).

However, sometimes the situation is different. Sometimes the lies that are told are serious, and we would like to detect them. Who would not have liked to know earlier that Mohammad Atta and 18 others came to the United States with the intention to carry out four coordinated suicide attacks on the New York Twin Towers, the Pentagon and the White House? In a similar vein, the police detective wants to know whether the suspect's alibi is reliable, the customs officer wants to know whether the traveler really has nothing to declare, the immigration officer wants to know whether the asylum seeker's life in his native country is indeed in danger as he claims, and the employer wants to know whether the candidate is indeed as capable as the candidate says. Being able to detect these sorts of lies would benefit individuals or the society as a whole.

In order to detect serious lies, researchers have been examining how liars respond and how they could be detected. There are four general approaches to detect lies. Investigators could measure someone's (i) physiological responses, (ii) observe their behaviour, (iii) analyse their speech, or (iv) measure their brain activity.

Throughout history, it has been assumed that lying is accompanied by physiological activity within the liar's body. The underlying assumption was that the fear of being detected was an essential element of deception (Trovillo, 1939). Early lie detection attempts were based on the idea that fear is associated with a dry mouth. Therefore, the Chinese in 1000 B.C., but also people in India and Western Africa, used to force suspected liars to chew rice powder and then to spit it out. If the resultant powder was dry then the person was judged to have been lying (Kleinmuntz & Szucko, 1984; Trovillo, 1939). Based on the same dry mouth assumption, the accused in north Bengal was told to prove his innocence by applying his tongue to a red-hot iron nine times. The full extent of this ordeal becomes clear when one realizes that the accused was also instructed to carry the red-hot iron in their hands (Trovillo, 1939).

Analyses of non-verbal behaviour also have a long history, and it also assumes fear underlies deception. A Hindu writing from 900 B.C. mentioned that liars rub the great toe along the ground and shiver and they rub the roots of their hair with their fingers (Trovillo, 1939), and Münsterberg (1908) described the utility of observing posture, eye movements, and knee jerks for lie detection purposes.

Lie detection through analysing speech also became apparent throughout history. In around 900 B.C., a papyrus of the Vedas described how to identify a poisoner. In addition to some physiological and behavioural cues, it says that a poisoner 'does not answer questions, or they give evasive answers; he speaks nonsense' (Trovillo, 1939, p. 849). Tardieu, a French forensic expert, already acknowledged in the 1850s that in children's alleged sexual abuse cases, certain characteristics in the story needs to be considered, such as 'quantity of detail' (Lamers-Winkelman, 1999). Walker (1886), an American forensic medical doctor, claimed that mere reliance upon the physical examination in alleged child sexual abuse cases is unreliable. Rather, according to Walker, children should be encouraged to tell their stories in their own words, and the way in which children tell their stories and the expressions they use are amongst the best guides to distinguish truth from deception in children (see Lamers-Winkelman, 1999).

Since the 1950s, the search for (non)verbal cues and physiological cues to deceit has accelerated. The development of methods to monitor neural activity non-invasively in humans, such as electroencephalography (EEG) and functional magnetic resonance imaging (fMRI), has enabled researchers to examine brain activity during deceit, the fourth way of detecting lies nowadays used to detect deceit. The use of EEG to detect deceit dates back to the late 1980s (Rosenfeld et al., 1988), whereas the first fMRI article on deception was published in 2001 (Spence et al., 2001).

THE PRESENT VOLUME

The field of 'deception detection' is one of the most expansive sub-fields of legal psychology. All major scientific journals in the field regularly publish papers on lie detection, and to date more than 150 articles about deception are published each year. Furthermore, most conferences on 'psychology and law' contain special seminars on how to detect deceit. Hence, it makes sense to now and then take stock of the field.

The present state-of-the-art volume differs from previous volumes in several ways. First, in addition to reviewing the most established approaches for detecting deceit, it also acknowledges a number of new challenges (e.g., how to discriminate between true and false intentions and how to covertly detect deceit). Second, the present volume takes a strong cognitive approach to deception detection. This in contrast to the more traditional anxiety-based approaches (basically, fear and/or anxiety is assumed to be stronger in liars than in truth tellers). The cognitive approach is visible by paying particular attention to the mental processes at play when lying and telling the truth. For example, the volume makes clear that concepts such as 'memory', 'cognitive load', 'reality monitoring', 'planning', 'episodic future thought', 'strategizing' and 'perspective-taking' are highly relevant for deception detection. Third, many of the chapters in the volume reflect a new wave in deception research – 'interviewing to detect deception'. For this new direction, the interviewer plays a vital role and the aim is to elicit and enhance cues to deceit by interviewing strategically (Vrij & Granhag, 2012). This new strand of research contrasts the traditional way of conducting deception detection research, in which observers assess short video clips in which there are few (if any) cues to deceit and truth.

The volume contains 14 chapters, organized into three main sections. The first section, 'Established Approaches', contains five chapters and offer comprehensive and up-to-date reviews of the most basic approaches to deception detection. The second section, 'Current Challenges', contains three chapters and draws attention to some current and future challenges in the field. The third and final section is 'Improving lie detection' and it contains six chapters. In this section, new and constructive approaches for detecting deceit are described and developed. All in all, we believe that the volume will be perceived as instructive for practitioners in the field and inspiring for academics.

REFERENCES

Aron, A., Dutton, D. G., Aron, E. N., & Iverson, A. (1989). Experiences of falling in love. *Journal of Social and Personal Relationships, 6*, 243–257.

DePaulo, B. M., Kashy, D. A., Kirkendol, S. E., Wyer, M. M., & Epstein, J. A. (1996). Lying in everyday life. *Journal of Personality and Social Psychology, 70*, 979–995.

Kleinmuntz, B., & Szucko, J. J. (1984). Lie detection in ancient and modern times: A call for contemporary scientific study. *American Psychologist, 39*, 766–776.

Lamers-Winkelman, F. (1999). Statement validity analysis: Its application to a sample of Dutch children who may have been sexually abused. *Journal of Aggression, Maltreatment & Trauma, 2*, 59–81.

Münsterberg, H. (1908). *On the witness stand: Essays on psychology and crime.* New York, NY: Doubleday.

Rosenfeld, J. P., Cantwell, B., Nasman, V. T., Wojdac, V., Ivanov, S., & Mazzeri, L. (1988). A modified, event-related potential-based guilty knowledge test. *International Journal of Neuroscience, 42*, 157–161.

Spence, S. A., Farrow, T. F. D., Herford, A. E., Wilkinson, I. D., Zheng, Y., & Woodruff, P. W. (2001). Behavioral and functional anatomical correlates of deception in humans. *Neuroreport, 12*, 2849–2853.

Trovillo, P. V. (1939). A history of lie detection, I. *Journal of Criminal Law and Criminology, 29*, 848–881.

Vrij, A., & Granhag, P. A. (2012). Eliciting cues to deception and truth: What matters are the questions asked. *Journal of Applied Research in Memory and Cognition, 1*, 110–117.

Walker, J. (1886). Reports, with comments, of twenty-one cases of indecent assault and rape upon children. *Archives of Pediatrics, 3*, 269–286.

Acknowledgements

We would like to thank all contributing authors for taking on their task so seriously. We used an external review system, where a group of international experts offered comments which sent the volume in the right direction. We would like to thank Lucy Akehurst (UK), Matthias Gamer (Germany), Maria Hartwig (USA), Jaume Masip (Spain), Ewout Meijer (the Netherlands), Henry Otgaar (the Netherlands), Teresa Schuhmann (the Netherlands) and Kristina Suchotzki (Belgium). We would also like to thank Femke Brankaert for helping us with the Index.

Section I

Deception Detection: Established Approaches

1

Verbal Lie Detection Tools: Statement Validity Analysis, Reality Monitoring and Scientific Content Analysis

ALDERT VRIJ

One approach to detecting lies that has a long history is to analyse speech content. In around 900 BC, a papyrus of the Vedas described how to identify a poisoner. In addition to some physiological and behavioural cues, it says that a poisoner 'does not answer questions, or they give evasive answers; he speaks nonsense' (Trovillo, 1939, p. 849). Tardieu, a French forensic expert, already acknowledged in the 1850s that in children's alleged sexual abuse cases, certain characteristics in the story needs to be considered, such as 'quantity of detail' (Lamers-Winkelman, 1999). Walker (1886), an American forensic medical doctor, claimed that mere reliance upon the physical examination in alleged child sexual abuse cases is unreliable. Rather, according to Walker, children should be encouraged to tell their stories in their own words, and the way in which children tell their stories and the expressions they

Detecting Deception: Current Challenges and Cognitive Approaches, First Edition.
Edited by Pär Anders Granhag, Aldert Vrij, and Bruno Verschuere.
© 2015 John Wiley & Sons, Ltd. Published 2015 by John Wiley & Sons, Ltd.

use are amongst the best guides to distinguish truth from deception in children (see Lamers-Winkelman, 1999).

Since the 1950s, the search for verbal cues to deceit has accelerated, and to date, a substantial number have been found to be diagnostic for deceit (DePaulo et al., 2003; Masip, Sporer, Garrido, & Herrero, 2005; Vrij, 2008). Some verbal cues are measured in isolation, but most are examined as part of verbal veracity assessment tools and this chapter discusses three of those tools: Statement Validity Analysis (SVA), Reality Monitoring (RM) and Scientific Content Analysis (SCAN). The focus is on those three tools because they are frequently used by practitioners and/or scholars. SVA is the most frequently researched verbal veracity tool to date and more than 50 studies have been published examining the working of this tool. It is also frequently used in daily life as SVA assessments are used as evidence in criminal courts in several European countries. RM is, to our knowledge, never used in real life but it is popular amongst scholars, perhaps because it has a solid theoretical background. The RM deception research body is substantial and more than 30 RM deception studies have been carried out to date. Conversely, SCAN is very popular in the field but has hardly been researched. This chapter provides only outlines of the three tools. For more detailed information about SVA, see Gumpert and Lindblad's (1999), Köhnken (2004), Raskin and Esplin (1991), Steller and Boychuk (1992) and Vrij (2005, 2008). For more detailed information about RM, see Masip et al. (2005), Sporer (2004) and Vrij (2008). For more detailed information about SCAN, see Armistead (2011), Driscoll (1994), Nahari, Vrij, and Fisher (2012) and Smith (2001).

The final section of this chapter compares the three tools by using the set of guidelines provided by the United States Supreme Court for admitting expert scientific evidence in (American) federal courts. These guidelines give good opportunity to summarize the key aspects of the tools, the extent to which they have been examined and the empirical and academic support each.

More than three verbal tools are available in the deception literature, of which two deserve special mention because they have potential. The Assessment Criteria Indicative of Deception (ACID) combines interview techniques aimed at eliciting cues to deception with the analysis of empirically derived content criteria (see Colwell, Hiscock-Anisman, and Fede (2013) for a review). The Aberdeen Report Judgment Scales are based on a factor analysis of RM and CBCA criteria and theoretical considerations such as autobiographical memory, the social psychology of attribution, and impression management and deception (see Sporer (2004, 2012) for overviews).

STATEMENT VALIDITY ANALYSIS

Statement Validity Analysis is a tool designed to determine the credibility of *child* witnesses' testimonies in trials for *sexual offences*. It is not surprising that a technique has been developed to verify whether or not a child has been sexually abused. It is often difficult to determine the facts in an allegation of sexual abuse, since often there is no medical or physical evidence. Frequently, the alleged victim and the defendant give contradictory testimony, and often there are no independent witnesses to give an objective version of events. This makes the perceived credibility of the defendant and alleged victim important. The alleged victim is in a disadvantageous position if he or she is a child, as adults have a tendency to mistrust statements made by children.

SVA assessments are accepted as evidence in some North American courts and in criminal courts in several Western European countries including Germany, the Netherlands, Spain and Sweden (Vrij, 2008). The tool originates from Sweden (Trankell, 1972) and Germany (Undeutsch, 1982) and consists of four stages (Vrij, 2008): (i) a case-file analysis; (ii) a semi-structured interview; (iii) a Criteria-Based Content Analysis (CBCA) that systematically assesses the quality of the transcribed interviews and (iv) an evaluation of the CBCA outcome via a set of questions (Validity Checklist). Much of the SVA research is concerned with the ability of CBCA, one of the four SVA stages, to discriminate between truth tellers and liars. Also the Validity Checklist, another stage of the SVA procedure, has attracted attention from researchers.

A Case-File Analysis

The SVA procedure starts with the analysis of the case file. A case file should include information about the child witness (e.g. his or her age, cognitive abilities, relationship to the accused person), the nature of the event in question and previous statements of the child and other parties involved. The case-file analysis gives the SVA expert insight into what may have happened and the issues that are disputed. The SVA analysis focuses on these disputed elements in the subsequent three stages.

A Semi-Structured Interview

The second stage of SVA is a semi-structured interview where the child provides his or her own account of the allegation. Conducting a proper interview is never an easy task, but interviewing young children is particularly difficult, because their descriptions of past events are notably incomplete (Bull, 2010; Goodman & Melinder, 2007). Therefore, interviewers routinely want more information than is initially provided (Kebbel & Milne, 1998), and interviewers have to ask further, specific questions to learn more about an event. The danger that interviewers face is that their questioning may become suggestive. In that case, the question suggests to the child what the answer should be and, subsequently, leads the child to providing that answer.

Special interview techniques based upon psychological principles have been designed to obtain as much information as possible from interviewees in a free narrative style without inappropriate prompts or suggestions. The UK Home Office (2002) and the American Professional Society on the Abuse of Children (1997) as well as many researchers provide guidance for good interviewing techniques (Bull, 2010; Fisher, 2010; Lamb, Hershkowitz, Orbach, & Esplin, 2008), but Raskin and Esplin (1991) deserve special mention as they outlined interview procedures specifically for SVA interviews. They stress the importance of the interviewer becoming as familiar with the case material as possible, and that the interview should take place in a supportive but neutral environment designed to maximize the performance level of the child witness. They further describe the importance of establishing rapport with the child prior to the interview (by asking the child about something pleasant or interesting that the interviewer knows the child has recently experienced) and the importance of motivating the child to be completely truthful during the interview, for example by discussing the differences between truths and lies. During the actual interview, the interviewer should take great care to use language and concepts that are appropriate for the age and cognitive development of the child. In addition, questions should be asked one at a time, and an answer should be obtained prior to asking the next question. Questions and comments that create expectations (criticism or praise) should be avoided.

The interview should start with a free narrative ('I understand there is a problem in your family and I need you to tell me about it so that I can help'), and the interviewer must be patient when the child starts answering the question (never interrupt the child). A child can be encouraged to say more through questions such as 'Did anything else happen?' The next phase includes asking open-ended questions used to elicit additional detail that seems necessary to complete the descriptions already given by the child ('You said something also happened in the car, tell me about that?'). Direct questioning should only be used if the elicited information requires clarifications ('So you said he was sitting next to you and then he put his thing inside you. How did that happen?' or 'Did he take your clothes off?'). Probing questions may be used to obtain information to evaluate alternative hypotheses ('You told me that he did that when you were only two, but you said you don't remember it. How do you know what happened?'). The interview should always end on a positive note that leaves the child feeling good, for example, by introducing a topic that is pleasant for the child to discuss, such as plans for the upcoming holiday or birthday.

CRITERIA-BASED CONTENT ANALYSIS

The interviews are audiotaped and transcribed, and the transcripts are used for the second part of SVA: *the CBCA*. Trained evaluators judge the presence or absence of 19 criteria (see Table 1.1). CBCA is based on the hypothesis, originally stated by Undeutsch, that a statement derived from memory of an actual experience differs in content and quality from a statement based on invention or fantasy, known as the *Undeutsch Hypothesis* (Steller, 1989). The presence of each criterion strengthens the hypothesis that the account is based on genuine personal experience. In other words, truthful statements will have more of the elements measured by CBCA than false statements. A theoretical foundation for the Undeutsch Hypothesis was presented by Köhnken (1989, 1996, 2004), who proposed that both cognitive and motivational factors influence CBCA scores.

With regard to cognitive factors, it is assumed that the presence of several criteria (Criteria 1–13) is likely to indicate genuine experiences as they are typically too difficult to fabricate. Therefore, statements which are coherent and consistent (*logical structure*), whereby the information is not provided in a chronological time sequence (*unstructured production*) and which contain a significant amount of detail (*quantity of detail*) are more likely to be true. Regarding details, accounts are more likely to be truthful if they include *contextual embeddings* (references to time and space: 'He approached me for the first time in the garden during the summer holidays'), *descriptions of interactions* ('The moment my mother came into the room, he stopped smiling'), *reproduction of speech* (speech in its original form: 'And then he asked: Is that your coat?'), *unexpected complications* (elements incorporated in the statement which are somewhat unexpected, e.g. the child mentions that the perpetrator had difficulty with starting the engine of his car), *unusual details* (details which are uncommon but meaningful, e.g. a witness who describes that the man she met had a stutter) and *superfluous details* (descriptions which are not

Table 1.1   The criteria-based content analysis criteria

General characteristics

1. Logical structure	Coherency of the statement in terms of not containing logical inconsistencies or contradictions.
2. Unstructured production	The presentation of the information in a (non) chronological order.
3. Quantity of details	The inclusion of specific descriptions of place, time, persons, objects and events.

Specific contents

4. Contextual embedding	Events being placed in time and location, and actions being connected with other daily activities and/or customs.
5. Descriptions of interactions	Information that interlinks at least the alleged perpetrator and witness.
6. Reproduction of conversation	Parts of the conversation are reported in original form or if the different speakers are recognizable in the reproduced dialogues.
7. Unexpected complications during the incident	Elements incorporated in the statement that are somewhat unexpected.
8. Unusual details	Details of people, objects or events that are unique, unexpected or surprising but meaningful in the context.
9. Superfluous details	Details in connection with the allegations that are not essential for the accusation.
10. Accurately reported details misunderstood	Mentioning of details that are beyond the interviewee's comprehension.
11. Related external associations	Events are reported that are not actually part of the alleged offence but are merely related to the offence.
12. Accounts of subjective mental state	Development and change of feelings experienced at the time of the incident. This criterion also includes reports of thoughts.
13. Attribution of perpetrator's mental state	Descriptions of the alleged perpetrator's feelings, thoughts or motives during the incident.

Motivation-related contents

14. Spontaneous corrections	Corrections that are made or information that is added to material previously provided in the statement without having been prompted by the interviewer.

Table 1.1 *(Cont'd)*

15. Admitting lack of memory	An unprompted interviewee admitting lack of memory by either saying 'I don't know' or 'I don't remember'.
16. Raising doubts about one's own testimony	Interviewee indicating that part of his or her description sounds odd, implausible, unlikely, etc.
17. Self-deprecation	Inclusion of personally unfavourable, self-incriminating details.
18. Pardoning the perpetrator	Failing to blame the perpetrator or excusing his or her behaviour.
Offence-specific elements	
19. Details characteristic of the offence	Description of elements of the crime that are known by professionals to be typical for the type of crime under investigation but are counter-intuitive for the general public.

Adapted with permission from Vrij (2008). © John Wiley & Sons, Ltd.

essential to the allegation, e.g. a witness who describes that the perpetrator was allergic to cats). Another criterion that might indicate truthfulness is when a witness speaks of details that are beyond the horizon of his or her comprehension, for example, when he or she describes the adult's sexual behaviour but attributes it to a sneeze or to pain (*accurately reported details misunderstood*). Finally, possible indicators of truthfulness are: if the child reports details which are not part of the allegation but are related to it (*related external associations*, e.g. a witness who describes that the perpetrator talked about the women he had slept with and the differences between them), when the witness describes his or her feelings or thoughts experienced at the time of the incident (*accounts of subjective mental state*), or describes the perpetrator's feelings, thoughts or motives during the incident (*attribution of perpetrator's mental state*: 'He was nervous, his hands were shaking').

Other criteria (Criteria 14–18) are more likely to occur in truthful statements for motivational reasons. A truthful person will not be as concerned with impression management as a deceiver. Compared to truth tellers, deceivers will be more keen to try to construct a report which they believe will make a credible impression on others, and will leave out information which, in their view, will damage their image of being a sincere person (Köhnken, 1999). As a result, a truthful statement is more likely to contain information that is inconsistent with the stereotypes of truthfulness. The CBCA list includes five of these so-called 'contrary-to-truthfulness-stereotype' criteria (Ruby & Brigham, 1998): *spontaneous corrections* (corrections made without prompting from the interviewer ('He wore black trousers, no sorry, they were green'), *admitting lack of memory* (expressing concern that some parts of the statement might be incorrect: 'I think', 'Maybe', 'I am not sure', etc.), *raising doubts about one's own testimony* (anticipated objections against the veracity of one's own testimony: 'I know this all sounds really odd'), *self-deprecation* (mentioning personally unfavourable, self-incriminating details: 'Obviously it was stupid of me to leave my door wide open because my wallet was clearly visible on my desk') and *pardoning the perpetrator* (making excuses for the perpetrator or failing to blame him or her, such as a girl who says she now feels sympathy for the defendant who possibly faces imprisonment).

The final criterion relates to *details characteristic of the offense*. This criterion is present if a description of events is typical for the type of crime under investigation but is counter-intuitive for the general public. For example, a witness describes feelings that professionals know are typical for victims of incestuous relationships but that seem counter-intuitive and odd to the layman.

THE VALIDITY CHECKLIST

A CBCA evaluation itself is not sufficient to draw conclusions about the truthfulness of a statement, because CBCA scores may be affected by factors other than the veracity of the statement. Take for example the age of the interviewee. Cognitive abilities and command of language develop throughout childhood, making it gradually easier to give detailed accounts of what has been witnessed (Davies, 1991, 1994; Fivush, Haden, & Adam, 1995). Therefore, all sorts of details are less likely to occur in the statements of young children. Also, children under eight years old may have difficulty in viewing the world from somebody else's perspective (Flavell, Botkin, Fry, Wright, & Jarvis, 1968); thus Criterion 13 *accounts of perpetrator's mental state* is unlikely to occur in the statements of young children. Finally, younger children have less developed meta-cognitive and meta-memorial capabilities (i.e. knowing whether or not they know or remember an answer, Walker & Warren, 1995), so they are less likely to be aware of gaps in their memories (Criterion 15).

The fourth and final phase of the SVA method is to examine whether any of these alternative explanations might have affected the presence of the CBCA criteria in the transcripts. For this purpose, a checklist, the Validity Checklist, has been compiled, which comprises 11 issues (called 'external factors' hereafter) that are thought to possibly affect CBCA scores. By systematically addressing each of the external factors addressed in the Validity Checklist, the evaluator explores and considers alternative interpretations of the CBCA outcomes. Each affirmative response that the evaluator gives to an external factor raises a question about the validity of the CBCA outcome.

Detailed descriptions of the external factors mentioned in the Validity Checklist are provided by Raskin and Esplin (1991), Steller (1989), Steller and Boychuk (1992) and Yuille (1988). Slightly different versions of the Validity Checklist exist (different authors have used somewhat different versions). The Validity Checklist presented below is that published by Steller and colleagues (Steller, 1989; Steller & Boychuk, 1992). SVA evaluators consider the following external factors:

(1) appropriateness of language and knowledge, for example mental capability of the child; (2) appropriateness of affect shown by the interviewee; (3) interviewee's susceptibility to suggestion; (4) evidence of suggestive, leading or coercive questioning; (5) overall adequacy of the interview; (6) motives to report, for example, whether the interviewee's relationship with the accused, or other people involved, suggests possible motives for a false allegation; (7) context of the original disclosure or report, for example, whether there are questionable elements in the context of the original disclosure; (8) pressures to report falsely, such as indications that others suggested, coached, pressured or coerced the interviewee to make a false report; (9) consistency with the law of nature, whether the described events are unrealistic; (10) consistency with other statements, whether there are major elements in the statement that are inconsistent or contradicted by another statement made by this interviewee; and (11) consistency with other evidence, for example, whether there are major elements in the statement that are contradicted by reliable physical evidence or other concrete evidence.

In the fourth stage of the SVA procedure, *evaluation of the CBCA outcome*, the evaluator systematically addresses each of the external factors mentioned in the Validity Checklist, and explores and considers alternative interpretations of the CBCA outcomes.

SVA: Research

Despite the fact that SVA assessments are used as evidence in court in several countries, it is unclear how accurate these assessments are because no reliable data regarding the accuracy of SVA assessments in real-life cases are currently available. To examine the accuracy of SVA assessments in real-life cases, it is necessary to know what truly happened in the disputed event. Obtaining this so-called ground truth is difficult because it can only be determined via case facts, such as medical evidence or other evidence, which indisputably links, or does not link, the alleged perpetrator to the crime. Such case facts are often never present in sexual abuse cases. Instead, researchers often use 'soft' evidence as ground truth (such as confessions). It is a common problem in deception field studies that researchers do not know what truly happened in the cases that are included in their field study.

Research has been carried out in the form of laboratory studies, but it has mainly been focused on the third phase of SVA: the accuracy of CBCA assessments. Vrij (2008) reviewed the available CBCA literature, and a summary of this review is presented here. In those studies, either children, but more often undergraduate students, told the truth or lied for the sake of the experiment. Such studies have revealed similar results for adults and children. In alignment with the CBCA assumption, many CBCA criteria were more often present in truthful statements than in fabricated reports. Of the individual criteria, Criterion 3, *quantity of details*, received the most support. The amount of details was calculated in 29 studies (field studies and laboratory studies combined), and in 22 of those studies (76%), truth tellers included significantly more details into their accounts than liars. Moreover, in not a single study did truth tellers include significantly less details into their statements than liars. This is impressive support for Criterion 3. Other criteria that received strong support were Criterion 4, *contextual embeddings* (truth tellers included more contextual embeddings in 16 out of 26 studies examining this criterion), and Criterion 6, *reproduction of conversation* (truth tellers included more reproductions of conversations in 15 out of 25 studies examining this criterion). A total CBCA score was reported in 20 studies, and truth tellers obtained higher CBCA scores than liars in 16 out of those 20 studies, whereas in none of the studies did liars obtain a higher CBCA score than truth tellers. This represents strong support for the CBCA total score.

In 19 laboratory studies, CBCA accuracy rates for classifying truth tellers and liars were calculated. The results revealed that 71% of the truths and 71% of the lies were correctly classified by using CBCA assessments (Vrij, 2008), whereas 50% accuracy rate can be expected by chance alone (by tossing a coin). Whether this reflects the accuracy of CBCA assessments in real-life criminal investigations is unknown. Students or children who tell lies and truths in an experiment are different from children who tell truths and lies in criminal investigations, and the accuracy scores therefore do not necessarily reflect the accuracy scores in criminal investigations. Three early CBCA field studies have reported accuracy rates, and two of them yielded very high accuracy rates (Esplin, Boychuk, & Raskin, 1988; Parker & Brown, 2000). However, the ground truth in those two studies is unknown, and the results are therefore unreliable. Fortunately, two CBCA field studies have been published more recently (both involving child witnesses) in which ground truth was established in a satisfactory manner. In Akehurst, Manton, and Quandte (2011), only a low number of fabricated cases ($N = 10$) were included in the study, almost certainly because it is difficult to establish ground truth. In that study, two experts rated the transcripts. One expert classified 81% of the fabricated cases correctly, whereas the other rater classified 60% of the fabricated cases correctly. Roma, San Martini, Sabatello, Tatarelli, and Ferracuti (2011) included many cases in their field study (60 true and 49 false cases). Trained CBCA coders examined the presence or absence of 14 criteria in the transcribed interviews. True cases included considerably more CBCA criteria ($M = 7.63$) than false cases ($M = 4.08$), and this difference was substantial, $d = 2.67$.

There are reasons to believe that applying the Validity Checklist is sometimes problematic. It is possible to question the justification of some of the external factors listed on the Validity Checklist, for example *inappropriateness of affect*. This refers to whether the affect displayed by the child when being interviewed (usually nonverbal behaviour) is inappropriate for the child's alleged experiences. This external factor implies that the notion of appropriate affect displayed by victims of sexual abuse exists, whereas it does not. That is, in interviews, some sexually abused victims express distress that is clearly visible to outsiders, whereby others appear numbed and cues of distress are not clearly visible (Burgess, 1985; Vrij & Fischer, 1997). The communication styles represent a personality factor and are not related to deceit (Littmann & Szewczyk, 1983). Yet, emotional victims are more readily believed than victims who report their experience in a controlled manner (Baldry & Winkel, 1998; Baldry, Winkel, & Enthoven, 1997; Bollingmo, Wessel, Eilertsen, & Magnussen, 2008; Bothwell & Jalil, 1992; Hackett, Day, & Mohr, 2008; Kaufmann, Drevland, Wessel, Overskeid, & Magnussen, 2003; Rose, Nadler, & Clark, 2006; Vrij & Fischer, 1997; Wessel, Drevland, Eilertsen, & Magnussen, 2006).

Some other external factors are difficult to measure. Take for example *susceptibility to suggestion*. Statements of suggestible children could be problematic to interpret because suggestible children may be inclined to provide information that confirms the interviewer's expectations but is, in fact, inaccurate. To examine a child's susceptibility to suggestion, the interviewer is recommended to ask the witness a few leading questions at the end of the interview (Landry & Brigham, 1992; Yuille, 1988). Interviewers should hereby only ask questions about irrelevant peripheral information, because asking questions about central information could damage the quality of the statement. Being allowed only to ask questions about peripheral information is problematic, as it may say little about the witness' suggestibility regarding core issues of his or her statement. Children show more resistance to suggestibility for central parts than peripheral parts of an event (Dalton & Daneman, 2006; Davies, 1991; Goodman, Rudy, Bottoms, & Aman, 1990).

It is difficult, if not impossible, to determine the exact impact that many external factors have on CBCA scores. A good illustration is the field study conducted by Lamers-Winkelman and Buffing (1996). In this study, raters were instructed to take the age of the child into account when calculating CBCA scores. Nevertheless, six criteria positively correlated with age. In other words, even after being instructed to correct CBCA scores for age, the results still showed age-related effects with older children obtaining higher CBCA scores than younger children.

Given these difficulties in measuring the external factors and in examining the exact impact of these external factors on CBCA scores, it is clear that the Validity Checklist procedure is more subjective and less formalized than the CBCA procedure. It is therefore not surprising that if two experts disagree about the truthfulness of a statement in a German criminal case, they are likely to disagree about the likely impact of Validity Checklist external factors on that statement (Vrij, 2008, personal communication). One study revealed that Swedish experts sometimes use the Validity Checklist incorrectly, and this could be due to the difficulties with applying it (Gumpert & Lindblad, 1999). First, although SVA experts sometimes highlight the influence of Validity Checklist issues on children's statements in general, they do not always discuss how these issues might influence the statement of the particular child they are asked to assess. Second, although experts sometimes indicate possible external influence on statements, they are inclined to rely upon the CBCA outcome, and tend to judge high-quality statements as truthful and low-quality statements as fabricated.

The latter, ignoring the Validity Checklist and solely relying on CBCA scores, is unfortunate. Most aspects mentioned on the Validity Checklist are relevant when making veracity judgements based on CBCA scores. For example, research has convincingly demonstrated that total CBCA scores are age dependent. With increased age, children obtain higher total CBCA scores (see Vrij (2008) for a list of 14 studies examining the CBCA–age relationship). The difficulties and problems in using the Validity Checklist do not mean that these factors do not have an influence on children's reports or that they should be dismissed.

SVA Summary

Although SVA assessments are used as evidence in (criminal) courts to evaluate the veracity of child witnesses' testimonies in trials for sexual offences, the accuracy of these assessments is unknown. However, research has shown that CBCA-trained evaluators achieve around 70% accuracy. The Validity Checklist is difficult to apply for a variety of reasons, yet it is a vital element of SVA and should not be dismissed.

REALITY MONITORING

People sometimes try to determine whether they have actually experienced an event they have in mind, or whether this memory is based on imagination. The processes by which a person attributes a memory to an actual experience (external source) or imagination (internal source) is called Reality Monitoring (Johnson, Foley, Suengas, & Raye, 1988; Johnson & Raye, 1981). Although the RM concept is not related to deception, scholars believe that RM can be used as a lie detection tool and have examined this. To our knowledge, the RM lie detection tool is not used by practitioners.

The core of RM is that memories based on real experiences differ in quality from memories based on fiction. In their seminal work on memory characteristics, Marcia Johnson and Carol Raye (1981) argued that memories of real experiences are obtained through perceptual processes. They are therefore likely to contain *sensory information*: details of smell, taste or touch, visual details and details of sound; *contextual information*: spatial details (details about where the event took place and about how objects and people were situated in relation to each other) and temporal details (details about the time order and duration of events) and *affective information*: details about people's feelings throughout the event. These memories are usually clear, sharp and vivid. By contrast, memories about imagined events are derived from an internal source and are therefore likely to contain *cognitive operations*, such as thoughts and reasonings ('I must have had my coat on, as it was very cold that night'). They are usually vaguer and less concrete. There is empirical support for this general RM assumption. For example, in some studies, participants were asked to think about an experienced event or about an imagined event. They were then asked to complete the Memory Characteristics Questionnaire which examines the quality of their memory. Participants in the real memory conditions had clearer memories that included more sensory information than participants in the imagined memory conditions (Gordon, Gerrig, & Franklin, 2009; Johnson et al., 1988).

Research has shown that people use these textual properties also to judge whether *somebody else's* memory (Interpersonal RM) is externally or internally derived (Johnson, 2006; Johnson, Bush, & Mitchell, 1998; Johnson & Suengas, 1989). Indeed, one of the verbal criteria observers report they rely most upon when detecting lies is 'richness in details' (Strömwall, Granhag, & Hartwig, 2004; Vrij, 2008; Vrij, Akehurst, & Knight, 2006). The richer an account is perceived to be in detail, the more likely it is to be believed (Bell & Loftus, 1989; Johnson et al., 1988).

From 1990 onwards, scholars have examined whether RM analyses can be used to discriminate between truths and lies. The assumption those scholars make is that truths are recollections of experienced events whereas lies are recollections of imagined events. Obviously not all lies are descriptions of events that a person did not experience. Many lies are not about events, but are about people's feelings, opinions or attitudes. And even when people lie about events (about their actions and whereabouts), they can sometimes describe events that they have actually experienced. For example, a burglar who denies having committed a burglary last night can claim that he went to the gym instead. He can then describe a truthful visit he made to the gym (but on another occasion).

Researchers have examined whether truthful statements about experienced events differ in terms of RM criteria from deceptive statements that are based on events that the liar imagined. The typical procedure is that liars and truth tellers are interviewed, and these interviews are taped and transcribed. RM experts check for the presence of RM criteria in these transcripts. A standardized set of RM deception criteria has not been developed to date, and different researchers use different criteria and sometimes use different definitions for the same criterion. However, most researchers include the following criteria in their RM veracity assessment tool (Vrij, 2008): *clarity and vividness* of the statement: is the report clear, sharp and vivid instead of dim and vague? *perceptual information:* the presence of sensory information in a statement, such as sounds ('He really shouted at me'), smells ('It smelled of rotten fish'), tastes ('The chips were very salty'), physical sensations ('It really hurt') and visual details ('I saw the nurse entering the ward'); *spatial information:* information about locations ('It was in a park') or the spatial arrangement of people and/

or objects ('The man was sitting to the left of his wife') and *temporal information:* information about when the event happened ('It was early in the morning') or explicitly described sequences of events ('When he heard all that noise, the visitor became nervous and left').

Other criteria that are part of the RM tool are *affect:* how the witness felt during the event ('I was scared'), *reconstructability of the story:* is it possible to reconstruct the story based on the information given and *realism:* is the story plausible, realistic and does it make sense. The final RM criterion is *cognitive operations:* descriptions of inferences made by the participant at the time of the event ('It appeared to me that she didn't know the layout of the building') or inferences/opinions made when describing the event ('She looked smart'). All criteria are thought to be more present in truthful than in deceptive accounts, except for the cognitive operations criterion, which is thought to be present more in deceptive than in truthful accounts. The criteria are also presented in Table 1.2.

Reading the content of several CBCA and RM criteria suggests that there is some overlap between the CBCA list and RM criteria, a view empirically supported by Sporer (2004) who carried out correlational and factorial analyses on several data sets. The RM criteria *spatial*

Table 1.2 The reality monitoring criteria

Clarity	Clarity and vividness of the statement
Sensory (perceptual) information	Details about what the interviewee saw, heard, smelled, touched or tasted.
Spatial detail	Information about locations or the spatial arrangement of people and/or objects.
Temporal detail	Information about when the event happened or explicitly describes a sequence of events.
Affect	Information about how the interviewee felt during the event.
Reconstructability of the story	Is it possible to reconstruct the event on the basis of the information that is given?
Realism	Is the story plausible, realistic and does it make sense?
Cognitive operations	Descriptions of inferences made by the interviewee at the time of the event or inferences/opinions made when describing the event. The presence of a cognitive operation suggests deceit.

Adapted with permission from Vrij (2008). © John Wiley & Sons, Ltd.

information and *temporal information* are related to CBCA Criterion 4, *contextual embeddings*. The difference is that *spatial information* and *temporal information* are two separate criteria in RM whereas they are combined into one criterion in CBCA. The RM criterion *affect* is related to *CBCA* Criterion 12, *subjective mental state*, although the CBCA criterion not only includes affect but also thoughts. The RM criterion *realism* is related to CBCA Criterion 1, *logical structure*. A difference, however, is that RM criterion *realism* takes plausibility into account whereas CBCA criterion *logical structure* does not. The sound detail in RM (part of the *perceptual information* criterion) is different from CBCA Criterion 6, *reproduction of conversation*. CBCA Criterion 6 is more restricted and only includes speech that is reported in its original form, whereas the RM criterion *sound* refers to sound in general. Thus the two phrases 'He said: Are you OK, you look so pale?' and 'He asked how I felt' both count as a sound detail in RM, whereas the latter phrase does not count as a conversation detail in CBCA because it is not verbatim. In addition, a car horn would count as a sound detail in RM but not as a conversation detail in CBCA.

RM: Research

Masip et al. (2005) and Vrij (2008) reviewed the RM deception research (all laboratory studies). Vrij (2008) reviewed the results of 30 samples and found that, in terms of individual criteria, in particular the idea that truth tellers recall more *perceptual information* and more *spatial information* and *temporal information* received support.

In 10 studies, RM was used to discriminate truth tellers from liars. The average truth accuracy rate was 72% and the average lie accuracy rate was 66% (Vrij, 2008), whereas 50% accuracy rate can be expected by chance alone. At least two more studies have been published since Vrij's (2008) review which reported accuracy rates (Nahari et al., 2012, in press). These two studies obtained similar accuracy rates to the first 10 studies (71 and 63% total accuracy).

These RM truth and lie accuracy rates are similar to those obtained with CBCA. In fact, in most of those studies ($N = 8$), researchers carried out RM and CBCA analyses, which makes a comparison of the two tools possible. The findings are inconclusive. In three studies, CBCA analyses resulted in superior total accuracy rates, and in the other five studies, the best accuracy rates were achieved with RM analyses. The average total accuracy rate for RM in those eight studies is slightly higher (68.13%) than the average total accuracy rate for CBCA (63.63%).

There are restrictions in using an RM veracity assessment tool. For example, the tool cannot be used with young children. In some circumstances, children do not differentiate between fact and fantasy as clearly as adults do, for several reasons including that children have a richer imagination than adults (Lindsay, 2002). Children may therefore be better than adults at imagining themselves performing acts. It is probably also difficult to use the RM tool when people talk about events that happened a long time ago. Over time, cognitive operations may occur in memories of experienced events because they facilitate the remembering of events (Roediger, 1996). Someone who drove fast in a foreign country may try to remember this by remembering the actual speed his speedometer indicated; alternatively, he could remember this by logical reasoning and by deducing that he must have driven fast because he drove on the motorway. Imagined memories, on the other hand, can become more vivid and concrete over time if people try to visualize what might have happened (Manzanero & Diges, 1996).

RM Summary

RM is based on solid memory theory. It is popular amongst researchers, but not used in real life by practitioners. The RM tool achieves around 70% accuracy, which is similar to CBCA. RM cannot be used under all circumstances.

SCIENTIFIC CONTENT ANALYSIS

SCAN, developed by Avinoam Sapir, a former polygraph examiner in the Israeli police, is used worldwide and in countries such as Australia, Belgium, Canada, Israel, Mexico, the Netherlands, Qatar, Singapore, South Africa, the United Kingdom, and the United States (Vrij, 2008). It is used by federal law enforcement (including the Federal Bureau of Investigation (FBI)), military agencies (including the U.S. Army Military Intelligence), secret services (including the Central Intelligence Agency (CIA)) and other types of investigators (including social workers, lawyers, fire investigators and the American Society for Industrial Security) (Bockstaele, 2008; www.lsiscan.co.il). http://www.lsiscan.com/id29.htm provides a full list of past participants of SCAN courses. According to (the American version of) the SCAN website (www.lsiscan.com), SCAN courses are mostly given in the United States and Canada (on a weekly basis in those countries). In addition, online courses are also available.

In the SCAN procedure, the interviewee is requested to write a detailed description of all his/her activities during a critical period of time in such a way that a reader without background information can determine what actually happened. The handwritten statement is then analysed by a SCAN expert on the basis of a list of criteria. It is thought that some SCAN criteria are more likely to occur in truthful statements than in deceptive statements, whereas other criteria are more likely to occur in deceptive statements than in truthful statements (Sapir, 1987/2000). However, despite its name, *Scientific* Content Analysis, SCAN is an a-theoretical and no theoretical justification is given as to why truth tellers and liars would differ from each other in the stated ways.

There is not a fixed list of SCAN criteria, and different experts seem to use different sets of criteria. The list of 12 criteria presented in Table 1.3 are those that are most emphasized in workshops on the technique (Driscoll, 1994), used in research (Smith, 2001) or were used frequently by SCAN users in a field observation (Bogaard, Meijer, Vrij, Broers, & Merckelbach, in press). *Denial of allegations* refers to whether the interviewee directly denies the allegation in the statement. Denials are perceived as truthful. *Social introduction* refers to how the persons described in the statement are introduced. Honest social introductions are thought to be unambiguous (e.g. 'My wife Lisa...'), whereas a failure to introduce someone (e.g. 'We went outside' without mentioning who 'we' are) is interpreted as the writer trying to hide something. It may also indicate tension between the people to whom the ambiguity refers. *Spontaneous corrections* refers to the presence of corrections in the statement, such as crossing out what has been written. Although explanations and additions are allowed, interviewees are explicitly instructed not to cross anything out. A failure to follow this instruction is believed to indicate deceit. *Lack of conviction or memory* is the interviewee being vague about certain elements in the statement ('I believe...', 'I think...', 'kind of...') or when the interviewee writes that he or she cannot remember something. SCAN users interpret these phrases as suspicious. *Structure of the statement* refers to the balance of the statement. It is thought that in a truthful statement the first 20% is used to describe activities leading up to the event, the next 50% to describe the actual event and the final 30% to discuss what happened after the event. Thus, a 10-line statement is thought to comprise 2 lines to introduce the event, 5 lines to describe the event and 3 lines about the aftermath. The more unbalanced a statement, it is suggested the greater the probability that the statement is deceptive.

Emotions refers to whether there are emotions described in the statement. This criterion also refers to *where* the emotions are mentioned in the statement. It is thought that deceivers will mention emotions just before the climax of the story, whereas truth tellers are more likely to mention emotions throughout the story, but particularly after

Table 1.3 The scientific content analysis criteria

1. Denial of allegations	Does the interviewee directly deny the allegation in the statement? Truthful interviewees are more likely to do this.
2. Social introduction	How are the persons introduced who are described in the statement. They can be unambiguous (e.g. 'My friend, by the name of Phil…') or ambiguous (e.g. 'We went outside') without saying who 'we' are. Ambiguous introductions indicate a lie.
3. Spontaneous corrections	Corrections in statements, such as crossing out what has been written. Corrections are seen as sign of deceit.
4. Lack of conviction and memory	The interviewee is vague about certain elements in the statement ('I think it was on the back of the chair but I just can't remember'), or reports that she/he cannot remember something. Lack of memory indicates deceit.
5. Structure of statement	The balance of the statement. It is thought that in a truthful statement the first 20% is used to describe activities leading up to the event, the next 50% to describe the actual event and the final 30% to discuss what happened after the event. The more unbalanced a statement, the greater the probability that the statement is deceptive.
6. Emotions	Description of emotions. Important is the position of the emotions in the statement: just *before* the climax of the story (liars), or *throughout* the story (truth tellers) and *after* the climax of the story (truth tellers).
7. Objective and subjective time	How different time periods are covered in a statement. Objective time is the actual duration of events described in the statement, whereas subjective time is the amount of words spent to describe these events. It is thought that in a truthful statement, the objective and subjective time will correspond with each other, unlike in a deceptive statement.

(Continued)

Table 1.3   *(Cont'd)*

8. Out-of-sequence and extraneous information	Does the statement recount the events in chronological order (out-of-sequence information)? A deviation of the chronological order indicates deceit. Also, does the statement contain information that does not seem relevant (extraneous information)? The presence may indicate deceit because interviewees could include extraneous information to hide more important information.
9. Missing information	The inclusion of words that indicate that some information has been left out, such as 'sometime after', 'finally', 'later on' and 'shortly thereafter'. Inclusion of those words indicates deceit.
10. First person singular past tense	The format in which a statement is written. It is thought that truthful statements are written in the first person singular, past tense because the interviewee describes an event that has taken place (e.g. 'At the time I just saw it happen, I just jumped down and picked the laptop up straight away'). Deviations from this norm (e.g. 'It is the blue one') when referring to a lost item should raise suspicion.
11. Pronouns	The use of pronouns ('I', 'my', 'he', 'his', 'they', 'their', etc.) in the statement. Pronouns signal commitment, responsibility and possession. Omitting pronouns ('Left the house' rather than 'I left the house') suggests reluctance of the writer to commit himself/herself to the described action and thus indicates deceit.
12. Change in language	Change of terminology or vocabulary in the statement. A change in language indicates that something has altered in the mind of the writer. For example, if an interviewee refers in his statement to all conversations he had as 'conversations' except one conversation which he describes as a 'discussion', it is likely that she/he perceived this conversation differently from the other conversations.

Adapted with permission from Vrij (2008). © John Wiley & Sons, Ltd.

the climax of the story. *Objective and subjective time* refers to how different time periods are covered in a statement. Objective time is the actual duration of events described in the statement, whereas subjective time is the amount of words spent describing these events. It is thought that in a truthful, but not in a deceptive statement, the objective and subjective time will correspond with each other. For example, if someone devotes five lines in a statement to describe a 30-minute period and then three lines to describe a subsequent 2-hour period, the objective and subjective time do not correspond and this may indicate deceit. *Out-of-sequence and extraneous information* refers first of all to whether the statement recounts the events in chronological order. A deviation of the chronological order may be deceptive. It also refers to extraneous information that does not seem relevant. It is thought that examinees could include extraneous information to hide more important information.

Missing information refers to phrases in the statement that indicate that some information has been left out. Examples are the use of words such as 'sometime after', 'finally', 'later on' and 'shortly thereafter'. Missing information is seen as a sign of deceit. *First person, singular tense* refers to the format in which a statement is written. It is thought that truthful statements are written in the first person singular, past tense because the writer describes an event that has taken place ('I saw the smoke coming out of the window'). Deviations from this norm are viewed with suspicion. *Pronouns* include words such as 'I', 'my', 'he', 'his', 'they' and 'their'. Pronouns signal commitment, responsibility and possession. Omitting pronouns ('Left the house' rather than 'I left the house') suggests reluctance on the writer's part to commit himself/herself to the described action. The use of 'we' when 'I' is appropriate is believed to suggest that the writer is trying to absolve himself/herself of personal responsibility. Leaving out pronouns that indicate possession ('my', etc.) suggests that the writer denies ownership. *Change of language* refers to the change of terminology or vocabulary in the statement. A change in language indicates that something has altered in the mind of the writer. For example, if a suspect describes in his statement all conversations he had as 'conversations' but one conversation as a 'discussion', it is considered likely that he perceived this conversation differently from the other conversations. When a change of language is noticed in a statement, a SCAN user should contemplate whether the sequence of events justifies such a change. If the SCAN expert can think of a justification, then she/he may consider that the interviewee may be truthful; if the expert cannot think of a justification, she/he should consider that the interviewee may be deceptive.

There is overlap between some SCAN criteria and some CBCA criteria although, intriguingly, SCAN and CBCA users often draw different conclusions about the veracity of a statement when a criterion is present. *Spontaneous corrections* is similar to CBCA Criterion 14, *spontaneous corrections*, but CBCA experts believe that spontaneous corrections indicate truthfulness whereas SCAN experts interpret it a sign to deceit. *Lack of conviction or memory* is similar to CBCA Criterion 15, *lack of memory*. Again, CBCA experts interpret lack of memory as a sign of truthfulness and SCAN experts as a sign of deceit. *Emotions* is similar to CBCA Criterion 12, *accounts of subjective mental state*. However, unlike CBCA, in SCAN, this criterion also refers to when the emotions are mentioned in the statement. *Out-of-sequence and extraneous information* is a combination of two CBCA criteria: *unstructured production* (Criterion 2) and *superfluous details* (Criterion 9). CBCA experts rate these criteria as signs of truthfulness and SCAN experts rate them as signs of deceit.

SCAN: Research

Research on SCAN is scarce. Given how often SCAN is used in real life, this is worrying and SCAN research is therefore urgent (Heydon, 2011). Only five SCAN studies have been published to date. In a field study, 30 written statements voluntarily given by suspects immediately prior to their polygraph tests were analysed (Driscoll, 1994). The SCAN expert allocated 73% of the truthful and 95% of the deceptive statements correctly. These accuracy scores are high and often mentioned by SCAN users. However, the study had an important limitation as acknowledged by the author of the paper himself. For each suspect, it is unknown whether he or she was actually telling the truth or lying. In technical terms, the *ground truth* was uncertain, which makes interpreting the results of this field study problematic.

A second SCAN field study was carried out in 2001 for the British Home Office (Smith, 2001). Three groups of SCAN users with different levels of experience, a fourth group of experienced detectives not trained in SCAN and a fifth group of newly recruited officers also not trained in SCAN analysed 27 real-life statements. As was the case in the first field study, ground truth was poorly established, which makes interpretation of the accuracy rates problematic. The three groups of SCAN users performed well and correctly classified at least 80% of the truths and 75% of the lies. However, so did the experienced detectives untrained in SCAN, and so the study therefore showed no benefit in using SCAN. The newly recruited officers performed worse than the SCAN groups and the experienced detectives but this may have little to do with lie detection skills. Smith's sample included only a small number of statements believed to be true and, as a result, a sceptical observer who had a lie bias and was inclined to judge a statement as deceptive was more likely to obtain a high accuracy rate. Research has indicated that training and experience tend to result in a lie bias (Meissner & Kassin, 2002), and the newly recruited officers were the least trained and experienced officers in the study.

Armistead (2011) challenged Smith's (2001) data analyses and believes that Smith may not have come to the conclusion that SCAN users were as accurate as experienced lie detectors who are not trained in SCAN if she had analysed the data differently. He also criticized her decision to include infrequent SCAN users in the sample. According to Armistead, SCAN is not a template that can be implemented well without thorough practice. Armistead noted that a common experience of new graduates is to consult with Sapir himself or more experienced SCAN users for a substantial period of time after attending the SCAN training course. Smith's field study also revealed that different SCAN experts used different SCAN criteria to justify their decision of whether or not a statement was deceptive. In other words, there was a lack of standardization in the application of SCAN amongst SCAN users. Lack of standardization is a serious problem, as it becomes unclear what the SCAN method actually entails: the way SCAN is used highly depends on the individual who applies it.

Porter and Yuille (1996) carried out a laboratory SCAN experiment in which participants did or did not commit a mock theft and were interviewed about this alleged crime. They examined three SCAN criteria: *Structure of the statement, missing information* and *first person singular, past tense*. Truthful and deceptive statements did not differ from each other on these three criteria. However, this experiment was also limited. First, it tested only a small number (three) of SCAN criteria. Second, participants gave oral statements that were subsequently transcribed. It means that the procedure did not follow one of the basic principles of SCAN, the request to write down a statement. In a fourth study, verbal criteria including some SCAN criteria (e.g. *verb tense*) were examined (Bachenko, Fitzpatrick, & Schonwetter, 2008). However, the results for the individual criteria were not discussed. In the final published SCAN study (Nahari et al., 2012), a laboratory experiment, truth tellers truthfully wrote down their activities during the last half hour, whereas liars reported a fabricated story. The statements were analysed with SCAN and, by way of comparison, also with RM. SCAN did not distinguish truth tellers from liars above the level of chance but RM did. With RM analyses, 71% of truth tellers and liars were correctly classified.

As mentioned above, there is some overlap between CBCA and SCAN criteria. For example, the criteria *spontaneous corrections, lack of memory, out-of-sequence information* and *extraneous information* appear on both lists, but the predictions about how these criteria discriminate between truth tellers and liars differ. In CBCA, the occurrence of those cues is perceived as an indicator of truth, whereas in SCAN, the same criterion is seen as an indicator of deceit. There is a substantial amount of CBCA research regarding these individual criteria (all laboratory studies) and they all give support only to the CBCA assumptions (Vrij, 2008).

To summarize SCAN research, two field studies with poor ground truth have been published. The findings of one study were favourable for SCAN, but the findings of the other were not, as the same high performance was achieved by non-SCAN users. That study also showed a lack of standardization in the way users apply SCAN. The SCAN laboratory experiments and the CBCA laboratory experiments that examined some individual SCAN criteria showed no support for SCAN.

SCAN Summary

SCAN is popular amongst practitioners and is widely used. There is not much research into it, but research carried out to date has shown that it lacks standardization and that it is subjective in that how it is used depends on the individual SCAN user. In addition, research has yet to demonstrate that SCAN actually works.

A SVA, RM AND SCAN COMPARISON

This section compares the three verbal veracity tools discussed in this chapter. To give structure to this comparison, the three tools are discussed by addressing the five criteria that are used by the United States Supreme Court for admitting expert evidence in American federal courts. The five criteria together address the theoretical underpinning and accuracy of the tools as well as the view of the scientific community about the tools. The following five criteria were used in the *Daubert* case (Honts, 1994): (1) Is the scientific hypothesis testable? (2) Has the proposition been tested? (3) Is there a known error rate? (4) Has the hypothesis and/or technique been subjected to peer review and publication? and (5) Is the theory upon which the hypothesis and/or technique is based generally accepted in the appropriate scientific community? In this section, one question was added to this list which

Table 1.4   A summary of the three tools based on the Daubert guidelines

	CBCA	RM	SCAN
(1) Is the scientific hypothesis testable?	Yes	Yes	Yes
(2) Has the proposition been tested?	Yes	Yes	Scarcely
(3) Is there a known error rate?[a]	Yes, 30%	Yes, 30%	No
(4) Has the hypothesis and/or technique been subjected to peer review and publication?	Yes	Yes	Barely
(5) Has research supported the hypothesis and/or technique?	Yes	Yes	No
(6) Is the theory upon which the hypothesis and/or technique is based generally accepted in the appropriate scientific community?	Unknown	Unknown	Unknown

Adapted with permission from Vrij (2008). © John Wiley & Sons, Ltd.
[a]Based on laboratory studies only.

seems important in a section that compares the three tools: has research supported the hypothesis and/or technique? Table 1.4 summarizes the answers to these questions for SVA, RM and SCAN assessments.

Question 1: Is the Scientific Hypothesis Testable?
The prediction that truthful statements will differ in quality from false statements because liars have difficulty in fabricating information and attempt to avoid looking suspicious (the rationale underlying CBCA) can easily be tested in laboratory research. The same applies to the underlying assumption of RM that memories based on real experiences differ in quality from memories based on fiction, which results in verbal differences between truth tellers and liars. SCAN has no theoretical rationale, and no justification is given as to why the SCAN criteria would differentiate truth tellers from liars. However, the hypothesis that truth tellers and liars do differ from each other in terms of SCAN criteria can be tested. Although testing the underlying rationales in field studies is possible in principle, in reality, it is difficult given the problems with establishing the truth or falsity of statements beyond doubt (ground truth). The answers are therefore 'yes' for CBCA, RM and SCAN.

Question 2: Has the Proposition Been Tested?
The answer to the second *Daubert* question is affirmative for CBCA and RM research. A substantial number of CBCA and RM studies have

been carried out, although in most studies adults rather than children participated (this is relevant for CBCA as that tool is designed for use with children). There have only been a few CBCA field studies conducted and several of those are of poor quality. No field studies exist that focus on the entire set of RM criteria. There are only five SCAN studies published to date and most of those have serious limitations. Although several CBCA studies have examined criteria that are also on the SCAN list, the SCAN tool as a whole has been scarcely examined to date. The answer for SCAN as a whole is thus 'scarcely'.

Question 3: Is There a Known Error Rate?

There are known error rates for CBCA and RM judgements made in laboratory research. These error rates are about 30% for both tools. An error rate for SCAN is not available. As mentioned earlier, SVA assessments are used as evidence in criminal courts in several European countries. The standard of proof set in those courts is 'beyond reasonable doubt'. An error rate of about 30% in that context is too high.

Question 4: Has the Hypothesis and/or Technique Been Subjected to Peer Review and Publication?

A growing number of CBCA and RM studies have been published in peer-reviewed journals, both laboratory studies and (for CBCA) field studies. Although some CBCA studies have examined some SCAN criteria, peer-reviewed studies about SCAN as a whole are almost lacking. The answer to the fourth *Daubert* question is thus 'yes' for CBCA and RM research, and 'barely' for SCAN research.

Question 5: Has Research Supported the Hypothesis and/or Technique?

Empirical studies provide general support for CBCA and RM, and the answer for CBCA and RM is therefore 'yes'. SCAN studies are scarce and, if we disregard the field study that lacked ground truth, do not support SCAN. The CBCA studies that examined SCAN criteria do not support the SCAN assumptions either. The answer is therefore 'no' for SCAN.

Question 6: Is the Theory upon Which the Hypothesis and/or Technique is Based Generally Accepted in the Appropriate Scientific Community?

Several authors have expressed serious doubts about the SVA method (Brigham, 1999; Davies, 2001; Lamb et al., 1997; Pezdek & Taylor, 2000; Rassin, 1999; Ruby & Brigham, 1997; Wells & Loftus, 1991). For example, Lamb et al. (1997, p. 262) who carried out a reliable field study with the ground truth being well established concluded that '... the level of precision clearly remains too poor to permit the designation of CBCA as a reliable and valid test suitable for the courtroom'. However, since then two CBCA field studies have been published which showed that CBCA analyses are a valuable tool in assessing child sexual abuse cases. Authors have also been critical about SCAN; see, for example, Heydon (2008, 2011), Nahari et al. (2012), Smith (2001), Verschuere (2008a, 2008b) and Verschuere, Meijer, and Vrij (2010). Scholars' views on RM seem to be more positive, and critical articles about the use of RM as a lie detection tool have not yet emerged. Of course, RM is not used by practitioners in the field and it may be that scholars who are sceptical about the technique do not feel the urge to criticize it. To answer this *Daubert* question properly, one needs to know the opinion of the appropriate scientific community. To gather the views of the scientific community, surveys amongst scholars are required, as has been done about physiological (polygraph) lie detection (Iacono & Lykken, 1997). The appropriate scientific community has not been consulted about verbal lie detection tools to date. The answer to this *Daubert* question is thus 'unknown' for all tools.

Final Verdict

The known CBCA error rate (based on laboratory studies only) is 30%, which is not beyond reasonable doubt, the standard of proof regularly set in criminal courts. This error rate, which amounts to almost a one in three chance of being wrong, makes me conclude that SVA assessments should not be allowed as evidence in criminal courts. I am aware that this firm standpoint will be challenged by SVA proponents. Their main argument is that SVA assessments need to be compared with other evidence presented in criminal courts that may be even less accurate (Köhnken, 2004). Indeed, if judges and jurors make intuitive decisions, the error rate is in all likelihood higher. A meta-analysis of lie detection performance by naïve observers showed that they obtained on average a 54% accuracy rate, which represents a 46% error rate, considerably higher than the CBCA error rate. Therefore, replacing CBCA assessments with intuitive judgements would make matters considerably worse.

I expect that more people working in the criminal justice system will be sensitive to the 'If not SVA, what is the alternative?' argument. However, there are arguments against this point of view. For example, in all likelihood, judges, jurors and defendants will perceive the evidence that SVA experts present in court as strong. In cases where the defendant is innocent but the SVA expert considers the accusation

made against the defendant to be truthful, this may easily lead to a
guilty jury verdict and, as a result, a wrongful conviction. It could also
lead to a false confession if a defendant comes to the conclusion that
the SVA expert's verdict means that she/he can no longer avoid conviction. Defendants sometimes falsely confess if they believe that a conviction is certain because a confession may lead to a more lenient
sentence (Vrij, 2008). Therefore, in my view, if the evidence presented
in a criminal court is likely to be influential, a high accuracy level is
necessary. If SVA assessments are accepted as evidence in criminal
courts, then, at the very least, SVA experts should present the problems and limitations associated with their assessments when giving
their expert testimony, so that judges, jurors, prosecutors and solicitors
can make a considered decision about the validity of their expert testimony. These considerations do not apply to RM and SCAN because RM/
SCAN assessments are not introduced as evidence in court.

The answers to the six questions do not really differ from each other
for CBCA and RM and the two tools are comparable. A possible advantage of RM is that it is based on sound theory and that it has a stronger
theoretical rationale than CBCA. Another advantage of RM is that it is
quicker to use and easier to teach (Vrij, 2008). However, in terms of
accuracy, CBCA and RM are probably similar. SCAN is the most problematic tool of the three. It is not based on any theory which is in itself
problematic. A theory can explain why a tool works and when it works.
Without an underlying theory, such questions cannot be answered.
SCAN research has hardly been carried out, and the study SCAN users
cite as support (Driscoll, 1994) is of poor quality. Other, more experimentally sound studies found no support for the SCAN tool (Nahari et
al., 2012) or contradict the SCAN assumptions (many CBCA studies).
Given these findings, it is worrying that SCAN is endorsed and used by
so many practitioners.

REFERENCES

Akehurst, L., Manton, S., & Quandte, S. (2011). Careful calculation or a leap of
    faith? A field study of the translation of CBCA ratings to final credibility
    judgements. *Applied Cognitive Psychology, 25*, 236–243.
American Professional Society on the Abuse of Children. (1997). *Investigative
    interviewing in cases of alleged child abuse*. Chicago, IL: Author.
Armistead, T. W. (2011). Detecting deception in written statements: The British
    Home Office study of scientific content analysis (SCAN). *Policing: An
    International Journal of Police Strategies & Management, 34*, 588–605.
Bachenko, J., Fitzpatrick, E., & Schonwetter, M. (2008). Verification and
    implementation of language-based deception indicators in civil and criminal

narratives. In Association for Computational Linguistics (Ed.), *Proceedings of the 22nd International Conference on Computational Linguistics (Coling 2008)* (pp. 41–48). Stroudsburg, PA: Author.

Baldry, A. C., & Winkel, F. W. (1998). Perceptions of the credibility and eventual value of victim and suspect statements in interviews. In J. Boros, I. Munnich, & M. Szegedi (Eds.), *Psychology and criminal justice: International review of theory and practice* (pp. 74–82). Berlin, Germany: De Gruyter.

Baldry, A. C., Winkel, F. W., & Enthoven, D. S. (1997). Paralinguistic and non-verbal triggers of biased credibility assessments of rape victims in Dutch police officers: An experimental study of 'nonevidentiary' bias. In S. Redondo, V. Garrido, J. Perze, & R. Barbaret (Eds.), *Advances in psychology and law* (pp. 163–174). Berlin, Germany: Walter de Gruyter.

Bell, B. E., & Loftus, E. F. (1989). Trivial persuasion in the courtroom: The power of (a few) minor details. *Journal of Personality and Social Psychology, 56*, 669–679.

Brigham, J. C. (1999). What is forensic psychology, anyway? *Law and Human Behavior, 23*, 273–298.

Bockstaele, M. (2008). Scientific content analysis (SCAN). Een nuttig instrument by verhoren? (SCAN: A useful investigative tool?) In L. Smets & A. Vrij (Eds.), *Het analyseren van de geloofwaardigheid van verhoren* (Credibility judgements in interviews) (pp. 105–156). Brussels, Belgium: Politeia.

Bogaard, G., Meijer, E. H., Vrij, A., & Merckelbach, H. (in press). SCAN criteria derived from field data. *Psychology, Crime, & Law*.

Bollingmo, G. C., Wessel, E. O., Eilertsen, D. E., & Magnussen, S. (2008). Credibility of the emotional witness: A study of ratings by police investigators. *Psychology, Crime & Law, 14*, 29–40.

Bothwell, R., & Jalil, M. (1992). The credibility of nervous witnesses. *Journal of Social Behavior and Personality, 7*, 581–586.

Bull, R. (2010). The investigative interviewing of children and other vulnerable witnesses: Psychological research and working/professional practice. *Legal and Criminological Psychology, 15*, 5–24.

Burgess, A. W. (1985). *Rape and sexual assault: A research book*. London, England: Garland.

Colwell, K., Hiscock-Anisman, C. K., & Fede, J. (2013). Assessment criteria indicative of deception: An example of the new paradigm of differential recall enhancement. In B. S. Cooper, D. Griesel, & M. Ternes (Eds.), *Applied issues in investigative interviewing, eyewitness memory, and credibility assessment* (pp. 259–292). New York, NY: Springer.

Dalton, A. L., & Daneman, M. (2006). Social suggestibility to central and peripheral misinformation. *Memory, 14*, 486–501.

Davies, G. M. (1991). Research on children's testimony: Implications for interviewing practice. In C. R. Hollin & K. Howells (Eds.), *Clinical approaches to sex offenders and their victims* (pp. 177–191). New York, NY: Wiley.

Davies, G. M. (1994). Children's testimony: Research findings and policy implications. *Psychology, Crime, & Law, 1*, 175–180.

DePaulo, B. M., Lindsay, J. L., Malone, B. E., Muhlenbruck, L., Charlton, K., & Cooper, H. (2003). Cues to deception. *Psychological Bulletin, 129*, 74–118.

Driscoll, L. N. (1994). A validity assessment of written statements from suspects in criminal investigations using the SCAN technique. *Police Studies, 17*, 77–88.

Esplin, P. W., Boychuk, T., & Raskin, D. C. (1988, June). *A field validity study of criteria-based content analysis of children's statements in sexual abuse cases.*

Paper presented at the NATO Advanced Study Institute on Credibility Assessment, Maratea, Italy.

Fisher, R. P. (2010). Interviewing cooperative witnesses. *Legal and Criminological Psychology, 15*, 25–38.

Fivush, R., Haden, C., & Adam, S. (1995). Structure and coherence of preschoolers' personal narratives over time: Implications for childhood amnesia. *Journal of Experimental Child Psychology, 60*, 32–56.

Flavell, J. H., Botkin, P. T., Fry, C. K., Wright, J. C., & Jarvis, P. T. (1968). *The development of role-taking and communication skills in children*. New York, NY: Wiley.

Goodman, G. S., & Melinder, A. (2007). Child witness research and forensic interviews of young children: A review. *Legal and Criminological Psychology, 12*, 1–20.

Goodman, G. S., Rudy, L., Bottoms, B., & Aman, C. (1990). Children's concerns and memory: Issues of ecological validity in the study of children's eyewitness testimony. In R. Fivush & J. Hudson (Eds.), *Knowing and remembering in young children* (pp. 249–284). New York, NY: Cambridge University Press.

Gordon, R., Gerrig, R. J., & Franklin, N. (2009). Qualitative characteristics of memories for real, imagined and media-based events. *Discourse Processes, 46*, 70–91.

Gumpert, C. H., & Lindblad, F. (1999). Expert testimony on child sexual abuse: A qualitative study of the Swedish approach to statement analysis. *Expert Evidence, 7*, 279–314.

Hackett, L., Day, A., & Mohr, P. (2008). Expectancy violation and perceptions of rape victim credibility. *Legal and Criminological Psychology, 13*, 323–334.

Heydon, G. (2008). The art of deception: Myths about lie detection in written statements. In L. Smets & A. Vrij (Eds.), *Het analyseren van de geloofwaardigheid van verhoren* (pp. 171–182). Brussels: Politeia.

Heydon, G. (2011). Are police organisations suspending their disbelief in scientific content analysis (SCAN)? *IIIRG Bulletin, 1*, 8–9.

Home Office Communication Directorate. (2002). *Achieving best evidence in criminal proceedings: Guidance for vulnerable or intimidated witnesses, including children*. London, England: Author.

Honts, C. R. (1994). Assessing children's credibility: Scientific and legal issues in 1994. *North Dakota Law Review, 70*, 879–903.

Iacono, W. G., & Lykken, D. T. (1997). The validity of the lie detector: Two surveys of scientific opinion. *Journal of Applied Psychology, 82*, 426–433.

Johnson, M. K. (2006). Memory and reality. *American Psychologist, 61*, 760–771.

Johnson, M. K., Bush, J. G., & Mitchell, K. J. (1998). Interpersonal reality monitoring: Judging the sources of other people's memories. *Social Cognition, 16*, 199–224.

Johnson, M. K., Foley, M. A., Suengas, A. G., & Raye, C. L. (1988). Phenomenal characteristics of memories for perceived and imagined autobiographical events. *Journal of Experimental Psychology: General, 117*, 371–376.

Johnson, M. K., & Raye, C. L. (1981). Reality monitoring. *Psychological Review, 88*, 67–85.

Johnson, M. K., & Suengas, A. G. (1989). Reality monitoring judgments of other people's memories. *Bulletin of the Psychonomic Society, 27*, 107–110.

Kaufmann, G., Drevland, G. C., Wessel, E., Overskeid, G., & Magnussen, S. (2003). The importance of being earnest: Displayed emotions and witness credibility. *Applied Cognitive Psychology, 17*, 21–34.

Kebbel, M. R., & Milne, R. (1998). Police officers' perception of eyewitness factors in forensic investigations. *Journal of Social Psychology, 138*, 323–330.

Köhnken, G. (1989). Behavioral correlates of statement credibility: Theories, paradigms and results. In H. Wegener, F. Lösel, & J. Haisch (Eds.), *Criminal behavior and the justice system: Psychological perspectives* (pp. 271–289). New York, NY: Springer-Verlag.

Köhnken, G. (1996). Social psychology and the law. In G. R. Semin & K. Fiedler (Eds.), *Applied social psychology* (pp. 257–282). London, Great Britain: Sage.

Köhnken, G. (1999, July). Statement Validity Assessment. Paper presented at the pre-conference program of applied courses 'Assessing credibility' organised by the European Association of Psychology and Law, Dublin, Ireland.

Köhnken, G. (2004). Statement validity analysis and the 'detection of the truth'. In P. A. Granhag & L. A. Strömwall (Eds.), *Deception detection in forensic contexts* (pp. 41–63). Cambridge, England: Cambridge University Press.

Lamb, M. E., Hershkowitz, I., Orbach, Y., & Esplin, P. W. (2008). *Tell me what happened: Structured investigative interviews of child victims and witnesses.* Chichester, UK/Hoboken, NJ: Wiley.

Lamb, M. E., Sternberg, K. J., Esplin, P. W., Hershkowitz, I., Orbach, Y., & Hovav, M. (1997). Criterion-based content analysis: A field validation study. *Child Abuse and Neglect, 21*, 255–264.

Lamers-Winkelman, F. (1999). Statement validity analysis: Its application to a sample of Dutch children who may have been sexually abused. *Journal of Aggression, Maltreatment & Trauma, 2*, 59–81.

Lamers-Winkelman, F., & Buffing, F. (1996). Children's testimony in the Netherlands: A study of statement validity analysis. In B. L. Bottoms & G. S. Goodman (Eds.), *International perspectives on child abuse and children's testimony* (pp. 45–62). Thousand Oaks, CA: Sage Publications.

Landry, K., & Brigham, J. C. (1992). The effect of training in criteria-based content analysis on the ability to detect deception in adults. *Law and Human Behavior, 16*, 663–675.

Lindsay, D. S. (2002). Children's source monitoring. In H. L. Westcott, G. M. Davies, & R. H. C. Bull (Eds.), *Children's testimony: A handbook of psychological research and forensic practice* (pp. 83–98). Chichester, UK: Wiley.

Littmann, E., & Szewczyk, H. (1983). Zu einigen Kriterien und Ergebnissen forensisch-psychologischer Glaubwürdigkeitsbegutachtung von sexuell misbrauchten Kindern und Jugendlichen [On some criteria and results of the forensic-psychological credibility assessment of sexually abused children and youths/adolescents]. *Forensia, 4*, 55–72.

Manzanero, A. L., & Diges, M. (1996). Effects of preparation on internal and external memories. In G. Davies, S. Lloyd-Bostock, M. McMurran, & C. Wilson (Eds.), *Psychology, law, and criminal justice: International developments in research and practice* (pp. 56–63). Berlin, Germany: Walter de Gruyter.

Masip, J., Sporer, S., Garrido, E., & Herrero, C. (2005). The detection of deception with the reality monitoring approach: A review of the empirical evidence. *Psychology, Crime, and Law, 11*, 99–122.

Meissner, C. A., & Kassin, S. M. (2002). 'He's guilty!': Investigator bias in judgments of truth and deception. *Law and Human Behavior, 26*, 469–480.

Nahari, G., Vrij, A., & Fisher, R. P. (2012). Does the truth come out in the writing? SCAN as a lie detection tool. *Law and Human Behavior, 36*, 68–76.

Nahari, G., Vrij, A., & Fisher, R. P. (in press). Exploiting liars' verbal strategies by examining the verifiability of details. *Legal and Criminological Psychology.*

Parker, A. D., & Brown, J. (2000). Detection of deception: Statement validity analysis as a means of determining truthfulness or falsity of rape allegations. *Legal and Criminological Psychology, 5*, 237–259.

Pezdek, K., & Taylor, J. (2000). Discriminating between accounts of true and false events. In D. F. Bjorklund (Ed.), *Research and theory in false memory creation in children and adults* (pp. 69–91). Mahwah, NJ: Erlbaum.

Porter, S., & Yuille, J. C. (1996). The language of deceit: An investigation of the verbal clues to deception in the interrogation context. *Law and Human Behavior, 20*, 443–459.

Rassin, E. (1999). Criteria-based content analysis: The less scientific road to truth. *Expert Evidence, 7*, 265–278.

Raskin, D. C., & Esplin, P. W. (1991). Statement validity assessment: Interview procedures and content analysis of children's statements of sexual abuse. *Behavioral Assessment, 13*, 265–291.

Roediger, H. L. (1996). Memory illusions. *Journal of Memory and Language, 35*, 76–100.

Roma, P., San Martini, P., Sabatello, U., Tatarelli, R., & Ferracuti, S. (2011). Validity of criteria-based content analysis (CBCA) at trial in free-narrative interviews. *Child Abuse and Neglect, 35*, 613–620.

Rose, M. R., Nadler, J., & Clark, J. (2006). Appropriately upset? Emotion norms and perceptions of crime victims. *Law and Human Behavior, 30*, 203–219.

Ruby, C. L., & Brigham, J. C. (1998). Can criteria-based content analysis distinguish between true and false statements of African-American speakers? *Law and Human Behavior, 22*, 369–388.

Sapir, A. (1987/2000). *The LSI course on scientific content analysis (SCAN)*. Phoenix, AZ: Laboratory for Scientific Interrogation.

Smith, N. (2001). *Police Research Series Paper: Vol. 135. Reading between the lines: An evaluation of the scientific content analysis technique (SCAN)*. London, UK: UK Home Office, Research, Development and Statistics Directorate.

Sporer, S. L. (2004). Reality monitoring and detection of deception. In P. A. Granhag & L. A. Strömwall (Eds.), *Deception detection in forensic contexts* (pp. 64–102). Cambridge, England: Cambridge University Press.

Sporer, S. L. (2012). *Making the subjective objective? Computer-assisted quantification of qualitative content cues to deception*. Retrieved from http://aclweb.org/anthology/W/W12/W12-0412.pdf

Steller, M. (1989). Recent developments in statement analysis. In J. C. Yuille (Ed.), *Credibility Assessment* (pp. 135–154). Deventer, the Netherlands: Kluwer.

Steller, M., & Boychuk, T. (1992). Children as witnesses in sexual abuse cases: Investigative interview and assessment techniques. In H. Dent & R. Flin (Eds.), *Children as witnesses* (pp. 47–73). New York, NY: Wiley.

Strömwall, L. A., Granhag, P. A., & Hartwig, M. (2004). Practitioners' beliefs about deception. In P. A. Granhag & L. A. Strömwall (Eds.), *Deception detection in forensic contexts* (pp. 229–250). Cambridge, England: Cambridge University Press.

Trankell, A. (1972). *Reliability of evidence*. Stockholm, Sweden: Beckmans.

Trovillo, P. V. (1939). A history of lie detection. *Journal of Criminal Law and Criminology, 29*, 848–881.

Undeutsch, U. (1982). Statement reality analysis. In A. Trankell (Ed.), *Reconstructing the past: The role of psychologists in criminal trials* (pp. 27–56). Deventer, the Netherlands: Kluwer.

Verschuere, B. (2008a). Een misleidende recensie gedetecteerd: Weerwoord (A misleading review detected: A reply). *Panopticon, 6*, 44–47.

Verschuere, B. (2008b). Leugens en hun detectie (boekbespreking) [Lies and their detection (book review)]. *Panopticon, 3*, 96–98.

Verschuere, B., Meijer, E., & Vrij, A. (2010). *Verbale leugendetectie* (Verbal le detection). In P. J. van Koppen, H. Merckelbach, M. Jelicic, & J. W. De Keijser (Eds.), *Reizen met mijn Rechter (Traveling with my judge)* (pp. 705–722). Deventer, the Netherlands: Kluwer.

Vrij, A. (2005). Criteria-based content analysis: A qualitative review of the first 37 studies. *Psychology, Public Policy, and Law, 11*, 3–41.

Vrij, A. (2008). *Detecting lies and deceit: Pitfalls and opportunities* (2nd ed.). Chichester, UK: John Wiley and Sons.

Vrij, A., Akehurst, L., & Knight, S. (2006). Police officers', social workers', teachers' and the general public's beliefs about deception in children, adolescents and adults. *Legal and Criminological Psychology, 11*, 297–312.

Vrij, A., & Fischer, A. (1997). The role of displays of emotions and ethnicity in judgements of rape victims. *International Review of Victimology, 4*, 255–265.

Walker, A. G., & Warren, A. R. (1995). The language of the child abuse interview: Asking the questions, understanding the answers. In T. Ney (Ed.), *True and false allegations in child sexual abuse: Assessment and case management* (pp. 153–162). New York, NY: Brunner-Mazel.

Walker, J. (1886). Reports, with comments, of twenty-one cases of indecent assault and rape upon children. *Archives of Pediatrics, 3*, 269–286, 321–341.

Wells, G. L., & Loftus, E. F. (1991). Commentary: Is this child fabricating? Reactions to a new assessment technique. In J. Doris (Ed.), *The suggestibility of children's recollections* (pp. 168–171). Washington DC: American Psychological Association.

Wessel, E., Drevland, G., Eilertsen, D. E., & Magnussen, S. (2006). Credibility of the emotional witness: A comparison of ratings by laypersons and court judges. *Law and Human Behavior, 30*, 221–230.

Yuille, J. C. (1988). The systematic assessment of children's testimony. *Canadian Psychology, 29*, 247–262.

2

New Findings in Non-Verbal Lie Detection

CHARLES F. BOND, TIMOTHY R. LEVINE AND MARIA HARTWIG

Ours is far from being the first chapter written on non-verbal lie detection. The topic was of interest since ancient times, and it remains of interest today. Vrij (2008) offered a thorough treatment of non-verbal lie detection. We will not review Vrij's excellent discussion here. Instead, we offer a selective review of the most recent work on attempts at lie detection from behaviour in hope of providing new insights through meta-analysis. We consider failed attempts to detect lies, as well as lie detection successes. We mention, in passing, lie detection from certain aspects of speech, but will leave to others the consideration of speech-based lie detection systems (e.g. statement validity analysis).

To provide a background, we begin by recalling some of the classic theories of non-verbal lie detection. We then consider current work on cues to deception, determinants of deception judgement and the accuracy of non-verbal lie detection. Although parts of the chapter review work that was previously published, we offer several new contributions. In particular, we document a decline effect in non-verbal deception cues, isolate audible from visible components of apparent honesty

Detecting Deception: Current Challenges and Cognitive Approaches, First Edition.
Edited by Pär Anders Granhag, Aldert Vrij, and Bruno Verschuere.
© 2015 John Wiley & Sons, Ltd. Published 2015 by John Wiley & Sons, Ltd.

showing that various cues to honesty are inter-correlated and present a meta-analytic comparison of explicit and implicit lie detection.

THEORETICAL HISTORY

There have been many theories of deception. Here we consider four of those formulations: leakage theory, four-factor theory, self-presentational theory and interpersonal deception theory. Three of the four predict observable differences in non-verbal behaviour between honest and deceptive communicators.

Non-Verbal Leakage

The first and perhaps the most influential theory of deception was initially described by Paul Ekman and Wallace Friesen in their classic 1969 article titled 'Nonverbal leakage and clues to deception'. In their paper, Ekman and Friesen made a distinction between deception clues and leakage. Deception clues signal that deception is in progress but are not informative about the information being concealed. Leakage, in contrast, gives away the concealed information. Expressed differently, the truth leaks out.

Ekman's theory focuses only on high-stakes lie, not inconsequential or white lies. According to this theory, deception must produce an emotional response in a liar that can be signalled behaviourally, and this is expected only for lies of consequence. In the original version of leakage, lies may be signalled in different parts of the body. The likelihood that deception will be signalled in a particular part of the body is a function of the non-verbal sending capacity of that body part and amount of feedback people receive about the body part. According to Ekman, the face has more non-verbal sending capacity than any other part of the body. However, people receive a lot of feedback about their facial expressions. Thus, people are aware of their face and exercise control over their facial expressions. Deception is unlikely to be signalled in the face except for fleeting signs of expressions that are being suppressed. These brief displays of suppressed emotion are called micro-expressions.

According to Ekman and Friesen (1969), the legs and feet 'are a primary source of both leakage and deception clues' (p. 99). 'Leakage in the legs/feet could include aggressive foot kicks, flirtatious leg displays, autoerotic or soothing leg squeezing, abortive restless flight movements. Deception clues can be seen in tense leg positions, frequent shift of leg posture, and in restless or repetitive leg and foot acts' (p. 99). This is because although the legs have limited sending capacity, we are less aware of what our feet are doing.

This reasoning gave rise to Ekman's idea of leakage hierarchy. In brief, he suggested that the utility of leakage and deception clues is inversely related to sending capacity and feedback. In other words, the less aware we are of a behaviour, the more likely the behaviour is to signal a lie.

Subsequent scientific data have not been supportive of the original leakage theory, and subsequent work by Ekman and his colleagues shifted to focus more on the face and micro-expressions. Even with these modifications, however, leakage theory remains controversial (e.g. Weinberger, 2010).

Four-Factor Theory

Zuckerman, DePaulo, and Rosenthal (1981) introduced a framework that has since come to be known as 'four-factor theory'. According to this theory, deception is not directly associated with any particular verbal or non-verbal behaviour. Instead, deception is directly associated with four psychological factors: emotions, arousal, cognitive effort and attempted behavioural control. These factors, in turn, may give rise to behavioural differences that distinguish truths from lies.

According to Zuckerman and colleagues (1981), people have emotional responses to their lies. Liars feel guilty and fear detection. These emotions may be conveyed non-verbally. For example, liars might show negative facial expressions.

Second, Zuckerman and colleagues maintain that deception is physiologically arousing. It is this arousal, in fact, that a polygraph measures. Arousal is reflected in increased heart rate, blood pressure and skin conductance. Arousal as a function of deception may produce recognizable behaviours such as eye blinking, high-pitched speech and fidgeting.

Third, deception may be cognitively demanding. This could be true for several reasons. First, formulating a lie may itself be demanding (Vrij et al., 2009). Second, liars must ensure that their stories are internally consistent as well as consistent with external information. These information management considerations may contribute to cognitive load (Hartwig, Granhag, Strömwall, & Doering, 2010). Third, liars must suppress the truth, which may require mental effort. Theoretically, the cognitive effort of lying should lead to longer response latencies, more pauses, more speech errors and fewer gestures.

Fourth, Zuckerman and colleagues also suggested that deceivers may attempt to avoid behaviours that give their lie away and instead present behaviours that appear honest. The net result of this attempted

control can be behaviour that appears stiff, rehearsed or overly controlled or discrepancies between what one part of the body is doing and
another.

In the theory by Zuckerman et al. (1981), these four factors provide
the basis for predicting the sorts of behavioural difference that might
be useful in lie detection. These factors help explain why non-verbal
deception cues exist and provide a rationale for further research on the
topic. As we will see in subsequent sections, like leakage theory, four-
factor theory too has failed to receive strong and consistent support.

Self-Presentational Theory

DePaulo (1992; see also DePaulo et al., 2003) offered a very different
take on non-verbal behaviour as related to deception. She shifted focus
from uncontrollable behaviours to purposefully controlled actions.
DePaulo regards non-verbal deception behaviours as forms of self-
presentation, that is, as vehicles for managing the impressions people
convey. These non-verbal behaviours can be strategic and goal directed.
More generally, self-presentation can be, but need not be, deceptive.
Rather than conveying impressions that are completely false, people
more often edit their images in subtle ways.

From DePaulo's (1992) perspective, people try to manage their non-
verbal behaviours. Thus, these behaviours are rarely unconscious
expressions of an individual's internal states. Instead, they reflect self-
presentation goals. People want others to believe what they say, and
they want others to regard them favourably. People learn to do this
over time, and adults typically have the skills needed to enact credible
presentations. Even so, there are individual differences in skill at self-
presentation and differences in individuals' concerns with the impressions they convey. As a rule, people play along with, and give the
appearance of accepting others' self-presentations. But there are limits
to the range of self-presentations that can be successfully conveyed
and limits to what others will publicly accept.

In DePaulo's view, people usually see their lies as minor, and
may experience little anxiety, guilt, regret or fear of detection while
lying. Liars want to be believed, but so do truth-tellers. Everyone
self-presents. Although some lies are not as convincing as truths, and
sometimes liars' performances appear pre-packaged, rarely do a liar's
behaviours constitute proof of deception. In sum, according to DePaulo's
self-presentational theory, both liars and truth-tellers engage in strategic control of their behaviour in order to convey a truthful impression.
Hence, DePaulo's theory of deception emphasizes similarities rather
than difference between liars and truth-tellers. Although the

self-presentation theory of deception has fared better empirically than its predecessors, it, unfortunately, offers little guidance for improving deception detection in practice.

Interpersonal Deception Theory

Following Stiff and Miller (1986), Buller and Burgoon (1996) sought to understand deception as a dynamic, interactive process. According to Buller and Burgoon's interpersonal deception theory, deception and suspected deception are commonplace. The process begins when a sender's expectations, goals, prior knowledge, skill set and behavioural repertoire combine to produce a communication that is true or false. The communication is accompanied by an initial behavioural display. Deceptive messages include the core deceptive content plus strategic actions aimed at making the deception believable, as well as non-strategic behaviours that might betray the lie. Senders' initial behavioural displays are judged by receivers who exhibit initial behavioural displays of their own and who may be suspicious. Based on initial suspicion and an assessment of sender behaviour displays, receivers may adjust their behavioural displays strategically. Senders may respond. Senders and receivers actively monitor each other and make behavioural adjustments over time so as to achieve their desired communicative goals. However, senders may leak indications of deceit and receivers' indications of suspicion in a dynamic series of moves and countermoves. The outcome is a successful or unsuccessful deception.

Interpersonal deception theory offers 18 theoretical propositions. We will not enumerate them here. Theoretically, deception depends on interactivity in a communication context. Face-to-face communication is maximally interactive and other contexts for communication are constraining. According to this theory, some of the important factors in interpersonal deception are access to social cues, immediacy of communication, feelings of relational engagement, conversational demands and spontaneity. Like its predecessors, interpersonal deception theory has proven controversial (e.g. DePaulo, Ansfield, & Bell, 1996).

EMPIRICAL EVIDENCE FOR NON-VERBAL CUES TO DECEPTION

Having reviewed classic theories on cues to deception, let us turn to empirical work on behavioural cues to deception. Recall that three of the theories predict differences in non-verbal behaviours while one (self-presentation) predicts few substantial differences. Do people behave in systematically different ways when they are lying compared to when they are telling the truth? Researchers have studied an extensive list of behaviours for their utility as deception cues. Their typical research method is to solicit deceptive statements from participants in laboratory studies (e.g. by asking them to deliberately distort their opinions, attitudes or emotions or to provide false descriptions of events) and to compare the behaviour of these liars to that of participants who have been instructed to tell the truth. Researchers have also studied cues to deception in real-life statements, for example, during police interrogations in which suspects truthfully or deceptively denied involvement in a crime (e.g. Mann, Vrij, & Bull, 2002; for an alternative approach see Ten Brinke & Porter, 2012).

Meta-Analytic Summary

In the most comprehensive synthesis of the literature on cues to deception to date, DePaulo and colleagues (2003) conducted a meta-analysis of 1,338 estimates of 158 behaviours. The analysis included both verbal and non-verbal behaviours. Overall, the results showed that behavioural signs of deception are weak and inconsistent. Many behaviours that people believe to be indicative of lying were not in fact reliably linked to deception. For example, people express the belief that liars' avert their gaze – in contrast, the meta-analysis showed that gaze aversion is not related to lying. Also, despite widespread beliefs (Strömwall, Granhag, & Hartwig, 2004), liars are not prone to fidgeting, nor do they display frequent posture shifts or self-grooming behaviours. Although some behaviours are statistically linked to deception, the links are not strong and the results vary from study to study.

A Decline Effect

Having studied the DePaulo et al. (2003) meta-analysis on cues to deception, we noticed an unexpected trend. For each of 158 distinct behaviours, DePaulo and colleagues reported two things: the number of times the behaviour had been studied as a possible deception cue and the relationship of that behaviour to deception. They measured the relationship of a behaviour to deception as a weighted standardized mean difference. Here we take the absolute value of each weighted mean d from tables in DePaulo et al. to assess the strength of each deception cue (irrespective of its direction). We wondered if the strength of a deception cue might be related to the number of times it had been studied, imagining that deception researchers might focus their investigative efforts on the strongest cues.

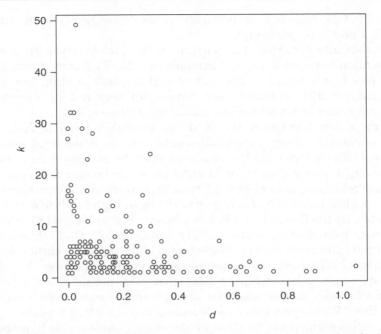

Figure 2.1 A decline effect in cues to deception. The scatterplot depicts a decline effect in cues to deception. Each data point represents one of the 158 cues in the DePaulo et al. meta-analysis. The horizontal axis of the plot is the number of times a cue had been studied at the time of the DePaulo et al. meta-analysis (*k*). On the *y*-axis is the absolute strength of the cue (as an absolute weighted mean *d*). As the scatterplot shows, the strongest cues to deception have rarely been studied, and that the most widely studied cues are weak.

For a relevant scatterplot, see Figure 2.1. There are 158 data points in the figure, one for each of the cues in the DePaulo et al. meta-analysis. On the horizontal axis of the plot is the number of times a cue had been studied at the time of DePaulo et al. meta-analysis (*k*). On the *y*-axis is the absolute strength of the cue (as an absolute weighted mean *d*).

An inspection of the graph suggests that the strongest cues to deception have rarely been studied, and that the most widely studied cues are weak. Response length, for example, has been studied more often than any other cue ($k = 49$). It has a very small relationship to deception ($d = 0.03$). Response latency and eye contact have each been studied 32 times, and they too have very small relationships to deception ($d = 0.02$ and 0.01, respectively). By contrast, the strongest cues to deception are foot movement changes, pupillary changes and issue-related reporting

($d = 1.05$, 0.90 and 0.87, respectively). These have rarely been studied ($k = 2$, 1 and 1, respectively).

Statistically speaking, the pattern in the plot involves an inverse correlation between k and d, Pearson's $r = -.26$. By a conventional significance test with cue as the unit of analysis, this relationship is significant, $p < .005$. Because the relationship may not be linear, the Pearson r may be an underestimate of the decline effect.

A more complete description of the scatterplot is possible. Note that cues of varying strength are studied once or twice. Some weak cues are studied once or twice, and some strong cues are studied once or twice. However, the only cues to be studied often are weak cues. Thus, the inverse relationship in Figure 2.1 shows a pattern of non-constant variance – at low levels of k, d is highly variable. At high levels of k, it is less variable. By the Breusch and Pagan test with cue as the unit of analysis, this heteroskedasticity is statistically significant, $\chi^2 (1) = 12.92, p < .001$.

Why do the most widely studied cues show a weak relationship to deception? Why have investigators rarely studied the cues that show the strongest relationship to deception? Or, perhaps the question should be: why do the cues that are researched most appear weaker over time? We suspect that as a deception cue is studied repeatedly, the cumulative estimate of its strength declines. To assess this hypothesis, we used data graciously provided by Bella DePaulo. These are the raw meta-analytic data from which the DePaulo et al. (2003) tables were constructed. For each effect-size estimate entering into the DePaulo et al. results, we noted which cue the effect concerned, the date of the effect-size, the effect-size itself and a meta-analytic weight. DePaulo provided us with data on 158 cues to deception. However, 43 of those cues had been studied only once. These were omitted from the analyses below because these could not change over time.

Our goal was to determine whether the cumulative estimate of the strength of a deception cue declines as the cue is studied more often. To assess this hypothesis, we grouped the effect size estimates for a given cue by year. We noted, for each cue in each year, the weighted mean for all effect sizes observed prior to and including that year. We took the absolute value of this cumulative effect size estimate. We then predicted this estimate of cue strength from the number of years the cue had been studied (e.g. from 4, if it was an estimate of cue strength from all effect sizes observed in the first 4 years the cue was studied). We used data from the 115 cues in the DePaulo et al. (2003) meta-analysis that had been studied more than once, entering all of the data into a single linear regression equation that included 114 dummy variables to control for cue. Results showed that, in fact, cumulative estimates of cue strength are smaller the more years a cue has been studied.

The standardized partial regression coefficient for the cumulative cue strength estimate on years of study is $-.27$, $t(526) = -5.84$, $p < .001$.

To illuminate this longitudinal trend, we noted two estimates of cue strength for each of the 115 cues in our regression equation: (1) an estimate of absolute cue strength for all effects observed in the first year for which DePaulo et al. have data and (2) an estimate of absolute cue strength for all effects observed in the final year for which the meta-analysts have data. Results show that estimates of cue strength were stronger the first year the cue was studied than the final year the cue was studied (absolute weighted mean $d = 0.34$ vs. 0.23; for the difference, $t(114) = 2.49$, $p < .01$, by a conventional test with cue as the unit of analysis).

Deception cues become weaker the longer they are studied. This may reflect a more general phenomenon. The so-called *decline effect* is a tendency for scientific findings to decrease in strength over time. Such effects have been observed in medicine and biology (McMahon, Holly, Harrington, Roberts, & Green, 2008; Ozonoff, 2011), and here we seem to be observing a decline effect in non-verbal behaviour cues. There is currently no generally agreed-upon explanation for the decline effect. Schooler (2011) notes some prosaic explanations for the effect, such as regression to the mean (i.e. self-correction from extreme values over time) or publication bias, meaning that the publication of novel findings may be more likely if these effects are large, whereas follow-up studies on an established phenomenon may pass the bar of peer review even if the effects are smaller. We are not able to test any of these explanations using our data; however, we point the reader to Lehrer (2010) for a popular discussion of the effect, and to Ioannidis (2005) for statistical explanations.

In sum, research on non-verbal cues that distinguish truths from lies finds that such cues tend to be weak and inconsistent and, to the extent there is empirical support for such cues, that support systematically diminishes as research accumulates. Consequently, classic theories such as leakage, four-factor theory and interpersonal deception theory which predict behavioural displays linked, albeit indirectly, to the act of lying lack convincing empirical support. Fortunately, more recent research has moved in different directions.

CONTEMPORARY RESEARCH

Having reviewed past theory and research on deception cues, let us note a few emphases in current research. There is a continuing quest for deception cues. Cognizant that cues to deception are generally weak, researchers have tried to elicit stronger cues. They use strategic questioning methods (e.g. Levine, Shaw, & Shulman, 2010). It has long been assumed that certain questions may evoke different psychophysiological responses from liars and truth-tellers (e.g. Honts, 2004). More recently, this idea has been explored in the context of lie detection from behaviours.

In this new wave of research, studies have examined the effect of various forms of strategic questions on audible and visible behavioural cues (Vrij & Granhag, 2012). These questioning methods emphasize cognitive rather than emotional differences in the psychological processes of liars and truth-tellers (Vrij, Granhag, & Porter, 2010). Some methods are designed to elicit verbal cues to deception. For example, the strategic use of evidence (SUE) framework posits that liars and truth-tellers have different information management strategies, and that liars' strategies of verbal evasion and concealment can be exploited through systematic use of available evidence (Granhag & Hartwig, 2008). By posing questions about the information that liars are motivated to conceal without revealing that one possesses this information, a questioner may lead liars to contradict these facts in their attempts to distance themselves from incriminating information (Hartwig, Granhag, Strömwall, & Vrij, 2005). Other methods of eliciting verbal cues to deception are based on the premise that liars prepare some, but not all, of their responses. It might thus be possible to create difficulties for liars in producing plausible accounts by asking them unanticipated questions that they are unlikely to be prepared to answer (Vrij & Granhag, 2012). Unanticipated questions have been found to produce inconsistencies between the statements of pairs of liars (Vrij et al., 2009), as well as less detailed accounts from single liars (Lancaster, Vrij, Hope, & Waller, 2012).

Other strategies may produce differences in liars and truth-tellers' demeanour. The cognitive load approach assumes that lying can be more cognitively demanding than telling the truth (Gamer, 2011; Vrij, Ennis, Farman, & Mann, 2010; however, see McCornack, 1997). The strategy is to impose additional cognitive load on senders, hoping that liars will display more pronounced signs of mental strain, as they are already taxed by the burden inherent in lying. Cognitive load has been operationally defined in various ways in empirical research, for example, by asking senders to provide their statements in reverse chronological order (Vrij, Leal, Mann, & Fisher, 2012; Vrij et al., 2008) or by asking them to maintain eye contact with the interviewer (Vrij, Mann, Leal, & Fisher, 2010). As predicted, cognitive load manipulations strengthen visual cues to deception. For example, in a study by Vrij and colleagues (2008), liars in a reverse order recall condition showed more pronounced signs of being taxed in that they were more prone to speech hesitations. They also spoke at a slower rate and made more speech errors. Liars and truth-tellers in the control (i.e. normal chronological order recall) condition did not differ in these respects. In sum, an emerging body of work suggests that both verbal and non-verbal cues to deception may become more pronounced if lie-catchers take a strategic approach to interacting with targets.

Finally, some approaches to strategic questioning eschew non-verbal cues completely and instead focus on message content (e.g. Blair, Levine, & Shaw, 2010; Levine, Blair, & Clare, 2013). Such approaches seek to illicit honest verbal responses and content that can be fact-checked.

NON-VERBAL DETERMINANTS OF DECEPTION JUDGEMENTS

Although most research continues to focus on cues useful in accurately detecting deception, arguably the strongest recent findings are those that link non-verbal behaviours with judgements of deception. Researchers have recently focused on and analysed individual differences in appearing honest or deceptive (Levine 2010; Levine et al., 2011). From a psychometric analysis of results from hundreds of studies, Bond and DePaulo (2008) concluded that the primary determinant of a deception judgement is the sender's demeanour. Some people appear more honest than others. They appear more honest when they are lying, and also when they are telling the truth. Individual differences in apparent honesty are large. In studies where people are judged as lying or truth-telling, the standard deviation from sender to sender in percentage truth judgements received is over 11%, and this is an estimate that corrects for measurement error. These individual differences are evident throughout the extensive research literature on deception judgements – people differ widely in apparent honesty when they tell motivated lies, when they engage in deceptive interactions and when their lies are detectable. When Person A judges the truthfulness of Person B, the largest single determinant of the judgement is Person B's demeanour.

Levine et al. (2011) reported a series of experiments on individual differences in demeanour. They began by videotaping people who were telling lies and truths, and solicited deception judgements of these videotapes from undergraduates. Using the undergraduates' judgements, they identified the people on the videotape who were perceived as most and least deceptive. The researchers then created two videotapes – a veracity-matched tape and a veracity-mismatched tape. On the veracity-matched tape were people who appeared honest and were telling the truth, as well as people who appeared dishonest and were lying. On the veracity-mismatched tape were people who appeared dishonest but were telling the truth, as well as people who appeared honest but were lying. The investigators solicited deception judgements to these two specially constructed tapes from a variety of judges – American undergraduates, Koreans and U.S. government security agents. Without exception, the judges were highly accurate in discriminating lies from truths on the veracity-matched tape. These accuracy rates were invariably above 70%. Without exception, the judges were highly inaccurate when judging the veracity-mismatched tape. Their accuracy rates were invariably under 45%. Deception judgements can be more strongly affected by a sender's apparent truthfulness than the sender's actual truthfulness, as these experiments dramatically show.

Individual differences among liars can be explicated in terms of cues that predispose people to appear more or less honest. Hartwig and Bond (2011) cumulated relevant research and found that many cues are correlated with a person's apparent honesty. For example, people are judged to be lying if they appear incompetent and if their remarks do not place events within context. In general, behavioural, verbal and impressionistic cues are more strongly related to a person's apparent deception than the person's actual deception. Further, Levine and colleagues (2011) found that the cues to apparent honesty are highly inter-correlated.

Here we seek to extend the understanding of individual differences in apparent honesty. We do so by examining differences in apparent honesty in different deception media. Some people may *look* more honest than others when they are seen lying. Some may *sound* more honest than others when they are heard lying. Moreover, there may be individual differences in the convincingness of verbal content – some people's words may appear more honest than others' when read on a transcript. We wondered whether people who *look* honest *sound* honest and whether their words appear honest when read.

To address the generality of individual differences in the honesty of a person's demeanour, we searched for studies in which a given individual was judged for deceptiveness in more than one medium. From each of these studies, we attempted to extract a Pearson product–moment correlation coefficient between a person's apparent honesty when judged in one deception medium and that person's apparent honesty when judged in a second medium. In many studies that would otherwise be relevant, no such correlation could be extracted. It could, however, be extracted from 12 documents. Here the unit of analysis is a target person. Typically, each person tells a lie and a truth and the percentage of times the person is judged deceptive is averaged across these two messages before being correlated across media. In other studies, message veracity was manipulated across target persons. In this latter case, we analysed a partial cross-medium correlation, controlling for message veracity. We converted each r to a Fisher's Zr and cumulated the Zrs using standard meta-analytic fixed-effects techniques.

Here we assess the consistency of individual differences in apparent honesty across four media: audiovisual, audio-only, video-only and verbal transcript. The results of this meta-analysis appear in Table 2.1. On each line of the table are results for the relationship of a person's apparent honesty in one medium with that person's apparent honesty in a second medium. The first line, for example, displays the relationship of a person's apparent honesty in an audio-only medium with his/her apparent honesty in a video-only medium. As we see there, the more honest a person sounds, the more honest the person looks, r corresponding to the weighted mean Fisher's $Z = .36, p < .05$.

In fact, individual differences in apparent honesty are consistent across all four of the media in Table 2.1. People who look honest not only sound honest, their words appear honest in a transcript. Each correlation in the table is positive and statistically significant. Many of the lies of everyday life are told face-to-face, that is, in an audiovisual medium. It is interesting to note that a person's apparent honesty in the audiovisual medium is strongly correlated with how honest that person sounds ($r = .67$) and less strongly correlated with how honest that person looks ($r = .44$); for the difference, $Z = 4.34, p < .001$. Indeed, audiovisual impressions of honesty are at least as highly correlated with impressions of honesty from words in a written transcript ($r = .58$)

Table 2.1 Individual differences in apparent honesty across deception media

Media[a]	k	N	r	95% CI
A with V	6	222	.36	(0.24, 0.48)
A with T	3	78	.51	(0.32, 0.66)
V with T	3	78	.34	(0.11, 0.53)
A with AV	10	264	.67	(0.59, 0.73)
V with AV	15	474	.44	(0.36, 0.52)
T with AV	4	90	.58	(0.37, 0.68)

[a]Each line depicts the relationship of a person's apparent honesty in one medium with the person's apparent honesty in a second medium. The media are symbolized as follows: A (audio-only), V (video-only), T (transcript) and AV (audiovisual).

as they are with visible impressions of honesty (again, $r = .44$). These results suggest words and voice figure heavily in the face-to-face deception judgements of everyday life. This is true despite the fact that people in 58 countries worldwide believe that they can detect lies through gaze aversion and a number of other visible cues (Global Deception Research Team, 2006).

LIE DETECTION ACCURACY

Although deception researchers have an interest in the determinants of naïve deception judgements, the public at large focuses on a different issue: lie detection. We end this chapter by discussing contemporary issues in the accuracy of deception judgements.

Can people infer deception from behaviour? Most studies suggest that human lie detection abilities are limited. Indeed, a recent meta-analysis synthesized several decades of research on human ability to detection deception (Bond & DePaulo, 2006). This study included 206 studies in which nearly 25,000 judgements of deception were made. The average accuracy rate was 54%, which is hardly impressive given that the accuracy rate obtained by simply guessing is 50%. Moreover, results did not vary much from study to study. The highest variability in accuracy rates occurred in studies that had the smallest samples. A few small samples produced very high accuracy rates, and a few produced very low accuracy rates. This would be expected by chance.

Are certain individuals especially gifted at non-verbal lie detection? A large-scale statistical compilation reveals no lie detection wizards. Indeed, the Bond and DePaulo (2008) meta-analysis concluded that people barely differ from one another in the ability to detect lies. Correcting for measurement error, the standard deviation across perceivers in percentage of lies detected is less than 1%. Bond and DePaulo found that the most successful judges of deception in the accumulated research literature are no more successful than would be expected under a simple statistical model. Relatedly, Leach et al. (2009) found that individual performances on lie detection tests are not generally stable over time.

Although most researchers have concluded that people are poor at detecting lies, O'Sullivan, Frank, Hurley, and Tiwana (2009) claim that certain people are adept at detecting certain lies. In particular, the authors claim that police officers are good at spotting consequential, high-stakes deception. In support of this contention, O'Sullivan et al. reviewed 23 studies of deception detection by 31 groups of police officers. Each detection task was coded as involving high- or low-stakes lies. O'Sullivan and colleagues report that police officers average 67.2% accuracy when judging high-stakes lies and 55.2% accuracy when judging low-stakes lies.

O'Sullivan et al.'s (2009) portrayal of the literature conflicts sharply with the results from formal meta-analyses. Whereas O'Sullivan et al. assert as fact that college students are inferior to older adults in lie detection, the meta-analysis by Aamodt and Custer (2006) found no relationship between age and accuracy, $r = -.03$. In their large-scale meta-analysis, Bond and DePaulo (2006) examined the impact on lie detection accuracy of both motivation and judge expertise. Neither of these factors had a significant effect. Accuracy for unmotivated lies was 53.4% compared to 53.3% for motivated lies.

Several factors likely explain the discrepancy between the results of large-scale meta-analyses and O'Sullivan et al.'s (2009) smaller and less formal literature review. The first issue is the sample sizes associated with the evidence cited by O'Sullivan et al. The three highest accuracy rates that support O'Sullivan's conclusions derive from samples with less than 24 judges. Sampling error may, in part, explain these results. Second, and more importantly, O'Sullivan et al. cherry-picked findings consistent with their view. As they wrote in their method: 'Where more than one mean accuracy was available for several different tests from the same group of subjects, the lie scenario resulting in the highest mean accuracy was used' (p. 532). For example, they report the accuracy obtained by Porter, Woodworth, and Birt (2000) as 77%. The parole officers in the Porter et al. study were tested four times. Yes, they scored 76.7% on one test, but 40.4% on another test. Third, O'Sullivan and colleagues' highest accuracy rate (88%) reflected data collected by O'Sullivan herself. Those data were never peer-reviewed, and no relevant procedural details have been made public. Fourth, a number of the people whom O'Sullivan et al. credited with accurate lie detection were allowed to score their own tests (Bond, 2008). In sum, because O'Sullivan et al.'s conclusions rest on the opportunistic selection of favourable accuracy rates from small samples, many will be sceptical of their claims.

As the review already mentioned shows, it is apparent that many deception judgements are wrong. Why are people so often inaccurate when they attempt to infer deception from behaviour? Two answers to this question have been proposed: (1) there is insufficient behavioural evidence of deception and (2) people tend to rely on the wrong cues when judging lies. To assess these two possibilities, Hartwig and Bond (2011) conducted a series of meta-analyses. They used Brunswik's lens model, which is an analytic framework to examine predictions of criteria that are probabilistically related to cues (Brunswik, 1952). Results suggested that the principal cause of inaccuracy in deception judgements is the minute behavioural differences between liars and truth-tellers. Given the meagre evidence at their disposal, those who must infer deception from behaviour do nearly as well as they can.

In their meta-analysis of cues to deception, DePaulo and colleagues (2003) found that deception can be detected to a statistically significant degree by some global impressions, such as impressions of the liar's vocal and verbal involvement, cooperation and ambivalence. Indeed, the meta-analysts found that impressionistic cues are generally more strongly linked to deception than more minute behavioural cues. The reason for this pattern is not clear. It is possible that deception is associated with complex psychological processes that give rise to subtle changes in broad constellations of behaviour rather than displays of particular, isolated cues. Relatedly, it might be that perceivers who are instructed to rate behaviours on general dimensions such as degree of involvement or cooperation rely more on intuitive processes, and that such processes are better equipped to evaluate deception. Several lines of research support this speculation (Albrechtsen, Meissner, & Susa, 2009; Anderson, DePaulo, Ansfield, Tickle, & Green, 1999; DePaulo & Morris, 2004). For example, a meta-analysis on the accuracy–confidence relationship in deception judgements showed that people's confidence levels were higher when they had been exposed to a true statement compared to a deceptive one, regardless of the veracity judgement that they made. It seems that perceiving true statements may be accompanied by an intuitive feeling of certainty, which is misinterpreted by perceivers as a meta-cognitive judgement rather than what it actually is: an indicator of the veracity of the message. Moreover, research suggests that people feel more suspicious when they hear a lie, even though the explicit judgement of veracity they ultimately make is not accurate (Anderson, DePaulo, & Ansfield, 2002). Indirect measures of deception are not invariably helpful, however (Klaver, Lee, Spidel, & Hart, 2009).

Can lies be detected more accurately with indirect methods than explicit deception judgements? We seek a research-based answer to this question, an answer that incorporates as much relevant evidence as possible. For purposes of comparing direct with indirect lie detection, we used results from three published meta-analyses: the DePaulo et al. (2003) meta-analysis of cues to deception, the Bond and DePaulo (2006) meta-analysis of explicit deception judgements and an earlier DePaulo, Charlton, Cooper, Lindsay, and Muhlenbruck (1997) meta-analysis on confidence in deception judgements.

From Bond and DePaulo (2006), we obtained a grand estimate of lie/truth discrimination accuracy from explicit judgements. Data in 384 samples yield an average accuracy of $d = 0.39$ (as a standardized mean difference). From DePaulo et al. (1997), we obtained an estimate of lie/truth discrimination from confidence in explicit deception judgements (whether or not the judgements were correct). As DePaulo et al. note, people in the eight samples they analysed were more confident when judging truthful messages than deceptive messages, and this yielded a standardized mean difference between lies and truths of $d = 0.30$. The 2003 meta-analysis by DePaulo and colleagues provided data on 158 cues to deception. Many of these cues, however, were objective behavioural measures, not observers' impressions. From the descriptions in appendix A of DePaulo et al. (2003), we identified 17 cues that were subjective impressions of liars and truth-tellers. From table 14 in the same review, we abstracted data on the strength of subjective measures of six additional cues. Altogether, the DePaulo et al. meta-analysis provided us with data on 23 indirect measures of deception. We noted the strength of each of these subjective deception cues (as an absolute mean weighted d), as well as the number of samples in which the measure had been studied.

For relevant results, see Table 2.2. In the table are 25 lines – 1 for each of 25 potential ways to discriminate lies from truths. We have

Table 2.2   Lie–truth discrimination with **direct** and indirect measures

Cue #	Cue name	k	d
50	Cooperative	3	0.66
92	Thinking hard	1	0.61
90	Indifferent	2	0.59
19/25	Audible immediacy	7	0.55
	Direct judgements	**384**	**0.39**
91	Not spontaneous	2	0.35
14	Ambivalent	7	0.34
4	Details	10	0.32
	Judgement confidence	8	0.3
31	Vocal uncertainty	10	0.3
121	Relaxed face	1	0.29
27	Eye contact	5	0.28
61	Nervous	16	0.27
12	Plausibility	9	0.23
54	Pleasant face	5	0.2
49	Friendly	6	0.16
17	Expressive face	3	0.12
53	Pleasant voice	4	0.11
15	Attentive	6	0.08
115	Competent	3	0.08
26	Non-verbal immediacy	4	0.07
51	Attractive	6	0.06
64	Relaxed posture	4	0.05
86	Shield face	4	0
93	Serious	4	0

arranged these from the strongest to the weakest methods for lie detection. Note that each deception cue extracted from DePaulo et al. is identified by a number those meta-analysts assigned.

Results of this comparative meta-analysis are easy to summarize. Relative to 24 indirect measures of lie detection, explicit judgements perform well. Explicit judgements are better than 20 indirect measures of lie detection. As a lie detector, explicit judgements appear to perform worse than only four indirect measures. None of the four high-performing indirect measures of deception has been widely studied. Having documented a decline effect in non-verbal deception cues, we will watch with interest the results of additional research into the perceived cooperativeness, cognitive busyness, indifference and audible involvement of liars and truth-tellers. In the meantime, it is apparent that explicit deception judgements (however fallible) provide better lie/truth discrimination than many indirect measures.

CONCLUSION

Here we have reviewed theories and recent research on non-verbal lie detection. We have made a few new contributions. We have documented a tendency for deception cues to decline over time. We have found that individual differences in apparent honesty generalize over deception media, and have discovered that direct judgements yield better lie detection than many indirect methods.

REFERENCES

References prefixed by an asterisk provided data for the meta-analysis of Table 2.1.

Aamodt, M. G., & Custer, H. (2006). Who can best catch a liar?: A meta-analysis of individual differences in detecting deception. *The Forensic Examiner*, *15*(1), 6–11.

Albrechtsen, J. S., Meissner, C. A., & Susa, K. J. (2009). Can intuition improve deception detection performance? *Journal of Experimental Social Psychology*, *45*, 1052–1055.

Anderson, D. E., DePaulo, B. M., & Ansfield, M. E. (2002). The development of deception detection skill: A longitudinal study of same-sex friends. *Personality and Social Psychology Bulletin, 28*, 536–545.

Anderson, D. E., DePaulo, B. M., Ansfield, M. E., Tickle, J. J., & Green, E. (1999). Beliefs about cues to deception: Mindless stereotypes or untapped wisdom? *Journal of Nonverbal Behavior, 23*, 67–89.

Blair, J. P., Levine, T. R., & Shaw, A. J. (2010). Content in context improves deception detection accuracy. *Human Communication Research, 36*, 423–442.

Bond, C. F., Jr. (2008). A few can catch a liar, sometimes: Comment on Ekman and O'Sullivan (1990) and on Ekman, Frank, and O'Sullivan (1999). *Applied Cognitive Psychology, 22*, 1298–1300.

*Bond, C. F., Jr., & Atoum, A. O. (2000). International deception. *Personality and Social Psychology Bulletin, 26*, 385–395.

*Bond, C. F., Jr., Omar, A. S., Mahmoud, A., & Bonser, N. (1990). Lie detection across cultures. *Journal of Nonverbal Behavior, 14*, 189–204.

Bond, C. F., Jr., & DePaulo, B. M. (2006). Accuracy of deception judgements. *Personality and Social Psychology Review, 10*, 214–234.

Bond, C. F., Jr., & DePaulo, B. M. (2008). Individual differences in judging deception: Accuracy and bias. *Psychological Bulletin, 134*, 477–492.

*Bond, C. F., Jr., Thomas, B. J., & Paulson, R. M. (2004). Maintaining lies: The multiple-audience problem. *Journal of Experimental Social Psychology, 40*, 29–48.

*Bond, G. D. (2006). *Detecting expert and novice deception detection behaviors with eye tracking and pathfinder networks* (Unpublished doctoral dissertation). New Mexico State University, Las Cruces, NM.

Brunswik, E. (1952). *The conceptual framework of psychology*. Chicago, IL: University of Chicago Press.

Buller, D. B., & Burgoon, J. K. (1996). Interpersonal deception theory. *Communication Theory, 6*, 203–242.

*Castillo, P. A. (2011). *Cultural and cross-cultural factors in judgements of credibility* (Unpublished doctoral dissertation). Charles Sturt University.

*Christensen, D. (1980). *Decoding of intended versus unintended nonverbal messages as a function of social skill and anxiety* (Unpublished doctoral dissertation). University of Connecticut, Storrs, CT.

DePaulo, B. M. (1992). Nonverbal behavior and self-presentation. *Psychological Bulletin, 111*, 203–243.

DePaulo, B. M, Ansfield, M. E., & Bell, K. L. (1996). Theories about deception and paradigms for studying it: A critical appraisal of Buller and Burgoon's Interpersonal Deception Theory. *Communication Theory, 6*, 297–310.

DePaulo, B. M., Charlton, K., Cooper, H., Lindsay, J. L., & Muhlenbruck, L. (1997). The accuracy-confidence relation in the detection of deception. *Personality and Social Psychology Review, 1*, 346–357.

DePaulo, B. M., Lindsay, J. J., Malone, B. E., Muhlenbruck, L., Charlton, K., & Cooper, H. (2003). Cues to deception. *Psychological Bulletin, 129*, 74–118.

DePaulo, B. M., & Morris, W. L. (2004). Discerning lies from truths: Behavioral cues to deception and the indirect pathway of intuition. In P. A. Granhag & L. A. Strömwall (Eds.), *The detection of deception in forensic contexts* (pp. 15–40). Cambridge, UK: Cambridge University Press.

Ekman, P., & Friesen, W. V. (1969). Nonverbal leakage and clues to deception. *Psychiatry, 32*, 88–106.

*Ekman, P., Friesen, W. V., O'Sullivan, M., & Scherer, K. (1980). Relative importance of face, body, and speech in judgements of personality and affect. *Journal of Personality and Social Psychology, 38*, 270–277.

*Frank, M. G., & Ekman, P. (2005). Appearing truthful generalizes across different deception situations. *Journal of Personality and Social Psychology, 86*, 486–495.

Gamer, M. (2011). Detection of deception and concealed information using neuroimaging techniques. In B. Verschuere, G. Ben-Shakhar, & E. Meijer (Eds.), *Memory detection: Theory and application of the concealed information test* (pp. 90–113). Cambridge, UK: Cambridge University Press.

Global Deception Research Team. (2006). A world of lies. *Journal of Cross-Cultural Psychology, 37*, 60–74.

Granhag, P. A., & Hartwig, M. (2008). A new theoretical perspective on deception detection: On the psychology of instrumental mind-reading. *Psychology, Crime & Law, 14*, 189–200.

Hartwig, M., & Bond, C. F., Jr. (2011). Why do lie-catchers fail? A lens model meta-analysis of human lie judgements. *Psychological Bulletin, 137*, 643–659.

Hartwig, M., Granhag, P. A., Strömwall, L. A., & Doering, N. (2010). Impression and information management: On the strategic self-regulation of innocent and guilty suspects. *Open Criminology Journal, 3*, 10–16.

Hartwig, M., Granhag, P. A., Strömwall, L. A., & Vrij, A. (2005). Detecting deception via strategic disclosure of evidence. *Law and Human Behavior, 29*, 469–484.

Honts, C. R. (2004). The psychophysiological detection of deception. In P. A. Granhag & L. A. Strömwall (Eds.), *The detection of deception in forensic contexts* (pp. 103–123). Cambridge, UK: Cambridge University Press.

Ioannidis, J. P. A. (2005). Why most published research findings are false. *PLoS Medicine, 2*, 696–701.

*Kassin, S. M., Meissner, C. A., & Norwick, R. J. (2005). 'I'd know a false confession if I saw one': A comparative study of college students and police investigators. *Law and Human Behavior, 29*, 211–227.

Klaver, J. R., Lee, Z., Spidel, A., & Hart, S. D. (2009). Psychopathy and deception detection with indirect measures. *Legal and Criminological Psychology, 14*, 171–182.

*Krauss, R. M., Geller, V., & Olson, C. T. (1976). *Modalities and cues in the detection of deception.* Paper presented at the Meeting of the American Psychological Association, Washington, DC.

Lancaster, G. L. J., Vrij, A., Hope, L., & Waller, B. (2012). Sorting the liars from the truth tellers: The benefits of asking unanticipated questions. *Applied Cognitive Psychology, 27*, 107–114.

Leach, A. M., Lindsay, R. C. L., Koehler, R., Beaudry, J., Bala, N. C., Lee, K., & Talwar, V. (2009). The reliability of lie detection performance. *Law and Human Behavior, 33*, 96–109.

Lehrer, J. (2010, December 13). The truth wears off. *New Yorker*.

Levine, T. R. (2010). A few transparent liars: Explaining 54% accuracy in deception detection experiments. In C. Salmon (Ed.), *Communication yearbook 34* (pp. 40–61). London, UK: Routledge.

Levine, T. R., Blair, J. P., & Clare, D. (2013). Diagnostic utility: Experimental demonstrations and replications of powerful question effects and smaller question by experience interactions in high stake deception detection. *Human Communication Research, 40*, 262–289.

Levine, T. R., Serota, K. B., Shulman, J., Clare, D. D., Park, H. S., Shaw, A. S., ... Lee, J. H. (2011). Sender demeanor: Individual differences in sender believability have a powerful impact on deception detection judgements. *Human Communication Research, 37*, 377–403.

Levine, T. R., Shaw, A., & Shulman, H. C. (2010). Increasing deception detection accuracy with strategic questioning. *Human Communication Research, 36,* 216–231.

McCornack, S. A. (1997). The generation of deceptive messages: Laying the groundwork for a viable theory of interpersonal deception. In J. O. Greene (Ed.), *Message production: Advances in communication theory* (pp. 91–126). Mahwah, NJ: Lawrence Erlbaum.

McMahon, B., Holly, L., Harrington, R., Roberts, C., & Green, J. (2008). Do larger studies find smaller effects? The example of studies for the prevention of conduct disorder. *European Child & Adolescent Psychiatry, 17,* 432–437.

Mann, S., Vrij, A., & Bull, R. (2002). Suspects, lies and videotape: An analysis of authentic high-stakes liars. *Law and Human Behavior, 26,* 365–376.

*O'Sullivan, M., Ekman, P., Friesen, W., & Scherer, K. R. (1985). What you say and how you say it: The contribution of speech content and voice quality to judgements of others. *Journal of Personality and Social Psychology, 48,* 54–62.

O'Sullivan, M., Frank, M. G., Hurley, C. M., & Tiwana, J. (2009). Police lie detection accuracy: The effect of lie scenario. *Law and Human Behavior, 33,* 530–538. doi:10.1007/s10979-008-9166-4.

Ozonoff, S. (2011). The first cut is the deepest: Why do the reported effects of treatments decline over trials? *Journal of Child Psychology & Psychiatry, 52,* 729–730.

Porter, S., Woodworth, M., & Birt, A. R. (2000). Truth, lies, and videotape: An investigation of the ability of federal parole officers to detect deception. *Law and Human Behavior, 24*(6), 643-658. doi: 10.1023/A:1005500219657.Schooler, J. (2011). Unpublished results hide the decline effect. *Nature, 470,* 437.

Stiff, J. B., & Miller, G. R. (1986). Come to think of it … Interrogative probes, deceptive communication, and deception detection. *Human Communication Research, 12,* 339–357.

*Streeter, L. A., Krauss, R. M., Geller, V., Olsen, C., & Apple, W. (1977). Pitch changes during attempted deception. *Journal of Personality and Social Psychology, 35,* 345–350.

Strömwall, L. A., Granhag, P. A., & Hartwig, M. (2004). Practitioners' beliefs about deception. In P. A. Granhag & L. A. Strömwall (Eds.), *The detection of deception in forensic contexts* (pp. 229–250). New York, NY: Cambridge University Press.

Ten Brinke, L., & Porter, S. (2012). Cry me a river: Identifying the behavioral consequences of extremely high-stakes interpersonal deception. *Law and Human Behavior, 36,* 469–477.

Vrij, A. (2008) *Detecting lies and deceit: Pitfalls and opportunities* (2nd ed.). Cheshire, UK: Wiley.

Vrij, A., Ennis, E., Farman, S., & Mann, S. (2010a). People's perceptions of their truthful and deceptive interactions in daily life. *Open Access Journal of Forensic Psychology, 2,* 6–42.

Vrij, A., & Granhag, P. A. (2012). Eliciting cues to deception and truth: What matters are the questions asked. *Journal of Applied Research in Memory and Cognition, 1,* 110–117.

Vrij, A., Granhag, P. A., & Porter, S. B. (2010b). Pitfalls and opportunities in nonverbal and verbal lie detection. *Psychological Science in the Public Interest, 11,* 89–121.

Vrij, A., Leal, S., Granhag, P. A., Mann, S., Fisher, R. P., Hillman, J., & Sperry, K. (2009). Outsmarting the liars: The benefit of asking unanticipated questions. *Law and Human Behavior*, *33*, 159–166.

Vrij, A., Leal, S., Mann, S., & Fisher, R. P. (2012). Imposing cognitive load to elicit cues to deceit: Inducing the reverse order technique naturally. *Psychology, Crime & Law*, *18*, 579–594.

Vrij, A., Mann, S., Fisher, R. P., Leal, S., Milne, B., & Bull, R. (2008). Increasing cognitive load to facilitate lie detection: The benefit of recalling an event in reverse order. *Law and Human Behavior, 32*, 253–265.

Vrij, A., Mann, S., Leal, S., & Fisher, R. P. (2010c). 'Look Into My Eyes': Can an instruction to maintain eye contact facilitate lie detection? *Psychology, Crime, & Law*, *16*, 327–348.

Weinberger, S. (2010). Intent to deceive? Can the science of deception detection help to catch terrorists? *Nature, 465*, 412–415.

Zuckerman, M., DePaulo, B. M., & Rosenthal, R. (1981). Verbal and nonverbal communication of deception. In L. Berkowitz (Ed.), *Advances in experimental social psychology* (Vol. 14, pp. 1–59). New York, NY: Academic Press.

3

The Polygraph: Current Practice and New Approaches

EWOUT H. MEIJER AND BRUNO VERSCHUERE

Of all deception detection tools, the polygraph has the longest tradition. First described almost 100 years ago (Larson, 1932; Marston, 1917), it is used in many countries worldwide, most notably in the United States with more recently European countries following suit (Meijer & van Koppen, 2008). Still, the use of the polygraph for the detection of deception has been debated in the scientific literature for almost as long as it exists. In this contribution, we highlight the promises and perils of the use of the polygraph for the detection of deception. We first critically discuss the rationale, accuracy and application of the widely used control question polygraph test, including its increased use in sex offender management. We then describe the current status, challenges and potential applications of a different testing format used in conjunction with the polygraph, namely, the concealed information test (CIT). This type of test has also been referred to as 'memory detection' and is typically employed to show the presence or absence of crime-related information in suspects.

Detecting Deception: Current Challenges and Cognitive Approaches, First Edition.
Edited by Pär Anders Granhag, Aldert Vrij, and Bruno Verschuere.
© 2015 John Wiley & Sons, Ltd. Published 2015 by John Wiley & Sons, Ltd.

We also highlight recent research on a potential new application of the CIT, namely, to extract information that is unknown to the investigative authorities, from either individuals or groups of suspects.

THE POLYGRAPH

The words 'polygraph' and 'lie detector' are often used synonymously. The term polygraph is derived from Latin – with poly meaning 'many' or 'multiple' and graph meaning 'write' – and technically refers only to the recording device that is used for registering different physiological parameters. Polygraphs used for lie detection tests used to be briefcase-sized instruments that registered physiological signals with multiple pens writing on a lengthy roll of paper. Nowadays, they have been largely replaced by small amplifier/digitizers combined with a laptop for the recording. The sensors attached to the subject are generally (1) two expendable bands positioned around the thorax and the abdomen measuring respiration, (2) two electrodes attached to the inside of the hand measuring electrodermal activity and (3) an inflatable cuff positioned around the upper arm registering blood pressure. These physiological parameters co-vary with a number of psychological processes, including attention, stress and emotion. Consequently, inferences about psychological processes can be made from polygraph recordings. It is widely accepted that there is no unique physiological pattern associated with lying and that lying can therefore not be directly inferred from polygraph recordings (Lykken, 1998; Raskin, 1979, 1986). Still, lying can be indirectly inferred from the recordings, when obtained during an appropriate interrogation technique.

THE CONTROL QUESTION TEST

The most widely used polygraph interrogation technique is known as the control question test (CQT) (Reid, 1947). In this type of test, the suspect answers several questions while connected to the polygraph. Among these questions are relevant and control questions. The relevant questions specifically deal with the incident under investigation, for example, 'On the 24th of May, did you stab your wife?' The control questions have a more generic nature but also deal with undesirable behaviour, for example, 'In the first 25 years of your life, have you ever done anything illegal?' It is reasoned that the questions posing the greatest threat to failing the test will elicit the strongest physiological responses (Horowitz, Kircher, Honts, & Raskin, 1997). The crucial assumption is that the relevant questions are most threatening for guilty suspects, whereas the control questions form the biggest threat to innocent suspects. This latter assumption requires some explanation.

A CQT is preceded by a lengthy interview that serves to convince the suspect that the polygraph can determine to an extremely high degree of accuracy whether the suspect is lying or not. It is implied that an innocent examinee can confidently and honestly answer 'no' to the relevant questions. After all, the polygraph will show that this is the truth. In addition, the interview serves to manoeuvre the examinee into answering 'no' to the control questions by suggesting that confessing illegal activities will negatively influence the test outcome (for an example of the interview, see Box 3.1). As a result, the innocent examinee is assumed

---

Box 3.1: An example of the pretest interview as given by Offe and Offe (2007) in an experiment where the theft of a €50 voucher is the incident under investigation

I am going to ask you some questions to find out what your history concerning this matter looks like. I want to give you the reason, too, why I have to ask you such indiscrete questions. I want to find out whether one would consider you capable of an action such as removing a voucher for €50 based on your history or not. In a nutshell, I want to know whether such an action, taking something of monetary value out of a closed room, fits your personality profile or not.

These personal questions also have to be answered entirely truthfully. The more of these questions you can truthfully negate, the better it is for you, because then one can say that such an action does not fit your personality profile. If, however, you have to truthfully answer yes, then I will have to continue asking what the context was, so that I can get an impression of whether these were small and harmless delinquencies or whether there were some serious ones as well. Depending on what you tell me, it may begin to become imaginable that you may have done what we are talking about here as well.

The personal questions have nothing to do with whether you have taken the voucher or not. In order to make that clear from the beginning of every question, each personal question will start with 'In the first 25 years of your life, ...,' so that you will know right away, 'this is about my past'. For the result of the polygraph examination, it is important that you answer these questions truthfully as well.

to show the strongest physiological responses to the control questions, fearing that his/her deceptive answer to this question will get him/her convicted for the crime under investigation.

The CQT has been criticized on several grounds, but it is especially the assumption that innocent suspects will be most concerned about the control questions that is controversial. After all, the stress-inducing effect is not a feature of the control questions themselves, but rather a consequence of how their function is explained to the suspect. As a consequence, the accuracy of the test depends largely on the skills of the polygrapher rather than on the test itself. According to proponents of the CQT, a skilled polygrapher is capable of formulating control questions and creating an atmosphere in which an innocent examinee will indeed perceive the control questions as more stressful than the relevant questions (Raskin & Honts, 2002). CQT critics argue that this assumption has no grounding in psychological or psychophysiological research, nor is it convincing in its inner logic. In addition, the critics argue that the reliance on the skills of the polygrapher emphasizes the unstandardized nature of the CQT (Ben-Shakhar, 2008; Fiedler, Schmid, & Stahl, 2002; Iacono, 2008b; Lykken, 1998).

ACCURACY

To what extent the problems with the CQT result in erroneous outcomes remains under dispute. Part of this dispute traces back to the difficulties that characterize this type of research. In a typical laboratory study, half of the participants are instructed to commit some kind of mock crime (e.g. 'steal' money from a desk in an office), while the other half remain innocent (e.g. go to the same office and wait there for 5 minutes). Subsequently, all participants are tested with a CQT and the test outcome is determined for each examinee. In such a laboratory study, participants do not face severe consequences when failing the test. This is especially problematic given that threat of these consequences is likely to influence the magnitude of the physiological responses. An innocent suspect may, for example, perceive a relevant question (but also a control question) in a real-life test as much more threatening than a participant in a laboratory study. Laboratory studies therefore lack ecological validity. Field studies that analyse real-life polygraph test outcomes have greater ecological validity but are plagued by other problems. Most importantly, they lack an objective criterion of guilt or innocence (i.e. ground truth). Often, criteria such as a conviction or a confession are used to determine the error rate. But both criteria are suboptimal given that they may be influenced by the results of the CQT. In many cases, a suspect is only interrogated – and confronted with the outcome of the polygraph test – if the outcome of the test yields that he or she is deceptive. This ensures that a confession will always match a deceptive test outcome, resulting in a sampling bias overestimating the validity of the CQT (Iacono, 1991, 2008a; Mangan, Armitage, & Adams, 2008; Verschuere, Meijer, & Merckelbach, 2008; see also section 'Pseudoscience').

Keeping the limitations of laboratory and field studies in mind, accuracy estimates of the CQT derived from laboratory studies range from 74 to 82% for guilty examinees, with a 7–8% false negative rate (guilty participants erroneously classified as innocent), and 61–83% for innocent examinees, with a false positive rate (innocent participants erroneously classified as guilty) varying from 10 to 16%. Estimates derived from field studies range from 84 to 89% for guilty examinees, with 1–13% false negatives, and 59–75% for innocent examinees, with 5–29% false positives (see Table 3.1). It should be noted that these percentages do not necessarily add up to 100% because of an inconclusive category. This inconclusive outcome occurs when the magnitude of the reactions to the relevant and the control questions is similar, and no conclusion regarding deception is made.

More recently, a panel of 14 leading American scientists reviewed the literature on the accuracy of the CQT. The National Research Council (NRC) did not report accuracy in terms of percentage correct decisions. This is because percentage correct decisions rely on an arbitrary cut-off point. The choice of where the cut-off is placed depends on the preference to reduce either the false positive ratio or the false negative ratio. Rather, the NRC expressed accuracy in terms of the area under the receiver operating characteristic curve (ROC a) that can vary from 0.5 (chance level) to 1 (perfect accuracy). The 37 laboratory studies and 7 field studies that passed the minimum standards for review showed a ROC a of 0.85 and 0.89, respectively. It led the panel to conclude that 'specific-incident polygraph tests can discriminate lying from truth telling at rates well above chance, though well below perfection' (National Research Council, 2003, p. 4). This conclusion was highly similar to a U.S. government report that was published 20 years earlier (Office of Technology Assessment, 1983), which concluded that '... the polygraph detects deception at a rate better than chance, but with error rates that could be considered significant'.

The aforementioned allows for a number of important conclusions. First, there are a certain number of degrees of freedom when it comes to selecting data on which accuracy estimates are based. Inconclusive outcomes can, for example, be counted as errors or not. Also, with the

Table 3.1 Overview of the accuracy figures yielded by laboratory and field studies for the control question and concealed information polygraph test

	n studies	Guilty examinee			Innocent examinee		
		Test outcome correct	Test outcome incorrect	Test outcome inconclusive	Test outcome correct	Test outcome incorrect	Test outcome inconclusive
CQT laboratory studies							
Office of Technology Assessment (1983)	12	74	7	19	60	16	24
Kircher, Horowitz, and Raskin (1988)	14	74	8	18	66	12	22
Ben-Shakhar and Furedy (1990)	9	80	7	13	63	15	22
Honts (2004)	11	82	7	11	83	10	7
CQT field studies							
Office of Technology Assessment (1983)	10	87	11	2	75	19	6
Ben-Shakhar and Furedy (1990)	9	84	13	3	72	23	5
Honts (2004)	4	89	1	10	59	12	29
CIT laboratory studies							
Ben-Shakhar and Furedy (1990)	10	84	16		94	6	
Elaad (1998)	15	81	19		96	4	
Lykken (1998)	8	88	12		97	3	
MacLaren (2001)	22	76	24		83	17	
CIT field studies							
Elaad (1990)	1	42	58		98	2	
Elaad et al. (1992)	1	76	24		94	6	

Reproduced with permission from Meijer and Versschuere (2010). © Taylor & Francis.

pros and cons of laboratory and field studies in mind, different authors apply different inclusion and exclusion criteria for studies they base their evaluation of the CQT's accuracy on. As a consequence, accuracy estimates between reviews vary dramatically. Second, even though the *exact* accuracy remains unknown, the CQT performs above chance level, meaning its outcome contains diagnostic information about deception. Third, the accuracy figures highlight that the error rate of the CQT can be substantial. Finally, with the cut-off points used in practice, the test is especially prone to false positive outcomes. This is problematic for application in the legal arena, as it is alien to legal doctrine abbreviated in the so-called Blackstone maxim: 'Better that ten guilty persons escape than that one innocent suffer' (Blackstone, 1882; see also Volokh, 1997).

PSEUDOSCIENCE

The NRC report cited earlier also contains some other noteworthy conclusions. For example, the council concluded that 'Research on the polygraph has not progressed over time in the manner of a typical scientific field. It has not accumulated knowledge or strengthened its scientific underpinnings in any significant manner' (p. 213). This absence of progress can, at least in part, be explained by the fact that the use of the polygraph is almost exclusively in the hands of practitioners who lack ties to academia. Historically, the CQT has been largely developed outside academia, and the examiners administering the tests are most often law enforcement officials without any academic background in psychology, physiology or psychophysiology. Without such a background, it is difficult to fully comprehend the scientific literature on polygraph testing. Hence, polygraph examiners almost exclusively rely on what they are trained at polygraph schools which is that the CQT is highly accurate. The British and European Polygraph Association, for example, claims that 'research has shown that the accuracy of computerized polygraph testing is 98%' (http://europeanpolygraph.org/faqs.htm. Retrieved 12th August 2014).

When conducting tests in the field, selective feedback may further strengthen their perception of the CQT being nearly infallible (Vrij, 2008). A closer look at how the CQT is employed in the field may help to understand this. Typically, a 'deception indicated' test outcome is followed by an interrogation during which the suspect is confronted with the test outcome. If the suspect confesses during this interrogation, this provides the examiner with the feedback that the test outcome was correct. If it was an innocent suspect who failed the test, a confession is unlikely. This does not, however, prove the test outcome wrong, as the examiner may uphold the belief that the suspect is indeed guilty, but he or she just did not confess. If the outcome of the test is 'no deception indicated', no subsequent interrogation takes place. In case of a guilty suspect escaping detection, this error will go unnoticed, as the absence of an interrogation ensures the absence of a confession. Thus, this mechanism of selective feedback ensures occasional feedback on correct decisions while preventing feedback in the cases of an incorrect outcome, thereby explaining the perceived infallibility of the polygraph by examiners. It also makes the following conclusion from the NRC report a little less remarkable: 'What is remarkable, given the large body of relevant research, is that claims about the accuracy of the polygraph made today parallel those made throughout the history of the polygraph: practitioners have always claimed extremely high levels of accuracy, and these claims have rarely been reflected in empirical research' (p. 107).

DISCLOSURE: JOB APPLICANTS AND SEX OFFENDERS

Historically, the most widely studied application of the CQT is in criminal investigations, but more recently, it has also gained popularity in the treatment and monitoring of sex offenders. Polygraph tests are used to monitor offenders' activities in the community (e.g. during a parole), as well as to gain a more comprehensive understanding of their historical sexual interests and behaviours (English, Jones, Patrick, & Pasini-Hill, 2003). In contrast to tests in criminal investigations where the offence is known and the question is whether the suspect committed it, the sex offender is questioned about incidents of which it is unknown whether they have taken place at all. This type of test bears close resemblance to the application of the polygraph in personnel screening, used in the United States to screen job applicants and monitor employees of government agencies whose work involves security risks (e.g. FBI applicants or nuclear scientists; Krapohl, 2002). As there is no longer a specific incident under investigation, the relevant questions are phrased in a very broad way (e.g. 'Have you had unsupervised contact with children over the last 3 months?'). Relevant and control questions (e.g. 'Have you done anything over the last 3 months that would concern your probation officer?'; Grubin, Madsen, Parsons, Sosnowski, & Warberg, 2004, p. 213) now become much more similar than in specific incident testing. As a consequence, it becomes much more ambiguous which question poses the greatest threat to the subject, and diagnostic decisions therefore become less accurate (National Research Council, 2003).

Despite these concerns, several reports have suggested that the polygraph is highly successful in obtaining previously undisclosed information (e.g. Ahlmeyer, Heil, McKee, & English, 2000; Emerick & Dutton, 1993; English et al., 2003; Gannon, Wood, Pina, Vasquez, & Fraser, 2012; Grubin, 2010; Grubin et al., 2004; Wilcox & Sosnowski, 2005). This includes information on the number of previous offences, age of the first offence, number of victims and prevalence of high-risk behaviours. It is important to realize that the capability of the polygraph to obtain new information is more related to its intimidating effect than to its accuracy. According to Abrams and Abrams (1993), for example, there are three points in time when sex offenders can disclose information: (1) when they are told that they will face a test in the near future, (2) during the pretest interview and (3) during the confrontation with the test outcome. Note that the first two points are before the polygraph test is actually conducted. Indeed, both Gannon and colleagues (2012) and Grubin and colleagues (2004) report that most information was disclosed during the pretest interview, well before the sensors of the polygraph were actually connected. Apparently, the expectation of an upcoming polygraph test is sufficient to make offenders disclose information. This means that disclosure of new information may have little to do with the polygraph as a method for the detection of deception per se. More likely, it is the questioning and the intimidation by the lie detector that makes the examinee bring up new information (see also Gannon, Keown, & Polaschek, 2007; Meijer, Verschuere, Merckelbach, & Crombez, 2008).

Little is known about the effects of newly disclosed information on treatment success. This is especially relevant as many studies used a design where participation in the polygraph treatment programme was voluntary. Given this voluntary nature, the offenders included in these programmes may represent a subgroup of highly motivated (and perhaps quickly disclosing) offenders, and similar disclosure rates may have been obtained by a thorough interview (Meijer et al., 2008).[1] In a first study investigating effect of disclosure on treatment

---

[1]The exception is the study by Gannon et al. (2012) which is based on data from a programme involving mandatory polygraph testing. Yet, these authors used information supplied by the polygraph offender managers, and note that 'It is possible that polygraph offender managers may have felt more motivated or "expected" to provide large numbers of disclosures compared to comparison offender managers' (p. 8).

success, McGrath, Cumming, Hoke, and Bonn-Miller (2007) compared
5-year re-offence rates of a group of 104 adult male sex offenders who
received community cognitive-behavioural treatment, correctional
supervision and periodic polygraph compliance exams with a matched
group of 104 sex offenders who received the same type of treatment
and supervision services but no polygraph exams. In line with earlier
studies, polygraph testing resulted in the disclosure of previously
withheld high-risk behaviours, and the vast majority of the treatment providers and supervision officers rated the tests as 'helpful' or
'very helpful' (see also Gannon et al., 2012; Grubin, 2010). Still, their
data did not provide much support for an effect of polygraph tests on
recidivism. The authors obtained recidivism data and classified each
incident as either sexual, violent or other. The only significant difference was found for violent incidents: the number of individuals in the
polygraph group charged with committing a new violent offence was
significantly lower than in the no-polygraph group (2.9 vs. 11.5%).
There were no significant between-group differences for the number
of individuals charged with a new sexual (5.8 vs. 6.7%) or other
offences (35.6 vs. 29.8%). There was also no significant difference in
overall recidivism when combining sexual, violent or other (39.4 vs.
34.6%). Finally, the number of individuals known to have violated
their supervision conditions did not differ between groups (51.9 vs.
45.2%), nor did the number of individuals who returned to prison
(47.1% in the polygraph vs. 38.5% in the no-polygraph group). Based
on these findings, the authors argued that the polygraph's 'widespread
use has far outpaced empirical examination of its effectiveness'
(McGrath et al., 2007, p. 391).

THE FUTURE OF THE CQT

While applied for over half a century, little effort and progress has
been made to increase the theoretical underpinning and validity of
the CQT. Many think that with the advancement of technology, polygraph tests will become more accurate. The review by the NRC, however, contradicts this idea. In their review, CQT accuracy of the
selected polygraph studies was plotted against the year of publication
(National Research Council, 2003, p. 346). If technological advancement would lead to an increased accuracy, a positive trend should be
apparent. This was not the case. Erroneous outcomes of the CQT
occur because the polygraph traces do not allow for distinguishing,
for example, between an innocent's fear of false detection and a

guilty's fear of detection. This problem is not solved by technologically more sophisticated measuring device or more advanced scoring algorithms. Without substantial changes to the CQT question format, polygraph tests will not reach extremely high accuracy (National Research Council, 2003).

CONCEALED INFORMATION

In the late 1950s, a professor of psychology and strong opponent of the CQT, David Lykken, developed an alternative application of the polygraph which he named the guilty knowledge test (GKT) (Lykken, 1959; see also Munsterberg, 1908). It is nowadays commonly referred to as the CIT (Verschuere, Ben-Shakhar, & Meijer, 2011). During a CIT, test questions do not directly address the incident under investigation. Rather, all questions concern details of the crime, presumably only known to the police and to the perpetrator. Answer alternatives to these questions are presented serially, while physiological signals are recorded. These answer alternatives include the correct answer but also several plausible but incorrect answers (e.g. 'Was the victim killed with a (a) gun, (b) knife, (c) rope, (d) bat or (e) ice pick?'). For a guilty suspect, the correct alternative is salient and will elicit an enhanced physiological response. When multiple questions, each pertaining to different details, are presented to the suspect and he or she shows a pattern of stronger responding to the correct alternative, knowledge of intimate details of the crime is determined, from which involvement can be inferred. For an innocent suspect, all alternatives are equally plausible and will elicit similar physiological responses. There are two ways to ensure that the different alternatives are equally plausible. First, like with an Oslo confrontation, all alternatives can be presented to a panel of naïve participants with the question to guess which alternative is correct (Doob & Kirschenbaum, 1973). Second, the alternatives can be presented to the suspect before the actual test in a previewing session (Verschuere & Crombez, 2008).

THEORY

The CIT theory is that '... for the guilty subject only, the "correct" alternative will have a special significance ... which will tend to produce a stronger orienting reflex than that subject will show to other alternatives' (Lykken, 1974, p. 728). The orienting reflex (OR) is also referred to as the 'What is it?' or the 'What's to be done?' reflex and is elicited by novel and/or significant stimuli (Sokolov, 1963). The organism orients to these potentially important stimuli in order to analyse them more thoroughly and to prepare for appropriate responding. Indeed, for the guilty only, the correct items are of special significance and will grasp attention. The OR is associated with a specific pattern of physiological responding – increase in skin conductance, heart rate deceleration and respiratory suppression (Lynn, 1966) – that can be made visible by a polygraph. With some exceptions, research findings have generally supported the idea that orienting accounts for differential responding in the CIT (Verschuere & Ben-Shakhar, 2011).

ACCURACY

One of the main advantages of the CIT is that the probability of a false positive test outcome is fully under the control of the examiner. A false positive test outcome means that, merely by chance, a pattern of stronger responding to the correct alternatives has occurred. The probability of this happening depends on two factors. The first factor concerns the test's properties; the false positive probability is inversely related to the number of questions and the number of answer alternatives per question. The second factor that determines false positive probability is how one defines 'a pattern of stronger responding'. When a guilty test outcome requires the suspect to respond maximally to the correct alternatives of all five questions, the probability of this happening by chance is smaller than when one requires a maximal response for only three out of the five correct alternatives. This control over false positive probability has important implications. For one thing, it allows the examiner to set the false positive probability at an arbitrary low level, as prescribed by legal doctrine in most civilized countries. It also allows for calculation of the probability that a guilty test outcome is incorrect. This is essential information if an incriminating test outcome is introduced in court proceedings, as it allows for proper weighing.

The CIT originally described by Lykken (1959) used only skin conductance responding (SCR) as the dependent measure. This measure has by far received the most attention in CIT research and has shown to be robust in discriminating between guilty and innocent participants (see Table 3.1). Elaad (1998), for example, reviewed 15 mock crime studies and found average detection rates of 81% for guilty examinees and 96% for the innocent. Similar accuracy rates were reported by Ben-Shakhar and Furedy (1990), who reviewed 10 mock crime studies and found detection rates of 84 and 94%, respectively. A more recent review showed similar results with successful detection of 76% of participants with concealed knowledge and slightly lower detection, 83%, of those without (MacLaren, 2001). The two available field studies (Elaad, 1990; Elaad, Ginton, & Jungman, 1992) show equally high detection of innocent suspects (98 and 94%, respectively) but somewhat lower detection accuracy among guilty suspects (42 and 76%, respectively). Meta-analytic research on 80 studies showed very large effects ($d = 1.55$; Ben-Shakhar & Elaad, 2003). Finally, in its 2003 report, the NRC selected 13 studies that passed their minimum standards, yielding an area under the ROC curve of 0.88.

Except for the two available field studies mentioned earlier (Elaad, 1990; Elaad et al., 1992), CIT accuracy estimates are derived from laboratory studies typically including undergraduate students asked to perform some kind of mock crime. This poses a threat to the ecological validity of the bulk of the CIT research, as many factors differ substantially between laboratory and field settings (see also Ben-Shakhar, 2012). A number of studies experimentally manipulated some of these factors in order to shed light on the direction of the effects these factors may cause. First, motivation is likely to substantially differ between a laboratory and a field setting. The meta-analysis by Ben-Shakhar and Elaad (2003), however, showed that motivation (e.g. by promising a monetary incentive for passing the test) was actually positively associated with detection efficiency, meaning that data from laboratory studies may in fact be an underestimation of the real effect size.

Needless to say, intact memory for crime details is a prerequisite for a successful CIT. Several factors that have been shown to affect memory differ between laboratory and field settings. For one thing, memory decays with time, and whereas the time between the (mock) crime and the CIT is typically a matter of minutes in laboratory studies, it can be days, months or even years in real life. Several authors (Carmel, Dayan, Naveh, Raveh, & Ben-Shakhar, 2003; Gamer, Kosiol, & Vossel, 2010; Nahari & Ben-Shakhar, 2011; Peth, Vossel, & Gamer, 2012) looked at this and varied the delay between the mock crime and the CIT. These studies show that such a delay indeed lowers the accuracy of the CIT. Yet, this effect is primarily present for peripheral items (details that are not essential to the execution of the mock crime such as the poster on the wall). Memory for central items remained much more intact, stressing the importance of using central details when conducting a CIT (see also Meijer, Verschuere, & Ben-Shakhar, 2011). Another factor that likely to substantially differ between laboratory and field setting is stress levels during the crime (Verschuere, Meijer, & De Clercq, 2011). Eyewitness research has shown that that increased stress causes an attention narrowing resulting in superior encoding of central details while undermining the encoding of peripheral details (Christianson, 1992). In a recent study, Peth et al. (2012) manipulated the level of emotional arousal by confronting half of the guilty participants with a confederate during execution of a mock crime. Yet, stress had no impact on CIT accuracy (see also Bradley & Janisse, 1981; Kugelmass & Lieblich, 1966).

Given the experimental nature of these studies, they do not allow for conclusions about the accuracy of the CIT in the field. Yet, they also do not lend strong support for the notion that accuracy in the field will be substantially lower as long as central details are used. Still, the lack of field data hinders real-life application of the CIT (Ben-Shakhar, 2012; Ben-Shakhar & Kremnitzer, 2011). One point that should be addressed here, however, is that the factors differing between laboratory and field setting may influence the false negative rate, but they are unlikely to influence the false positive rate of the CIT. Many other, more widely accepted forms of forensic evidence such as fingerprints, DNA or confessions are typically used as challenge tests: presence of such evidence is indicative of guilt, but absence is not indicative of innocence. The CIT outcome should be handled in a similar manner: an information present outcome is indicative of guilt, while an information absent outcome is less indicative of innocence (see also Meijer et al., 2011).

APPLICATION OF THE CIT

Despite its controllable false positive rate and its firm grounding in orienting theory (Verschuere, Crombez, De Clercq, & Koster, 2004), the CIT is only rarely used in the field, with Japan being the only exception (Hira & Furumitsu, 2002; Nakayama, 2002; Osugi, 2011). This limited use can, at least in part, be attributed to the difficulty of formulating sufficient appropriate test items. These items need to fulfil two requirements. To begin with, the details asked need to be known to the culprit and the investigating authorities. Second, these items may not have been exposed to an innocent suspect, for example, through prior interrogation, or the media. Estimations of the number of cases that meet these criteria are given by Podlesney (1993, 2003). This author examined the files of FBI examinations in which a CQT was performed for usable CIT items. The first study (Podlesney, 1993) showed that in 8 out of the 61 files (13%), sufficient usable items were present. The second study (Podlesney, 2003) examined 758 files and found this to be the case in 51 of them (7%). At first glance, these statistics do not look very encouraging. It should be noted, however, that Podlesney's estimation is based on a retrospective review of case records. This way of post hoc determination of possible test is likely to underestimate potential application, because the information in these records was not selected with a CIT in mind (see also Lykken, 1998). Furthermore, discussions about applicability seem to be dictated by the issue of whether the CIT can fully replace the CQT (e.g. Ben-Shakhar, 1991). This, however, should not be the primary question. The relevant question that should be answered is whether a CIT can be applied in a substantial proportion of the cases. With this question in mind, Podlesney's data sketch a much more optimistic picture. After all, it shows that in difficult cases (otherwise, a CQT would not have been necessary), a CIT would have been possible in approximately 10% of the cases. This figure should be regarded as the lower-bound estimate as it is based on incomplete file records. In a regular forensic context, the applicability of the CIT seems amply enough to yield a positive cost/benefit analysis. The large-scale use of the CIT in Japan has, in any case, shown that successful implementation is indeed possible (Hira & Furumitsu, 2002; Nakayama, 2002; Osugi, 2011).

NEW APPROACHES: THE SEARCHING AND GROUP CIT

As outlined earlier, in a typical CIT, a suspect is tested for intimate knowledge of a crime known only to the investigative authorities and the perpetrator. A relatively new application of the CIT principle has become known as the searching CIT (S-CIT) (Osugi, 2011; see also Raskin, 1989). This variant can be employed when the correct alternative is not known to the investigative authorities, but rather is the topic of investigation. If that is the case, a series of answer options are presented to the suspect, and the option that evokes the largest response is considered to be the correct one. As such, the S-CIT can be used, for example, to locate a victim's body (Nakayama, 2002) or find the location of illegal substances (MacLaren, 2001) when the perpetrators are known.

Experimental research on the S-CIT has only recently commenced. Meijer, Smulders, and Merckelbach (2010) investigated the S-CIT in a laboratory setting using undergraduate students as participants. These authors applied the S-CIT to a group of suspects rather than to individuals. The idea behind this was that whereas lie detection techniques are typically geared towards testing individuals, many of today's security threats come from organized groups such as terrorist networks or criminal organizations. In these cases, there are often multiple suspects who are likely to possess the same critical information. Twelve participants were provided with the date, location and target of an upcoming mock terrorist act with instructions not to reveal the information under any circumstances. The S-CIT showed that the mean responding of the group to the correct answers was stronger than that to all the other options, and as such, the plan could be extracted from the group as a whole.

In the study by Meijer and colleagues (2010), all participants received all the information with regard to the mock attack. In real life, however, not all members of a group of suspects who are on the radar of the investigative authorities may hold all the relevant information. Breska, Ben-Shakhar, and Gronau (2012) re-examined three datasets to investigate to what extent the S-CIT could be applied to groups that consisted of both guilty and innocent participants. Two sets of algorithms were tested, both based on the assumption that individuals who share the same concealed information would demonstrate a similar pattern of differential responses across items (for details of these algorithms, see Breska et al., 2012). Both sets of algorithms achieved a detection accuracy similar to the standard CIT analysis. For the SCR measure, for example, the standard CIT analysis yielded an area under the ROC curve of 0.99, 0.89 and 0.82 for the three respective datasets. For the new algorithms, the area under the curve ranged from 0.97 to 0.99 for dataset 1, from 0.88 to 0.91 for dataset 2 and from 0.73 to 0.80 for dataset 3. In addition, the algorithms were highly robust even when including a large number of unknowledgeable participants.

Finally, given the multiple choice-like format of the CIT, only a limited number of items can be presented. As the starting point for the S-CIT is that the correct option is unknown, choosing what items to include poses a challenge. To test a potential solution to this problem, Meijer, Bente, Ben-Shakhar, and Schumacher (2013) applied a dynamic questioning approach to the group S-CIT. Twenty groups of five participants were invited to the lab, and each group was asked to plan a mock terrorist attack based on a list of potential countries, cities and streets. The dynamic questioning approach entailed simultaneous data recording and direct online analysis of the data in each group of five, allowing follow-up questions to be based on the outcome of the previous question. For example, a first question regarding the location of the attack could ask about the country where the attack would take place. If the reaction to the option 'Italy' exceeded the threshold, the question was followed up by presenting five cities in Italy, allowing to sequentially zoom in on the exact location. Results showed that in 19 of the 20 groups, the country was correctly detected using this procedure. In 13 of these remaining 19 groups, the city was correctly detected. In 7 of these 13, the street was also correctly detected. The question about the country resulted in no false positives (out of 20), the question about the city resulted in two false positives (out of 19), while the question about the streets resulted in two false positives (out of 13). Furthermore, the two false positives at the city level also yielded a false positive at the street level. These results indicated that – despite the modest effect sizes – this dynamic questioning approach can still help to unveil plans about a mock terrorist attack.

THE FUTURE OF THE CIT

Unlike with the CQT, the CIT is characterized by an active and flourishing research tradition. Ongoing efforts include (1) researching into its theoretical underpinning, (2) investigating the effect factors such as stress and memory decay have on its accuracy as well as (3) introducing additional and new measures such as finger pulse volume, the P300 component of the ERP, fMRI and reaction times. With regard to these new measures, it is important to realize that the strength of the CIT lies in its design that offers appropriate protection of the innocent and that this property is relatively independent of the dependent measure or technology. The lack of application outside of Japan can primarily be attributed to problems of a practical nature. Implementing the CIT requires specific changes to the way cases are handled to ensure relevant details are collected but also kept from innocent suspects. This includes, for example, visiting the crime scene at an early stage to collect details but also making sure these details are not shared with the suspect during any interrogation that precedes the CIT. Because of the low probability of false positive errors, the CIT can be tested under field situations relatively safely. After all, the risk of incriminating an innocent suspect is small. It is unlikely, however, that investigative authorities will successfully implement the method on their own, and researchers should be willing to invest in assisting the investigative authorities with implementation of the CIT.

CONCLUDING REMARKS

The use of the CQT for the detection of deception is highly controversial. Strong claims about its accuracy and utility almost exclusively come from practitioners. Academics, on the other hand, are mostly sceptical. Practitioners who are involved in the use of polygraph tests, whether it is in law enforcement, sex offender treatment or any other application, should keep in mind that the inner logic of the CQT is weak and that an innocent examinee may also respond to the relevant questions. In specific incident (i.e. crime) testing, where the offence is known, its accuracy has been shown to exceed chance level. The error rate is, however, substantial, and in screening situations (i.e. sex offender monitoring and treatment), where the offence is unknown, the error rate is most likely higher. The problems associated with the CQT are of a logical nature and will not be solved by new sensors or advanced scoring algorithms. Despite its strong underpinnings in theory and empirical data, the CIT is hardly used in the field. Due to its low false positive rate, the CIT can safely be applied in the field. For successful application, researchers need to assist investigative authorities, which will hopefully result in an increase in the amount of available field data.

REFERENCES

Abrams, S., & Abrams, J. B. (1993). *Polygraph testing of the pedophile*. Portland, OR: Ryan Gwinner Press.

Ahlmeyer, S., Heil, P., McKee, B., & English, K. (2000). The impact of polygraphy on admissions of victims and offenses in adult sexual offenders. *Sexual Abuse: A Journal of Research and Treatment, 12*, 123–138.

Ben-Shakhar, G. (1991). Future prospects of psychophysiological detection: Replacing the CQT by the GKT. In J. R. Jennings, P. K. Ackles, & M. G. H. Coles (Eds.), *Advances in psychophysiology* (Vol. 4, pp. 193–199). London, UK: Jessica Kingsley.

Ben-Shakhar, G. (2008). The case against the use of polygraph examinations to monitor post-conviction sex offenders. *Legal and Criminological Psychology, 13*, 191–207.

Ben-Shakhar, G. (2012). Current research and potential applications of the concealed information test: An overview. *Frontiers in Psychology, 3*, 342.

Ben-Shakhar, G., & Elaad, E. (2003). The validity of psychophysiological detection of information with the Guilty Knowledge Test: A meta-analytic review. *Journal of Applied Psychology, 88*, 131–151.

Ben-Shakhar, G., & Furedy, J. J. (1990). *Theories and applications in the detection of deception: A psychophysiological and international perspective*. New York, NY: Springer-Verlag.

Ben-Shakhar, G., & Kremnitzer, M. (2011). The CIT in the courtroom: Legal aspects. In B. Verschuere, G. Ben-Shakhar, & E. Meijer (Eds.), *Memory detection: theory and application of the Concealed Information Test* (pp. 276–290). Cambridge, UK: Cambridge University Press.

Blackstone, W. (1882). *Commentaries on the laws of England* (3rd ed.). London, UK: Murray.

Bradley, M. T., & Janisse, M. P. (1981). Extraversion and the detection of deception. *Personality and Individual Differences, 2*, 99–103.

Breska, A., Ben-Shakhar, G., & Gronau, N. (2012). Algorithms for detecting concealed knowledge among groups when the critical information is unavailable. *Journal of Experimental Psychology Applied, 18*, 292–300.

Carmel, D., Dayan, E., Naveh, A., Raveh, O., & Ben-Shakhar, G. (2003). Estimating the validity of the Guilty Knowledge Test from simulated experiments: The external validity of Mock Crime studies. *Journal of Experimental Psychology: Applied, 9*, 261–269.

Christianson, S. A. (1992). Emotional stress and eyewitness testimony: A critical review. *Psychological Bulletin, 112*, 284–309.

Doob, A. N., & Kirschenbaum, H. M. (1973). Bias in police lineups-partial remembering. *Journal of Police Science and Administration, 1*, 187–293.

Elaad, E. (1990). Detection of guilty knowledge in real-life criminal investigations. *Journal of Applied Psychology, 75*, 521–529.

Elaad, E. (1998). The challenge of the Concealed Knowledge Polygraph Test. *Expert Evidence, 6*, 161–187.

Elaad, E., Ginton, A., & Jungman, N. (1992). Detection measures in real-life criminal guilty knowledge tests. *Journal of Applied Psychology, 77*, 757–767.

Emerick, R. L., & Dutton, W. A. (1993). The effect of polygraphy on the self report of adolescent sex offender: Implications for risk assessment. *Annals of Sex Research, 6*, 83–103.

English, K., Jones, L., Patrick, D., & Pasini-Hill, D. (2003). Sexual offender containment: Use of the postconviction polygraph. *Annuals New York Academy of Sciences, 989*, 411–427.

Fiedler, K., Schmid, J., & Stahl, T. (2002). What is the current truth about polygraph lie detection. *Basic and Applied Social Psychology, 24*, 313–324.

Gamer, M., Kosiol, D., & Vossel, G. (2010). Strength of memory encoding affects physiological responses in the Guilty Action Test. *Biological Psychology, 83*, 101–107.

Gannon, T. A., Keown, K., & Polaschek, D. L. (2007). Increasing honest responding on cognitive distortions in child molesters: The bogus pipeline revisited. *Sex Abuse, 19*, 5–22.

Gannon, T. A., Wood, J., Pina, A., Vasquez, E., & Fraser, I. (2012). *The evaluation of the mandatory polygraph pilot*. Ministry of Justice Research Series 14/12. London, UK: Ministry of Justice.

Grubin, D. (2010). A trial of voluntary polygraphy testing in 10 english probation areas. *Sexual Abuse: A Journal of Research and Treatment, 22*, 266–278.

Grubin, D., Madsen, L., Parsons, S., Sosnowski, D., & Warberg, B. (2004). A prospective study of the impact of polygraphy on high-risk behaviors in adult sex offenders. *Sexual Abuse: A Journal of Research and Treatment, 16*, 209–222.

Hira, S., & Furumitsu, I. (2002). Polygraphic examinations in Japan: Application of the guilty knowledge test in forensic investigations. *International Journal of Police Science & Management, 4*, 16–27.

Honts, C. R. (2004). The psychophysiological detection of deception. In P. A. Granhag & L. A. Strömwall (Eds.), *The detection of deception in forensic contexts* (pp. 103–126). Cambridge, UK: Cambridge University Press.

Horowitz, S. W., Kircher, J. C., Honts, C. R., & Raskin, D. C. (1997). The role of comparison questions in physiological detection of deception. *Psychophysiology, 34*, 108–115.

Iacono, W. G. (1991). Can we determine the accuracy of polygraph tests. In J. R. Jennings, P. K. Ackles, & M. G. H. Coles (Eds.), *Advances in psychophysiology* (Vol. *4*, pp. 201–207). London, UK: Jessica Kingsley.

Iacono, W. G. (2008a). Accuracy of polygraph techniques: Problems using confessions to determine ground truth. *Physiology & Behavior, 95*, 24–26.

Iacono, W. G. (2008b). Effective policing – Understanding how polygraph tests work and are used. *Criminal Justice and Behavior, 35*, 1295–1308.

Kircher, J. C., Horowitz, S. W., & Raskin, D. C. (1988). Meta-analysis of mock crime studies of the control question polygraph technique. *Law and Human Behavior, 12*, 79–90.

Krapohl, D. J. (2002). The polygraph in personnel screening. In M. Kleiner (Ed.), *Handbook of polygraph testing* (pp. 217–236). San Diego, CA: Academic Press.

Kugelmass, S., & Lieblich, I. (1966). Effects of realistic stress and procedural interference in experimental lie detection. *Journal of Applied Psychology, 50*(3), 211–216.

Larson, J. A. (1932). *Lying and its detection: A study of deception and detection tests*. Chicago, IL: University of Chicago Press.

Lykken, D. T. (1959). The GSR in the detection of guilt. *Journal of Applied Psychology, 43*, 385–388.

Lykken, D. T. (1974). Psychology and the lie detector industry. *American Psychologist, 29*, 725–739.

Lykken, D. T. (1998). *A tremor in the blood*. New York, NY: Plenum Press.

Lynn, R. (1966). *Attention, arousal and the orienting reaction*. New York, NY: Pergamon.

MacLaren, V. V. (2001). A quantitative review of the guilty knowledge test. *Journal of Applied Psychology, 86*(4), 674–683.

Mangan, D. J., Armitage, T. E., & Adams, G. C. (2008). A field study on the validity of the Quadri-Track Zone Comparison Technique. *Physiology and Behavior, 95*, 17–23.

Marston, W. M. (1917). Systolic blood pressure symptoms of deception. *Journal of Experimental Psychology Human Learning and Memory, 2*, 117–163.

McGrath, R. J., Cumming, G. F., Hoke, S. E., & Bonn-Miller, M. O. (2007). Outcomes in a community sex offender treatment program: A comparison between polygraphed and matched non-polygraphed offenders. *Sex Abuse, 19*, 381–393.

Meijer, E. H., Bente, G., Ben-Shakhar, G., & Schumacher, A. (2013). Detecting concealed information from groups using a dynamic questioning approach: Simultaneous skin conductance measurement and immediate feedback. *Frontiers in Psychology, 4*, 68.

Meijer, E. H., Smulders, F. T., & Merckelbach, H. L. (2010). Extracting concealed information from groups. *Journal of Forensic Sciences, 55*, 1607–1609.

Meijer, E. H., & van Koppen, P. J. (2008). Lie detectors and the law: The use of the polygraph in Europe. In D. Canter & R. Zukauskiene (Eds.), *Psychology and law: Bridging the gap* (pp. 31–50). Aldershot, UK: Ashgate.

Meijer, E. H., Verschuere, B., & Ben-Shakhar, G. (2011). Practical guidelines for developing a CIT. In B. Verschuere, G. Ben-Shakhar, & E. H. Meijer (Eds.), *From deception detection to memory detection: Theory and application of the Concealed Information Test* (pp. 293–302). Cambridge, UK: Cambridge University Press.

Meijer, E. H., Verschuere, B., Merckelbach, H. L., & Crombez, G. (2008). Sex offender management using the polygraph: A critical review. *International Journal of Law and Psychiatry, 31*, 423–429.

Munsterberg, H. (1908). *On the witness stand*. New York, NY: McClure.

Nahari, G., & Ben-Shakhar, G. (2011). Psychophysiological and behavioral measures for detecting concealed information: The role of memory for crime details. *Psychophysiology, 48*, 733–744.

Nakayama, M. (2002). Practical use of the Concealed Information Test for criminal investigation in Japan. In M. Kleiner (Ed.), *Handbook of polygraph testing* (pp. 49–86). San Diego, CA: Academic Press.

National Research Council. (2003). *The polygraph and lie detection. Committee to review the scientific evidence on the polygraph. Division of behavioral and social sciences and education.* Washington, DC: The National Academic Press.

Offe, H., & Offe, S. (2007). The comparison question test: Does it work and if so how? *Law and Human Behavior, 31*, 291–303.

Office of Technology Assessment. (1983). *Scientific validity of polygraph testing: A research review and evaluation.* Washington, DC: US Government Printing Office.

Osugi, A. (2011). Daily application of the Concealed Information Test: Japan. In B. Verschuere, G. Ben-Shakhar, & E. Meijer (Eds.), *Memory detection: theory and application of the Concealed Information Test* (pp. 253–275). Cambridge, UK: Cambridge University Press.

Peth, J., Vossel, G., & Gamer, M. (2012). Emotional arousal modulates the encoding of crime-related details and corresponding physiological responses in the Concealed Information Test. *Psychophysiology, 49*, 381–390.

Podlesney, J. A. (1993). Is the guilty knowledge technique applicable in criminal investigations? A review of FBI case records. *Crime Laboratory Digest, 20*, 57–61.

Podlesney, J. A. (2003). A paucity of operable case facts restricts applicability of the guilty knowledge technique in FBI criminal polygraph examinations. *Forensic Science Communications, 5*, Retrieved 10 October 2013 from http://www.fbi.gov/hq/lab/fsc/backissu/july2003/podlesny.htm. Accessed 6 June 2014.

Raskin, D. C. (1979). Orienting and defensive reflexes in the detection of deception. In H. D. Kimmel, E. H. van Olst, & J. F. Orlebeke (Eds.), *The orienting reflex in humans* (pp. 587–605). Hillsdale, NJ: L. Erlbaum Associates.

Raskin, D. C. (1986). The polygraph in 1986: Scientific, professional and legal issues surrounding application and acceptance of polygraph evidence. *Utah Law Review, 29*, 29–74.

Raskin, D. C. (1989). Polygraph techniques for the detection of deception. In D. C. Raskin (Ed.), *Psychological methods in criminal investigation and evidence* (pp. 247–296). New York, NY: Springer.

Raskin, D. C., & Honts, C. R. (2002). The comparison question test. In M. Kleiner (Ed.), *Handbook of polygraph testing* (pp. 1–47). San Diego, CA: Academic Press.

Reid, J. E. (1947). A revised questioning technique in lie detection tests. *Journal of Criminal Law and Criminology, 37*, 542–547.

Sokolov, E. N. (1963). *Perception and the conditioned reflex.* Oxford, NY: Pergamon.

Verschuere, B., & Ben-Shakhar, G. (2011). Theory of the Concealed Information Test. In B. Verschuere, G. Ben-Shakhar, & E. H. Meijer (Eds.), *Memory detection: theory and application of the Concealed Information Test* (pp. 128–148). Cambridge, UK: Cambridge University Press.

Verschuere, B., Ben-Shakhar, G., & Meijer, E. H. (Eds.). (2011a). *Memory detection: theory and application of the Concealed Information Test.* Cambridge, UK: Cambridge University Press.

Verschuere, B., & Crombez, G. (2008). Deja vu! The effect of previewing test items on the validity of the Concealed Information polygraph Test. *Psychology, Crime & Law, 14*, 287–297.

Verschuere, B., Crombez, G., De Clercq, A., & Koster, E. H. (2004). Autonomic and behavioral responding to concealed information: Differentiating orienting and defensive responses. *Psychophysiology, 41*, 461–466.

Verschuere, B., Meijer, E. H., & De Clercq, A. (2011b). Concealed information under stress: A test of the orienting theory in real-life police interrogations. *Legal and Criminological Psychology, 16*, 348–356.

Verschuere, B., Meijer, E., & Merckelbach, H. (2008). The quadri-track zone comparison technique: It's just not science a critique to Mangan, Armitage, and Adams (2008). *Physiology and behavior, 95*, 27–28.

Volokh, A. (1997). n Guilty men. *University of Pennsylvania Law Review, 146*, 173–211.

Vrij, A. (2008). *Detecting lies and deceit. Pitfalls and opportunities*. Chichester, UK: Wiley.

Wilcox, D. T., & Sosnowski, D. E. (2005). Polygraph examination of British sexual offenders: A pilot study on sexual history disclosure testing. *Journal of Sexual Aggression, 11*, 3–23.

4

Forensic Application of Event-Related Brain Potentials to Detect Guilty Knowledge

WILLIAM G. IACONO

Although the control or comparison question technique (CQT) is the most commonly employed lie detection method used in specific incident forensic investigations, it has many serious limitations, including a weak theoretical rationale and inadequate empirical foundation (Iacono & Patrick, 2014). The CQT's key deficiency is the questioning format which involves contrasting responses to relevant questions to so-called control or comparison questions. Relevant questions go to the heart of the matter under investigation and represent direct queries regarding involvement in a crime, for example, 'On the night of March 15, did you take Fisbee's attaché case?' Control questions involve probable lies concerning denied misdeeds from a person's past, for example, 'Have you ever taken something of value from someone who trusted you?' Autonomic nervous system (ANS) responses to these paired questions are examined to determine which one elicits a stronger reaction, with larger responses to relevant questions indicating deception and larger responses to control questions indicating truthfulness. The primary problem with this format is that the control question does not provide

Detecting Deception: Current Challenges and Cognitive Approaches, First Edition.
Edited by Pär Anders Granhag, Aldert Vrij, and Bruno Verschuere.
© 2015 John Wiley & Sons, Ltd. Published 2015 by John Wiley & Sons, Ltd.

an adequate psychological control for the emotional impact of the accusation contained in the relevant question, an imbalance that makes the innocent vulnerable to false positive outcomes. A second major problem is that countermeasures can be used by the guilty to augment responses to the control question (e.g. by performing mental arithmetic when the control question is presented), leading to false negative outcomes. Attempts to improve CQT administration have focused on recording and scoring procedures and have failed to come to grips with the fundamental weakness in the questioning format. Thus, the CQT is unlikely to be improved by substituting brain recordings for the ANS measures. In the 60 years elapsing since the CQT was introduced, determining its error rate has proved intractable, a situation that is unlikely to change in the future.

Fortunately, there is a well-researched, theoretically sound alternative to the CQT that also has potential applicability to specific incident investigations. First introduced by David Lykken (1959) as the guilty knowledge test (GKT), and now commonly referred to as the concealed information test (CIT), this method involves determining if a suspect is concealing knowledge specific to the commission of a crime. As introduced by Lykken, the GKT involved recording the galvanic skin response (GSR) while presenting a series of multiple choice questions wherein one of the alternatives in each question involved guilty knowledge. Consider the theft of Fisbee's attaché case. Fisbee's co-workers knew it was likely to contain the proceeds from his cash-only business, but unknown to even his closest friends, in addition to the $2000 cash, the case included a number of other items, including a pistol, a dispenser marked 'Police Strength Pepper Spray', a diamond necklace, four gold American eagle $50 coins, a guidebook to vacationing in Barbados and a pornographic magazine. A sample GKT item might take the form: 'If you took Fisbee's attaché case, then you'd know what was inside the case. Did you find a (a) sapphire ring, (b) hunting knife, (c) gold coins, (d) bible, (e) cell phone?' Not knowing what the case contained, the innocent would be expected to respond randomly to these alternatives. In contrast, the guilty person, aware the case contained the gold coins, would be expected to give the largest response to this item. Because an innocent person could respond most strongly to the guilty alternative by chance and the guilty person may not recognize the relevant item, a well-constructed GKT would have many questions and would be scored to determine how consistently the strongest response occurred to the guilty alternatives. It is obvious that with a sufficient number of questions, innocent people can be expected to have little chance of failing a GKT because the non-guilty knowledge alternatives provide proper control for the substantive information contained in the guilty knowledge item. Also obvious is that on a GKT with many items, if the examinee responded most strongly to the guilty alternative on every item, there would be little room for doubt that the test subject possessed guilty knowledge. However, whether the guilty are detected depends heavily on whether those investigating a crime can identify memorable facts that the guilty will recognize.

Unlike the CQT, the GKT is likely to be improved by substituting electroencephalographic (EEG) brain event-related potentials (ERPs) for the recording of ANS measures like electrodermal activity, blood pressure and respiration that are common to polygraph recording systems. In this chapter, I have considered how adoption of the GKT might be furthered by using brain waves, in particular the P300 ERP, to assess recognition memory. Because most of the research on the GKT is based on ANS measures, I will necessarily refer to it as appropriate because it provides the foundation for the development of a P300-GKT. Although work on a P300-GKT has been ongoing for over two decades, my aim in writing this chapter is not to provide a comprehensive review of this work which has been recently summarized and critiqued in other sources (Farwell, 2012; Farwell & Richardson, 2013; Iacono, 2008; Krapohl, 2011; Meegan, 2008; Meijer, Ben-Shakar, Verschuere, & Donchin, 2012; Rosenfeld, 2005, 2011). Rather, my goal is to build on what has been accomplished by considering what remains to be done to increase the field applicability of these methods. This includes consideration of tactical strategy needed to encourage the interest of law enforcement authorities as well as needed basic and applied research that would support field applications of the P300-GKT.

THE CASE FOR THE P300-GKT

The GKT was introduced about a decade after the CQT. Like its predecessor, it has been around for over a half century, but unlike the CQT, it has generated substantial interest among academic psychologists, an interest that has been growing stronger in recent years. Embedded in this body of work has been the coupling of the GKT to ERP measures, a topic that has gained ground recently. In their meta-analysis of the ANS-GKT literature, Ben-Shakhar and Elaad (2003) examined 80 laboratory studies and concluded 'that the GKT has excellent potential as an applied method for detecting information and for differentiating between individuals possessing guilty knowledge and those who do not' (p. 147). In addition, they noted that the GKT produced especially strong results in studies that optimized the application of the GKT, with accuracy improved when several ANS indices were used in combination rather than relying on a single index.

There is reason to believe that ERPs have advantages over ANS measures and that they could make the GKT even more accurate. With an ANS-GKT, it takes a minute or longer to administer each multiple choice question because it takes several seconds for the ANS response to fully materialize and additional time (15–30 seconds) must be provided to allow for recovery to baseline between the administration of alternatives. Although examinees are typically told to respond 'no' to each alternative when presented, this can be accomplished rather mechanically without paying careful attention to item content. To the extent this occurs, it would reduce accuracy for the guilty by reducing the perceived salience of the guilty information. In addition, by augmenting responses to one or two of the non-guilty alternatives in each question, the ANS-GKT can be defeated by countermeasures.

The most studied and promising brainwave-based GKT involves recording the P300 wave from one or more scalp electrodes. This wave is so named because in certain simple stimulus paradigms, it has an onset or peak latency of about 300 ms. As stimulus complexity increases, the latency is increased, such that the P300 present in GKT studies is likely to occur much later, perhaps peaking at 500–600 ms. P300 is sensitive to the rarity and meaningfulness of a stimulus, and the amplitude varies with the strength of recognition memory (Johnson, Pfefferbaum, & Kopell, 1985). In the GKT context, the elicitation of P300 is based on the fact that the guilty knowledge items in a GKT (called probes) are presented less frequently than the non-guilty knowledge items (called foils) and that they thus stand out as meaningful to the guilty. Because the brain response is superimposed on the background EEG signal that is continually present in brain wave recordings, in order to resolve the response and determine its amplitude, the ERPs to all of the probe stimuli are averaged together, and the same is done for all of the foil stimuli. This averaging process causes the random background 'EEG noise' to cancel out, leaving the ERP response to the stimulus clearly defined. For both the innocent and the guilty, because the foils occur with high frequency and they have no special significance, they are not associated with a strong P300 response. For the innocent, the probes are not recognized as having any more meaning than the foils, so the average response to the probes matches the average response of the foils. For the guilty, the probes should elicit a pronounced P300 wave, rendering the probe ERP clearly distinct from the foil ERP. Although there are variations of this P300-GKT paradigm, they have in common the expectation that only the guilty will respond differentially to the probes and foils.

In a P300-GKT, stimuli are presented only briefly on a computer screen and typically must be monitored closely because they require timed manual responses that vary according to stimulus content. The ERPs elicited by these stimuli appear within milliseconds of their presentation and are fully resolved in well under 2 seconds. The pace of stimulus presentation coupled with the rapid development of the brain response and the requirement of a speeded manual response all make more difficult the application of countermeasures. If countermeasures are attempted, it is reasonable to believe they could be detected if they altered the timing and morphology of the brain response or the distribution of manual reaction times. In addition, the ERP-GKT can be constructed to include control stimuli (called targets) that involve information known by the person taking the test (e.g. such as crime facts that are publicly known to be true). Target stimuli, like the probes, are presented infrequently, but because they are recognized by both the guilty and innocent, they elicit a P300 response in anyone taking the test. The responses to these targets can be monitored to determine the validity of an individual test administration by showing that a person is paying attention and producing P300 waves to stimuli that are intended to elicit them. Indeed, using a behavioural GKT paradigm based on measures of reaction time, Noordraven and Verschuere (2013) found that the degree to which targets and foils produced a strong response difference predicted mock crime classification accuracy for guilty participants. This study needs to be extended to the P300-GKT to determine if as expected given the theoretical foundation for the P300-GKT, a test has greater sensitivity in the detection of guilty knowledge when the difference in P300 response to the foils and targets is large. Not surprisingly, in a meta-analysis of both ANS-GKT and P300-GKT studies, the P300-GKT produced stronger effects (Meijer et al., 2012; summarized in Ben-Shakhar, 2012; see also Matsuda, Nittono, & Ogawa, 2011). Taken together, what 50 years of research with the ANS-GKT has taught us along with what we know so far about the P300-GKT points to great promise for marrying brain wave recording with the GKT format.

IMPORTANT PERSPECTIVE FOR MOVING FORWARD WITH THE DEVELOPMENT OF A FIELD-APPLICABLE P300-GKT

Although many laboratories have published research in this area (e.g. Lefebvre, Marchand, Smith, & Connolly, 2007; Matsuda et al., 2011; Meijer, Smulders, Merckelbach, & Wolf, 2007; van Hoof, Brunia, & Allen, 1996), two laboratories have done the most to define the field. One of these laboratories is led by Dr. Lawrence Farwell as a part of a company called Government Works based in Massachusetts (http://www.governmentworks.com/bws/index.asp). Farwell's lab employs a type of P300-GKT called 'brain fingerprinting' that is based on a paper published by Farwell and Donchin (1991) and for which there are U.S. government patents. One goal of this company is to generate income by providing brain fingerprinting services to clients, including those accused of wrongdoing. Another objective is to have the results of these tests admitted into legal proceedings as scientific evidence. Perhaps the most famous of Farwell's cases involved an Iowa prison inmate named Terry Harrington who was convicted of murder and sentenced to life in prison. Harrington was released after serving about 20 years following his passing a P300-GKT. Although the results of the test did not directly lead to the overturning of Harrington's conviction by the Iowa Supreme Court, an evidentiary hearing was held to evaluate the results (*Harrington v. Iowa*, 1997), and there is no question that Harrington's passing the test led to a chain of events leading to his freedom. This case generated national attention, including the CBS television segment '60 Minutes' and discussion of the precedence established by the case in several law journals (Greeley & Illes, 2007). In a subsequent case covered by a PBS documentary, death row inmate Jimmie Ray Slaughter (*State v. Slaughter*, 2004) passed a brain fingerprinting test and attempted to use it to overturn his conviction (the appeal failed and Slaughter was eventually executed). The publicity surrounding the Harrington and Slaughter cases provided a boost to brain fingerprinting, leading to considerable additional press coverage of Farwell's work, including notation on Farwell's web page that he was selected by *TIME* magazine as one of *TIME*'s 100 Innovators of the 21st Century.

In addition to endeavouring to sell the application of brain fingerprinting, Farwell has received government grants and carried out studies to evaluate the effectiveness of his methods (summarized in Farwell, 2012). Promoting the application of brain fingerprinting, Farwell has made claims that are seldom seen among academics who, by and large, tend to be self-effacing and circumspect about the interpretations justified by their research. On the May 2013 version of his corporate web page, these included referring to his 'invention' of brain fingerprinting as an 'infallible witness' and 'game-changing science', 'proven over 99% accurate in criminal investigations' and 'tested and proven at the FBI, the CIA, and the US Navy'. Most academics have no stomach for such unqualified, incautious self-promotion. Farwell has been criticized regarding the validity of many of the claims he has made about brain fingerprinting (Rosenfeld, 2005) and recently has been asked to retract a key paper he published in support of his approach (Meijer et al., 2012). Farwell's influence has derived from a combination of entrepreneurship and publicity seeking as much as it has from the science supporting his work.

The other primary laboratory is led by Professor J. Peter Rosenfeld at Northwestern University. Beginning with Rosenfeld, Nasman, Whalen, Cantwell, and Mazzeri (1987), this laboratory has generated over two dozen empirical papers involving the P300-GKT. As Ben-Shakhar (2012) has noted, 80% of the P300-GKT research comes out of the Rosenfeld lab. This impressive body of programmatic research, summarized in Rosenfeld (2011), has done much to identify and define salient issues pertinent to the development of a P300-GKT. Unlike Farwell's commercial enterprise and efforts to apply the P300-GKT to real-life cases, Rosenfeld's research is aimed at providing insight into factors that affect the design and accuracy of P300-based assessments and includes the development and evaluation of different P300-GKT paradigms. Although this programme of research can be characterized as addressing the basic science behind memory detection, it has a translational emphasis linking it to applied considerations.

Given their contrasting objectives, it is perhaps not surprising that Farwell and Rosenfeld have been critical of each other's work. It is not my goal to weigh their arguments to pick winners and losers. Although it is fair to hold Farwell's work to rigorous standards and he has an obligation to back his claims or cease making them, I do not believe that Farwell's brain fingerprinting approach should be delegitimized because his self-promoting style is off-putting. Farwell's contribution derives from many years of work trying to adapt his version of the P300-GKT to real-world application, and this work needs to be examined for what we can learn from it to further foster this goal. By the same token, Farwell derives no legitimacy by implying that Rosenfeld's work can be dismissed because it does not measure up to the standards Farwell has set for the development of a field-applicable version of the P300-GKT (Farwell, 2012; Farwell & Richardson, 2013). The goals of the Rosenfeld lab are not identical to Farwell's, and criticizing the work without recognizing this difference fails to appreciate the richness of knowledge gained for Rosenfeld's body of research.

In what follows, I have considered how to increase the likelihood of adopting P300-GKT methods for practical application in forensic investigations. Included is reliance on my own work with the ANS- and P300-GKT, as well as 30 years of experience working with the police and legal profession on detection deception. This includes my serving as an expert witness in dozens of criminal proceedings involving lie detection as well as serving as a pro bono witness in support of Terry

Harrington's appeal of his murder conviction. It also includes my having worked to encourage responsible use of polygraph tests by the police (Iacono, 2008) and field application of the P300-GKT (Iacono, 2008, 2011). Finally, it should be noted that a comprehensive text that offers important perspective and many thoughtful suggestions related to furthering the use of the GKT has recently become available (Verschuere, Ben-Shakhar, & Meijer, 2011). Because this volume deals with the GKT broadly, it provides important foundation (only some of which will be echoed here) for this chapter's focus on advancing the P300-GKT.

OPTIMIZING THE P300-GKT

There are several important practical and scientific questions that must be satisfactorily addressed for the P300-GKT to be broadly embraced for fieldwork.

Under What Circumstances Is a GKT Applicable?

This question applies to any GKT. Some authors have implied that the GKT is appropriate for such a small fraction of crimes that its practical utility is negligible. Examining U.S. federal government investigative files, Podlesny (1993) concluded a GKT would be perhaps applicable in only about 15% of cases. However, as Iacono and Lykken (2009) have pointed out, prior to the discovery of fingerprints or DNA, inspection of police records for such evidence probably would have turned up few suitable cases. But once their value became apparent, investigative procedures were enhanced to ensure the collection of this evidence when it was available. If investigators were trained to systematically collect guilty knowledge evidence, it is almost certain that many cases would yield useful items, and the quality and quantity of guilty knowledge material would likely be enhanced as well. A crime with a victim who is competent to provide testimony regarding crime details has strong potential for a GKT. The GKT may be especially useful with sex crimes provided that the victim can recount the details. Premeditated, carefully planned crimes and those with unusual details may also lend themselves to GKTs. These recommendations are in line with those of Osugi (2011) who, based on experience with the GKT in Japan, noted that the culprit's own deliberate actions, unexpected events pertinent to the commission of the crime and items associated with strong emotion are especially memorable.

Whatever the GKT items are, they cannot involve information that has been disclosed to the public or been leaked to suspects in the course of interrogation and investigation of the crime (Gamer, 2010). Every GKT subject should have the opportunity to review guilty knowledge items to affirm that none of the probes can be recognized and that none have special significance either personally or because they stand out among the foils. Items that are identified as significant should be explained by the suspect. The explanations should be verified as plausible because their unexplained identification would be tantamount to a confession. To avoid inadvertently incriminating themselves, subjects who may have been unwittingly exposed to crime information and remain unaware of how they came to possess it, after item review, should be allowed to refuse the test without explanation.

What Is Required for Law Enforcement to Embrace the P300-GKT?

Given this chapter's emphasis on laying the foundation for field applications of the P300-GKT, consideration of what it will take for law enforcement to accept and rely on this approach is paramount. Importantly, Krapohl (2011) noted that there is a culture among polygraph examiners that works against the GKT. There are many factors that feed into a resistance to adopt the GKT, and they include superficial or non-existent training in the guilty knowledge method and a high comfort level with the familiar CQT which has recognized investigative utility. Krapohl notes an additional strike against the GKT derives from its historical advocacy by the late David Lykken, who besides developing and promoting the GKT was an outspoken and well-known critic of the CQT.

In addition, influential scientists who are proponents of the CQT have argued against the GKT. In their chapter titled 'The Case for Polygraph Tests', Honts, Raskin, and Kircher (2009) drew a strong contrast between the CQT, which they find to be a valid application of psychological science, and the GKT, which they concluded has 'demonstrably low accuracy ... useful only as a vehicle for laboratory research' (p. 317).

Clearly, the professional polygraph community appears unlikely to advocate for the adoption of the GKT. Moreover, even examiners who are favourably disposed to the GKT have neither the skills nor training to administer the P300-GKT. Hence, those working outside the traditional polygraph community with expertise in brain electrophysiological methods are in the best position to develop the field application of the P300-GKT. Acceptance from the professional polygraph community will be more likely if the P300-GKT is advocated as an adjunctive tool that can supplement rather than replace existing methods.

However, to it is not necessary to couple the introduction and use of the P300-GKT to police polygraph units. Many police departments, even in large cities, do not have polygraph units, and even if they did, the procedures recommended here for application of the P300-GKT involve a different type of expertise than is typically found among polygraph examiners. Compared to polygraph examiners, detectives who investigate crimes are more likely to be interested in and supportive of scientists' efforts to apply the P300-GKT in fieldwork. However, no matter what type of collaboration is established with law enforcement, the important questions will be as follows: under what circumstances is the P300-GKT likely to have utility, and what is the incremental value of the new information derived from the P300-GKT over and above all the other evidence available in a case?

Another consideration involves the need for P300-GKT proponents to demonstrate its value for inculpating the guilty rather than promoting it as a method that protects the innocent from false positive outcomes. Good police work generates leads intended to resolve cases with convictions. A test that produces virtually no false positives but for which false negatives are a problem is unlikely to be valued by law enforcement. There are many reasons why GKTs might be passed by the guilty. Even if the P300-GKT was 100% effective in the detection of memories stored in the brain, there remains no way to know for certain what crime-related information was memorialized. At best, a P300-GKT might represent a well-reasoned attempt to develop items that contain salient probes, but there is no way of being certain that the chosen probes are indeed appropriate in any given case. Information that is not remembered because it was not encoded or has been forgotten cannot be detected. Career criminals who commit many crimes may not have distinct memories associated with a particular crime under investigation.

Nonetheless, certain crimes, because they were meticulously planned and associated with salient evidence likely to be memorialized, make obvious candidates for P300-GKT case studies (Iacono, 2011; Lykken, 1981). The one P300-GKT case study that has received the most attention, the Harrington case (*Harrington v. Iowa*, 1997), was a passed test. Although the cascade of events following this result led to Harrington's eventual freedom, Harrington's P300-GKT was nonetheless based on items whose validity was vigorously challenged during the appeal proceedings, raising fears that real-life applications of the P300-GKT will lead to the undoing rather than enhancing of police work. What is needed is one or more cases that solve a crime and lead to the conviction of a suspect. In addition, it will be important for those advocating for the P300-GKT to emphasize that the results pertain to the probabilistic possession of knowledge, not guilt, and are thus designed to provide crime-relevant evidentiary information rather than be dispositive. Viewed from this perspective, a P300-GKT that is considered to be 'passed' is not indicative of innocence but rather shows that the subject did not possess the knowledge covered by the test items. Although innocence is consistent with this result, it is also possible that the items are not tapping the memory of a guilty person.

What Is Required for P300-GKT Results to Be Admissible in Legal Proceedings?

To be admissible in the U.S. court as scientific evidence, key considerations are whether the Frye (*Frye v. United States*, 1924) or Daubert (*Daubert v. Merrell Dow Pharmaceuticals*, 1993) legal standards are met. These include (1) general acceptance of the technique in the scientific community, (2) being supported by a testable theory, (3) having undergone peer review and (4) having a known error rate. Ben-Shakhar and colleagues have evaluated the GKT according to these standards (Ben-Shakhar & Kremnitzer, 2011), recently concluding that it would be premature to recommend admissibility without further field study. This tempered recommendation stemmed primarily from concerns that standard #4 was not met, especially because the false negative error rate in field applications is unknown.

Although a stronger foundation supporting the validity of passed tests is clearly desirable, there is little reason to doubt the results of a failed test if the P300-GKT is administered under circumstances insuring that the innocent are not exposed to the guilty knowledge (Iacono, 2008). Failed P300-GKTs have obvious probative value and appear to meet criterion #4. Iacono and Lykken (1997) surveyed scientific opinion regarding the validity of the ANS-GKT and found that 77–81% of the members of the Society for Psychophysiological Research and the general psychology division of the American Psychological Association agreed that the GKT 'is based on scientifically sound psychological principles or theory'. In addition, Iacono and Lykken included a question asking whether it was reasonable to conclude that a 10-item GKT in which the strongest response occurred to the guilty knowledge alternative in 8 of the 10 items (a result expected <1% of the time by chance) indicated knowledge of the crime scene. Seventy-two percent agreed such a conclusion was reasonable.

Failed tests thus appear to meet current standards for admissibility. How courts will respond to attempts to admit failed tests can only be determined by developing cases in which P300-GKT evidence is likely to be brought before the court. A possible concern is how courts would view admitting the results of a test that could be used only to inculpate a defendant since the error rate of a passed test is indeterminate (Meegan, 2008). However, this imbalanced evidentiary situation is not unlike others that come before the court. Fingerprints on a murder weapon are incriminating, but fingerprints have no evidentiary value when the weapon has been wiped clean.

What Research Questions Need to Be Answered for the P300-GKT?

How Can Valid Items Be Identified?

Probably no other topic is more in need of research than what material is appropriate for developing GKT items. The Japanese have much experience in this regard, but differences in culture and legal procedure between other countries and Japan make additional research important. Laboratory research, while pointing to the importance of certain factors, is unlikely to be entirely satisfactory. For instance, Carmel, Dayan, Naveh, Raveh, and Ben-Shakhar (2003) found that details central to the commission of a mock crime (like what was stolen) were recalled better than peripheral details (such as room decorations), and this differential memorial sensitivity became stronger with the passage of time between crime commission and the GKT. This innovative investigation clearly points to the importance of understanding how attention to details and memory over time are likely to co-vary, but it is not an adequate substitute for understanding what is likely to be remembered in real crimes. There are simply too many factors to cover adequately in laboratory research. In the Harrington P300-GKT case, for example, the test was administered decades after the crime was committed, and the alleged crime was murder. Neither of these facts is ever likely to be adequately simulated in a laboratory study.

Training in GKT item development should include familiarity with what is known about the formation and recall of crime-related memories (e.g. Christianson, 2007). However, it may be possible to carry out field studies on GKT item appropriateness that provide insight into the development and maintenance of crime-related memory by studying those involved in crimes that have already been adjudicated. This could be achieved without ever administering a psychophysiological test, increasing the feasibility and cost-effectiveness of the research. Work with selected incarcerated felons who confessed to their crime constitutes one group that could be used for this purpose. The point would be to examine their files, interview those who investigated the case and interview those involved in the same crime (informants such as witnesses, co-offenders, victims) to generate GKT items. Some of the items could be deliberately chosen because they were leaked during the investigation. These items would provide a baseline against which to determine the effectiveness of hypothetically appropriate GKT items that contain information the felon would presumably be reviewing for the first time. The experiment would call for the culprit to choose the correct alternatives in the GKT with a reward for every correct choice. A follow-up interview could be conducted to explore how the felon came to remember certain items and not others. Different kinds of items could be evaluated, for example, words versus pictures, with the latter including crime scene images manipulated in Photoshop to create foils. Individual difference characteristics could be tabulated along with the outcome, including time elapsing since the crime, use of drugs and alcohol, IQ, past history of criminal involvement (including involvement in similar crimes that might weaken memory of details specific to the investigated crime), etc. Some of the informants in these studies could also be subjects in such memory experiments. Also of interest is how crime knowledge varies as a function of situational characteristics such as type of crime and crime circumstances (e.g. degree of planfulness, stress experienced during the crime). The resulting database of information that would eventually become available could then be used to guide real-life GKT item development.

An aspect of item development that has not received the emphasis it deserves concerns the skill of the investigator in obtaining suitable information. Because there is no reason for the person administering a GKT to know the answer to the questions, the psychophysiological test should be administered by a technician who has the skills to administer a standardized test protocol and insure that quality psychophysiological data are collected. The GKT thus does not require a polygraph operator in the sense that a CQT does; rather, it requires a forensic data collection investigator who visits the crime scene, interviews informants, examines collected evidence and constructs the test items, but does not administer the test. The training of this GKT investigator is thus very important. Part of the training regimen should include evaluation of archival data from past cases to determine how well the trainee can reproduce successful tests previously administered by accomplished investigators. Once trained, the GKT investigator should undergo continued evaluation by keeping track of hit rates and performing periodic reliability checks.

How Well Are Known Memories Identified as Present?

Farwell (2012) has argued forcefully that in order to determine how well the P300-GKT performs, it is essential to show that those being tested did in fact remember the guilty knowledge that was being assessed with the P300 recording. Rosenfeld (2011), by contrast, has emphasized the need for ecological validity, noting that in real life individuals do not rehearse the items that are going to be on their tests. It is important that the ability of the P300-GKT to detect memories the person actually has be separated from the likelihood that a P300-GKT optimized to detect such memories can be used to detect crime-relevant guilty knowledge in suspects. Unless this step is taken, it would not be known to what degree detection inaccuracy is due to a deficient P300 protocol versus poor memory. Needed are laboratory studies to determine how well the P300-GKT procedure works in identifying known memories in cooperative people who can verify that they have the memory. This would tell us how well the procedure works under optimized circumstances, and only procedures that have extremely high accuracy under ideal circumstances should be considered for their field effectiveness. Although such laboratory studies can involve training subjects on the details of a mock crime so they achieve 100% accuracy (e.g. as Farwell has done), they may also involve evaluating subjects who have committed a mock crime to determine both how well they can recall crime details and how accurately they can identify the probes. With these data in hand, the effectiveness of the P300-GKT can be evaluated in terms of how well it detects those with varying degree of memory. In addition, ERPs to remembered probes can be averaged, post hoc, separately from those not remembered, again to determine how well the procedure works in identifying known information.

An important element of the structure of the P300-GKT concerns test length and developing understanding how the results may vary as a function of the number of probes. While there is no downside to having a large number of high-quality items, in real life, the number of items is likely to be limited (Elaad, 1990), some items are likely to better than others, and having a long test with a mix of good and poor items could increase the probability of false negative outcomes, further undermining the potential credibility of this application. While this matter can be addressed to some extent using mock crime participants, an improved research design would involve application of the P300-GKT to those involved in adjudicated crimes to determine how the P300 signal strength varies with the number and quality of items. Although P300-GKT studies based on subjects involved in real-life crimes have not been conducted to address this particular question, this approach has been shown to be feasible by Farwell, Richardson, and Richardson (2013) who have profitably carried out P300-GKT work with those involved in felony crimes.

How Well Do Countermeasures Work with an Optimized P300-GKT?

More laboratory studies examining the effectiveness of countermeasures are needed. Countermeasure effectiveness can best be evaluated if the focus is on how well they can be used to defeat the detection of known memories using an optimized protocol. This research also needs to take into account how countermeasure effectiveness can be minimized by altering the test format and/or test scoring as well as identifying signs of countermeasure use that reduce confidence in the test outcome. The goal should be to use countermeasure research to further optimize the protocol both to make it countermeasure resistant and to identify ERP (e.g. altered morphology, latency shifts) and behavioural measures (e.g. slowed reaction time, misidentification of targets) that indicate the likely use of countermeasures. For field use, it is not necessary to require every P300-GKT to end with a definitive result. Inconclusive outcomes, including those based on the possible use of countermeasures, are to be encouraged to minimize classification errors. A simple-to-execute countermeasure involves adopting strategies to enhance the significance of foils so the probe P300 is more likely to resemble the foil P300. This strategy, however, would also make the response to the target more like that of the foils. For this reason, tests where the P300 response to the target and the foils is similar should be judged inconclusive (see also Noordraven & Verschuere, 2013, discussed previously).

Several studies have found that countermeasures are a potential threat and that their detection may not be easy (Mertens & Allen, 2008; Rosenfeld, Soskins, Bosh, & Ryan, 2004). Extending these studies, Farwell et al. (2013) examined 12 participants from real crime cases involving 14 tests (9 of which corresponded to being guilty). Some of these individuals were trained in the countermeasure procedures used in the Mertens and Allen and Rosenfeld studies and offered a $100,000 reward for beating the test with a false negative result. All 14 tests were correctly classified indicating that the countermeasures were ineffective. A possible issue in this study concerns how motivating the allure of a large reward was, whether subjects saw it as a credible incentive and whether it could have had the opposite of the intended effect by leading subjects to believe such a large reward was offered only because it was unattainable no matter their efforts to use countermeasures. What would have made the study more convincing would have been a debriefing questionnaire in which subjects indicated they did indeed use the countermeasures and that they found the reward to be a credible motivator. Such post-test querying has been important in countermeasure studies using the CQT. When debriefing questions have been included in CQT studies designed to assess countermeasure effectiveness, many participants have admitted not following through with their countermeasure assignments (e.g. Honts & Alloway, 2007; Honts & Schweinle, 2009). Farwell (2012) has also argued against the likelihood that countermeasures are an issue by noting that in his research, after conducting about 200 brain fingerprinting tests under a wide variety of circumstances, there have been no errors.

Of note, Rosenfeld and colleagues (Lui & Rosenfeld, 2009; Rosenfeld et al., 2008; see Rosenfeld, Hu, Labkovsky, Meixner, & Winograd, 2013 for a review) have developed novel P300-GKT methods that appear to be resistant to countermeasures as well as to provide an opportunity to detect when they are being used (Meixner et al., 2013). More of this type of counter-countermeasure research is highly desirable. Also of note, as important as it is to evaluate fully countermeasure effects because they contribute to the false negative error rate, their use would not change the confidence to be placed in a failed test.

What Is the Known Error Rate?
Beginning with Lykken (1974), academic psychology has heaped criticism on the extraordinary accuracy claims made by the polygraph profession regarding the CQT. Chief among the criticisms is the charge that the research used to support the claims is of poor quality and methodologically inadequate. Four factors in particular have been advanced as important to the design of an adequate validity study, and they apply as well to evaluation of the P300-GKT:

1. *Laboratory versus field studies.* Laboratory studies also cannot approximate the circumstances that entail standing accused, which would likely include anxiety over being tested that could manifest as poor performance on a P300-GKT, motivation to beat the test that leads to inventive application of countermeasures and interrogation about the crime that could both enhance and alter memories. Only field studies carried out in real-life circumstances can circumvent this problem. As noted, there have been P300-GKTs administered in actual criminal cases, but hit rates have been derived almost exclusively from laboratory investigation. The sole exception is a Japanese study by Miyake, Mizutani, and Yamahura (1993) which is better viewed as proof in principle that the P300-GKT can be deployed for field tests rather than as a report from which valid accuracy estimates can be derived.

2. *Blind evaluation of test results.* To avoid any possibility that the P300-GKT technician administering the test may influence the outcome, the technician must be blind to the case information, including the answers to the test questions. Scoring of the results must also be carried out blindly. The only field tests carried out to date, however, do not appear to meet this criterion.

3. *A gold standard for what constitutes ground truth.* Because it is possible that legal adjudication is less accurate than the P300-GKT, legal outcomes are unlikely to be accepted as ground truth. In the CQT literature, the gold standard has become confessions. Confessions inculpate the guilty and clear innocent co-suspects in

the same case. Although confessions may occasionally be false, their association with a failed test adds to their credibility because in addition to taking responsibility for the crime, the confessor has been found to have knowledge that the culprit should possess if guilty.

4. *Confessions must be independent of test outcome.* As has been noted for the CQT literature, if suspects are only asked to confess after failing a lie test, the confession will necessarily confirm the outcome. Missing would be errors in which the guilty pass their test because they would not be interrogated to confess. Also missing would be errors from the innocent who fail the test because they would be unlikely to confess during an interrogation. Under the circumstances, the only tests that are confirmed are ones where the test by necessity was correct, resulting in inflated accuracy estimates. What is needed are tests confirmed by confessions that arise independently from the administration of the test. These types of confessions are difficult, but not impossible to obtain. Patrick and Iacono (1991) were able to obtain them by reviewing files prepared by detectives investigating cases where an individual had taken a CQT polygraph. Confessions would appear in these files often because a person investigated for another crime confessed to the crime covered by the polygraph. Sometimes, it was learned that there was no crime because an item reported as stolen was later found (e.g. a daughter away at college borrowed her mother's jewellery without telling her). And of course, it is possible that with subsequent investigation and the accumulation of evidence, a confession would come from the person who took the test.

What Is the Best Protocol?

Needed are more laboratory studies that compare the memory detection efficiency of competing protocols and that evaluate how parametric variations of a given protocol affect results. Given the existing literature, there is good reason to believe that the top candidate P300-GKT protocols all have high accuracy (80% or better), so discriminating among them will require using much larger sample sizes than typically have been used, ideally with at least 100 subjects tested on each protocol. An important aspect of this programme of research will be to evaluate how different scoring methods fare when applied to the same protocol, a question that has been approached in several studies (e.g. Abootalebi, Moradi, & Khalilzadeh, 2009; Allen & Iacono, 1997; Mertens & Allen, 2008; Rosenfeld et al., 2004; Rosenfeld, Sweet, Chuang, Ellwanger, & Song, 1996). With an optimized laboratory-based procedure in hand, field research is needed to further optimize the method for applied memory detection.

MOVING FORWARD WITH REAL-LIFE APPLICATION
OF THE P300-GKT

Simply stated, the idealized goal of an applied P300-GKT research programme should be to develop an applicable technique that is optimized
to produce the lowest possible error rate. In the absence of the type of
thorough evaluation that would be desirable before formally launching
the P300-GKT as a forensic tool, should there be an injunction against
the use of the P300-GKT in real-life criminal investigations?

It is my recommendation that field application of the P300-GKT proceed in parallel with the research programme outlined in the preceding
sections. There is little doubt that these real-life case applications will
sputter along with uneven results, but occasionally, cases will emerge
that can be evaluated as admissible evidence. Although imperfect, the
adversarial legal process can be used to determine if select cases meet
scientific standards for admissibility based on the state of P300-GKT
research at the time such cases come before the court. Strong candidate
cases will likely involve failed P300-GKTs, perhaps to invalidate the
testimony of a witness whose claims against a defendant are in dispute,
thus lessening the court's possible concern about using the P300-GKT
to incriminate a possibly innocent defendant. In certain limited circumstances, passed P300-GKTs could also come before the court. For
instance, turning to the case of Fisbee's attaché case that was described
at the beginning of this chapter, if the best P300-GKT currently available
and administered according to acknowledged best practice standards in
existence at the time showed that targets (e.g. '$2000', 'attaché case')
elicited strong P300 responses compared to foils and ERPs to the probes
(e.g. 'pepper spray', 'gold coins') closely resembled those to the foils,
might not this result be seen as having evidentiary value?

At present, Farwell's brain fingerprinting protocol appears to be the
frontrunner for these types of case study applications. Unlike Rosenfeld's
research programme which approximates the type of systematic laboratory study I am advocating here for optimizing the P300-GKT, Farwell's
laboratory has only minimally explored how parametric variations of
his procedure affect results. His work has contributed little incremental
knowledge regarding the optimization of the brain fingerprinting procedure. Nevertheless, it has the advantage of being the only procedure
that has been used in criminal investigations and legal proceedings.
In addition, it has been consistently applied for over two decades in a
number of empirical studies (at least six involving peer review publication; (Farwell & Donchin, 1991; Farwell & Smith, 2001; Farwell et al.,
2013)). The procedure is based on a sensible rationale, and detailed
information is now available regarding how to structure and administer a test (Farwell, 2012).

Important questions have been raised about the adequacy of Farwell's brain fingerprinting procedure (Meijer et al., 2012; Rosenfeld, 2011). Farwell and colleagues addressed many of these concerns in a reply (Farwell & Richardson, 2013) and have provided argument for why others using Farwell's P300-GKT methodology fail to obtain hit rates commensurate with those reported by Farwell (Farwell, 2012; Farwell & Richardson, 2013). Countering criticism that much of his work is unpublished, Farwell and colleagues (2013) recently published a monograph that includes four empirical studies. Although Farwell et al. identify this recent work as involving 'field/real-life' studies, they are not traditional field studies in that few of their subjects (at most 12, all from their 'Study 2'; the number cannot be determined from the information provided) were undergoing criminal investigation at the time of the P300-GKT, and for only these few was there any real-life consequence associated with the test outcome. Nevertheless, these studies went well beyond typical mock crime experiments with college student volunteers. In addition to participants involved in legal proceedings, subjects included FBI agents tested on information the agents possessed that was not accessible to the general public, bomb making/disposal experts tested on their unique knowledge and individuals tested on their life experiences (some involving past crimes) with probes developed through interviews with someone familiar with the subject. No classification errors were made in a total of 76 tests spread across these studies. While more can be done to evaluate brain fingerprinting and this report could have provided better detail, the body of work by Farwell and associates bolsters the promise of the P300-GKT for field application.

CONCLUSION

Because the development and evaluation of the P300-GKT is an ongoing enterprise, the P300-GKT is a moving target, with science unlikely to provide a final appraisal of the P300-GKT. Nonetheless, in the half century elapsing since Lykken introduced the GKT, an impressive body of knowledge related to the ANS-GKT has emerged, laying a strong foundation for the P300-GKT. P300-GKT work has been ongoing for over 20 years, and there is evidence supporting its potential high accuracy. The P300-GKT will not be applicable in all crimes, but there is good reason to believe it will be applicable in many crimes, especially if personnel trained in GKT item development are given the opportunity to investigate them. The P300-GKT is now being advanced for forensic application, and even if it is not used as courtroom evidence, it has the potential to be used advantageously as an investigative tool in much the same way that the CQT is used to assist police work. Although there are likely to be cases where confidence in the validity of a particular outcome should be doubted, the question I am raising is whether there are also likely to be cases where confidence in the outcome is high. I believe the answer is 'yes', and that scientists with interest in this question can begin to formulate the criteria they feel must be satisfied in a particular case before they would decide it is likely to have probative value. While passed tests will no doubt rise above this threshold on occasion, to win over the law enforcement community, failed tests need to advance through the legal system to demonstrate the inculpatory value of the P300-GKT.

ACKNOWLEDGEMENT

I would like to thank Francis X. Shen for comments on an earlier version of this chapter.

REFERENCES

Abootalebi, V., Moradi, M. H., & Khalilzadeh, M. A. (2009). A new approach for EEG feature extraction in P300-based lie detection. *Computer Methods and Programs in Biomedicine, 94*(1), 48–57.

Allen, J. J., & Iacono, W. G. (1997). A comparison of methods for the analysis of event-related potentials in deception detection. *Psychophysiology, 34*(2), 234–240.

Ben-Shakhar, G. (2012). Current research and potential applications of the concealed information test: An overview. *Frontiers in Psychology, 3*, 342. doi:10.3389/fpsyg.2012.00342

Ben-Shakhar, G., & Elaad, E. (2003). The validity of psychophysiological detection of information with the Guilty Knowledge Test: A meta-analytic review. *The Journal of Applied Psychology, 88*(1), 131–151.

Ben-Shakhar, G., & Kremnitzer, M. (2011). The concealed information test in the courtroom: Legal aspects. In B. Verschuere, G. Ben-Shakhar, & E. Meijer (Eds.), *Memory detection: Theory and application of the concealed information test* (pp. 276–292). Cambridge, UK: Cambridge University Press.

Carmel, D., Dayan, E., Naveh, A., Raveh, O., & Ben-Shakhar, G. (2003). Estimating the validity of the guilty knowledge test from simulated experiments: The external validity of mock crime studies. *Journal of Experimental Psychology: Applied, 9*(4), 261–269.

Christianson, S. A. (2007). *Offenders' memories of violent crimes*. West Sussex, England: Wiley.

Daubert v. *Merrell Dow Pharmaceuticals*, (1993).

Elaad, E. (1990). Detection of guilty knowledge in real-life criminal investigation. *Journal of Applied Psychology, 75*(5), 521–529.

Farwell, L. A. (2012). Brain fingerprinting: A comprehensive tutorial review of detection of concealed information with event-related brain potentials. *Cognitive Neurodynamics, 6*(2), 115–154.

Farwell, L. A., & Donchin, E. (1991). The truth will out: Interrogative polygraphy ("lie detection") with event related brain potentials. *Psychophysiology, 28*(5), 531–547.

Farwell, L. A., & Richardson, D. C. (2013). Brain fingerprinting: Let's focus on the science-a reply to Meijer, Ben-Shakhar, Verschuere, and Donchin. *Cognitive Neurodynamics, 7*(2), 159–166.

Farwell, L. A., Richardson, D. C., & Richardson, G.M. (2013). Brain fingerprinting field studies comparing P300-MERMER and P300 brainwave responses in the detection of concealed information. *Cognitive Neurodynamics, 7*(4), 263–299.

Farwell, L. A., & Smith, S. S. (2001). Using brain MERMER testing to detect knowledge despite efforts to conceal. *Journal of Forensic Sciences, 46*(1), 1–9.

Frye v. *United States*, (1924).

Gamer, M. (2010). Does the Guilty Actions Test allow for differentiating guilty participants from informed innocents? A re-examination. *International Journal of Psychophysiology, 76*(1), 19–24.

Greeley, H. T., & Illes, J. (2007). Neuroscience-based lie detection: The urgent need for regulation. *American Journal of Law & Medicine, 33*(2), 377–431.

Harrington v. Iowa, 109 F. 3d 1275 - Court of Appeals, 8th Circuit C.F.R. (1997).

Honts, C. R., & Alloway, W. R. (2007). Information does not affect the validity of a comparison question test. *Legal and Criminal Psychology, 12*(2), 311–320.

Honts, C. R., Raskin, D. C., & Kircher, J. C. (2009). The case for polygraph tests. In D. L. Faigman, M. J. Saks, J. Sanders, & E. K. Cheng (Eds.), *Modern scientific evidence: The law and science of expert testimony* (Vol. 5, pp. 297–341). Eagan, MN: Thomson Reuters/West.

Honts, C. R., & Schweinle, W. (2009). Information gain of psychophysiological detection of deception in forensic and screening settings. *Applied Psychophysiology and Biofeedback, 34*(3), 161–172.

Iacono, W. G. (2008a). The forensic application of "brain fingerprinting:" why scientists should encourage the use of P300 memory detection methods. *The American Journal of Bioethics, 8*(1), 30–32.

Iacono, W. G. (2008b). Effective policing: Understanding how polygraph tests work and are used. *Criminal Justice and Behavior, 35*(10), 1295–1308.

Iacono, W. G. (2011). Encouraging the use of the guilty knowledge test (GKT): What the GKT has to offer law enforcement. In B. Verschuere, G. Ben-Shakhar, & E. Meijer (Eds.), *Memory detection: Theory and application of the concealed information test* (pp. 12–23). Cambridge, UK: Cambridge University Press.

Iacono, W. G., & Lykken, D. T. (1997). The validity of the lie detector: Two surveys of scientific opinion. *Journal of Applied Psychology, 82*(3), 426–433.

Iacono, W. G., & Lykken, D. T. (2009). The case against polygraph tests. In D. L. Faigman, M. J. Saks, J. Sanders, & E. K. Cheng (Eds.), *Modern scientific evidence: The law and science of expert testimony* (Vol. 5, pp. 342–406). Eagan, MN: Thomson Reuters/West.

Iacono, W. G., & Patrick, C. J. (2014). Employing polygraph assessment. In I. B. Weiner & R. K. Otto (Eds.), *The handbook of forensic psychology* (4th ed., pp. 613–658). Hoboken, NJ: John Wiley & Sons.

Johnson, R., Jr., Pfefferbaum, A., & Kopell, B. S. (1985). P300 and long-term memory: Latency predicts recognition performance. *Psychophysiology, 22*(5), 497–507.

Krapohl, D. J. (2011). Limitations of the concealed information test in criminal cases. In B. Verschuere, G. Ben-Shakhar, & E. Meijer (Eds.), *Memory detection: Theory and application of the concealed information test* (pp. 151–170). Cambridge, UK: Cambridge University Press.

Lefebvre, C. D., Marchand, Y., Smith, S. M., & Connolly, J. F. (2007). Determining eyewitness identification accuracy using event-related brain potentials (ERPs). *Psychophysiology, 44*(6), 894–904.

Lui, M., & Rosenfeld, J. P. (2009). The application of subliminal priming in lie detection: Scenario for identification of members of a terrorist ring. *Psychophysiology, 46*(4), 889–903.

Lykken, D. T. (1959). The GSR in the detection of guilt. *Journal of Applied Psychology, 43*(6), 385–388.

Lykken, D. T. (1974). Psychology and the lie detector industry. *American Psychologist, 29*(10), 725–739.

Lykken, D. T. (1981). *A tremor in the blood: Uses and abuses of the lie detector.* New York, NY: McGraw-Hill.

Matsuda, I., Nittono, H., & Ogawa, T. (2011). Event-related potentials increase the discrimination performance of the autonomic-based concealed information test. *Psychophysiology, 48*(12), 1701–1710.

Meegan, D. V. (2008). Neuroimaging techniques for memory detection: Scientific, ethical, and legal issues. *The American Journal of Bioethics, 8*(1), 9–20. doi:10.1080/15265160701842007

Meijer, E. H., Ben-Shakar, G., Verschuere, B., & Donchin, E. (2012). A comment on Farwell (2012): Brain fingerprinting: A comprehensive tutorial review of detection of concealed information ith event-related brain potentials. *Cognitive Neurodynamics, 7*(2), 155–158.

Meijer, E. H., Smulders, F. T., Merckelbach, H. L., & Wolf, A. G. (2007). The P300 is sensitive to concealed face recognition. *International Journal of Psychophysiology, 66*(3), 231–237. doi:10.1016/j.ijpsycho.2007.08.001

Meixner, J. B., Labkovsky, E., Rosenfeld, J. P., Winograd, M., Sokolovsky, A., Weishaar, J., & Ullmann, T. (2013). P900: A putative novel ERP component that indexes countermeasure use in the P300-based concealed information test. *Applied Psychophysiology and Biofeedback, 38*(2), 121–132.

Mertens, R., & Allen, J. J. B. (2008). The role of psychophysiology in forensic assessments: Deception detection. *Psychophysiology, 45*(2), 286–298.

Miyake, Y., Mizutani, M., & Yamahura, T. (1993). Event-related potentials as an indicator of detecting information in field polygraph examinations. *Polygraph, 22*(2), 131–149.

Noordraven, E., & Verschuere, B. (2013). Predicting the sensitivity of the reaction time-based concealed information test. *Applied Cognitive Psychology, 27*(3), 328–335. doi:10.1002/acp.2910

Osugi, A. (2011). Daily application of the concealed information test: Japan. In B. Verschuere, G. Ben-Shakhar, & E. Meijer (Eds.), *Memory detection: Theory and application of the concealed information test* (pp. 253–275). Cambridge, UK: Cambridge University Press.

Patrick, C. J., & Iacono, W. G. (1991). Validity of the control question polygraph test: The problem of sampling bias. *Journal of Applied Psychology, 76*(2), 229–238.

Podlesny, J. A. (1993). Is the guilty knowledge polygraph technique applicable in criminal investigations? A review of FBI case records. *Crime Laboratory Digest, 20*, 57–61.

Rosenfeld, J. P. (2005). 'Brain fingerprinting': A critical analysis. *Scientific Review of Mental Health Practice, 4*(1), 20–37.

Rosenfeld, J. P. (2011). P300 in detecting concealed information. In B. Verschuere, G. Ben-Shakar, & E. Meijer (Eds.), *Memory detection: Theory and application of the concealed information test* (pp. 63–89). Cambridge, UK: Cambridge University Press.

Rosenfeld, J. P., Hu, X., Labkovsky, E., Meixner, J., & Winograd, M. R. (2013). Review of recent studies and issues regarding the P300-based complex trial protocol for detection of concealed information. *International Journal of Psychophysiology, 9*(2), 118–134. doi:10.1016/j.ijpsycho.2013.08.012

Rosenfeld, J. P., Labkovsky, E., Winograd, M., Lui, M. A., Vandenboom, C., & Chedid, E. (2008). The Complex Trial Protocol (CTP): A new, countermeasure-resistant, accurate, P300-based method for detection of concealed information. *Psychophysiology, 45*(6), 906–919. doi:PSYP708 [pii]

Rosenfeld, J. P., Nasman, V. T., Whalen, R., Cantwell, B., & Mazzeri, L. (1987). Late vertex positivity in event-related potentials as a guilty knowledge indicator: A new method of life detection. *The International Journal of Neuroscience, 34*(1–2), 125–129.

Rosenfeld, J. P., Soskins, M., Bosh, G., & Ryan, A. (2004). Simple, effective countermeasures to P300-based tests of detection of concealed information. *Psychophysiology, 41*(2), 205–219.

Rosenfeld, J. P., Sweet, J. J., Chuang, J., Ellwanger, J., & Song, L. (1996). Detection of simulated malingering using forced choice recognition enhanced with event-related potential recording. *The Clinical Neuropsychologist, 10*(2), 163–179.

Slaughter v. State, 2005. Court of criminal Appeals of Oklahoma, No. PCD-2004-277.

van Hoof, J. C., Brunia, C. H. M., & Allen, C. J. (1996). Event-related potentials as indirect measures of recognition memory. *International Journal of Psychophysiology, 21*(1), 15–31.

Verschuere, B., Ben-Shakar, G., & Meijer, E. (Eds.). (2011). *Memory detection: Theory and application of the concealed information test*. New York, NY: Cambridge University Press.

5

Deception Detection Using Neuroimaging

Giorgio Ganis

Empirical studies on deception can be placed on a continuum (Figure 5.1), independently of the methods they employ. At the top end of this continuum, there are studies that focus on understanding deception by testing general theories at the group level. For example, questions that might be examined at this level are whether lies about oneself are different from lies about other people (Ganis, Morris, & Kosslyn, 2009) or whether certain cognitive control processes are engaged during deception (Christ, Van Essen, Watson, Brubaker, & McDermott, 2009). In contrast, at the bottom end of the continuum, there are studies that focus on methods to detect deception in single subjects with field validity. For example, one may want to find methods to determine if a suspect has revealed classified information to an unauthorized party. Between these two extremes, there are studies that focus on theory-based methods and paradigms that could eventually lead to field applications. Neuroimaging methods to investigate deception have been used since 2001 (Spence et al., 2001), and most

Detecting Deception: Current Challenges and Cognitive Approaches, First Edition.
Edited by Pär Anders Granhag, Aldert Vrij, and Bruno Verschuere.
© 2015 John Wiley & Sons, Ltd. Published 2015 by John Wiley & Sons, Ltd.

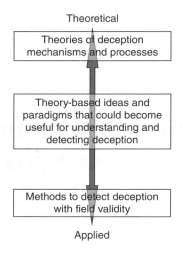

Figure 5.1 Schematic of the deception research continuum, from theoretical (top) to field applications (bottom).

of the published work has focused on the top half of the deception research continuum (Abe, Suzuki, Mori, Itoh, & Fujii, 2007; Abe et al., 2008; Baumgartner, Fischbacher, Feierabend, Lutz, & Fehr, 2009; M. A. Bhatt, Lohrenz, Camerer, & Montague, 2010; S. Bhatt et al., 2009; Browndyke et al., 2008; Davatzikos et al., 2005; Fullam, McKie, & Dolan, 2009; Gamer, Bauermann, Stoeter, & Vossel, 2007; Gamer, Klimecki, Bauermann, Stoeter, & Vossel, 2012; Ganis, Kosslyn, Stose, Thompson, & Yurgelun-Todd, 2003; Ganis, Rosenfeld, Meixner, Kievit, & Schendan, 2011; Ganis et al., 2009; Hakun et al., 2009; Ito et al., 2011, 2012; Jin et al., 2009; Kaylor-Hughes et al., 2011; Kireev, Korotkov, & Medvedev, 2012; Kozel, Johnson, Grenesko et al., 2009; Kozel, Johnson, Laken, et al., 2009; Kozel, Laken, et al., 2009; Kozel, Padgett, & George, 2004; Kozel et al., 2004; Kroliczak, Cavina-Pratesi, Goodman, & Culham, 2007; Langleben et al., 2002; Lee, Raine, & Chan, 2010; Lee et al., 2009; Lee et al., 2002; Lee et al., 2005; Liang et al., 2012; Marchewka et al., 2012; McPherson, McMahon, Wilson, & Copland, 2012; Mohamed et al., 2006; Monteleone et al., 2009; Nunez, Casey, Egner, Hare, & Hirsch, 2005; Phan et al., 2005; Sip et al., 2010; Spence, Kaylor-Hughes, Farrow, & Wilkinson, 2008; Spence et al., 2001). The focus of this chapter is on the technical aspects of deception detection, and so it will review and discuss the minority of neuroimaging studies in the bottom half of the research continuum that have addressed this issue.

THEORETICAL FRAMEWORK

Detecting deception is just an instance of the more general case of mental state detection in which one tries to detect the presence of a mental state of interest in a person. Thus, it is useful to discuss deception detection within the more general framework of mental state detection. The fundamental problem facing mental state detection is that one does not have direct access to the mental states of other people. To get around this problem, mental state detection methods postulate the existence of an internal process (which we will refer to as 'internal process X') that can act as a proxy for the mental state of interest (Figure 5.2). In the ideal case, this internal process X acts as a perfect proxy and is engaged if and only if the mental state of interest is present. Arousal is an example of an internal state that has been used as a proxy for deceptive mental states in the control question test (CQT) polygraphic tradition (Saxe, 1991). Similarly, the orienting reflex (Sokolov, 1963) is an example of an internal process that has been used as a proxy for a recognition mental state within the CIT tradition (Lykken, 1959). The internal process X can be monitored by measuring a set of variables $V_1, ..., V_N$, which may include behavioural indices (e.g. response times, eye fixation times), peripheral psychophysiological indices as in the case of the polygraph (e.g. electrodermal responses), electrophysiological indices (e.g. event-related potentials) or cerebral haemodynamic indices (e.g. blood–oxygen level-dependent signals). These measures are then analysed using technique-specific analytical methods, and the results of these analyses can be used to infer the presence of the mental state of interest.

In practice, the correlation between internal processes that can be measured and complex mental states such as deception is far from perfect because there is uncertainty and variability at various steps in the inferential chain. First, the internal process X may be triggered

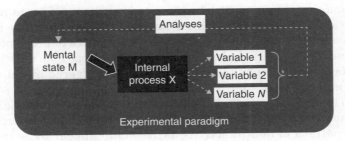

Figure 5.2   Theoretical framework illustrating the logic of deception detection methods.

by other mental states that have nothing to do with the mental state of interest. For example, arousal can be triggered by deceptive mental states in guilty suspects who may be afraid of getting caught, but it can also be triggered by non-deceptive mental states in innocent individuals who are telling the truth but may be anxious about being unjustly accused (Lykken, 1998). This situation can lead to false positives in which a deceptive mental state is incorrectly inferred. Second, there may be internal processes other than X that are associated with the mental state of interest that are not being monitored. This situation can lead to false negative cases, that is, cases in which the presence of a deceptive mental state is missed.

It is important to remember that the process of mental state detection always takes place within the context of an experimental paradigm or setting. One of the functions of the experimental paradigm is to impose constraints on the number of possible mental states within the testing session so as to strengthen the link between internal process X and mental state of interest. For instance, even if internal process X may be triggered by several non-deceptive mental states in unconstrained situations, a suitable experimental paradigm may be able to minimize the chance that such non-deceptive mental states occur during the testing session (e.g. by manipulating cognitive load), thus reducing the possibility of false positives.

NEUROIMAGING APPROACH

Within this theoretical framework, the neuroimaging approach postulates that the internal process X associated with deceptive mental states is a neural process occurring in the brain, and that such a process can be measured more directly than would be possible with behavioural or peripheral psychophysiological methods by using brain imaging (Figure 5.3). The most common form of brain imaging is functional magnetic resonance imaging (fMRI), the only method reviewed in this chapter, though other techniques exist (e.g. positron-emission tomography and near-infrared spectroscopy). fMRI measures changes in regional cerebral blood flow triggered by changes in neural activity with high spatial resolution (Logothetis & Wandell, 2004). Thus, to the extent that the internal process X is spatially specific, that is, to the extent that it can be fully characterized by a spatial pattern of neural activity, fMRI would appear to be the technique of choice for measuring it. However, the haemodynamic signals

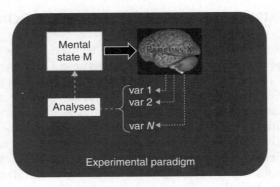

Figure 5.3 Theoretical framework illustrating the logic of neuroimaging-based deception detection methods.

measured with fMRI are slow and integrate neural information over several seconds, and so important temporal properties of internal process X may be smeared or not present in the fMRI signal (Logothetis & Wandell, 2004). fMRI activation is typically measured by time-locking the fMRI time series to the onset of the events of interest and by averaging several tens of trials to increase the signal-to-noise ratio of the data. However, analyses of event-related fMRI time series are usually more complex than those used for event-related potentials because there is substantial signal overlap between temporally adjacent trials which needs to be removed by using statistical models (Dale, 1999).

One advantage of the neuroimaging approach is that typically one measures tens of thousands of variables from the brain. For example, a typical fMRI dataset has one time series per voxels, and there may be over one hundred thousand voxels in an fMRI volume. This means that the information acquired with these methods is very rich and in principle could be used to discriminate between subtle differences, relative to the few time series one can obtain with standard peripheral measures (e.g. skin conductance). The other side of the coin, however, is that much of the data collected during an fMRI session is not obviously related to the internal process X one is interested in monitoring, and so the problem of how to zoom onto the subset of information that is important for distinguishing deceptive and non-deceptive mental states arises. This is a critical machine learning problem, present whenever highly multidimensional datasets are analysed (Jin et al., 2009).

fMRI STUDIES OF DECEPTION DETECTION

The number of fMRI studies that have focused on the detection of deception and that have carried out single-subject analyses to quantify the accuracy of the methods is still quite small, and so a formal meta-analysis is not possible at this stage. Accuracy is often measured by building a statistical classification model and by determining how well it discriminates deceptive from non-deceptive cases. One key issue in quantifying the accuracy is that of generalization to new cases. Indeed, it is not sufficient to show that a statistical model is very accurate in classifying cases that were used to generate the model itself because of overfitting: the model will fit not only data but also noise present in the data in order to maximize classification (Kriegeskorte, Simmons, Bellgowan, & Baker, 2009). This means that even perfect classification on the data that is used to generate the model can nonetheless generalize very poorly to a new dataset (e.g. to a different group of people). Thus, generalization is usually assessed by measuring how well the model performs in classifying data that was not used to build the classification model (test dataset). The accuracy rates reported usually are an average of sensitivity (proportion of deceptive cases correctly classified as deceptive) and specificity (proportion of honest cases correctly classified as honest).

ACCURACY OF fMRI-BASED DECEPTION DETECTION

This section will summarize the fMRI studies conducted so far that have quantified deception detection accuracy (Table 5.1). The first single-subject analyses on detecting deception with fMRI were reported in three papers published around the same time in 2005 (Davatzikos et al., 2005; Kozel et al., 2005; Langleben et al., 2005), which will be described in some detail. The fMRI study by Langleben and collaborators employed pictures of playing cards as stimuli and a modified concealed information test in 22 participants. Data from additional four participants were used to assess generalization. There were several types of cards, including the following. The first type was a 'lie' card, a card each participant took from an envelope given to him or her before the test, with the instructions to lie about possessing it. The second type was a 'truth' card, also from the same envelope as the lie card, but with instructions to tell the truth about possessing it. The third type was a set of distractor cards, and participants were instructed to be truthful about not possessing any of these cards. Findings showed that several brain regions were differentially engaged by the lie, relative to

Table 5.1   Accuracy rates for fMRI studies that performed single-subject analyses

Study	Accuracy (%)	Sensitivity (%)	Specificity (%)	Comments
Langleben et al. (2005)	76.5	68.8	83.7	
Davatzikos et al. (2005)	88.6	90.9	86.4	Reanalysis of Langleben et al. (2005)
Kozel et al. (2005)	90	NA	NA	
Kozel, Laken et al. (2009)	86	NA	NA	
Kozel, Johnson, Grenesko, et al. (2009) Exp 2	69	NA	NA	
Kozel, Johnson, Grenesko, et al. (2009) Exp 1	66.7	100	33.3	
Jin et al. (2009)	65–87	55–90	70–87	Reanalysis of Kozel et al. (2005)
Nose et al. (2009)	84.2	84.2	84.2	
Monteleone et al. (2009)	85.5	71	100	Reanalysis of Phan et al. (2005)
Ganis et al. (2011)	100	100	100	

'Indeterminate' cases have been excluded from the calculations.

the truth condition. Only two areas were more engaged by lies than truth telling, the inferior lateral prefrontal cortex (BA 44 and 47) and parts of the medial superior prefrontal cortex (BA 9). All other regions were more active during honest than deceptive responses, and they included the inferior parietal lobule bilaterally (BA 40), the superior parietal lobule (BA 1–5), the precuneus (BA 7), numerous prefrontal regions (BA 4, 6, 9, 24, 32, 44) as well as the cerebellum and subcortical regions (striatum and left thalamus). Statistical analyses were carried out on these regions of interest (ROIs) to determine single-subject accuracy. A linear classification model was built using these results that included 14 ROIs, as well as 3 two-way interactions and 1 three-way interaction. When the final model was tested for generalization in a group of four additional participants not used to generate the classification model, results showed an accuracy of 76.5% (sensitivity of 68.8% and specificity of 83.7%).

The paper by Davatzikos and collaborators was a reanalysis of the data collected in the study just described, using machine learning procedures (non-linear support vector machines) to discriminate patterns of brain activation elicited by deceptive and truthful responses. These procedures did not define ROIs in advance, based on group contrasts, but instead used information from the entire brain simultaneously (after reducing dataset size by averaging activation in nearby voxels) to compute discrimination functions that maximally would distinguish between deceptive and honest responses. The first analysis modelled single trials for all subjects together, training a classifier on 99% of all trials and testing its performance on the remaining 1% to assess generalization. Results showed an accuracy at testing of 87.9% (90% sensitivity and 85.8% specificity). A limitation of this analysis was that it did not truly test across-participant generalization because the training set included some trials from each of the participants. An additional generalization analysis was conducted in which a classifier was trained on the average data for 21 participants (with each participant providing two datasets, one for deceptive and one for honest responses) and tested it on the left-out participant. Somewhat surprisingly, the results were essentially unchanged and indicated that predictive accuracy at testing was 88.6% (90.9% sensitivity, 86.4% specificity).

A different experimental and analytical paradigm was used by Kozel and collaborators (2005). Participants took part in a mock crime scenario during which they were instructed to 'steal' either a watch or a ring and hide the item in a locker. Thus, this experimental paradigm attempted to simulate a real case situation more closely than paradigms based on playing cards. During the fMRI scan, participants were instructed to deny having stolen either item (therefore lying about one of the items and telling the truth about the other). Furthermore, they were instructed to respond honestly to a set of neutral and control questions. The contrast between deceptive and honest responses resulted in numerous clusters of brain regions, three of which were selected as ROIs for the single-participant analyses: right anterior cingulate, right inferior frontal and orbitofrontal and right middle frontal. For each participant, the difference between the number of voxels active in the deceptive versus honest response conditions within the three ROIs was computed. A positive number (i.e. more voxels active during the deceptive than honest condition) was counted as a correct classification, a negative number as a wrong classification, and a zero as 'indeterminate'. The results on the group of 30 participants used to build the ROI model (combining the three ROIs) showed an accuracy of 93%. The generalization results to a new group of 31 participants not used in building the ROI model showed a slightly lower accuracy of 90%. Note that this accuracy only refers to sensitivity, since it was not possible to estimate specificity because deceptive and honest responses were not tested separately (only their difference within each participants was).

The same ring/watch paradigm was used in two additional experiments by the same group. In the first study (Kozel, Johnson, Grenesko, et al., 2009), the accuracy was 69% (including an indeterminate participant), much lower than the one reported in the previous study, whereas in the second study (Kozel, Laken, et al., 2009), it was comparable and equal to 86%.

Another study by this same group was based on a more elaborate mock sabotage scenario involving, among other things, picking up an envelope marked 'confidential' and destroying a CD with 'crime evidence' on it (Kozel, Johnson, Grenesko, et al., 2009). A no-crime group of participants simply picked up the envelope and were told that someone else had destroyed criminal evidence stored on a CD. Analyses used the ROIs defined previously (Kozel et al., 2005) and the same methods used in that study. Results showed that all participants in the crime group who were lying were correctly classified as being deceptive (i.e. sensitivity was 100%, with nine out of nine participants classified correctly). However, only 33% of the participants in the no-crime group were classified as being honest (i.e. specificity was 33%, with only 5 out of 15 participants classified correctly). These numbers resulted in an overall accuracy of 66.7%.

Not surprisingly, the accuracy of these results has been shown to depend to some extent on the choice of features used by the machine classification methods (Jin et al., 2009). This study reanalysed data from a previous study (Kozel et al., 2005) using classification without and with feature selection. Methods without feature selection include all data in the analyses and attempt to reduce the dimensionality of the data, for instance, by performing principal component analyses. In contrast, methods with feature selection perform classification in a subset of the data. Accuracy results using classification without feature selection were consistently below 60%. The method used in a previous study was also employed (Davatzikos et al., 2005), but this also resulted in poor accuracy of less than 60%, for reasons that are unclear. In contrast, classification with feature selection was consistently between 65 and 80%.

Nose, Murai, and Taira (2009) conducted a study using a concealed information test paradigm in which participants were asked to hide having seen a card (probe) they selected before the study. Note that even in this case participants are lying, as they are attempting to convince the experimenter that they do not have knowledge about the probe. During the fMRI scan, participants performed a target detection task while the probe card was presented randomly in a stream of irrelevant cards. A control group without concealed information about the probe was also tested. In the concealed information group, several regions were found to be more engaged by the probe than irrelevant items: the ventrolateral prefrontal cortex bilaterally (BA 47), the left inferior frontal cortex (BA 44), the right middle frontal gyrus (BA 9) and the right intraparietal lobule (BA 40). A single-subject analysis using a one-out method was carried out on the right ventrolateral prefrontal cortical region of interest. The results showed an accuracy of 84.2% (with both sensitivity and specificity at 84.2%).

One-out single-subject analyses were also performed by Monteleone and collaborators (2009) on the data collected from 14 participants in a previous study (Phan et al., 2005). The study used a card paradigm very similar to that used in an earlier study by a different group (Langleben et al., 2002). Each participant was tested against the model generated using the contrast between deceptive and honest cases using the remaining 13 participants. Results showed that the region that best discriminated between deceptive and honest cases was in the medial prefrontal cortex (including BA 32), with an accuracy of 85.5% (sensitivity of 71% and specificity of 100%).

Finally, single-subject analyses were carried out in an fMRI study by our group (Ganis et al., 2011). This study was a modified concealed information test in which participants lied about their own date of birth (probe) within a stream of irrelevant dates. Probes engaged a number of brain regions more than irrelevants, including some of the same prefrontal, parietal and subcortical regions found in other studies. Importantly, one-out generalization analyses showed that activation in 3 regions (including the medial prefrontal BA 32 and lateral prefrontal BA 45 and BA 47 bilaterally) defined in a separate group of 12 participants could be used to classify deceptive and honest cases with an accuracy of 100%.

The accuracy results of this set of studies are reported in Table 5.1: the average accuracy is 82% (SD = 10%), with an average sensitivity of 84% (SD = 13%) and an average specificity of 81% (SD = 22%). It is clear that, while these rates are substantially better than chance, they are not much better than the rates found using polygraphic measures in laboratory studies using comparable paradigms (Vrij, 2008).

DO fMRI DECEPTION DETECTION RESULTS REPLICATE?

An important issue that has received little attention so far is the extent to which the results of fMRI deception detection studies replicate within and between laboratories. There have been only very few attempts at replications using the same methods and procedures, in part because the resources required to carry out these types of studies are substantial and there is a relatively low pay-off in conducting replication studies. Yet, this is a critical issue for any potential applications.

The first study series that included a replication is the work by Kozel, Laken, Johnson, et al. (2009), which replicated a previous study using the same paradigm and methods but a different MRI scanning facility (Kozel et al., 2005). The accuracy achieved in the replication study using the classification model generated with data from the original study was very similar to that found in the testing dataset of the original study (86 vs. 90%, respectively). However, a third study using a very similar paradigm (Kozel, Laken, et al., 2009) produced a much lower accuracy (69%). Among the potential reasons for this discrepancy are the following: (i) the lack of neutral questions that were instead used in the original study, possibly resulting in lower power; (ii) participant fatigue, since the task was conducted at the end of another test in the replication (Kozel, Johnson, Grenesko, et al., 2009), but not in the original study (Kozel et al., 2005); and (iii) the lack of monetary reward for participants in the replication study. Regardless of the reasons, this suggests that slight changes in the experimental paradigm can produce large variations in accuracy rates, even in these simple and controlled laboratory settings. Empirical evidence in support of this suggestion comes from two studies by the same group, which differed only slightly between each other but found largely different sets of brain regions when comparing deceptive and honest responses (Langleben et al., 2002, 2005). For instance, the anterior cingulate and inferior parietal activations found in the original study were not found in the later study. Furthermore, in the later study, the parietal lobes showed greater activation during honest compared to deceptive responses, the exact opposite of what was found in the original study. Clearly, if one had used the results of the early study to build a classification model and used that on the data from the second study, accuracy would have been very low because of the different brain regions implicated.

The second deception detection dataset with a built-in replication is from our own work (Ganis et al., 2011). In this study, two groups of participants were tested. The first group (ROI group) performed the same modified concealed information task as the second group to define ROIs to be used in the main analysis in order to avoid circularity (Kriegeskorte et al., 2009). Seven out of 14 activation foci found comparing deceptive and honest cases overlapped between the two groups with an extent of more than 40 voxels. Classification accuracy on the second group using three of the ROIs defined in the first group was 100%, suggesting that fMRI replicability may not be an issue, provided that the same stimuli and tasks are used.

Although the dependence of brain imaging results on small changes in paradigms is not necessarily a weakness of the technique, since it may simply reflect its sensitivity, it may pose a problem for potential applications. Indeed, the lack of clear understanding of how subtle changes in the deception paradigms affect the precise pattern of brain activation and accuracy rates could make it very difficult to apply this work complex and variable real-life situations.

fMRI DECEPTION DETECTION AND FIELD VALIDITY

Another important issue is the extent to which the laboratory results can be generalized to field situations, with all their complexity. First, not unlike work done with other techniques, all fMRI paradigms used until now have been far from anything resembling a realistic situation that may involve reputation damage and other social or financial punishments. For example, to date, there have been no fMRI studies investigating the effect of important variables such as the motivation to lie or the perceived 'gullibility' of the target of deception on accuracy rates (Vrij, 2008). Interestingly, deception detection accuracy in the study with perhaps the most elaborate mock crime scenario used so far (Kozel, Johnson, Grenesko, et al., 2009) was rather low (67%), as described earlier. Thus, at the moment, there is no evidence as to whether the fMRI laboratory methods used so far would be useful to detect deception in field situations.

Second, like all other methods to detect deception, fMRI uses evidence based on what a person believes is true and based on what one remembers, and our memories are not perfectly reliable. This is especially true for temporally remote memories, because memory is a constructive process. An extreme case is that of false memories, and the question here is whether it is possible to distinguish a person who is lying from a person who is simply making an objectively false statement based on a false memory. Although one fMRI study has shown that it is possible to differentiate deception from false memories in group data (Abe et al., 2008), it is unclear whether these differences are large and reliable enough to be used in single-subject analyses and in more ecologically valid paradigms.

Third, in addition to the important question of the reliability of memory, in field situations, potential suspects are motivated to deploy countermeasures, that is, methods to beat deception detection procedures. Within the theoretical framework of deception detection outlined earlier, countermeasures usually work by triggering internal process X

(Figure 5.3) in the absence of a deceptive mental state, thus weakening the deception detection inferential chain. A classic countermeasure in the CQT polygraphic tradition is to increase arousal intentionally by biting one's tongue right after comparison questions, so as to reduce the difference between comparison and relevant questions. Physical countermeasures of this kind are not very effective with fMRI scans because the motion artefacts they produce would be easy to spot, but mental countermeasures that rely on inducing specific changes in brain activation during key parts of the scan can be highly problematic. Indeed, recent work by our group has shown that mental countermeasures can dramatically reduce the accuracy of deception detection methods during a modified concealed information test (Ganis et al., 2011). As described earlier, in the main condition of this study, participants lied about their own date of birth. In a second condition, participants were instructed to generate countermeasures during a subset of the irrelevant dates. The countermeasures consisted of specific mental actions (imperceptibly moving the index finger, middle finger or left toe) to be carried out upon seeing three of the irrelevant dates, as done in previous ERP work (Rosenfeld, Soskins, Bosh, & Ryan, 2004). The main purpose of these mental actions was to make these irrelevant dates more salient in order to decrease the difference in saliency between the probe and the irrelevant dates. Sensitivity fell from 100 to 33%, when participants used these countermeasures, providing evidence that these methods may be quite vulnerable to cognitive countermeasures. Although this study was specific to the paradigm employed and to the countermeasures used, it suggests that cognitive countermeasures could be effective at disrupting fMRI-based deception detection methods more generally. At minimum, this is another issue that needs additional investigation before field applications are proposed.

CONCLUSIONS

This chapter reviewed briefly fMRI-based paradigms and methods that could be used to detect deception in single participants. Even without considering the important practical issues involved in having to carry out these tests at suitable MRI facilities, the evidence suggests that current methods and paradigms are not even remotely suitable for field applications. First, their accuracy is not higher, on average, than that found for less expensive methods based on psychophysiological measures such as skin conductance (Vrij, 2008). Second, the dependence of the accuracy results on the details of the paradigms suggests that it may be difficult to devise general and robust methods for deception detection in realistic situations. The effect of important variables such as various types of individual differences (Ganis et al., 2003, 2009), social context (Sip, Roepstorff, McGregor, & Frith, 2008) and instructions to lie (Spence et al., 2008) on the reliability of deception detection in single subjects has been completely unexplored. It is likely that multiple paradigms and methods may need to be used for different situations. Third, the vulnerability of these fMRI-based methods to cognitive countermeasures further decreases the appeal of these methods.

fMRI-based methods to study deception are still young (compared, e.g., to polygraphic methods) as they have been used only for the last 10 years. Thus, it is reasonable to expect that significant progress will be made in the field and in the accuracy and robustness of these methods in the future. What is unique to the neuroimaging approach, relative to other methods, is the richness of the data it collects. Thus, one of the main challenges of this approach, and where most of the progress is likely to occur, is in the domain of signal processing and machine learning to better exploit the information contained in neuroimaging datasets.

ACKNOWLEDGEMENTS

This research was funded in part by the UoP International Research, Networking and Collaboration Award and by a Marie Curie Career Integration Grant (CoND) to Giorgio Ganis.

REFERENCES

Abe, N., Okuda, J., Suzuki, M., Sasaki, H., Matsuda, T., Mori, E., ... Fujii, T. (2008). Neural correlates of true memory, false memory, and deception. *Cerebral Cortex, 18*(12), 2811–2819.

Abe, N., Suzuki, M., Mori, E., Itoh, M., & Fujii, T. (2007). Deceiving others: Distinct neural responses of the prefrontal cortex and amygdala in simple fabrication and deception with social interactions. *Journal of Cognitive Neuroscience, 19*(2), 287–295.

Baumgartner, T., Fischbacher, U., Feierabend, A., Lutz, K., & Fehr, E. (2009). The neural circuitry of a broken promise. *Neuron, 64*(5), 756–770.

Bhatt, M. A., Lohrenz, T., Camerer, C. F., & Montague, P. R. (2010). Neural signatures of strategic types in a two-person bargaining game. *Proceedings of the National Academy of Sciences of the United States of America, 107*(46), 19720–19725.

Bhatt, S., Mbwana, J., Adeyemo, A., Sawyer, A., Hailu, A., & Vanmeter, J. (2009). Lying about facial recognition: An fMRI study. *Brain and Cognition, 69*(2), 382–390.

Browndyke, J. N., Paskavitz, J., Sweet, L. H., Cohen, R. A., Tucker, K. A., Welsh-Bohmer, K. A., ... Schmechel, D. E. (2008). Neuroanatomical correlates of malingered memory impairment: Event-related fMRI of deception on a recognition memory task. *Brain Injury, 22*(6), 481–489.

Christ, S. E., Van Essen, D. C., Watson, J. M., Brubaker, L. E., & McDermott, K. B. (2009). The contributions of prefrontal cortex and executive control to deception: Evidence from activation likelihood estimate meta-analyses. *Cerebral Cortex, 19*(7), 1557–1566.

Dale, A. (1999). Optimal experimental design for event-related fMRI. *Human Brain Mapping, 8*, 109–114.

Davatzikos, C., Ruparel, K., Fan, Y., Shen, D. G., Acharyya, M., Loughead, J. W., ... Langleben, D. D. (2005). Classifying spatial patterns of brain activity with machine learning methods: Application to lie detection. *Neuroimage, 28*(3), 663–668.

Fullam, R. S., McKie, S., & Dolan, M. C. (2009). Psychopathic traits and deception: Functional magnetic resonance imaging study. *British Journal of Psychiatry, 194*(3), 229–235.

Gamer, M., Bauermann, T., Stoeter, P., & Vossel, G. (2007). Covariations among fMRI, skin conductance, and behavioral data during processing of concealed information. *Human Brain Mapping, 28*(12), 1287–1301.

Gamer, M., Klimecki, O., Bauermann, T., Stoeter, P., & Vossel, G. (2012). fMRI-activation patterns in the detection of concealed information rely on memory-related effects. *Social Cognitive and Affective Neuroscience, 7*(5), 506–515.

Ganis, G., Kosslyn, S. M., Stose, S., Thompson, W. L., & Yurgelun-Todd, D. A. (2003). Neural correlates of different types of deception: An fMRI investigation. *Cerebral Cortex, 13*(8), 830–836.

Ganis, G., Morris, R., & Kosslyn, S. M. (2009). Neural processes underlying self- and other-related lies: An individual difference approach using fMRI. *Society for Neuroscience, 4*(6), 539–553.

Ganis, G., Rosenfeld, J. P., Meixner, J., Kievit, R. A., & Schendan, H. E. (2011). Lying in the scanner: Covert countermeasures disrupt deception detection by functional magnetic resonance imaging. *Neuroimage, 55*(1), 312–319.

Hakun, J. G., Ruparel, K., Seelig, D., Busch, E., Loughead, J. W., Gur, R. C., & Langleben, D. D. (2009). Towards clinical trials of lie detection with fMRI. *Society for Neuroscience, 4*(6), 518–527.

Ito, A., Abe, N., Fujii, T., Hayashi, A., Ueno, A., Mugikura, S., ... Mori, E. (2012). The contribution of the dorsolateral prefrontal cortex to the preparation for deception and truth-telling. *Brain Research, 1464*, 43–52.

Ito, A., Abe, N., Fujii, T., Ueno, A., Koseki, Y., Hashimoto, R., ... Mori, E. (2011). The role of the dorsolateral prefrontal cortex in deception when remembering neutral and emotional events. *Neuroscience Research, 69*(2), 121–128.

Jin, B., Strasburger, A., Laken, S. J., Kozel, F. A., Johnson, K. A., George, M. S., & Lu, X. (2009). Feature selection for fMRI-based deception detection. *BMC Bioinformatics, 10*(Suppl 9), S15.

Kaylor-Hughes, C. J., Lankappa, S. T., Fung, R., Hope-Urwin, A. E., Wilkinson, I. D., & Spence, S. A. (2011). The functional anatomical distinction between truth telling and deception is preserved among people with schizophrenia. *Criminal Behaviour and Mental Health, 21*(1), 8–20.

Kireev, M. V., Korotkov, A. D., & Medvedev, C. V. (2012). [fMRI study of deliberate deception]. *Fiziologiia Cheloveka, 38*(1), 41–50.

Kozel, F. A., Johnson, K. A., Grenesko, E. L., Laken, S. J., Kose, S., Lu, X., ... George, M. S. (2009a). Functional MRI detection of deception after committing a mock sabotage crime. *Journal of Forensic Sciences, 54*(1), 220–231.

Kozel, F. A., Johnson, K. A., Laken, S. J., Grenesko, E. L., Smith, J. A., Walker, J., & George, M. S. (2009b). Can simultaneously acquired electrodermal activity improve accuracy of fMRI detection of deception? *Society for Neuroscience, 4*(6), 510–517.

Kozel, F. A., Johnson, K. A., Mu, Q., Grenesko, E. L., Laken, S. J., & George, M. S. (2005). Detecting deception using functional magnetic resonance imaging. *Biological Psychiatry, 58*(8), 605–613.

Kozel, F. A., Laken, S. J., Johnson, K. A., Boren, B., Mapes, K. S., Morgan, P. S., & George, M. S. (2009c). Replication of functional MRI detection of deception. *Open Forensic Science Journal, 2*, 6–11.

Kozel, F. A., Padgett, T. M., & George, M. S. (2004a). A replication study of the neural correlates of deception. *Behavioral Neuroscience, 118*(4), 852–856.

Kozel, F. A., Revell, L. J., Lorberbaum, J. P., Shastri, A., Elhai, J. D., Horner, M. D., ... George, M. S. (2004b). A pilot study of functional magnetic resonance imaging brain correlates of deception in healthy young men. *Journal of Neuropsychiatry and Clinical Neurosciences, 16*(3), 295–305.

Kriegeskorte, N., Simmons, W. K., Bellgowan, P. S., & Baker, C. I. (2009). Circular analysis in systems neuroscience: The dangers of double dipping. *Nature Neuroscience, 12*(5), 535–540.

Kroliczak, G., Cavina-Pratesi, C., Goodman, D. A., & Culham, J. C. (2007). What does the brain do when you fake it? An FMRI study of pantomimed and real grasping. *Journal of Neurophysiology, 97*(3), 2410–2422.

Langleben, D. D., Loughead, J. W., Bilker, W. B., Ruparel, K., Childress, A. R., Busch, S. I., & Gur, R. C. (2005). Telling truth from lie in individual subjects with fast event-related fMRI. *Human Brain Mapping, 26*(4), 262–272.

Langleben, D. D., Schroeder, L., Maldjian, J. A., Gur, R. C., McDonald, S., Ragland, J. D., ... Childress, A. R. (2002). Brain activity during simulated deception: An event-related functional magnetic resonance study. *Neuroimage, 15*(3), 727–732.

Lee, T. M., Au, R. K., Liu, H. L., Ting, K. H., Huang, C. M., & Chan, C. C. (2009). Are errors differentiable from deceptive responses when feigning memory impairment? An fMRI study. *Brain and Cognition, 69*(2), 406–412.

Lee, T. M., Liu, H.-L., Chan, C. C., Ng, Y. B., Fox, P. T., & Gao, J. H. (2005). Neural correlates of feigned memory impairment. *Neuroimage, 28*(2), 305–313.

Lee, T. M., Liu, H.-L., Tan, L.-H., Chan, C. C. H., Mahankali, S., Feng, C.-M., ... Gao, J.-H. (2002). Lie detection by functional magnetic resonance imaging. *Human Brain Mapping, 15*, 157–164.

Lee, T. M., Raine, A., & Chan, C. C. (2010). Lying about the valence of affective pictures: An fMRI study. *PLoS One, 5*(8), e12291.

Liang, C. Y., Xu, Z. Y., Mei, W., Wang, L. L., Xue, L., Lu de, J., & Zhao, H. (2012). Neural correlates of feigned memory impairment are distinguishable from answering randomly and answering incorrectly: An fMRI and behavioral study. *Brain and Cognition, 79*(1), 70–77.

Logothetis, N. K., & Wandell, B. A. (2004). Interpreting the BOLD signal. *Annual Review of Physiology, 66*, 735–769.

Lykken, D. (1959). The GSR in the detection of guilt. *Journal of Applied Psychology, 43*, 385–388.

Lykken, D. (1998). *A tremor in the blood: Uses and abuses of the lie detector.* New York, NY: Plenum.

Marchewka, A., Jednorog, K., Falkiewicz, M., Szeszkowski, W., Grabowska, A., & Szatkowska, I. (2012). Sex, lies and fMRI-gender differences in neural basis of deception. *PLoS One, 7*(8), e43076.

McPherson, B., McMahon, K., Wilson, W., & Copland, D. (2012). 'I know you can hear me': Neural correlates of feigned hearing loss. *Human Brain Mapping, 33*(8), 1964–1972.

Mohamed, F. B., Faro, S. H., Gordon, N. J., Platek, S. M., Ahmad, H., & Williams, J. M. (2006). Brain mapping of deception and truth telling about an ecologically valid situation: Functional MR imaging and polygraph investigation – initial experience. *Radiology, 238*(2), 679–688.

Monteleone, G. T., Phan, K. L., Nusbaum, H. C., Fitzgerald, D., Irick, J. S., Fienberg, S. E., & Cacioppo, J. T. (2009). Detection of deception using fMRI: Better than chance, but well below perfection. *Society for Neuroscience, 4*(6), 528–538.

Nose, I., Murai, J., & Taira, M. (2009). Disclosing concealed information on the basis of cortical activations. *Neuroimage, 44*(4), 1380–1386.

Nunez, J. M., Casey, B. J., Egner, T., Hare, T., & Hirsch, J. (2005). Intentional false responding shares neural substrates with response conflict and cognitive control. *Neuroimage, 25*(1), 267–277.

Phan, K. L., Magalhaes, A., Ziemlewicz, T. J., Fitzgerald, D. A., Green, C., & Smith, W. (2005). Neural correlates of telling lies: A functional magnetic resonance imaging study at 4 Tesla. *Academic Radiology, 12*(2), 164–172.

Rosenfeld, J. P., Soskins, M., Bosh, G., & Ryan, A. (2004). Simple, effective countermeasures to P300-based tests of detection of concealed information. *Psychophysiology, 41*(2), 205–219.

Saxe, L. (1991). Science and the CQT polygraph. A theoretical critique. *Integrative Physiological and Behavioral Science, 26*(3), 223–231.

Sip, K. E., Lynge, M., Wallentin, M., McGregor, W. B., Frith, C. D., & Roepstorff, A. (2010). The production and detection of deception in an interactive game. *Neuropsychologia, 48*(12), 3619–3626.

Sip, K. E., Roepstorff, A., McGregor, W., & Frith, C. D. (2008). Detecting deception: The scope and limits. *Trends in Cognitive Sciences, 12*(2), 48–53.

Sokolov, E. N. (1963). Higher nervous functions; the orienting reflex. *Annual Review of Physiology, 25*, 545–580.

Spence, S. A., Farrow, T. F., Herford, A. E., Wilkinson, I. D., Zheng, Y., & Woodruff, P. W. (2001). Behavioural and functional anatomical correlates of deception in humans. *Neuroreport, 12*(13), 2849–2853.

Spence, S. A., Kaylor-Hughes, C., Farrow, T. F., & Wilkinson, I. D. (2008). Speaking of secrets and lies: The contribution of ventrolateral prefrontal cortex to vocal deception. *Neuroimage, 40*(3), 1411–1418.

Vrij, A. (2008). *Detecting lies and deceit* (2nd ed.). Chichester, UK: Wiley.

Section II

Current Challenges

6

Exploring the Nature and Origin of Beliefs about Deception: Implicit and Explicit Knowledge among Lay People and Presumed Experts

MARIA HARTWIG AND PÄR ANDERS GRANHAG

Deception scholars have studied lying and the detection of lies for roughly half a century. This research has examined a variety of questions. For example, how frequently do people lie in everyday life, and what motivates these lies (Cole, 2001; DePaulo & Kashy, 1998; DePaulo, Kashy, Kirkendol, Wyer, & Epstein, 1996; Jensen, Arnett, Feldman, & Cauffman, 2004; Serota, Levine, & Boster, 2010)? Are there behavioural signs of deception? How good are people at distinguishing between true and false statements? For meta-analyses of this work, see DePaulo et al. (2003) and Bond and DePaulo (2006, 2008), and for general overviews, see Vrij (2008a) and Granhag and Strömwall (2004).

This chapter focuses on beliefs about deceptive behaviour. That is, what behaviours do people associate with lying? In what ways do they believe that liars differ from truth tellers? The behaviours that people believe to be indicative of lying are called *subjective cues to deception* (in contrast to *objective*, i.e. actual cues to deception). Such beliefs are

Detecting Deception: Current Challenges and Cognitive Approaches, First Edition.
Edited by Pär Anders Granhag, Aldert Vrij, and Bruno Verschuere.
© 2015 John Wiley & Sons, Ltd. Published 2015 by John Wiley & Sons, Ltd.

of interest for at least two reasons. First, common reasoning about deception is of interest from a basic psychological perspective. Social psychologists have long examined naïve psychology (Heider, 1944; Kelley, 1973),
with a particular focus on how naïve reasoning may be plagued by shortcomings (Ross & Anderson, 1982). Second, beliefs about deceptive behaviour are of interest from an applied perspective, as judgements of veracity
are central in a number of settings, perhaps most prominently in the
legal system. This chapter provides an overview of the available research
on subjective cues to deception. We will discuss the methods employed to
map beliefs about lying and the populations in which these beliefs have
been studied. We will review the patterns emerging from the body of
work and gauge the accuracy of people's reasoning about deception
based on the literature on objective cues to deception. The chapter also
introduces and discusses a distinction between explicit and implicit
knowledge about deception. We conclude with a brief discussion of areas
where more empirical research may be warranted.

METHODS OF RESEARCH INTO SUBJECTIVE
CUES TO DECEPTION

Researchers have used a range of methodologies to examine subjective
cues to deception (Hartwig, 2011; Vrij, 2008a). The most frequently
used method is the survey approach, which prompts participants to
self-report on their beliefs about deception. Within this approach, there
are variations. In some studies, participants are provided with a list of
behaviours and asked to indicate if and how these behaviours are
related to deception (e.g. Colwell, Miller, Miller & Lyons, 2006; Taylor
& Hick, 2007). For example, people may be asked to rate whether lies
are more detailed than truths, whether the opposite is true or whether
there is no difference in the amount of detail between true and false
statements. The behaviours listed on these closed-ended question-
naires are typically drawn from the previous literature on subjective
cues to deception or research on actual indicators of deception (or both).
While some studies focus solely on people's beliefs about non-verbal
cues (e.g. Vrij & Semin, 1996), others examine beliefs about both verbal
and non-verbal behaviour (e.g. Akehurst, Köhnken, Vrij & Bull, 1996;
Strömwall & Granhag, 2003).

An alternative to the closed-ended approach is to ask participants
the open-ended question, 'How do people behave when they are lying?'
(e.g. Greuel, 1992). The obvious advantage of this approach is that participants may freely choose to report cues that they believe to be signs
of lying – that is, they are not confined to the cues selected by the

researchers. However, it is possible that this method does not capture the range of beliefs people hold, since it only measures the beliefs that happen to come to mind at the particular moment when the respondents are filling out the questionnaire (Marksteiner, Reinhard, Dickhäuser, & Sporer, 2012). Another disadvantage of this method is that it is time consuming. Researchers have to generate a coding scheme based on the responses to the open-ended question and categorize the beliefs according to this coding scheme. This may be an arduous process. To our knowledge, only one study has employed a hybrid methodology: in the cross-cultural survey by the Global Deception Research Team (2006), one sample of respondents were asked an open-ended question about behavioural indicators of deception. Based on the responses to this question, a questionnaire consisting of a series of closed-ended questions was developed and distributed to a second sample of respondents.

A second form of the self-report method is to ask participants who serve as lie-catchers in experimental studies to justify their judgement (e.g. 'Why did you think the person was lying/telling the truth?'). While some have suggested that this method may produce more valid results (Anderson, DePaulo, Ansfield, Tickle, & Green, 1999), others have argued that the cues generated in these studies are similar to those obtained from surveys where people are probed about cues to deception detached from an actual judgement situation (Marksteiner et al., 2012).

While the majority of the literature has relied on survey methods, researchers have also examined subjective cues to deception using non-self-report measures. These studies employ correlational metrics. That is, in these studies, researchers have correlated the behaviours of senders (i.e. liars or truth tellers) with perceiver's (i.e. lie-catcher's) judgements of deception (DePaulo, Stone & Lassiter, 1985; Kraut & Poe, 1980; Zuckerman, DePaulo, & Rosenthal, 1981). This method has a significant advantage, in that it does not assume that perceivers are consciously aware of, and hence capable of reporting on the cues they use to judge veracity. Later in this chapter, we will discuss the different patterns emerging from self-report and correlational studies and elaborate on the psychological and methodological implications of these different approaches.

MAJOR FINDINGS

The literature on beliefs about deceptive behaviour consists of a broad set of samples. A distinction can be made between studies that have examined laypeople's beliefs about cues to deception and those that have mapped the beliefs of various professional groups. The most widely studied group of professionals is police officers, but as we shall see, a variety of other practitioners who face the task of judging veracity in their professional life have also been studied. Sometimes, the beliefs of laypeople are compared to those held by professionals within the same study. Moreover, beliefs about deceptive behaviour have been studied not only in the Western world but in a range of other countries across the globe. We will begin this literature review by describing the results from studies on laypeople.

Laypeople's Beliefs about Deception

One of the first studies on subjective cues to deception was conducted by Zuckerman, Koestner, and Driver (1981). They asked a sample of American undergraduate students how a number of behaviours are related to deception. With regard to non-verbal behaviour, the respondents expressed the belief that liars avert their gaze. Further, they reported that lying is accompanied by increased self-manipulations (i.e. touching or scratching oneself), posture shifts and movements of legs and feet. In line with these findings, Akehurst et al. (1996) found that a sample of British laypeople endorsed the view that liars look away, that they move their hands and feet more and that they engage in self-manipulations more frequently than truth tellers. Vrij and Semin (1996) surveyed Dutch participants, who in general were found to associate gaze aversion with lying. They also expressed the beliefs that liars shift position more frequently than truth tellers; that they move their hands, feet and legs more; that they make more head and trunk movements; and that they speak at a faster rate than truth tellers. Granhag, Andersson, Strömwall, and Hartwig (2004) surveyed Swedish college students who reported that liars are more prone to gaze aversion, frequent body movements and self-manipulations.

In terms of paralinguistic and vocal behaviour, people generally express the view that liars' speech contains more frequent hesitations and speech errors (Akehurst et al., 1996), that their rate of speech is faster (Vrij, Akehurst, & Knight, 2006) and that their pitch of voice is higher than that of truth tellers (Granhag et al., 2004; Vrij & Semin, 1996). Further, people seem to believe that liars' pauses are shorter in duration (Granhag et al., 2004; Granhag, Strömwall, & Hartwig, 2005) and more frequent (Akehurst et al., 1996; Lakhani & Taylor, 2003).

Some surveys of laypeople have also included questions about verbal differences between liars and truth tellers. In a review of the literature on beliefs about deception, Strömwall, Granhag, and Hartwig (2004) pointed out that the data on beliefs about verbal behaviour is relatively

Table 6.1   Common explicit (self-reported) beliefs about deception

Explicit beliefs about deception

Non-verbal cues	Vocal/paralinguistic cues	Verbal cues
Gaze aversion	Speech hesitations	Implausibility
Fidgeting	Speech errors	Inconsistency
Posture shifts	High-pitched voice	Indirect statements
Illustrators	High speech rate	Non-immediate statements
Hand/finger movements	Speech latencies	
Foot/leg movements	Pause frequency	
Head movements		
Eye blinks		

The table is based on a qualitative review of the literature, drawing on the literature discussed here along with the syntheses provided by Granhag et al. (2004) and Vrij (2008a). For each cue listed, people tend to express the belief that more of that particular behaviour is displayed during deception.

scarce, at least in comparison to the data on non-verbal cues. Still, there are some patterns emerging from the available studies. For example, Vrij, Akehurst and Knight (2006) found that liars were believed to be evasive and that their statements tend to sound implausible, illogical and contradictory. Several studies have found that inconsistency of statements is a prominent subjective cue to deception (e.g. Granhag & Strömwall, 2000b; Granhag et al., 2004), a phenomenon labelled the consistency heuristic (Granhag & Strömwall, 1999, 2000a). The pattern of beliefs about the amount of details in true and false statements is inconsistent: Granhag et al. (2004) found that people believe that liars' statements are more detailed. In contrast, Akehurst et al.'s (1996), participants expressed the view that liars include fewer details. For an overview of beliefs about deceptive behaviour, see Table 6.1.

Cross-Cultural Consistency in Beliefs

The beliefs expressed by laypeople in the Western world show remarkable consistency. Laypeople in Europe and the United States express the belief that liars are gaze aversive and that they move more than truth tellers. They also believe that there are verbal indicators of deception (e.g. that deceptive statements tend to be inconsistent or contradictory) and that paralinguistic behaviours such as hesitations and speech errors accompany deception.

Are these beliefs cultural idiosyncrasies of Westerners, or do they generalize to other parts of the world as well? In order to answer this question, the Global Deception Research Team (2006) conducted a large-scale survey mapping cross-cultural similarities and differences in beliefs about cues to deception. As described earlier, the study employed a two-step methodology. In the first survey, respondents were asked the question 'How can you tell if people are lying?'. This question was posed to participants in 58 countries all over the world. The most prevalent response to this question was that liars are gaze aversive. This belief was expressed by over 60% of participants, and in 51 out of the 58 countries surveyed, it was the predominant belief. Other common beliefs were that liars are nervous, that lies can be detected on the basis of body movements and that liars' statements are incoherent. In the second survey, participants in 63 countries were asked to rate if and how a number of behaviours were related to deception. Again, the strongest belief that emerged was that liars avoid eye contact (a view expressed by over 70% of the respondents). Over 60% of the respondents endorsed the following beliefs: that liars shift posture more frequently than truth tellers, that they touch or scratch themselves and that they tell longer stories than truth tellers. On the basis of the response patterns, the authors concluded that there was considerable cross-cultural agreement in beliefs about lying. In particular, they highlighted the strong pan-cultural belief in gaze aversion as an indicator of deception (for a further discussion of cross-cultural aspects of deception, see Bond & Rao, 2004).

In summary, we have reviewed research showing substantial consistency in people's beliefs about deception. The available surveys show that people believe that liars look away, that they shift positions and fidget and that their speech is marred by hesitations and other speech disturbances.

Accuracy of People's Beliefs

Let us now compare these beliefs to the literature on objective cues to deception. To date, the most comprehensive synthesis of research on cues to deception was offered by DePaulo et al. (2003). We will rely on the data from this meta-analysis in order to gauge the accuracy of people's beliefs about cues to deception. Starting with the global belief in gaze aversion, the meta-analysis demonstrates that this belief is incorrect. DePaulo et al. wrote: 'It is notable that none of the measures of looking behavior supported the widespread belief that liars do not look their targets in the eye. The 32 independent estimates of eye contact produced a combined effect that was almost exactly zero $(d = .01)$' (p. 93). Moreover, contrary to people's beliefs, posture shifts are not systematically related to deception $(d = 0.05)$. As for the belief about self-manipulations, neither self-fidgeting $(d = -0.01)$ nor facial fidgeting $(d = 0.08)$ appear to be actual cues to deception. Fidgeting with an object does not occur more frequently when lying, $d = -0.12$ (indeed, the negative value suggests that fiddling with an object occurs somewhat less frequently when lying, but this difference is not statistically significant). Speech disturbances are not related to deception ($d = 0.00$), nor are pauses (silent pauses $d = 0.01$, filled pauses $d = 0.00$, mixed pauses $d = 0.03$).

With regard to verbal cues to deception, at least some of people's beliefs seem in line with the results from research on objective cues to deception. For example, the Global Deception Research Team (2006) found that people believe that liars' statements are incoherent. Indeed, DePaulo et al. (2003) found that deceptive statements make less sense, in that they are less logically structured ($d = -0.25$) and less plausible ($d = -0.20$). In Akehurst et al. (1996), participants expressed the belief that deceptive statements are less detailed. This belief is supported by the meta-analysis in which details were negatively associated with deception ($d = -0.30$).

However, there is also evidence of misconceptions when it comes to verbal cues to deception. In the global survey, a majority of respondents indicated that liars tell longer stories. This belief runs counter to the meta-analytic finding that there is no difference in response length between true and false statements ($d = -0.03$). As for the common belief in inconsistency as a cue to deception (e.g. Vrij, Akehurst, & Knight, 2006), research suggests that this belief is an oversimplification. In one study, consecutive deceptive statements were at least as consistent as true statements (Granhag & Strömwall, 1999). Moreover, deceptive statements given by pairs of senders are not necessarily more inconsistent than statements from truthful pairs (Strömwall, Granhag, & Jonsson, 2003; Vredeveldt & Wagenaar, 2013, but see Vrij et al., 2009).

In conclusion, the picture emerging from these comparisons is one of a mismatch between people's views of cues to deception and reality. Although people express some correct views about deceptive behaviour, the most prevalent beliefs about deception tend to be false. We will elaborate on the possible causes and implication of false beliefs about deception in a later section.

Professionals' Beliefs about Deception

As we described in the beginning of this chapter, mapping naïve reasoning about deception has merits in itself. However, from a forensic point of view, it might be of more interest to examine the beliefs of legal practitioners, as these beliefs may play an important role in how investigative processes unfold. For example, consider the case of Michael Crowe. He was 14 years old when his sister Stephanie was murdered. Crowe and his friends Joshua Treadway and Aaron Houser were arrested and charged with the murder. During lengthy interrogations, the police induced Michael Crowe to confess, but the charges were eventually dropped when another person was found with the victim's blood on his clothing. According to Johnson (2003), the boys were subjected to interrogation because the police investigators believed that Crowe's reaction to his sister's death was suspiciously void of emotion. Another example is the case of Jeffrey Deskovic, 16 years old at the time, became a suspect in the investigation of the murder of his 15-year-old classmate, who was found beaten, raped and strangled. Although there was no tangible evidence against him, Deskovic was interrogated aggressively and ultimately ended up providing self-incriminating statements. One of the reasons he was targeted for interrogation was the police investigators' impression that he was overly emotional in response to the victim's death. Deskovic was convicted of murder, even though it was known all along that the semen found at the crime scene did not match his. Deskovic spent almost 16 years in prison before his conviction was overturned, when another inmate (whose semen did match that found at the crime scene) confessed to the crime.

These examples illustrate the important point that police officers' beliefs about the characteristics of deceptive behaviour may constitute a pivotal point in the investigation process. Of course, the cases outlined earlier are extreme. Misjudgements of deception do not always lead to convictions of innocent people. However, if legal professionals consistently rely on invalid cues to deception, time and costly resources might be wasted.

Because of the importance of legal professionals' knowledge and judgements about deception, a considerable amount of research has been devoted to mapping their beliefs (for a previous overview, see Strömwall et al., 2004). What would one expect to find? Common sense suggests that legal professionals such as police officers, who routinely make judgements about deception and who may have special training, will be more knowledgeable about the psychology of deception than laypeople. Unfortunately, the data from studies with legal professionals does not support this view. A series of studies have compared the beliefs of laypeople to those expressed by legal professionals. Akehurst et al. (1996) compared the beliefs of their sample of laypeople to those expressed by British police officers and found that they did not differ significantly in their views about the characteristics of deceptive behaviour. Similarly, Vrij and Semin (1996) found that the beliefs of police officers, customs officers and prison guards were in line with those expressed by students. Masip and Garrido (2001) examined police officers and police students and found that the two groups expressed beliefs similar to those of laypeople. The primary difference between the experienced officers and the police students was that the beliefs of the former were more pronounced. Strömwall and Granhag (2003) surveyed Swedish police officers, prosecutors and judges. Again, police officers expressed the belief that liars are gaze aversive and prone to make many body movements and that their statements are inconsistent. While prosecutors and judges also endorsed the consistency heuristic, they expressed less pronounced beliefs with regard to gaze aversion and body movements. A study of American police officers replicated the finding that police officers associate deception with lack of eye contact and fidgeting (Colwell et al., 2006).

Beyond police officers and other legal professionals, there are surveys of a range of professionals outside the forensic domain. A few studies have examined beliefs about lying in the workplace. While some lies in the work domain may be fairly trivial, serious deception perpetrated by employees in businesses can have major consequences if undetected. Hart, Hudson, Fillmore, and Griffith (2006) surveyed managers and compared their beliefs about non-verbal cues to deception to those held by non-managers. They predicted that managers would hold more correct beliefs about deception due to their occupational experience. This prediction was not supported, as managers' beliefs did not differ from those of the non-managers. Moreover, the beliefs expressed by both groups were similar to those found in other studies. The respondents believed that liars are more gaze aversive than truth tellers; that they display more finger, hand, arm, foot and leg movements; and that they engage in more frequent posture shifts and shrugs. However, the managers differed in one respect: they expressed more confidence in their ability to judge deception than did non-managers. This finding is similar to those obtained in experimental studies of lie judgement accuracy. Presumed lie experts such as police officers display higher confidence in their judgement, but are not more accurate in distinguishing between truth and deception (Bond & DePaulo, 2006). In another study, Hart, Fillmore, and Griffiths (2010) mapped managers' and non-managers' beliefs about verbal and paraverbal cues to deception. Again, the beliefs of the two groups did not differ. The most strongly held beliefs concerned paralinguistic indicators in the form of speech disturbances and disfluencies. For example, the respondents expressed the view that speech interruptions, pauses and hectic speech are indicative of deception. In terms of verbal content, respondents reported the common belief that deceptive statements contain contradictions. Moreover, they stated that liars claim lack of memory and that they include unnecessary and unusual details. The latter beliefs are in direct contrast with frameworks such as Statement Validity Assessment (SVA; see Köhnken, 2004; Vrij, 2005).

As evidenced by well-publicized frauds and the subsequent collapse of corporations (e.g. Barings Bank, Enron), there may be significant monetary incentives to trigger deception in the financial domain and severe consequences of failure to detect deception. Unfortunately, there is little research on deception in the financial industry. One exception is a recent survey by Hartwig, Voss, and Wallace (in press). They mapped beliefs about deception held by a large sample of investment professionals from 76 countries all across the world. The respondents included portfolio managers, research analysts, consultants and financial advisors who were asked to rate how a number of different verbal and non-verbal behaviours were related to deception. In line with the typical findings, the most strongly expressed beliefs were that liars are gaze aversive and fidgety. When asked about the reliability of verbal and non-verbal behaviour as cues to deception, respondents expressed the view that non-verbal behaviour is more reliable.

Granhag et al. (2005) examined the beliefs of Swedish migration board officers and compared these beliefs to those expressed by students. The officers in the sample were responsible for handling and making decisions in asylum-seeking cases. Because physical evidence is rarely present in these cases, credibility judgements of the asylum seekers' statements are often central. Indeed, the officers in this study acknowledged this problem: when asked what the primary problem was in making decisions about asylum, the most frequent response concerned the difficulty of establishing veracity. Moreover, migration board officers and asylum seekers are with few exceptions members of different ethnic groups, which may complicate the process of judging veracity (see Bond & Rao, 2004; and Chapter 8 on cross-cultural deception detection in this volume). When asked about specific behavioural indicators of deception, migration board officers generally did not endorse the widespread stereotype that liars are gaze aversive. Further, they reported that verbal cues are more indicative of deception than non-verbal behaviour. These findings contrast with the beliefs of other groups of legal professionals. How can we explain unusual pattern of beliefs reported by migration board officers? Research on non-verbal communication shows that there are culturally dictated rules governing people's demeanour (Matsumoto, 1990, 2006). For example, these so-called display rules may hold that it is disrespectful to maintain eye contact with an authority figure. Indeed, Vrij and Winkel (1991) found that Black interviewees displayed more gaze aversion during a simulated police interview than White interviewees (see also Vrij & Winkel, 1992). A possible explanation for the finding that migration board officers do not trust gaze as a cue to deception is their professional experience of interactions with people from different cultural backgrounds. Perhaps these interactions sensitize them to the ambiguity of non-verbal behaviour in general and to the lack of validity of gaze aversion in particular. The beliefs of migration board officers convey a broader point: the decision-making environment may shape people's understanding of the dynamics of deception. We will return to this possibility shortly.

The review of the literature on professionals' beliefs about deception can be summarized as follows. Despite the intuitively appealing notion that these groups may be more knowledgeable about deceptive behaviour (either as a function of training or professional experience), the literature shows that they express similar beliefs as laypeople. That is, they too endorse the stereotype that liars betray their deception through gaze aversion, body movement and speech disturbances.

Other Beliefs about the Psychology of Deception

So far, we have described people's beliefs about particular behavioural indicators of deception. However, surveys have also asked respondents broader questions about the psychology of deception. For example, Strömwall and Granhag (2003) asked police officers, prosecutors and judges whether it is easier to detect deception when interviewing a person face-to-face, compared to judging an interviewee via videotape. All groups expressed the view that face-to-face interactions allow for more accurate judgements than passive observations. This belief is unsupported by research. In fact, experimental studies show that passive observers achieve similar or slightly higher hit rates than those engaged in a face-to-face interaction with the sender (Buller, Strzyzewski, & Hunsaker, 1991; Burgoon, Buller, White, Afifi, & Buslig, 1999; Feeley & de Turck, 1997; Granhag & Strömwall, 2001; also, see Bond & DePaulo, 2006, for a meta-analytic comparison). This finding held true even in a study where highly experienced police officers were allowed to question a mock suspect in the manner of their own choice (Hartwig, Granhag, Strömwall, & Vrij, 2004).

Granhag et al. (2004b) asked their respondents about the effect of producing a statement in reverse chronological order. That is, participants were asked whether liars find it easier or more difficult than truth tellers to tell their story backwards. Respondents indicated that liars find reverse-order recall more difficult. Recent research supports this belief. This research shows that lying may be more cognitively demanding than telling the truth (e.g. Vrij, Fisher, Mann, & Leal, 2006) and that lie-catchers can exploit this by imposing further cognitive load on targets, for example, by asking them to tell their story in reverse chronological order. Indeed, research shows that cues to deception become more pronounced and lie-catchers become more accurate when liars and truth tellers provide their statements in reverse chronological order (e.g. Vrij et al., 2008).

A few studies have asked participants to estimate their accuracy rate in detecting lies. In a survey of over 600 American law enforcement officers' beliefs about police interviews and interrogations, respondents reported an average deception detection accuracy rate of 77% (Kassin et al., 2007). In the survey of investment professionals, respondents indicated an accuracy rate of 68% in their professional life and a rate of 66% in their everyday life (Hartwig, Voss, & Wallace, in press). Given the stable finding that lie detection accuracy rates tend to hover only slightly above the level of chance (50%) (Bond & DePaulo, 2006; see also Bond & DePaulo, 2008), it seems that people's beliefs about their ability to detect deception is overly optimistic.

To our knowledge, only one study has asked respondents to estimate how frequently people lie. In the previously mentioned survey by Hartwig, Voss and Wallace (in press), respondents were asked to estimate the frequency of lies in everyday life and professional life. The average estimates were just over two lies a day in everyday life, and one and a half lies a day in their professional life. It is difficult to gauge the accuracy of this particular belief, given that it is methodologically challenging (if not impossible) to establish the prevalence of lying in everyday life nor people's professional lives. We cannot fully trust people's self-reports about how often they lie, given that lying is considered a highly undesirable behaviour (Anderson, 1968). Still, the available data on the frequency of lying is roughly in line with investment professionals' beliefs (e.g. DePaulo et al., 1996).

Criminals' Beliefs about Deception

As far as we know, only two studies have mapped criminals' beliefs about deception. However, the results of these studies are interesting and warrant some discussion. The previously mentioned survey by Vrij and Semin (1996) contained samples of presumed lie experts (customs officers, police detectives, patrol police officers and prison guards), college students and prisoners. While presumed lie experts and students were in general agreement and, as described earlier, expressed stereotypical beliefs about deceptive behaviour, criminals deviated markedly in their beliefs. For example, the most common response given by prisoners regarding gaze aversion was that liars and truth tellers do not differ. The same pattern was observed for several other behaviours. The most frequent response by prisoners concerning posture shifts and self-fidgeting was that there is no difference between liars and truth tellers in their display of these behaviours. As for hand and finger movements, prisoners expressed the belief that these movements tend to decrease during deception. This belief is supported by research on actual cues to deception (Vrij, 2008a).

Granhag et al.'s (2004) survey mapped the beliefs of college students, prison personnel and prison inmates. The results mirrored those found by Vrij and Semin (1996). Prison inmates expressed different views from those of prison personnel and students, and their beliefs were generally more in line with research on objective cues to deception. For example, prison inmates were significantly less convinced that deceptive statements are less consistent than truthful statements. They were also less convinced that liars move more than truth tellers – the most frequent response was that there is no difference in body movements between liars and truth tellers. Moreover, in contrast to the two other groups, prison inmates believed that verbal cues are more reliable than non-verbal behaviour, a belief that is supported by research (e.g. Vrij, 2008b).

A third study on prison inmates, which did not focus on beliefs but on judgement accuracy, lends further support to the notion that criminals differ from laypeople and presumed lie experts in their reasoning and judgements of deception. In a quasi-experimental study, prison inmates' judgements of true and false statements were compared to those of college students (Hartwig, Granhag, Strömwall, & Andersson, 2004). While students performed at chance level, prison inmates obtained an accuracy rate of 65%. This figure is higher than chance, and it exceeds hit rates typically observed in studies on human lie detection accuracy (Bond & DePaulo, 2006, 2008). Interestingly, while students did not display a judgement bias, prison inmates displayed a pronounced lie bias: 73% of their judgements were lie judgements. When asked what cues they based their judgements on, the most common cue mentioned by students was consistency. In contrast, prison inmates most often referred to the plausibility (or lack thereof) of the statement they had seen. The meta-analysis by DePaulo et al. (2003) shows that implausibility is indeed related to deception.

CAUSES OF CORRECT AND INCORRECT BELIEFS

The research reviewed in the section earlier suggests that criminals deviate from the patterns obtained in studies of laypeople and presumed lie experts. In general, their beliefs about deceptive behaviour appear less stereotypical and more realistic, and their ability to distinguish between true and false statements appears to be better than that of other groups. Of course, it is prudent to exercise some caution in interpreting these results, as the body of research is relatively small. However, if we accept these findings, they are in need of an explanation. Why would criminals differ from other groups in their beliefs about deception? And why would their beliefs be more realistic?

First, it is plausible that criminals live in a more deceptive environment, which may make them more alert to the possibility of being deceived (Vrij & Semin, 1996). Vrij and Semin argued that the ability to prevail in a deceptive environment may hinge on one's ability to avoid being duped (see also Strömwall et al., 2004). Furthermore, it is possible that the consequences of trusting the wrong person may be more severe than for non-criminals – this could explain the pronounced lie bias observed in the study by Hartwig, Granhag, Strömwall, and Andersson (2004).

It may also be that certain elements of the environment in which criminals live create less stereotypical and more correct beliefs about deception over time. In particular, decision-making research has pointed to the importance of feedback in order to improve reasoning and judgement (Einhorn, 1982). This notion, referred to as *the feedback hypothesis*, suggests that mere experience of making a certain type of judgement is not sufficient for improvement over time. Instead, systematic and reliable outcome feedback on the accuracy of one's judgements may be necessary for improvement to occur. It has been suggested that such outcome feedback may be more available in the environment of criminals (Vrij & Semin, 1996). It has been argued that criminals may receive clearer feedback on their impressions of trustworthiness and that they may also receive more reliable feedback from others about whether their own deceptive strategies work (e.g. as a function of experience of being interrogated; see Granhag et al., 2004).

The feedback hypothesis is not only of relevance for criminals and their beliefs about deception. It may also serve as a general framework to explain the perpetuation of stereotypical beliefs about deception. Hence, it can explain why legal professionals with extensive experience of judging veracity subscribe to faulty stereotypes about deceptive behaviour. If the environment does not provide clear feedback when a judgement is wrong, these stereotypes may not be subject to revision. For many legal professionals, the feedback structure is unreliable. For example, a police officer who believes a suspect is lying based on their stereotypical beliefs in gaze aversion and fidgeting could proceed to interrogate that suspect using manipulative and coercive interrogation techniques, which may lead to false confessions (Kassin et al., 2010). Through the elicitation of a confession, the belief in the validity of the cues may be strengthened – a case of confirmation bias (Findley &

Scott, 2007). In this particular example, the feedback is invalid. There are other situations where feedback is lacking. For example, when a police officer mistakenly believes that a person is telling the truth, he or she may dismiss that person and hence never find out that the statement was actually deceptive. Another example is customs officers, who rarely (if ever) receive feedback from travellers whom they decide not to stop and search. For a lengthier discussion of the role of feedback in the formation of beliefs about deception, see Strömwall et al. (2004), and for a general review of feedback in learning, see Hogarth (2001).

ORIGIN OF THE STEREOTYPE ABOUT DECEPTIVE BEHAVIOUR

The aforementioned reasoning can help understand when and why stereotypical beliefs are likely to be corrected (or perpetuated) by experience. But one might wonder where the stereotype of liars as nervous, fidgety and gaze aversive comes from in the first place. Why is this particular set of beliefs so widespread?

In order to provide some possible answers to this question, let us consider the psychological assumptions that underlie people's beliefs about deceptive behaviour; that is, what do these beliefs indicate about people's views of the state of mind of a liar? As we have described in detail, when asked about the characteristics of deceptive behaviour, people endorse cues like gaze aversion, fidgeting, posture changes and speech disfluencies. These behaviours are indicative of stress, nervousness, discomfort, shame and guilt. For example, research has shown that anxiety is related to gaze aversion (Grumet, 1983; Terburg, Aarts, & van Honk, 2012), fidgeting (Heerey & Kring, 2007), posture shifts (Jurich & Jurich, 1974) and speech disturbances (Ragsdale & Silvia, 1982). Thus, people seem to hold two assumptions about the psychology of deception: (1) liars experience negative emotions while lying, and (2) these emotions will be evident in behaviour, primarily in the form of non-verbal cues. What might be the basis for these naïve assumptions?

The Double Standard Hypothesis

In relation to their meta-analysis on lie judgement accuracy, Bond and DePaulo (2006) proposed a framework to understand the psychology of interpersonal deception. They placed morality at the forefront of their reasoning about deception. More specifically, they proposed that people's moral perspective on deception depends on whether they are the sender or the receiver of a lie. They note that as liars, people are pragmatic. Lying is a strategic activity, tailored to achieve desired goals. While, occasionally, lies may be gratuitous, the vast majority of lies are instrumental, told either in the interest of oneself or the presumed interest of others (e.g. DePaulo & Kashy, 1998). If lies are instrumental and goal oriented, they may be easily justified from the perspective of the liar and may therefore be accompanied by few qualms (DePaulo et al., 1996).

However, when people think of other people's lies, they take a different view: then lying is morally reprehensible, and the liar is perceived as a wrongdoer (Anderson, 1968). This perception may colour people's belief about what liars feel and consequently how they expect liars to behave. Bond and DePaulo (2006) wrote: 'People have a prescriptive stereotype of the liar – stricken with shame, wracked by the threat of exposure, liars leak signs of their inner torment. They fidget, avoid eye contact, and can scarcely bring themselves to speak' (p. 216). The important element of Bond and DePaulo's assertion is that they view beliefs about deception as *prescriptive* – that is, they represent people's beliefs about how liars *should* feel and behave. In sum, it is possible that the widely held stereotype about how liars behave is a form of projection; an attribution of mental states based on what people believe ought to be the case.

Bond and DePaulo's (2006) assertion that people judge others' lies more harshly than their own may not only explain the existence of the widespread stereotype of deceptive behaviour; it may also explain why this stereotype is faulty. If people readily justify their own lies and are not crippled by guilt while delivering them, it makes sense that they should not display signs of stress, guilt and shame.

When discussing the double standard hypothesis, Bond and DePaulo acknowledge that their meta-analysis of judgement accuracy is not a formal test of the hypothesis. Moreover, they state that they do not believe that a test 'for so obvious an idea is needed' (p. 231). While we believe that the double standard hypothesis has intuitive appeal, we disagree with their second assertion. That is, we do not believe that the hypothesis is obvious nor that it would not benefit from empirical examination. In fact, we believe that further exploration of the role of moral reasoning, from the perspective of both liars and lie-catchers, would be fruitful to further our understanding of deception. Of particular relevance for the current discussion, we believe that future research ought to examine the possibility that stereotypes about deceptive behaviour are rooted in moralistic reasoning. Such research may help answer the largely unexplored question of the ultimate origin of stereotypes about deceptive behaviour.

The Leakage Hypothesis

As we described earlier, it seems that people believe that the emotions they attribute to liars will be evident in their behaviour – a notion we can call *the leakage hypothesis*. In the psychological literature, this idea can be traced to Freud (1905, cited in Bond & DePaulo, 2006, p. 215), who wrote, 'No mortal can keep a secret. If his lips are silent, he chatters with his finger-tips; betrayal oozes out of him at every pore'. In more recent times, psychological theories of leakage have primarily been explored by Ekman and colleagues (Ekman, 2001; Ekman & Friesen, 1969; see also Porter, Ten Brinke, & Wallace, 2013; Ten Brinke & Porter, 2012).

It is possible that laypeople's belief in the leakage of cues is grounded in naïve morality, much like the belief that liars experience negative emotions. More specifically, it could be rooted in a general belief in the fairness of the world. The theory of a *belief in a just world* posits that people have a need to perceive the world as a fair place, in which people get what they deserve (Lerner, 1980). Decades of empirical research supports this theory, by showing that the belief in a just world drives how people respond to justice and injustice across a variety of settings (for a meta-analytic overview, see Hafer & Bègue, 2005). More generally, the belief in a just world concerns how people relate to notions of deservingness (Furnham, 2003; Lerner & Miller, 1978). In its simplest form, the theory holds that people believe that one gets what one deserves: bad things happen to bad people, and good things happen to good people (and not the other way around). Translated to the current context, the notion that lies will be evident in behaviour fits with a general notion of deservingness: to the extent that lying is perceived as bad behaviour, liars deserve to be found out. Expressed differently, the notion that people can lie effortlessly and without behavioural traces may violate the belief in a just world.

IMPLICIT AND EXPLICIT BELIEFS ABOUT DECEPTION

The bulk of this chapter has reviewed and discussed self-report data on people's beliefs about deceptive behaviour. It is fair to question whether this data is reliable – that is, whether people have insight into the thought processes that lead them to form judgements of deception. In other words, can we trust people's capacity to self-report on their knowledge about deceptive behaviour? This is a central question because of the conclusions that have been drawn from people's reporting of incorrect beliefs about deceptive behaviour. In fact, the finding that people express incorrect beliefs is frequently invoked as the primary explanation for the fact that human lie judgement accuracy is so poor (e.g. Colwell et al., 2006; Park, Levine, McCornack, Morrison, & Ferrara, 2002; Strömwall et al., 2004). The argument is straightforward: because people have faulty beliefs about deceptive behaviour, they rely systematically on incorrect cues to deception, and therefore, their judgement accuracy suffers. But what if people don't actually rely on the faulty beliefs they report?

In a seminal paper, Nisbett and Wilson (1977) argued that self-reports may be misleading simply because people may not have access to the processes that underlie their judgement and behaviour. While the argument sparked controversy at the time of its publication (e.g. Adair & Spinner, 1981; Smith & Miller, 1978), it is now empirically well established that a significant portion of cognitive processing occurs outside of conscious awareness (Bargh, 1997; Bargh & Chartrand, 1999; Hassin, Uleman, & Bargh, 2005; Wilson, 2009). In particular, there is evidence that social judgements are at least partly formed through implicit processes (DeCoster, Banner, Smith, & Semin, 2006; McConnell, 2001; Uleman, Blader & Todorov, 2005; Uleman, Saribay, & Gonzalez, 2008). If this is true, people might not be able to self-report accurately on how they arrived at the impression that a given person is deceptive.

As we alluded to in the beginning of the chapter, there is an alternative to self-report methodology. By correlating the behaviours of senders (i.e. liars and truth tellers) with the judgements of receivers (i.e. lie-catchers), it is possible to capture what we may call *implicit beliefs about deception*. For example, if a study using this correlational method finds a positive correlation between the extent to which senders' faces seem pleasant (as coded by independent observers) on the one hand and perceivers' judgements of truthfulness on the other, one can conclude that perceivers implicitly associate pleasant faces with truth telling. Using this approach, it is possible to shed light on beliefs about deception in several ways. First, it is possible to uncover notions about deception that people may not be consciously aware that they hold. Second, the correlational method may reveal discrepancies between people's self-reports and the cues they actually rely on when making judgements of deception and truth. Such discrepancies would be consistent with Nisbett and Wilson's (1977) assertion that self-knowledge is limited. For reviews of studies using the correlational method, see Malone (2001) and Zuckerman et al. (1981).

Meta-analytic Findings on Implicit Beliefs about Deception

Recently, Hartwig and Bond (2011) conducted a series of meta-analyses in order to examine implicit beliefs about deception. They referred to the behaviours that coincide with impression of deception as *cues to deception judgements* to distinguish them from cues to actual deception. Cues to deception judgements are simply the behaviours that correlate with lie-catchers' judgement that a person is lying. The study aimed to answer several questions. First, beyond self-reports, what are the behaviours that trigger judgements of deception? Second, to what extent are cues to deception judgements in line with actual cues to deception? Third, to what extent is the presumed lack of overlap between beliefs about deceptive behaviour and actual cues to deception responsible for inaccuracy in lie judgements?

In order to answer these questions, Brunswik's lens model was employed. The lens model is a framework to analyse judgements of variables that are probabilistically related to cues. In the lens model view, people attend to cues in order to make judgements. The extent to which a given cue is relied upon to make a judgement can be captured by a correlation coefficient (a so-called utilization coefficient). Also, cues may be related to the variable that the perceiver is attempting to predict, to an extent that can also be captured by a correlation coefficient (a so-called validity coefficient). Translated to the current contexts, in order to detect deception, people attend to cues. These cues may or may not be actually related to deception. The lens model holds that accuracy of judgements depends on two criteria being satisfied. First, there must be valid cues, in this case, to deception, and second, people must base their judgements on these valid cues in order to arrive at a correct judgement. For a comprehensive discussion of the theory and methodology of Brunswik's lens model, see Cooksey (1996) and Hursch, Hammond and Hursch (1964); and for previous application of the lens model to judgements of deception, see Fiedler and Walka (1993), Sporer (2007) and Sporer and Kupper (1995).

Let us return to the first question. What behaviours are the strongest cues to deception judgements? If we are to trust people's explicit beliefs about deceptive behaviour, the behaviours with the strongest utilization coefficients should be gaze aversion, fidgeting and speech disturbances. However, this is not what Hartwig and Bond's (2011) meta-analysis showed. Instead, results of the meta-analysis showed that people are judged as deceptive primarily based on impressionistic cues. These are measured by having raters, who are blind to the veracity of the statement they are seeing, judge the sender on various dimensions (for more information, see DePaulo et al., 2003). For example, people are judged as deceptive when they seem incompetent (correlation with judgements of deception $r = .59$) and ambivalent ($r = .49$) and when their statement appears implausible ($r = .47$) and is lacking in spontaneity ($r = .48$). People infer truthfulness from pleasant faces ($r = .44$), from senders who appear cooperative ($r = .41$) and friendly ($r = .35$) and from statements that are rich in details ($r = .37$). As for the cues commonly reported in surveys, the general pattern of results on the actual utilization of these cues might be surprising (Table 6.2). Most prominently, lack of eye contact is a far weaker cue to deception judgements than one would expect from survey research – the association between this cue and judgements of deception is $r = .15$. This cue is more weakly associated with deception than most of the 66 behavioural cues included in the meta-analysis. Gaze aversion is somewhat more strongly associated with judgements of deception ($r = .28$), but it is still weaker than 30 other cues to deception judgements in the meta-analysis. As for the belief that liars move and fidget more than truth tellers, these are far from the strongest cues to deception judgements. For postural shifts, the utilization coefficient is $r = .09$ (meaning that there is no tendency to infer truth rather than deception from postural shifts). Fidgeting is not strongly related to deception judgement either – the utilization coefficient for general fidgeting is $r = .03$ and for self-fidgeting is $r = .01$ (i.e. touching, rubbing or scratching oneself). Fidgeting with objects is associated with judgements of truthfulness ($r = .49$), although the sample size for this cue is small. Overall, the results suggest that there are substantial discrepancies between the cues people self-report and the cues they actually rely on.

As we described earlier, it has repeatedly been argued that there is a mismatch between subjective and actual cues to deception, meaning that people consistently rely on invalid cues (e.g. Strömwall et al., 2004). Brunswik's lens model allows for a formal test of this so-called wrong subjective cue hypothesis, through a comparison between utilization and validity coefficients. If a weak (or in a more extreme interpretation of the wrong subjective cue hypothesis, negative) correlation between the two sets of cues were to be found, the hypothesis would appear valid. In a second set of meta-analyses, Hartwig and Bond (2011) compared cues to deception judgements and cues to actual deception. They found a substantial positive correlation between utilization and validity coefficients ($r = 59$ in a meta-analysis using between-sample comparisons, and $r = .72$ in a within-sample comparison). These latter correlation coefficients suggest that, in general, the more strongly a behaviour is linked to deception (i.e. is an objective cue to lying), the more likely it is to be utilized by perceivers to make judgements of deception. Although these correlations are not perfect, they are fairly

Table 6.2 Implicit beliefs about deception

Behavioural cue	Correlation (r) with deception judgements
Implicit beliefs about deception	
Impressions of incompetence	.59
Impressions of ambivalence	.49
Lack of spontaneity	.48
Implausibility	.47
Unfriendly face	.44
Lack of cooperation	.41
Lack of details	.37
Lack of friendliness	.35
Commonly self-reported cues	
Eye blinks	.15
Lack of eye contact	.15
Postural shifts	.09
Speech disturbances	.09
High-pitched voice	.07
Fidgeting	.03
Illustrators	.03

The table is based on data from the meta-analysis by Hartwig and Bond (2011). The table lists a selection of behaviours that correlate strongly with deception judgements (most of which are measured impressionistically; see DePaulo et al., 2003), as well as the strengths of cues that are commonly self-reported cues to deception. For each cue listed, people tend to express the belief that more of that particular behaviour is displayed during deception.

strong, and they certainly do not support the notion that perceivers systematically rely on invalid cues.

To what extent does reliance on invalid cues contribute to poor lie judgement accuracy? Expressed differently, is accuracy in lie judgements primarily due to incorrect cue utilization or lack of validity in cues to deception? In order to answer this question, Hartwig and Bond conducted lens model analyses (see Karelaia & Hogarth, 2008) with the purpose of examining constraints on lie judgement accuracy. The results showed that even if perceivers displayed a perfect reliance on the most valid constellation of cues, their performance would not improve much. Instead, the results show that inaccuracy in lie judgements is primarily due to the weakness of behavioural cues to deception. For a recent discussion of how to overcome the problem of weak cues to deception, see Vrij and Granhag (2012).

The results of these meta-analytic patterns have important implications for our understanding of judgements of deception in general and for the psychology of beliefs about deception in particular. The discrepancy between people's self-reports of cues to deception and cues that actually impact on judgements indicates that people are largely unaware of what behaviours they rely on when attempting to distinguish between true and false statements. This implies that people's judgements of deception might be driven at least partly by intuitive and unconscious processes. Furthermore, it seems that these intuitive processes may be more accurate than people's explicit beliefs. The latter assertion is based on the observation that explicit beliefs about deception are largely inconsistent with the literature on actual cues to deception, while the cues that people actually rely on are fairly well in line with actual cues. In line with this argument, Albrechtsen, Meissner, and Susa (2009) found that increasing people's reliance on intuition improved accuracy in deception detection. More specifically, Albrechtsen and colleagues manipulated participants' reliance on intuitive (vs. deliberate) processes using a thin-slice manipulation (Study 1) and a dual-task manipulation (Study 2). Participants who were induced to rely on intuitive processes were 10–15% more accurate than the control conditions in detecting deception. Possibly, the manipulations may have lead participants to rely more on their implicit (and more correct) knowledge about deception, which lead to an increase in accuracy. This explanation is speculative, as Albrechtsen and colleagues did not analyse the cues that were associated with deception judgements.

Dual-process theory (Chaiken & Trope, 1999) suggests that there are two primary systems of cognition – a rapid, automatic, intuitive system (System 1) and a slow, deliberate, conscious system (System 2). Dual-process theory may explain the distinction between explicit and implicit beliefs about deception: it is possible that explicit beliefs about deception are the product of deliberate cognitive processes prompted by questions about the nature of deceptive behaviour, while in contrast, actual judgements of deception may be driven by automatic, intuitive processes.

The finding that explicit and implicit beliefs about deceptive behaviour differ has methodological implications. In simple terms, it seems we must be sceptical of people's self-knowledge about their decision making about deception. Of course, explicit beliefs about deception are of interest in themselves, and we do not discourage the use of self-report altogether. Still, we believe researchers should exercise caution when drawing conclusions from self-reports. If the aim is to map actual decision making, it may be more fruitful to employ decision analysis and process-tracing approaches (e.g. Juslin & Montgomery, 1999; Schulte-Mecklenbeck, Kühberger, & Ranyard, 2011).

CONCLUSIONS AND DIRECTIONS FOR FUTURE RESEARCH ON BELIEFS ABOUT DECEPTIVE BEHAVIOUR

In this chapter, we have discussed the available research on beliefs about deception. As we have shown, a substantial body of research demonstrates that people endorse a faulty stereotype about the characteristics of deceptive behaviour. This stereotype is held by laypeople across the globe, as well as by presumed lie experts. If people rely on this faulty stereotype, errors in lie judgements can be expected. Interestingly, recent research suggests that people's implicit knowledge about deceptive behaviour may be more accurate than their self-reported knowledge. However, the mechanisms behind this pattern are not understood. Below, we will outline some possible avenues for future research on this and other topics related to beliefs about deceptive behaviour.

Research has yet to establish the origin of the stereotype about deceptive behaviour. This stereotype has been amply documented, but as far as we know, not a single empirical study has focused on the source of this set of beliefs. We simply do not know where this widespread myth comes from, how it is shaped or how it spreads. Here, we have offered some possible explanations, but these remain speculative. We believe that future research ought to examine the basic question of the cause of the pan-cultural myth about deceptive behaviour.

Previously, we discussed the possibility that shortcomings in the feedback structure of both laypeople and presumed experts may explain why false beliefs are maintained. However, we believe further empirical research on the role of feedback in shaping beliefs about deception is warranted. Further, the finding that implicit beliefs about deception are fairly accurate complicates the interpretation of the feedback hypothesis. If it is true, as has been argued repeatedly (e.g. Granhag et al., 2004; Hartwig, Granhag, Strömwall and Andersson, 2004; Vrij & Semin, 1996), that feedback about judgements of deception is often lacking, it remains unclear why people's implicit beliefs about deception are reasonably in tune with actual deceptive patterns.

In this chapter, we introduced a distinction between explicit and implicit beliefs about deception. This distinction needs further empirical scrutiny. In particular, we believe that adopting a dual-process perspective may be fruitful in order to understand the interplay between explicit and implicit thoughts about deception. For example, under what conditions are implicit processes dominant? Are there conditions under which people's explicit beliefs about deception actually drive their judgements? Understanding what variables govern people's reliance on cues to deception is important from a basic perspective. Moreover, given the importance of accurate judgements of deception in real-life settings (Granhag & Strömwall, 2004), mapping the mechanisms that lead people to rely on more or less valid cues to deception may have significant practical benefits.

REFERENCES

Adair, J. G., & Spinner, B. (1981). Subjects' access to cognitive processes: Demand characteristics and verbal report. *Journal for the Theory of Social Behaviour, 11*, 31–52. doi:10.1111/j.1468-5914.1981.tb00021.x

Akehurst, L., Köhnken, G., Vrij, A., & Bull, R. (1996). Lay persons' and police officers' beliefs regarding deceptive behavior. *Applied Cognitive Psychology, 10*, 461–471.

Albrechtsen, J. S., Meissner, C. A., & Susa, K. J. (2009). Can intuition improve deception detection performance? *Journal of Experimental Social Psychology, 45*, 1052–1055. doi:10.1016/j.jesp.2009.05.017

Anderson, D. E., DePaulo, B. M., Ansfield, M. E., Tickle, J. J., & Green, E. (1999). Beliefs about cues to deception: Mindless stereotypes or untapped wisdom? *Journal of Nonverbal Behavior, 23*, 67–89.

Anderson, N. H. (1968). Likableness ratings of 555 personality-trait words. *Journal of Personality and Social Psychology, 9*, 272–279.

Bargh, J. A. (1997). The automaticity of everyday life. In R. S. Wyer Jr. (Ed.), *The automaticity of everyday life: Advances in social cognition* (pp. 1–61). Mahwah, NJ: Erlbaum.

Bargh, J. A., & Chartrand, T. L. (1999). The unbearable automaticity of being. *American Psychologist, 54*, 462–479. doi:10.1037/0003-066X.54.7.462 DOI:10.1037/0003-066X.54.7.462#_blank

Bond, C. F., Jr., & DePaulo, B. M. (2006). Accuracy of deception judgments. *Personality and Social Psychology Review, 10*, 214–234. doi:10.1207/s15327957pspr1003_2 DOI:10.1207/s15327957pspr1003_2#_blank

Bond, C. F., Jr., & DePaulo, B. M. (2008). Individual differences in judging deception: Accuracy and bias. *Psychological Bulletin, 134*, 477–492. doi:10.1037/0033-2909.134.4.477 DOI:10.1037/0033-2909.134.4.477#_blank

Bond, C. F., Jr., & Rao, S. R. (2004). Lies travel: Mendacity in a mobile world. In P. A. Granhag & L. A. Strömwall (Eds.), *The detection of deception in forensic contexts* (pp. 127–147). Cambridge, UK: Cambridge University Press.

Buller, D. B., Strzyzewski, K. D., & Hunsaker, F. G. (1991). Interpersonal deception: II. The inferiority of conversational partners as deception detectors. *Communication Monographs, 58*, 25–40.

Burgoon, J. K., Buller, D. B., White, C. H., Afifi, W., & Buslig, A. L. S. (1999). The role of conversational involvement in deceptive interpersonal interactions. *Personality and Social Psychology Bulletin, 25*, 669–685.

Chaiken, S., & Trope, Y. (1999). *Dual-process theories in social psychology*. New York, NY: Guilford Press.

Cole, T. (2001). Lying to the one you love: The use of deception in romantic relationships. *Journal of Social and Personal Relationships, 18*, 107–129. doi:10.1177/0265407501181005 DOI:10.1177/0265407501181005#_blank

Colwell, L. H., Miller, H. A., Miller, R. S., & Lyons, P. M., Jr. (2006). U.S. police officers' knowledge regarding behaviors indicative of deception: Implications for eradicating erroneous beliefs through training. *Psychology, Crime & Law, 12*, 489–503.

Cooksey, R. W. (1996). *Judgment analysis: Theory, methods, and applications.* New York, NY: Academic Press.

DeCoster, J., Banner, M. J., Smith, E. R., & Semin, G. R. (2006). On the inexplicability of the implicit: Differences in the information provided by implicit and explicit tests. *Social Cognition, 24*, 5–21. doi:10.1521/soco.2006.24.1.5

DePaulo, B. M., & Kashy, D. A. (1998). Everyday lies in close and casual relationships. *Journal of Personality and Social Psychology, 74*, 63–79. doi:10.1037/0022-3514.74.1.63

DePaulo, B. M., Kashy, D. A., Kirkendol, S. E., Wyer, M. M., & Epstein, J. A. (1996). Lying in everyday life. *Journal of Personality and Social Psychology, 70*, 979–995. doi:10.1037/0022-3514.70.5.979

DePaulo, B. M., Lindsay, J. J., Malone, B. E., Muhlenbruck, L., Charlton, K., & Cooper, H. (2003). Cues to deception. *Psychological Bulletin, 129*, 74–118.

DePaulo, B. M., Stone, J. L., & Lassiter, G. D. (1985). Deceiving and detecting deceit. In B. R. Schenkler (Ed.), *The self and social life* (pp. 323–370). New York, NY: McGraw-Hill.

Einhorn, H. J. (1982). Learning from experience and suboptimal rules in decision making. In D. Kahneman, P. Slovic, & A. Tversky (Eds.), *Judgment under uncertainty: Heuristics and biases* (pp. 268–283). Cambridge, UK: Cambridge University Press.

Ekman, P. (2001). *Telling lies: Clues to deceit in the marketplace, politics, and marriage* (3rd ed.). New York, NY: Norton.

Ekman, P., & Friesen, W. V. (1969). Nonverbal leakage and clues to deception. *Psychiatry: Journal for the Study of Interpersonal Processes, 32*, 88–106.

Feeley, T. H., & de Turck, M. A. (1997). *Perceptions of communications as seen by the actor and as seen by the observer: The case of lie detection.* Paper presented at the International Communication Association Annual Conference, Montreal, Canada.

Fiedler, K., & Walka, I. (1993). Training lie detectors to use nonverbal cues instead of global heuristics. *Human Communication Research, 20*, 199–223. doi:10.1111/j.1468-2958.1993.tb00321.x

Findley, K. A., & Scott, M. S. (2007). The multiple dimensions of tunnel vision in criminal cases. *Wisconsin Law Review, 2*, 291–397.

Furnham, A. (2003). Belief in a just world: Research progress over the past decade. *Personality and Individual Differences, 34*, 795–817. doi:10.1016/S0191-8869(02)00072-7

Global Deception Research Team. (2006). A world of lies. *Journal of Cross-Cultural Psychology, 37*, 60–74.

Granhag, P. A., Andersson, L. O., Strömwall, L. A., & Hartwig, M. (2004). Imprisoned knowledge: Criminals' beliefs about deception. *Legal and Criminological Psychology, 9*, 1–17.

Granhag, P. A., & Strömwall, L. A. (1999). Repeated interrogations: Stretching the deception detection paradigm. *Expert Evidence, 7*, 163–174. doi:10.1023/A:1008993326434

Granhag, P. A., & Strömwall, L. A. (2000a). Deception detection: Examining the consistency heuristic. In C. M. Breur, M. M. Kommer, J. F. Nijboer, & J. M. Reintjes (Eds.), *New trends in criminal investigation and evidence II* (pp. 309–321). Antwerp, Belgium: Intersentia.

Granhag, P. A., & Strömwall, L. A. (2000b). The effects of preconceptions on deception detection and new answers to why lie-catchers often fail. *Psychology, Crime & Law, 6*, 197–218.

Granhag, P. A., & Strömwall, L. A. (2001). Deception detection: Interrogators' and observers' decoding of consecutive statements. *The Journal of Psychology – Interdisciplinary and Applied, 135*, 603–620.

Granhag, P.A., & Strömwall, L.A. (2004). *The detection of deception in forensic contexts.* Cambridge: Cambridge University Press.

Granhag, P. A., Strömwall, L. A., & Hartwig, M. (2005). Granting asylum or not? Migration Board personnel's beliefs about deception. *Journal of Ethnic & Migration Studies, 31*, 29–50. doi:10.1080/1369183042000305672

Greuel, L. (1992). Police officers' beliefs about cues associated with deception in rape cases. In F. Loesel, D. Bender, & T. Bliesener (Eds.), *Psychology and law: International perspectives* (pp. 234–239). Berlin, Germany: de Gruyter.

Grumet, G. W. (1983). Eye contact: The core of interpersonal relatedness. *Psychiatry: Journal for the Study of Interpersonal Processes, 46*, 172–180.

Hafer, C. L., & Bègue, L. (2005). Experimental research on just-world theory: Problems, developments, and future challenges. *Psychological Bulletin, 131*, 128–167. doi:10.1037/0033-2909.131.1.128

Hart, C. L., Fillmore, D., & Griffith, J. (2010). Deceptive communication in the workplace: An examination of beliefs about verbal and paraverbal cues. *Individual Differences Research, 8*, 176–183.

Hart, C. L., Hudson, L. P., Fillmore, D. G., & Griffith, J. D. (2006). Managerial beliefs about the behavioral cues of deception. *Individual Differences Research, 4*, 176–184.

Hartwig, M. (2011). Methods in deception research. In B. Rosenfeld and S. Penrod (Eds.), *Research methods in forensic psychology.* Chichester: John Wiley and Sons.

Hartwig, M., & Bond, C. F., Jr. (2011). Why do lie-catchers fail? A lens model meta-analysis of human lie judgments. *Psychological Bulletin, 137*, 643–659.

Hartwig, M., Granhag, P. A., Strömwall, L. A., & Andersson, L. O. (2004a). Suspicious minds: Criminals' ability to detect deception. *Psychology, Crime & Law, 10*, 83–95.

Hartwig, M., Granhag, P. A., Strömwall, L. A., & Vrij, A. (2004b). Police officers' lie detection accuracy: Interrogating freely versus observing video. *Police Quarterly, 7*, 429–456.

Hartwig, M., Voss, J. A., & Wallace, D. B. (in press). Detecting lies in the financial industry: A survey of investment professionals' beliefs. *Journal of Behavioral Finance.*

Hassin, R. R., Uleman, J. S., & Bargh, J. A. (2005). *The new unconscious.* New York, NY: Oxford University Press.

Heerey, E. A., & Kring, A. M. (2007). Interpersonal consequences of social anxiety. *Journal of Abnormal Psychology, 116*, 125–134. doi:10.1037/0021-843X.116.1.125

Heider, F. (1944). Social perception and phenomenal causality. *Psychological Review, 51*, 358–373.

Hogarth, R. M. (2001). *Educating intuition.* Chicago, IL: University of Chicago Press.

Hursch, C. J., Hammond, K. R., & Hursch, J. L. (1964). Some methodological considerations in multiple-cue probability studies. *Psychological Review, 71*, 42–60. doi:10.1037/h0041729

Jensen, L. A., Arnett, J. J., Feldman, S. S., & Cauffman, E. (2004). The right to do wrong: Lying to parents among adolescents and emerging adults. *Journal of Youth and Adolescence, 33*, 101–112. doi:10.1023/B:JOYO.0000013422.48100.5a

Johnson, M. B. (2003). The interrogation of Michael Crowe: A film review focused on education and training. *American Journal of Forensic Psychology, 21*, 71–79.

Jurich, A. P., & Jurich, J. A. (1974). Correlations among nonverbal expressions of anxiety. *Psychological Reports, 34*, 199–204. doi:10.2466/pr0.1974.34.1.199

Juslin, P., & Montgomery, H. (1999). *Judgment and decision making: Neo-Brunswikian and process-tracing approaches*. Mahwah, NJ: Lawrence Erlbaum Associates.

Karelaia, N., & Hogarth, R. M. (2008). Determinants of linear judgment: A meta-analysis of lens model studies. *Psychological Bulletin, 134*, 404–426. doi:10.1037/0033-2909.134.3.404

Kassin, S. M., Drizin, S. A., Grisso, T., Gudjonsson, G. H., Leo, R. A., & Redlich, A. D. (2010). Police-induced confessions: Risk factors and recommendations. *Law and Human Behavior, 34*, 3–38. doi:10.1007/s10979-009-9188-6

Kassin, S. M., Leo, R. A., Meissner, C. A., Richman, K. D., Colwell, L. H., Leach, A., & La Fon, D. (2007). Police interviewing and interrogation: A self-report survey of police practices and beliefs. *Law and Human Behavior, 31*, 381–400. doi:10.1007/s10979-006-9073-5.

Kelley, H. H. (1973). The process of causal attribution. *American Psychologist, 28*, 107–128.

Köhnken, G. (2004). Statement validity analysis and the 'detection of the truth'. In P. A. Granhag & L. A. Strömwall (Eds.), *The detection of deception in forensic contexts* (pp. 41–63). Cambridge, UK: Cambridge University Press.

Kraut, R. E., & Poe, D. (1980). Behavioral roots of person perception: The deception judgements of customs inspectors and laymen. *Journal of Personality and Social Psychology, 39*, 784–798.

Kruglanski, A. W. (1996). Motivated social cognition: Principles of the interface. In E. Higgins & A. W. Kruglanski (Eds.), *Social psychology: Handbook of basic principles* (pp. 493–520). New York, NY: Guilford Press.

Kunda, Z. (1990). The case for motivated reasoning. *Psychological Bulletin, 108*, 480–498. doi:10.1037/0033-2909.108.3.480

Lakhani, M., & Taylor, R. (2003). Beliefs about the cues to deception in high- and low-stake situations. *Psychology, Crime & Law, 9*, 357–368.

Lerner, M. J. (1980). *The belief in a just world: A fundamental delusion*. New York, NY: Plenum Press.

Lerner, M. J., & Miller, D. T. (1978). Just world research and the attribution process: Looking back and ahead. *Psychological Bulletin, 85*, 1030–1051. doi:10.1037/0033-2909.85.5.1030

Malone, B. E. (2001). *Perceived cues to deception: A meta-analytic review* (Unpublished master's thesis). University of Virginia, Charlottesville, VA.

Marksteiner, T., Reinhard, M., Dickhäuser, O., & Sporer, S. (2012). How do teachers perceive cheating students? Beliefs about cues to deception and detection accuracy in the educational field. *European Journal of Psychology of Education, 27*, 329–350. doi:10.1007/s10212-011-0074-5

Masip, J., & Garrido, E. (2001, June). *Experienced and novice officers' beliefs about indicators of deception*. Paper presented at the 11th European Conference of Psychology and Law, Lisbon, Portugal.

Matsumoto, D. (1990). Cultural similarities and differences in display rules. *Motivation and Emotion, 14*, 195–214. doi:10.1007/BF00995569

Matsumoto, D. (2006). Culture and nonverbal behavior. In V. Manusov & M. L. Patterson (Eds.), *The Sage handbook of nonverbal communication* (pp. 219–235). Thousand Oaks, CA: Sage.

McConnell, A. R. (2001). Implicit theories: Consequences for social judgments of individuals. *Journal of Experimental Social Psychology, 37,* 215–227. doi:10.1006/jesp.2000.1445

Nisbett, R. E., & Wilson, T. D. (1977). Telling more than we can know: Verbal reports on mental processes. *Psychological Review,* 84, 231–259. doi:10.1037/0033-295X.84.3.231

Park, H. S., Levine, T. R., McCornack, S. A., Morrison, K., & Ferrara, M. (2002). How people really detect lies. *Communication Monographs, 69,* 144–157. doi:10.1080/714041710

Porter, S., Ten Brinke, L., & Wallace, B. (2012). Secrets and lies: Involuntary leakage in deceptive facial expressions as a function of emotional intensity. *Journal of Nonverbal Behavior, 36,* 23–37. doi:10.1007/s10919-011-0120-7

Ragsdale, J., & Silvia, C. F. (1982). Distribution of kinesic hesitation phenomena in spontaneous speech. *Language and Speech, 25,* 185–190.

Ross, L., & Anderson, C. A. (1982). Shortcomings in the attribution process: On the origins and maintenance of erroneous social assessments. In D. Kahneman, P. Slovic, & A. Tversky (Eds.), *Judgment under uncertainty: Heuristics and biases* (pp. 129–152). New York, NY: Oxford University Press.

Sato, T., Kikuchi, F., & Nihei, Y. (2007). Adolescent and young adult beliefs about deception. *Tohoku Psychologica Folia, 66,* 54–61.

Sato, T., & Nihei, Y. (2009). Sex differences in beliefs about cues to deception. *Psychological Reports, 104,* 759–769. doi:10.2466/PR0.104.3.759-769

Schulte-Mecklenbeck, M., Kühberger, A., & Ranyard, R. (2011). *A handbook of process tracing methods for decision research: A critical review and user's guide.* New York, NY: Psychology Press.

Serota, K. B., Levine, T. R., & Boster, F. J. (2010). The prevalence of lying in America: Three studies of self-reported lies. *Human Communication Research, 36,* 2–25. doi:10.1111/j.1468-2958.2009.01366.x

Slane, S., Dragan, W., Crandall, C. J., & Payne, P. (1980). Stress effects on the nonverbal behavior of repressors and sensitizers. *Journal of Psychology: Interdisciplinary and Applied, 106,* 101–109.

Smith, E. R., & Miller, F. D. (1978). Limits on perception of cognitive processes: A reply to Nisbett and Wilson. *Psychological Review,* 85, 355–362. doi:10.1037/0033-295X.85.4.355

Sporer, S. L. (2007). Evaluating witness evidence: The fallacies of intuition. In C. Engel & F. Strack (Eds.), *The impact of court procedure on the psychology of judicial decision making* (pp. 111–150). Baden-Baden, Germany: Nomos Verlag.

Sporer, S. L., & Kupper, B. (1995). Realitätsueberwachung und die Beurteilung des Wahrheitsgeshaltes von Erzaehlungen: Eine experimentelle Studie [Reality monitoring and the judgment of the truthfulness of accounts: An experimental study]. *Zeitschrift fuer Sozialpsychologie, 26,* 173–193.

Strömwall, L. A., & Granhag, P. A. (2003). How to detect deception? Arresting the beliefs of police officers, prosecutors and judges. *Psychology, Crime & Law, 9,* 19–36.

Strömwall, L. A., Granhag, P. A., & Hartwig, M. (2004). Practitioners' beliefs about deception. In P. A. Granhag & L. A. Strömwall (Eds.), *The detection of deception in forensic contexts* (pp. 229–250). New York, NY: Cambridge University Press.

Strömwall, L. A., Granhag, P. A., & Jonsson, A. (2003). Deception among pairs: 'Let's say we had lunch and hope they will swallow it!'. *Psychology, Crime & Law, 9*, 109–124. doi:10.1080/1068316031000116238

Taylor, R., & Hick, R. F. (2007). Believed cues to deception: Judgments in self-generated trivial and serious situations. *Legal and Criminological Psychology, 12*, 321–331.

Taylor, R., & Hill-Davies, C. (2004). Parents' and non-parents' beliefs about the cues to deception in children. *Psychology, Crime, & Law, 10*, 455–464. doi:10.1080/16683160310001634322

Ten Brinke, L., & Porter, S. (2012). Cry me a river: Identifying the behavioral consequences of extremely high-stakes interpersonal deception. *Law and Human Behavior, 36*, 469–477. doi:10.1037/h0093929

Terburg, D., Aarts, H., & van Honk, J. (2012). Memory and attention for social threat: Anxious hypercoding-avoidance and submissive gaze aversion. *Emotion, 12*, 666–672. doi:10.1037/a0027201

Uleman, J. S., Blader, S. L., & Todorov, A. (2005). Implicit impressions. In R. R. Hassin, J. S. Uleman, & J. A. Bargh (Eds.), *The new unconscious* (pp. 362–392). New York, NY: Oxford University Press.

Uleman, J. S., Saribay, S., & Gonzalez, C. M. (2008). Spontaneous inferences, implicit impressions, and implicit theories. *Annual Review of Psychology, 59*, 329–360. doi:10.1146/annurev.psych.59.103006.093707

Vredeveldt, A., & Wagenaar, W. A. (2013). Within-pair consistency in child witnesses: The diagnostic value of telling the same story. *Applied Cognitive Psychology*. doi: 10.1002/acp.2921

Vrij, A. (2005). Criteria-based content analysis: A qualitative review of the first 37 studies. *Psychology, Public Policy, & Law, 11*, 3–41. doi:10.1037/1076-8971.11.1.3

Vrij, A. (2008a). *Detecting lies and deceit: Pitfalls and opportunities* (2nd ed.). New York, NY: John Wiley & Sons.

Vrij, A. (2008b). Nonverbal dominance versus verbal accuracy in lie detection: A plea to change police practice. *Criminal Justice and Behavior, 35*(10), 1323–1336. doi:10.1177/0093854808321530

Vrij, A., Akehurst, L., & Knight, S. (2006). Police officers', social workers', teachers' and the general public's beliefs about deception in children, adolescents and adults. *Legal and Criminological Psychology, 11*, 297–312. doi:10.1348/135532505X60816

Vrij, A., Fisher, R., Mann, S., & Leal, S. (2006). Detecting deception by manipulating cognitive load. Trends in Cognitive Sciences, 10, 141–142.

Vrij, A., & Granhag, P. A. (2012). Eliciting cues to deception and truth: What matters are the questions asked. *Journal of Applied Research in Memory and Cognition, 1*, 110–117.

Vrij, A., Leal, S., Granhag, P. A., Mann, S., Fisher, R. P., Hillman, J., & Sperry, K. (2009). Outsmarting the liars: The benefit of asking unanticipated questions. *Law and Human Behavior, 33*, 159–166. doi:10.1007/s10979-008-9143-y

Vrij, A., Mann, S., Fisher, R. P., Leal, S., Milne, R., & Bull, R. (2008). Increasing cognitive load to facilitate lie detection: The benefit of recalling an event in reverse order. *Law and Human Behavior, 32*, 253–265. doi:10.1007/s10979-007-9103-y

Vrij, A., & Semin, G. R. (1996). Lie experts' beliefs about nonverbal indicators of deception. *Journal of Nonverbal Behavior, 20*, 65–80.

Vrij, A., & Winkel, F. W. (1991). Cultural patterns in Dutch and Surinam non-verbal behavior: An analysis of simulated police/citizen encounters. *Journal of Nonverbal Behavior, 15*, 169–184. doi:10.1007/BF01672219

Vrij, A., & Winkel, F. W. (1992). Cross-cultural police-citizen interactions: The influence of race, beliefs, and nonverbal communication on impression formation. *Journal of Applied Social Psychology, 22*, 1546–1559. doi:10.1111/j.1559-1816.1992.tb00965.x

Wilson, T. D. (2009). Know thyself. *Perspectives on Psychological Science, 4*, 384–389. doi:10.1111/j.1745-6924.2009.01143.x

Zuckerman, M., DePaulo, B. M., & Rosenthal, R. (1981a). Verbal and nonverbal communication of deception. In L. Berkowitz (Ed.), *Advances in experimental social psychology* (Vol. 14, pp. 1–59). New York, NY: Academic Press.

Zuckerman, M., Koestner, R., & Driver, R. (1981b). Beliefs about cues associated with deception. *Journal of Nonverbal Behavior, 6*, 105–114.

7

Discriminating between True and False Intentions

Erik Mac Giolla, Pär Anders Granhag and Aldert Vrij

Since 9/11, a renewed and fervent interest on crime prevention has emerged. A salient example comes from the ever-increasing measures being taken at airport security checks (e.g. the recent introduction of full-body scanners at a number of international airports; Milmo, 2010). Fundamental to crime prevention is an ability to ascertain the veracity of statements of intent. The psycho-legal study of true and false intentions aims to address this issue. It is, however, only in recent years that researchers have turned to this topic – the majority of past research on deception detection has focused on true and false statements about past events (Vrij, 2008). In brief, research on true and false intentions focuses on statements concerning future events. Specifically, a statement of true intent refers to a future action which a speaker *intends* to carry out, while a statement of false intent refers to a future action which a speaker *does not* intend to carry out. True and false statements of intent, just as with true and false statements of past actions, can vary in kind (e.g. outright lies, exaggerations, subtle lies; DePaulo, Kashy, Kirkendol, Wyer, & Epstein, 1996). Statements of intent however

Detecting Deception: Current Challenges and Cognitive Approaches, First Edition.
Edited by Pär Anders Granhag, Aldert Vrij, and Bruno Verschuere.
© 2015 John Wiley & Sons, Ltd. Published 2015 by John Wiley & Sons, Ltd.

have an additional dimension which must also be considered, insofar as the intended actions have not yet been performed.

Granhag (2010), drawing on research from social psychology (Malle, Moses, & Baldwin, 2001), defines an intention as an actor's mental state preceding a corresponding action. Intentions differ from related concepts like desires as they come with a commitment to perform the action in question and are often given some degree of thought and planning. In order to establish a focused research agenda, Granhag further delineated the definition of intention to refer only to single acts to be performed in the near future. Based on this stricter working definition, a statement of true intent refers to a single act one plans to perform in the near future. In contrast, a statement of false intent refers to a single act one claims, but does not in fact intend, to perform in the near future. A common use of a false intention in a legal context is a cover story. That is, a false statement about your future actions is given to mask the criminal actions you intend to carry out.

To date, some dozen studies have been implemented based on this stricter definition of intentions, most of which with a focus on cover stories (for a detailed review, see Granhag & Mac Giolla, 2014). Just as Granhag (2010) provided guidelines for the first round of studies on true and false intent, this chapter hopes to pave the way for a second round. Our aim is to highlight critical questions and new avenues of research and, where possible, offer advice on how these avenues can be approached. First, we provide a brief review of extant research. Following this, gaps in the research are highlighted, with a strong emphasis on different types of intentions and notable contextual variables.

WHERE WE ARE

The first studies on true and false intentions focused simply on (1) the ability to detect deceit when no specific methods are used (Vrij, Granhag, Mann, & Leal, 2011) and (2) how, in such situations, accuracy of veracity judgements compare to veracity judgements on past events (Vrij, Leal, Mann, & Granhag, 2011).

Vrij, Granhag, et al. (2011) conducted their study at an international airport using passengers as participants. Truth tellers were instructed to answer all interview questions about their upcoming trip truthfully. Liars were instructed to answer questions on their destination truthfully but were told to lie when answering questions on the purpose of their trip. Results showed a discrimination accuracy of approximately

70% (Vrij, Granhag, et al., 2011). This is markedly higher than what is typically found in deception studies, where accuracy rates are around 54% (Bond & DePaulo, 2006).

Vrij, Leal, et al. (2011) directly compared the deception detection accuracy for both statements of intent and statements on past behaviour. Participants were serving military and police officers. They were given a mission to collect and deliver a package. Intention-related interviews were conducted before they began their mission, and interviews about their past actions were conducted after they had completed the mission. Participants were interviewed a total of four times, twice on their intentions and twice on their past actions. In half of the interviews, they lied, and in the other half, they told the truth. Corroborating the findings of Vrij, Granhag, et al., results showed a discrimination accuracy of approximately 70% with regard to intentions. In contrast, and in line with previous research, a discrimination accuracy of approximately 55% was found for statements on past events.

Though these studies offer little in guidance with regard to theory, the differences in discrimination ability nonetheless highlight that statements about future and past events may differ in important ways. Since these pioneering studies, research on the topic has progressed steadily, and two broad approaches can be distinguished. First, researchers have extended deception detection techniques traditionally used by people speaking about past events to people speaking about future events. Second, researchers have sought to develop methods distinct for the study of true and false intent. These are based on theoretical approaches and assumptions not offered in the traditional setup on past events. It is primarily this latter approach that justifies a unique research field of true and false intentions.

Extending Past Approaches to Intentions

A number of deception detection techniques that have been applied to statements about past events have recently been extended to the study of true and false intentions, with mostly promising results.

Research on the strategic use of evidence (SUE) technique has shown that when evidence exists against a suspect, it can be strategically deployed in an interview to elicit cues to deceit (e.g. Granhag, Strömwall, Willén, & Hartwig, 2012; Hartwig, Granhag, Strömwall, & Kronkvist, 2006). The approach is built on the differing counter-interrogation strategies between truth-telling and lying suspects. Truth tellers will typically be more forthcoming and willing to provide information, while liars will be more evasive and withholding (Clemens, Granhag, & Strömwall, 2013; Granhag, Mac Giolla, Strömwall, & Rangmar, 2012).

The aim of the SUE technique is to strategically disclose evidence throughout an interview, so as to increase statement-evidence inconsistencies for liars, but not for truth tellers. For instance, a late disclosure of evidence could cause liars, due to their withholding strategies, to produce more inconsistencies than truth tellers. The SUE technique has been successfully extended to statements of intent (Clemens, Granhag, & Strömwall, 2011). The evidence, identical for both truth tellers and liars, was derived from the planning phase preceding the intention and included fingerprints on a folder and Internet browsing history. Liars interviewed with an early disclosure of evidence produced fewer statement-evidence inconsistencies compared to liars interviewed by the SUE technique. Despite these promising results, some caution should be raised. Although there are now a large number of studies on the SUE technique (see Chapter 10, in this volume), there is only one study on intent; there are still few field studies; and, as of yet, there are no countermeasure studies.

Like the SUE technique, the concealed information test (CIT; also known as the guilty knowledge test; Lykken, 1959) has also been successfully extended to statements of intent (see Meijer, Smulders, & Merckelbach, 2010; Meijer, Verschuere, & Merckelbach, 2010; Meixner & Rosenfeld, 2011; Noordraven & Verschuere, 2013). During a CIT, participants are presented with crime-related questions (e.g. 'What was the murder weapon?') and a number of plausible answers to those questions (typically around five answers are provided, e.g. *gun*, *knife*, etc.). Guilty suspects are expected to show a heightened arousal (usually measured with skin conductors) to the correct answer, while innocent suspects are expected to show similar responses to all answers (Verschuere, Ben-Shakhar, & Meijer, 2011). The CIT is theoretically supported by research on the human orienting reflex, which demonstrates that personally relevant information produces orienting responses (Sokolov, 1963; Verschuere, Crombez, De Clercq, & Koster, 2004). Since personally relevant information can relate just as easily to information on future events as to information on past events, it is not surprising that the CIT can be applied to statements of intent. For example, Meijer, Verschuere, et al. (2010) compared participants who had committed a mock crime to participants who intended to commit a mock crime. Six crime-related questions (e.g. 'What did you steel/what did you intend to steel?') each with six potential answers were asked. Participants with a criminal intent and participants who had already committed the crime showed similar orienting responses to the crime-relevant answers.

Of all the methods reviewed in this chapter, the CIT has the longest research tradition (over five decades) and is the most established in an applied setting. The most notable example of this is in Japan, where CITs are administered within police settings on a daily basis (Osugi, 2011). If we couple this strong tradition of research with the recent studies on CITs and intent, CITs perhaps represent the most ready-to-use approach to distinguish between true and false intent. With that said, CITs are not without criticism. For example, few field studies have been carried out on the topic; they are susceptible to countermeasures (but see recent work on countermeasure-resistant P300-based CITs; Rosenfeld et al., 2008; Meixner & Rosenfeld, 2010), are vulnerable to information leakage and can only be successfully applied in limited situations (Ben-Shakhar, 2012).

A related area of research has examined the visual attention orientation of individuals with malintent (i.e. malicious intent) (Wallace, 2013). Inspired by the CIT and the human orienting reflex, it was proposed that objects of personal relevance should capture people's visual attention to a greater extent than non-relevant objects. Results from a series of studies provide promising support for this claim. The results consistently showed that individuals with malintent would attend to malintent-relevant objects to a greater extent than individuals without malintent.

The Sheffield lie test (Suchotzki, Verschuere, Crombez, & De Houwer, 2013) and the autobiographical implicit association test (aIAT) (Agosta, Castiello, Rigoni, Lionetti, & Sartori, 2011) provide further examples of deception detection techniques that have been successfully extended to intentions. The study by Agosta et al. is particularly noteworthy as it distinguishes not only true intentions from false intentions, but also distinguishes intentions from the related concept of hopes. Extending the typical aIAT, Agosta et al. paired known true and false autobiographical statements (e.g. I am sitting in front of a computer/I am not sitting in front of a computer) with unknown true and false statements of intent (e.g. I will sleep in Padua/I will sleep in Milan). Faster response times were shown for congruent pairings (e.g. true known statement/true statement of intent) than for incongruent pairings (e.g. true known statement/false statement of intent). As noted, however, the authors also distinguished between true intentions and hopes. Based on Audi's (1973) classification, hopes were defined as desirable outcomes that were less probable than intentions (e.g. winning a lottery). Results showed that participants had faster response times for the congruent pairings of true intent and true known statements compared to the congruent pairings of hopes and true known statements.

Though the aIAT allowed for unique insights into the topic of true and false intent, its current applied value is called into question by countermeasure studies. These studies showed that it is possible to fake the aIAT with minimal instruction and practice (Hu, Rosenfeld, & Bodenhausen, 2012; Verschuere, Prati, & De Houwer, 2009). Others, however, have claimed that simple algorithms can be developed to catch such fakers (Agosta, Ghirardi, Zogmaister, Castiello, & Sartori, 2011). Though the approach is not without its merits, more research is needed on this topic before it should be recommended for use in an applied setting.

Some techniques, however, have not fared so well when applied to intent situations. Pavlidis, Eberhardt, and Levine (2002) demonstrated how thermal imaging technology could be used to distinguish between guilty suspects (who had committed a mock crime) and innocent suspects (who had not committed a mock crime). Using thermal imaging, a classification accuracy of 83% was achieved (75% of liars were classified as guilty; 90% of truth tellers were classified as innocent). The authors explained the findings with regard to the liars' fright/flight response, which resulted in warming around the eyes to a higher degree compared to truth tellers. In addition, the authors suggested that the technique may be usable in security screening situations, that is, situations concerning true and false intent. Warmelink et al. (2011) tested this claim in a recent study taking place at an international airport. The design was the same as that used by Vrij, Granhag, et al. (2011). Participants – passengers at the airport – answered questions about their forthcoming trip either truthfully or deceptively. Although results were in line with the underlying theory – insofar as liars showed more warming around the eyes than truth tellers – classification rates at 64% were unremarkable. Furthermore, simple veracity judgements reached a classification rate of 69% and thus outperformed the thermal imaging technique. Notably, the classification rates based on thermal imaging in Warmelink et al.'s study were lower than those observed by Pavlidis and colleagues. Whether the differences between the two studies were due to differences in the design, or whether they were due to lies being about past rather than future events, remains undetermined. Regardless of which answer is correct, the results question the generalizability of thermal imaging as an efficient screening tool. Similar difficulties were found when examining the now debunked neurolinguistic programming approach. In brief, the authors found no support for the claim that liars gaze to the right more than truth tellers (Mann et al., 2012). In sum, deception detection techniques are likely to successfully extend to situations of intent when there is a sound underlying theory that is independent of whether statements concern past or future events.

Intention-Specific Approaches

To date, research on intentions has availed of at least three distinct psychological research areas to help develop novel intention-specific deception detection techniques: research on goals, planning and episodic future thought (EFT).

Goals

Goals influence how we interact with our environment. Research on goals has demonstrated that goal activation is distinct from the activation of non-motivational constructs (Förster, Liberman, & Friedman, 2007). Intentions are closely related to the concept of goals: specifically, an intention activates a behavioural goal. Based on these findings, Ask, Granhag, Juhlin, and Vrij (2013) proposed that the distinct markers of goal-directed behaviour should only be evident for people with a true intention, as only a true intention should activate a behavioural goal. Specifically, Ask and colleagues examined whether the finding that objects are evaluated based on their utility for active goals would hold for true but not false intentions. Using an evaluative priming task, they demonstrated that truth tellers showed implicit positive evaluations of the goal-facilitative stimuli. Liars, in contrast, showed a neutral evaluation of the stimuli, in accordance with someone who would not have an active goal. A ROC analysis was used to gauge discrimination accuracy. It showed an area under the curve of 0.67 (significantly better than chance at 0.50). Although this discrimination accuracy is modest, the primary value of the study is in highlighting a viable direction for future research from the perspective of goal-directed behaviour.

Planning

Planning is a typical concomitant of a true intention (Malle et al., 2001). Liars, however, as their stated intentions are false, may be less likely to have planned for these or at least less likely to have planned to the same extent as a typical truth teller. This discrepancy between truth tellers' and liars' planning can be addressed in at least two ways. First, planning can be used as a theme for an unanticipated question. The unanticipated question approach is designed to ask questions that an interviewee is unlikely to have prepared an answer for. It should be devised so that a truth teller can recall the answer from memory but a liar must come up with an answer on the spot (Vrij et al., 2009). In an intention scenario, questions on the topic of one's intentions can be seen as anticipated (e.g. 'What do you intend to do on your trip?'), while questions on the planning of the intentions can be seen as unanticipated (e.g. 'How did you plan for your trip?'). Research examining this showed that truth tellers and liars provided similar answers for the anticipated questions on intentions. For the unanticipated questions, however, truth tellers provided longer and more detailed answers compared to liars (Sooniste, Granhag, Knieps, & Vrij, 2013). In a travel experiment, truth tellers and liars were interviewed about their alleged forthcoming trip (Warmelink, Vrij, Mann, Jundi, & Granhag, 2012). Anticipated questions about the purpose of the trip (e.g. 'What is the main purpose of your trip?') were followed by unanticipated questions about transport (e.g. 'How are you going to travel to your destination?'), planning ('What part of the trip was easiest to plan?') and the core event ('Keep in mind an image of the most important thing you are going to do on this trip. Please describe this mental image in detail'.). Compared to truth tellers, liars gave significantly more detail to the anticipated questions and significantly less detail to the unanticipated questions. The authors therefore cautioned that if one wishes to avail of the 'less detail indicates deceit' decision rule, it may be better to focus on answers to unanticipated questions.

Unanticipated questions, based on the planning phase of the stated intentions, have also been extended to cells of suspects with some success. With cells of suspects, the primary cue to deceit is within-group consistency. Studies have shown that, when interviewing groups of suspects, questions on planning produced larger differences between truth tellers and liars for measures of within-group consistency compared to questions on intentions (Mac Giolla & Granhag, 2014; Sooniste, Granhag, Strömwall, & Vrij, in press).

A second approach to the likely discrepancy between truth tellers' and liars' degree of planning is to directly focus on quality of plans. As truth tellers are typically more likely and more motivated to plan their intentions than liars, it follows that they should produce better plans. Based on this assumption, Mac Giolla, Granhag, and Liu-Jönsson (2013) examined whether markers of good planning behaviour (e.g. effective time allocation, implementation intention-related utterings and likelihood to speak of potential problems) would be more pronounced in statements of true intent compared to statements of false intent. As expected, truth tellers' statements were shown to consist of such markers to a greater extent than liars' statements.

Episodic Future Thought

A final area of research, distinguishing the study of true and false intentions from other forms of lies, concerns the concept of Episodic Future Thought(EFT) and mental images. EFT refers to our ability to pre-experience future events through mental simulation, with a strong focus on visual imagery (Szpunar, 2010). Just as planning is a typical concomitant of intentions, EFTs are a typical – often automatic – concomitant of planning. Therefore, since truth tellers are more likely to engage in detailed planning compared to liars, it follows that truth tellers should have EFTs related to their intentions to a greater extent than liars.

In their studies investigating this claim, Knieps and colleagues (Granhag & Knieps, 2011; Knieps, Granhag, & Vrij, 2013a, 2013b) had truth tellers plan a shopping trip in a nearby shopping mall, while liars used a shopping trip as a cover story to mask their criminal intention. Self-report measures showed that truth tellers were much more likely to have EFTs, and to have clearer EFTs, than liars. In essence, Knieps (2013) provides strong and consistent empirical support that – during an investigative interview – more truth tellers than liars report to have experienced a mental image during the planning phase. Differently put, if suspects do not report that they had a mental image activated during the planning phase, they are most likely lying about their stated intentions.

The series of studies reported by Knieps (2013) is, however, less clear when it comes to comparing the content of the descriptions of the mental images offered by liars and truth tellers. However, a similar study where more specific questions were used during the interview to probe the suspects' mental image provides more promising results (Warmelink, Vrij, Mann, & Granhag, 2013). Participants either lied or told the truth about a forthcoming trip. If participants indicated that they had a mental image of their trip, a number of specific (e.g. 'In your mental picture, where are you?') and general questions (e.g. 'Please tell me what you can see, hear, taste and feel'.) were asked. Results showed that truth tellers described their mental images with more spatial and temporal details compared to liars.

WHERE WE ARE GOING

To reiterate, the first round of research has availed of a rather strict working definition of intentions. In the following section, we will highlight variants of intentions and contextual factors that may influence suspect's reports. These variables offer new directions for research and new theoretical perspectives, which hopefully can result in novel deception detection techniques and a more complete research agenda.

Threats and Bluffs

As noted, the extant research on true and false intentions has focused on statements that denote lawful activities; when false, such statements are cover stories used to mask a genuine (e.g. criminal) intention.

Although this is an important area of research, with a value in a myriad of situations, an equally important area has been relatively ignored by psycho-legal research, namely, threats. Threats are statements of intent denoting criminal activities. They are a major concern for any security agency, with modern terrorism providing a particularly high-profile example. In such situations, an ability to assess whether a threat is authentic, or whether it is unfounded, is of utmost importance. Additionally, in many countries, simple verbal threats are punishable by law. When evaluating such threats, the intent of the speaker is paramount in determining subsequent legal actions (Crane, 2006). This highlights how distinguishing between a threat and a bluff is important at both the investigative phase and in the courtroom.

Importantly, true and false threats differ in a number of ways from true and false statements concerning lawful activities, thereby warranting specific research on the topic. First, as noted, cover stories denoting lawful activities typically mask other (e.g. criminal) intentions. With a false threat, however, there is no true intention being masked. For this reason, true and false threats offer a more straightforward categorization of true and false intent: the suspect is simply lying or telling the truth. Second, the content of a stated threat will differ considerably compared to statements concerning lawful activities: threats will likely consist of more negative and emotive language compared to statements of intent concerning lawful activities. Future research can shed light on whether these differences will change how interviewers should approach these sorts of situations.

Taking this direction one step further, it may also be constructive to examine people's statements about others' intentions. Operations with informants provide examples of situations where such research can be applied. In such human intelligence gathering situations, the accurate assessment of an informant's statement is critical (Meissner, Evans, Brandon, Russano, & Kleinman, 2010).

Abstractness and Planning

As noted, following the guidelines of Granhag (2010), the majority of studies have focused on specific rather than abstract intentions. That is, they have focused on future actions where the what, where, when and how are largely decided upon. It is, however, not difficult to think of situations where some or even all of these have been left undecided. Consider, for instance, a prisoner's parole hearing. One of the goals of a parole committee is to assess the prisoner's chances of recidivating. A great advantage in such a situation would be to accurately assess the veracity of the prisoner's stated intentions. In such a situation, the intentions, of both truth tellers and liars, may be considerably more abstract compared to the form of intentions hitherto studied. For instance, a prisoner may well intend to commit a future crime without having specifics decided upon. Others may intend to live lawfully, again, without accompanying specific plans.

Variation in specificity is a particular aspect associated with statements of intent (rather than statements about past events). Of course, with regard to past events, both questions and answers can refer to less or more specific aspects of an event. The event, however, has nonetheless occurred. Therefore, truth-telling suspects should be capable of speaking about the event in both abstract and specific terms. With regard to intentions, suspects will not always be capable of this. Degree and type of planning will affect how a suspect can speak about their intention. As an example, consider two friends who are taking a trip together. The trip was predominantly organized by one of the two. The planner should be able to speak of specifics in a way the other cannot. The planner could mention a specific café or art exhibit they intend to visit, while the other might speak more generally of seeing the sights. In other words, degree of planning should moderate people's capacity to speak about an event. Past research has shown that liars speak more abstractly about their claimed intentions than truth tellers (Vrij, Mann, Jundi, Hope, & Leal, 2012). Future research could examine if such findings hold when truth tellers' planning is limited.

The Post-planning Pre-action Interval

Thus far, intention studies have focused on acts to be carried out in the near future. In other words, the time between planning and action is brief. Social psychological research indicates that truth tellers and liars may markedly differ in situations with a longer and varying post-planning pre-action interval.

First, the intention superiority effect holds that intention-related constructs (e.g. tasks to be performed) are more salient in our minds than constructs of a non-motivational kind (e.g. tasks simply to be remembered, but not performed) (Goschke & Kuhl, 1993). In other words, intention-related information shows a heightened activation and accessibility (e.g. Penningroth, 2005). In addition, research demonstrates that future tasks that would benefit from forethought (broadly synonymous with the definition of intentions given earlier) commonly cause task-related spontaneous thoughts (Masicampo & Baumeister, 2011; Morsella, Ben-Zeev, Lanska, & Bargh, 2010). As an example, consider how we are often kept awake at night by tomorrow's duties. Since only truth tellers have a genuine intention, it seems reasonable that during the pre-action interval, truth tellers should show more intention-related chronic thought and have more intention-related spontaneous intrusions than liars. Preliminary support for this claim was found in a recent study. Participants were either told that they were to partake in an argument creation task (true intention) or that they were to lie about their intentions to partake in the task (false intention). Those with a true intention reported to have both more, and more distracting, task-related thoughts than those with a false intention (Mac Giolla, Granhag, & Ask, 2014, Experiment 1).

Second, construal level theory holds that people think more abstractly about distant-future events compared to near-future events (Trope & Liberman, 2003). Therefore, when an intention is to be carried out is likely to affect how suspects think, and in turn speak, about the event. The influence of temporal distance, however, is likely to differ between truth tellers and liars. Research on suspect counter-interrogation strategies shows that a common strategy for liars is to *stick to a cover story* (Clemens et al., 2013). As this is akin to learning a script, liars' thoughts about the event are likely to be quite rigid, reducing the typical effects of temporal distance. Truth tellers, in contrast, should adhere to the tenets of construal level theory and think about the future event in a more dynamic way. As the event draws nearer, they will be more likely to think about the event in concrete terms. In sum, truth tellers should think more often and more dynamically about the events associated with the stated intention. This may lead to notable differences in statement content when compared to liars. Such effects may be particularly telling over repeated interviews with large intervals between interviews.

Embedded Lies

Embedded lies are lies that are nested in otherwise true statements. For instance, instead of an outright fabrication, liars can recall an event they have experienced and simply alter some crucial details (e.g. the date or time of the event). Such lies are particularly difficult for people to uncover (Vrij, 2008). Furthermore, when given the opportunity, liars will often opt for these types of lies (Leins, Fisher, & Ross, 2013).

Just as with past events, embedded lies can occur with statements of intent: cover stories can denote acts that are largely intended with only slight alterations to mislead receivers. Worse still, the misleading element of a statement may not be what is said, but rather what is left out. Consider, for example, a terrorist who moves to a country under the guise of an international student. The cover story in such a situation is studying. However, it is likely that such individuals will often live the roles entailed in their cover stories – this, for example, is what is recommended in the so-called Manchester Manual, the al-Qaeda handbook that advises on terrorist behaviours. In other words, they will attend classes, write assignments and so on. For this reason, to a direct question such as 'What do you intend to do in this country?', a direct answer like 'study' is true, since the individual does intend to study. Yet, it is nonetheless misleading as a vital piece of information is omitted.

Psychological work on goals may provide avenues to help disentangle such half-truths. Most goal theories advance a hierarchical structure for the organization of goals, where base sub-goals aid in the eventual attainment of higher-order goals (Austin & Vancouver, 1996). The higher-order goals can be as abstract as 'being a good person', and the lowest sub-goals typically refer to concrete motor actions (Austin & Vancouver, 1996). Between these extremes, sub-goals can be held at any point along the spectrum. This perspective can help us frame statements of intent. In situations with embedded lies, those with a false intent may share many of the sub-goals of those with a true intent. At some stage on the spectrum, however, the goals of the liars must differ from the goals of the truth tellers. If we return to the example of the international student, truth tellers and liars may share similar lower-level goals, such as attending classes, passing exams, etc. On some occasions, they may even share some higher-level sub-goals such as graduating. The further one goes in the hierarchy, however, the less likely it becomes that a typical student will share the same goals as a student-would-be-terrorist. For instance, if asked questions such as 'What do you plan to do when you graduate?', liars' statements may be less likely to be imbedded and hence will be closer to outright lies. This approach can help interviewers better frame their questions during an interview. In situations when embedded lies may be expected, interviewers may be advised to include questions on higher-order end states. Furthermore, this approach could be combined with the unanticipated question approach or, more specifically, could aid in the development of unanticipated questions that are unlikely to be addressed by liars' cover stories.

Other work on goals could provide further insights. For instance, it may be possible to extend the work of Ask and colleagues (2013) who demonstrated how true but not false intentions display effects of goal-directed behaviour. They demonstrated that those with a true intention should positively evaluate goal-facilitative stimuli. Another marker of goal-directed behaviour is the automatic positive evaluation of end states (Förster et al., 2007). If the end states refer to the end states of higher-order goals, it may be possible to distinguish truth tellers from liars even with embedded lies. Alternatively, availing of such research may provide ways to analyse the content of answers directed towards end states (e.g. truth tellers may spontaneously speak more positively of end states than liars).

The Intention–Behaviour Gap

Decades of research investigating predictors of people's behaviour converge on one important finding: intentions do not guarantee action (Sheeran, 2002). Importantly, in the topic of true and false intentions, the intention–behaviour gap is only of relevance for those with a true intention – since those with a false intention will never attempt to bridge it. To date, research has minimized the gap for those with a true intention by having an achievable task coupled with a high level of motivation and commitment. In real-life settings, however, large variations of these variables can be expected and an intention–behaviour gap will be likely in many situations. Of interest is whether this can be exploited in an interview context. For example, in situations when a gap is more likely (e.g. when intention commitment is low; Sheeran, 2002), truth tellers may speak of doubts or hindrances with regard to their ability to achieve their stated intention. In contrast, liars may be more likely to ignore the gap, taking for granted that intentions will lead to action. Of course, past research shows that truth tellers will often take this for granted as well. Future research should address whether situations exist where liars will be more likely to do so than truth tellers. A first step from a research perspective is to vary the form of intention that truth tellers plan for and their relationship to it. This could include varying intention difficulty and the actor's ability, motivation and commitment.

A NOTE OF CAUTION: THE ELUSIVE NATURE OF INTENT

As time in office is coming to an end, politicians are regularly faced with their unkept promises. Disappointed voters feel that they were deceived during the elections. A common line of defence is, 'Really, our true intention was to [x], but then [y], and our priorities had to change'. The elusive nature of intentions can be seen in many other walks of life, and the legal arena is no exception. For example, accusations of tax fraud (and other white-collar crimes) are often met by the suspect admitting to the actions per se but leaving to the prosecutor the job of proving that the actions were premeditated (i.e. that he acted with criminal intent). On a related note, a recurrent dilemma in counterterrorism work is to know when to interrupt a surveilled illegal operation that is about to unfold (e.g. Bjørgo, 2013). In short, delaying the arrest until there is sufficient evidence to prove criminal intent must be balanced against the risk (and possible consequences) of suddenly losing track of the players involved. Furthermore, a person might, at a certain point in time (e.g. after having watched an upsetting debate on TV), express a serious threat against a person but later (e.g. the next day) decide not to follow through. The expressed intention was never acted upon, but might have been genuine when stated. In addition, an unfounded threat (false intent) might be used to obtain a very harmful effect, for example, a sense of fear in the individual who was threatened (true intent).

The legal field offers many opportunities and motives to study 'intent'. Irrespective of whether the issue is to assess past intentions ('Did he act with criminal intent in mind?') or to assess future intentions ('Is he telling the truth about his intentions?'), the different tasks seem to converge with regard to the complexity of the nature of intent.

CONCLUSIONS

Developing methods to distinguish between true and false intentions is not an easy task. The primary defence for conducting this type of research is the sheer amount of veracity judgements that are made about intentions on a daily basis. Border control, security personne and intelligence agencies provide salient examples. Nonetheless, research on the topic remains scarce.

In this chapter, we have reviewed a number of new approaches for discriminating between true and false intent. No matter how acute different operators' needs might be, one must remember that all these approaches are still underdeveloped. Hence, it makes little sense to provide any strong practical recommendations, and the different approaches should at best be seen as promising avenues for future research.

Researchers are perhaps unlikely to ever provide clear-cut diagnostic tools. However, considering the amount of judgements that are regularly made, even slight improvements of practitioners' classification rates could have tremendous positive effects. To date, as highlighted by the review of the extant literature, a number of advances have already been made. This first round of research has focused on (1) extending deception detection techniques traditionally used on statements concerning past actions to statements of intent and (2) developing novel approaches based on the unique psychological features of intentions. Our contention is that it is too early to choose one approach over the other; instead, both strands of research should be further developed. The next round of research should address a host of variants of intentions and contextual factors omitted in the first round. Whether these variables will result in novel and useable interview techniques remains an open question, but past research in related areas provides us with some degree of optimism.

REFERENCES

Agosta, S., Castiello, U., Rigoni, D., Lionetti, S., & Sartori, G. (2011). The detection and the neural correlates of behavioral (prior) intentions. *Journal of Cognitive Neuroscience, 23*, 3888–3902.

Agosta, S., Ghirardi, V., Zogmaister, C., Castiello, U., & Sartori, G. (2011). Detecting fakers of the autobiographical IAT. *Applied Cognitive Psychology, 25*, 299–306. doi: 10.1002/acp.1691

Ask, K., Granhag, P. A., Juhlin, F., & Vrij, A. (2013). Intending or pretending? Automatic evaluations of goal cues discriminate true and false intentions. *Applied Cognitive Psychology, 27*, 173–177. doi: 10.1002/acp.2893

Audi, R. (1973). Intending. *Journal of Philosophy, 70*, 387–403.

Austin, J. T., & Vancouver, J. B. (1996). Goal constructs in psychology: Structure, process, and content. *Psychological Bulletin, 120*, 338.

Ben-Shakhar, G. (2012). Current research and potential applications of the concealed information test: An overview. *Frontiers in Psychology, 3*, 342.

Bjørgo, T. (2013). *Strategies for preventing terrorism*. Hampshire, UK: Palgrave Macmillan.

Bond, C. F., & DePaulo, B. M. (2006). Accuracy of deception judgments. *Personality and Social Psychology Review, 10*, 214–234. doi: 10.1207/s15327957pspr1003_2

Clemens, F., Granhag, P. A., & Strömwall, L. A. (2011). Eliciting cues to false intent. *Law and Human Behavior, 35*, 512–522. doi: 10.1007/s10979-010-9258-9

Clemens, F., Granhag, P. A., & Strömwall, L. A. (2013). Counter-interrogation strategies when anticipating questions on intentions. *Journal of Investigative Psychology and Offender Profiling, 10*, 125–138. doi: 10.1002/jip.1387

Crane, P. T. (2006). 'True threats' and the issue of intent. *Virginia Law Review, 92*, 1225–1277.

DePaulo, B. M., Kashy, D. A., Kirkendol, S. E., Wyer, M. M., & Epstein, J. A. (1996). Lying in everyday life. *Journal of Personality and Social Psychology, 70*, 979–995.

Förster, J., Liberman, N., & Friedman, R. S. (2007). Seven principles of goal activation: A systematic approach to distinguishing goal priming from priming of non-goal constructs. *Personality and Social Psychology Review, 11*, 211–233. doi: http://dx.doi.org/10.1177/1088868307303029

Goschke, T., & Kuhl, J. (1993). Representation of intentions: Persisting activation in memory. *Journal of Experimental Psychology: Learning, Memory, and Cognition, 19*(5), 1211–1226.

Granhag, P. A. (2010). On the psycho-legal study of true and false intentions: Dangerous waters and some stepping stones. *The Open Criminology Journal, 3*, 37–43.

Granhag, P. A., & Knieps, M. (2011). Episodic future thought: Illuminating the trademarks of forming true and false intentions. *Applied Cognitive Psychology, 25*, 274–280. doi: http://dx.doi.org/10.1002/acp.1674

Granhag, P. A., & Mac Giolla, E. (2014). Preventing future crimes: Identifying markers of true and false intent. *European Psychologist, 19*(3), 156–206. doi: 10.1027/1016-9040/a000202

Granhag, P. A., Mac Giolla, E., Strömwall, L. A., & Rangmar, J. (2012a). Counter-interrogation strategies among small cells of suspects. *Psychiatry, Psychology and Law*, 1–8. doi: 10.1080/13218719.2012.729021

Granhag, P. A., Strömwall, L. A., Willén, R. M., & Hartwig, M. (2012b). Eliciting cues to deception by tactical disclosure of evidence: The first test of the Evidence Framing Matrix. *Legal and Criminological Psychology, 18*, 341–355.

Hartwig, M., Granhag, P. A., Strömwall, L. A., & Kronkvist, O. (2006). Strategic use of evidence during police interviews: When training to detect deception works. *Law and Human Behavior, 30*, 603–619. doi: http://dx.doi.org/10.1007/s10979-006-9053-9

Hu, X., Rosenfeld, J. P., & Bodenhausen, G. V. (2012). Combating automatic autobiographical associations: The effect of instruction and training in strategically concealing information in the autobiographical implicit association test. *Psychological Science, 23*, 1079–1085. doi: 10.1177/0956797612443834

Knieps, M. (2013). *True and false intentions: Mental images of the future* (Doctoral dissertation). Department of Psychology, University of Gothenburg, Sweden.

Knieps, M., Granhag, P. A., & Vrij, A. (2013a). Back to the future: Asking about mental images to discriminate between true and false intentions. *The Journal of Psychology, 147*, 619–640. doi: 10.1080/00223980.2012.728542

Knieps, M., Granhag, P. A., & Vrij, A. (2013b). Repeated visits to the future: Asking about mental images to discriminate between true and false intentions. *International Journal of Advances in Psychology, 2*, 93–102.

Leins, D. A., Fisher, R. P., & Ross, S. J. (2013). Exploring liars' strategies for creating deceptive reports. *Legal and Criminological Psychology, 18*, 141–151. doi: 10.1111/j.2044-8333.2011.02041.x

Lykken, D. T. (1959). The GSR in the detection of guilt. *Journal of Applied Psychology, 43*, 385–388.

Mac Giolla, E., & Granhag, P. A. (2014). Detecting false intent among small cells of suspects: Single vs. repeated interviews. *Journal of Investigative Psychology and Offender Profiling*. Advance online publication. doi: 10.1002/jip.1419

Mac Giolla, E, Granhag, P. A., & Ask, A. (2014). Intention related spontaneous thought: A cue to discriminate between true and false intent. Manuscript in preparation.

Mac Giolla, E., Granhag, P. A., & Liu-Jönsson, M. (2013). Markers of good planning behavior as a cue for separating true and false intent. *PsyCh Journal, 2*, 183–189.

Malle, B. F., Moses, L. J., & Baldwin, D. A. (2001). *Intentions and intentionality: Foundations of social cognition.* Cambridge, MA: The MIT Press.

Mann, S., Vrij, A., Nasholm, E., Warmelink, L., Leal, S., & Forrester, D. (2012). The direction of deception: Neuro-linguistic programming as a lie detection tool. *Journal of Police and Criminal Psychology, 27,* 160–166. doi: 10.1007/s11896-011-9097-8

Masicampo, E. J., & Baumeister, R. F. (2011). Unfulfilled goals interfere with tasks that require executive functions. *Journal of Experimental Social Psychology, 47*(2), 300–311.

Meijer, E. H., Smulders, F. T. Y., & Merckelbach, H. L. G. J. (2010a). Extracting concealed information from groups. *Journal of Forensic Sciences, 55,* 1607–1609. doi: 10.1111/j.1556-4029.2010.01474.x

Meijer, E. H., Verschuere, B., & Merckelbach, H. (2010b). Detecting criminal intent with the concealed information test. The *Open Criminology Journal, 3,* 44–47.

Meissner, C. A., Evans, J. R., Brandon, S. E., Russano, M. B., & Kleinman, S. M. (2010). Criminal versus HUMINT interrogations: The importance of psychological science to improving interrogation practice. *Journal of Psychiatry & Law, 38,* 215–249.

Meixner, J. B., & Rosenfeld, J. P. (2010). Countermeasure mechanisms in a P300-based concealed information test. *Psychophysiology, 47*(1), 57–65.

Meixner, J. B., & Rosenfeld, J. P. (2011). A mock terrorism application of the P300-based concealed information test. *Psychophysiology, 48,* 149–154.

Milmo, D. (2010, February 2). Full-body scanners already in use at Heathrow airport, says BAA. *The Guardian.* Retrieved from http://www.theguardian.com. Accessed 9 June 2014.

Morsella, E., Ben-Zeev, A., Lanska, M., & Bargh, J. A. (2010). The spontaneous thoughts of the night: How future tasks breed intrusive cognitions. *Social Cognition, 28*(5), 641–650.

Noordraven, E., & Verschuere, B. (2013). Predicting the sensitivity of the reaction time-based Concealed Information Test. *Applied Cognitive Psychology, 27,* 328–335. doi: 10.1002/acp.2910

Osugi, A. (2011). Daily application of the concealed information test: Japan. In B. Verschuere, G. Ben-Shakhar, & E. Meijer (Eds.), *Memory detection: Theory and application of the Concealed Information Test* (pp. 253–275). New York, NY: Cambridge University Press.

Pavlidis, I., Eberhardt, N. L., & Levine, J. A. (2002). Seeing through the face of deception. *Nature, 415,* 35.

Penningroth, S. (2005). Free recall of everyday retrospective and prospective memories: The intention-superiority effect is moderated by action versus state orientation and by gender. *Memory, 13*(7), 711–724.

Rosenfeld, J. P., Labkovsky, E., Winograd, M., Lui, M. A., Vandenboom, C., & Chedid, E. (2008). The Complex Trial Protocol (CTP): A new, countermeasure-resistant, accurate, P300-based method for detection of concealed information. *Psychophysiology, 45*(6), 906–919.

Sheeran, P. (2002). Intention – behavior relations: A conceptual and empirical review. *European Review of Social Psychology, 12,* 1–36.

Sokolov, E. N. (1963). *Perception and the conditioned reflex.* New York, NY: Macmillan.

Sooniste, T., Granhag, P. A., Knieps, M., & Vrij, A. (2013). True and false intentions: Asking about the past to detect lies about the future. *Psychology, Crime & Law,* 1–13. doi: 10.1080/1068316x.2013.793333

Sooniste, T., Granhag, P. A., Strömwall, L. A., & Vrij, A. (in press). Discriminating between true and false intent among cells of suspects. *Legal and Criminological Psychology*

Suchotzki, K., Verschuere, B., Crombez, G., & De Houwer, J. (2013). Reaction time measures in deception research: Comparing the effects of irrelevant and relevant stimulus–response compatibility. *Acta Psychologica, 144,* 224–231. doi: http://dx.doi.org/10.1016/j.actpsy.2013.06.014

Szpunar, K. K. (2010). Episodic future thought an emerging concept. *Perspectives on Psychological Science, 5,* 142–162.

Trope, Y., & Liberman, N. (2003). Temporal construal. *Psychological Review, 110,* 403.

Verschuere, B., Ben-Shakhar, G., & Meijer, E. (2011). *Memory detection: Theory and application of the Concealed Information Test:* Cambridge, UK: Cambridge University Press.

Verschuere, B., Crombez, G., De Clercq, A., & Koster, E. H. (2004). Autonomic and behavioral responding to concealed information: Differentiating orienting and defensive responses. *Psychophysiology, 41,* 461–466.

Verschuere, B., Prati, V., & De Houwer, J. (2009). Cheating the lie detector: Faking in the autobiographical implicit association test. *Psychological Science, 20,* 410–413. doi: 10.1111/j.1467-9280.2009.02308.x

Vrij, A. (2008). *Detecting lies and deceit: Pitfalls and opportunities* (2nd ed.). New York, NY: John Wiley & Sons Ltd.

Vrij, A., Granhag, P. A., Mann, S., & Leal, S. (2011). Lying about flying: The first experiment to detect false intent. *Psychology, Crime & Law, 17,* 611–620.

Vrij, A., Leal, S., Granhag, P. A., Mann, S., Fisher, R. P., Hillman, J., & Sperry, K. (2009). Outsmarting the liars: The benefit of asking unanticipated questions. *Law and Human Behavior, 33,* 159–166.

Vrij, A., Leal, S., Mann, S. A., & Granhag, P. A. (2011). A comparison between lying about intentions and past activities: Verbal cues and detection accuracy. *Applied Cognitive Psychology, 25,* 212–218. doi: http://dx.doi.org/10.1002/acp.1665

Vrij, A., Mann, S., Jundi, S., Hope, L., & Leal, S. (2012). Can I take your picture? Undercover interviewing to detect deception. *Psychology, Public Policy, and Law, 18,* 231–244. doi: 10.1037/a0025670

Wallace, D. B. (2013). *The effect of malintent on visual attention* (Unpublished doctoral dissertation). John Jay College of Criminal Justice, New York.

Warmelink, L., Vrij, A., Mann, S., & Granhag, P. A. (2013). Spatial and temporal details in intentions: A cue to detecting deception. *Applied Cognitive Psychology, 27,* 101–106.

Warmelink, L., Vrij, A., Mann, S., Jundi, S., & Granhag, P. A. (2012). The effect of question expectedness and experience on lying about intentions. *Acta Psychologica, 141*(2), 178–183.

Warmelink, L., Vrij, A., Mann, S., Leal, S., Forrester, D., & Fisher, R. P. (2011). Thermal imaging as a lie detection tool at airports. *Law and Human Behavior, 35,* 40–48.

8

Cross-Cultural Deception Detection

PAUL J. TAYLOR, SAMUEL LARNER, STACEY M. CONCHIE
AND SOPHIE VAN DER ZEE

The cultural diversity of people encountered by investigators who interact with the public has increased substantially over the last decade (Giebels & Taylor, 2009; Gould, 1997). This has inevitably meant that these investigators face a harder interpersonal challenge when answering key questions such as: has the suspect understood what is at stake; why do they avoid answering the question; and why are they being aloof and distant? In cross-cultural interactions, the usual challenges of an investigator's role are compounded by the need to decipher whether the behaviour of a suspect is indicative of deceit or a consequence of the suspect's culturally unique way of interacting.

The challenge investigators face stems from the fact that humans rely on culturally determined norms and expectations to guide their sense making during an interaction (Gudykunst, 1997; Tannen, 2006). These norms include differences in beliefs about how to interact with authority figures or those of the opposite sex (Rosenquist & Megargee, 1970), differences in the expression of emotions and thoughts (Scherer, Banse, & Wallbott, 2001), differences in what we

Detecting Deception: Current Challenges and Cognitive Approaches, First Edition.
Edited by Pär Anders Granhag, Aldert Vrij, and Bruno Verschuere.
© 2015 John Wiley & Sons, Ltd. Published 2015 by John Wiley & Sons, Ltd.

understand by 'crime' and 'lying' (Mealy, Stephan, & Urrutia, 2007; Ning & Crossman, 2007), differences in how we respond to others' attempts at influence (Beune, Giebels, & Taylor, 2010) and differences in the etiquette of interaction (e.g. turn taking) (Gumperz, 1982). In within-cultural interactions, such norms simplify the complex task of interaction by making it possible to anticipate the other person's behaviour. In cross-cultural interactions, the norms of one person are often not the norms underpinning the behaviour of their interlocutor. The result is that these contrasting foundations interfere with how behaviour is understood. In these conditions, investigators (and every-one else) become less confident in their ability to make appropriate inferences from an individual's behaviour (Black & Mendenhall, 1990).

The need to improve this situation is recognized by many law enforce-ment authorities. The U.K.'s Home Office and several Police Authorities list cultural differences and cultural awareness as one of the key issues in investigator training and development (Jones & Newburn, 2001). Similarly, in their report *Educing Information*, the U.S. Defence Intelligence Board acknowledged that current techniques and training 'takes a "one-size-fits-all" approach and fails ... to adapt the techniques to differences in age, ethnicity, or culture of the suspect' (Neuman & Salinas-Serrano, 2006, p. 230). They suggest that this must change to allow investigators to feel better equipped to handle the diversity of the individuals they encounter.

The need for improvement is also beginning to be recognized in research. Over the last decade, there has been a modest but steady increase in studies of other cultural groups, although, despite its clear relevance, very little research looking at interactions *across* cultures. In this chapter, we review the emerging literature as it relates to two aspects of deception. First, we examine cross-cultural judgements of deception and the interpersonal factors that moderate the accuracy of these judgements. We begin by examining cultural variation in people's perceptions of what constitutes deception, and we then review findings showing that people's subjective judgements about deception deterio-rate when they are made across cultures. We discuss dominant accounts for why this is the case and explore a number of moderators of this effect. We end by examining the roots of this poor performance and methods through which performance can be improved. We show how eight cultural norms lead to behaviours that appear suspicious to judges from other cultures, and we discuss how familiarity with such norms can reduce the extent of incorrect judgements.

Second, we review evidence suggesting that verbal and non-verbal cues to deception vary across cultures. In particular, we show that the observed variation in cues is consistent with what is known about cultural differences in three areas of social and cognitive functioning: self-construal as it varies across key cultural dimensions, such as individualism–collectivism; episodic memory and the cultural differences in the way people encode and retrieve their experiences; and interpersonal coordination and its association, at a subconscious level, with cooperation. We review recent work that demonstrates patterns of verbal and non-verbal correlates of deception that match the predictions made by these cultural differences. In some scenarios, these patterns show that the cues typically associated with deceit in Western student samples are associated with truthful accounts in samples from other cultures. In our conclusion, we speculate about likely areas of development of research in this area.

CROSS-CULTURAL JUDGEMENTS ABOUT DECEPTION

The question of whether or not people can recognize deception across cultures is important, in part, because it distinguishes between two accounts of what occurs in cross-cultural interactions (Bond, Omar, Mahmoud, & Bonser, 1990). One account is that differences in social norms and expectations may reduce the accuracy of judgements because judges cannot draw on their usual heuristics when making an inference. This explanation implies that deception detection is derived from a culture-specific code that must be understood in order for behaviour to be deciphered. An alternative, opposing account suggests that cues to deception may be consistent enough across individuals to remain effective despite the variance introduced by culture. Arguably, this second account is closer to the implicit assumption made by many researchers when they treat their participant groups as homogeneous; most university campuses do not contain a random sampling of cultures.

One of the first studies of deception detection accuracy involved Jordanian and U.S. undergraduate students who were videotaped giving either a genuine or fabricated description of somebody they liked or disliked (Bond et al., 1990). These videotapes were then watched by other Jordanian and U.S. students who were asked to identify the truthful and fabricated accounts. The student judges were able to identify deception with better than chance accuracy when judging their own culture, but not when judging across cultures. Specifically, the accuracy of within-cultural detection for the Jordanian and U.S. students averaged 56%, which is not untypical of the accuracies reported in research (Bond & DePaulo, 1996). The accuracy of cross-cultural judgements, however, averaged 49%. They may have well guessed.

This finding has since been replicated by a number of researchers. Bond and Atoum (2000) compared American, Jordanian and Indian students, as well as an illiterate Indian sample, and showed that an above chance accuracy rate for within-cultural judgements dropped to chance when judgements were made across cultures. Similarly, Lewis (2009) found that the accuracy of Spanish judges was 59% when making judgements about other Spanish students but only 51% when making judgements about U.S. students. In an interesting twist to this line of research, Park and Ahn (2007) showed that Korean and U.S. students based their judgements, in part, on how they felt others from their culture would evaluate the message rather than on some form of absolute criteria about behaviour. This implies that judgements are based on culturally determined cues, which may not remain valid across cultures.

So why does judgement accuracy decrease when judgements are made across cultures? One influential explanation is provided by the norm violation model, which proposes that people infer deception when the communicator violates what the receiver anticipates as being normative behaviour (Levine et al., 2000; see also Bond et al., 1992, who argue for a broader 'expectation violation model' in which suspicion is aroused by all behaviour that violates expectations, regardless of whether or not it is normative). These social norms may reflect non-verbal behaviour or 'display rules' (Ekman & Friesen, 1971) or paralinguistic behaviours, such as turn taking and intonation. When an interlocutor behaves in a way that is unusual and unexpected, a speaker seeks a plausible explanation for that behaviour. In the absence of other information, a plausible account becomes that the interlocutor is being duplicitous. For example, a comparison of Arabic and American conversations shows that Arabs are more likely to confront one another, sit closer to one another, touch one another, make more eye contact with one another and converse more loudly with one another than Americans (Watson & Graves, 1966). This can lead Americans to misinterpret their style as confrontational.

Cultural differences may also exist in the norms that dictate the purpose of certain behaviours and the interactions in which they should be used. Matsumoto and Kudoh (1993) found that Japanese students have a display rule to use smiles for social appropriateness more frequently than U.S. students and use smiles relatively less frequently to display true feelings of pleasure and joy. Such differences in normative non-verbal behaviour may in turn lead to differences in perceived credibility during cross-cultural interactions. Consistent with this idea, Bond et al. (1992) found that observers perceived actors who performed strange and unexpected behaviours (e.g. head tilting and staring) as more dishonest than those who did not perform such behaviours. This was true regardless of whether the actor was actually telling the truth or lying. Similarly, Vrij and Winkel (1991, 1994) videotaped Dutch and Surinam actors displaying typical Dutch or Surinam non-verbal behaviour while giving a statement about an event. When Dutch police officers rated their opinion of the suspiciousness of the videotaped actors, they tended to rate both Surinam and Dutch actors as more suspicious when they showed non-verbal behaviour that was consistent with Surinam norms, compared to when they displayed normative Dutch behaviour (i.e. a within-cultural judgement). This finding is interesting because it suggests that cross-cultural biases in behaviour can influence deception judgements above and beyond biases cued by visual appearance.

The studies described so far focus on non-verbal behaviour, but the impact of norm violations on veracity judgements has also been shown for verbal behaviour. McCornack, Levine, Soloqczuk, Torres and Campbell (1992) found that messages containing violations of one or more of Grice's (1975) four maxims (quality, quantity, relevance and manner) were rated by U.S. students as less honest than messages that did not violate the maxims. In a replication involving Hong Kong students, Yueng, Levine, and Nishiyama (1999) found the same association for violations of falsification (quality) and evasion (relevance), but no association for violations of omissions (quantity) and equivocation (manner). This difference suggests that Hong Kong and U.S. students have a different norm around what counts as a violation of the maxims, a difference that is presumably driven at least in part by culture. Lastly, in a clever demonstration of how personal norms drive such judgements, Sagarin, Rhoads, and Cialdini (1998) found that those who were induced to lie to their partners tended to see their partners as less honest than did people who did not lie to their partners.

CROSS-CULTURAL MODERATORS OF DECEPTION JUDGEMENTS

Although this research suggests that violations of norms can drive misjudgements of veracity across cultures, the picture is not so straightforward. One moderating factor is the existence of considerable cultural differences in the acceptability of deception. For example, Fu, Lee, Cameron, and Xu (2001) found that Chinese and Canadian students differed on their perception of lies about prosocial behaviour, with the Chinese endorsing lies as permissible modesty far more than the Canadians (Lee, Xu, Fu, Cameron, & Chen, 2001, found the same effect for children). Similarly, Nishiyama's (1995) study of business negotiations found that some everyday Japanese business acts, such as agreeing to save the other party's honour, would be considered deceptive by observers in the United States. Such differences in beliefs about acceptability impact on what people are prepared to lie about. Aune and Waters (1994) found that Samoans, who are dominantly collectivist in culture, were more likely to attempt deception for a group or for family concerns, while Americans, who are dominantly individualistic in culture, were more likely to deceive to protect self or a private issue. Similarly, Sims (2002) found that U.S. employees were more likely than Israeli employees to deceive for personal gain. These differences are likely to influence the extent to which different cues to deception are shown by different cultural groups, since each has a different expectation about what is acceptable and what should be hidden (Seiter, Bruschke, & Bai, 2002).

A second moderator of deception judgements is cultural differences in how perceptions of lying translate into differences in what is felt and thought by liars while deceiving. This is particularly true when comparing individualistic and collectivist participants because the latter group's social norm is such that they accept lying when it saves the honour of the interlocutor. For example, Seiter and Bruschke (2007) found that Americans expect to feel more guilty than Chinese participants when lying to various interaction partners across a range of different motivations. Similarly, in their study of Singaporean participants, Li, Triandis, and Yu (2006) showed a positive correlation between deception and collectivism in business negotiations. As might be expected for collectivist participants, this lying was particularly prevalent when the negotiation was around family issues.

Interestingly, the differences across cultures may be more specific than the broad differences found across individualistic and collectivist cultures. In his anthropological work, Abu-Lughod (1986) found that arousing guilt among Awlad Ali – a tribe of Bedouins living in the Egyptian side of the Western Desert – required unusual conditions. They experienced guilt only in situations that were perceived as shameful, which were primarily those in which an individual's autonomy is threatened. Thus, the experience of lying is likely quite unique for the Awlad Ali (Abu-Lughod, 1986).

A third moderator of deception judgements relates to evidence suggesting that people around the world have common misperceptions of what constitute signs of lying. In the most extensive survey of its kind (Global Deception Research Team, 2006), respondents from 75 countries using 43 languages were asked how they might tell when people are lying and completed a survey about lying stereotypes. The overwhelming finding was that over 65% of the participants listed avert gaze as a marker of lying, followed by cues such as nervousness and incoherence. When probed, they also reported strong beliefs about less eye contact, more shifting of posture, more self-touching and so on. This commonality in beliefs suggests that a common set of cues will be used by people of all cultures when making judgements about veracity, which contradicts the difference in rates of judgement accuracy observed across within- and cross-cultural comparisons. There are two dominant and as yet untested explanations for this. One is that people from different cultures interpret these cues in different ways; they are using the same cues but interpreting them according to a unique cultural code. The second is that people's reporting of cues bares little relation to what they actually use in their judgements (cf. Baumeister, Vohs, & Funder, 2007). That is, people are unable to accurately report what cues they are utilizing when making judgements, such that an external measure of their behaviour (e.g. through eye tracking) is required to ascertain what behaviours they are relying on (Hartwig & Bond, 2011).

A fourth moderator is that people's cross-cultural judgements of lying depend on which language the suspect is speaking when being judged. Cheng and Broadhurst (2005) had Cantonese and English postgraduate students identify liars and truth tellers giving their opinion on capital punishment. Compared to targets speaking in their native language, judges tended to identify people speaking in a second language as liars. The effect of this shift in judgements was to remove the 'truth bias', thereby increasing the correct identification of liars but also leading to more false accusations of truth tellers. This difference in the relative bias towards truth and lie has also been found by Da Silva and Leach (2013) who found that participants were more likely to exhibit a truth bias when observing native-language speakers, whereas they were more likely to exhibit a lie bias when viewing second-language speakers. Interestingly, in the Cheng and Broadhurst study, liars also reported less ability to control verbal and non-verbal behavioural cues when speaking a second language, suggesting that the cognitive load of interaction led them to resort to a culturally normative interaction style rather than the one made salient by their interaction partner.

A final, more positive twist in complexity about judgements of deception across cultures comes from evidence suggesting that performance can be improved by exposing individuals to other cultures. Collett (1971) showed that U.K. workers trained in the non-verbal behaviour of Arabs (the article's terminology) were subsequently liked better by their Arab interlocutors than those who did not receive the training. More recently, Castillo and Mallard (2012) investigated whether informing people about cultural differences in non-verbal behaviour could counteract cross-cultural bias in deception judgements. Sixty-nine Australian students were randomly assigned to receive no information, general information or targeted information about culture-specific behavioural norms prior to making credibility judgements of 10 video clips (5 consistent norms and 5 inconsistent norms). The results suggest that cross-cultural biases in deception judgements can occur but may also be prevented by providing appropriate examples prior to exposure.

CULTURAL ROOTS OF JUDGEMENT ERRORS

The research on improving performance raises the question of what it is about cultural differences in behaviour that leads to so many misjudgements. Zhou and Lutterbie (2005) suggest there are two approaches to answering this question and, as a consequence, two ways to think about improving judge performance. One approach is 'bottom up' and involves learning the theoretical frameworks and research findings available in the literature and then applying them to individual cases. The difficulty with this approach is that investigators must remember a significant amount of material and translate that material to the situation in front of them. In a high-pressured interaction, it is not realistic to expect a careful and considered application of aggregate findings about cultures to the behaviour of an individual (Eades, 1996). A second approach is to substitute prescriptive suggestions with a descriptive account in which the issues that are characteristically important to cross-cultural interactions are highlighted. In this top-down approach, the focus is on providing investigators an understanding of why differences are observed (i.e. information on *what* changes) rather than encouraging them to memorize a range of cultural differences (i.e. information about *how* communication changes).

Figure 8.1 gives an example of a top-down approach. In Figure 8.1, the top half, labeled as Communication features, provides a description of issues that have been shown to result in misunderstandings, while the bottom half, labeled as Learning points, summarizes the learning points that emerge from this research. The framework is structured according to four aspects of dialogue: orientation dialogue, which refers to communication used to establish interaction and the nature of the engagement; relational dialogue, which refers to behaviours that are geared to managing the relationship with the other party rather than handling any substantive issues (e.g. attempts to put them at ease);

Orientation dialogue	Relational dialogue	Problem-solving dialogue	Resolution dialogue
Small talk–dialogue that is tangential to the substance of interaction. Some cultures are not used to engaging in this way	**Story telling**–dialogue that appears rambling is appropriate contextualized storytelling for some cultures. Not all cultures use a linear story line when recounting	**Persuasion**–arguments and discussion are less central to some cultures and thus less effective as interaction tactics	**Resistance**–dialogue that attempts to delay or stall a solution can be used for other legitimate, cultural reasons
Role differences–perceived differences in status and action towards the other. Can lead to avoidance and/or aggression. It can also lead to memory conformity	**Empathizing**–dialogue that seeks to gain trust and get the other 'on side' is not effective in all cultures because it is perceived as patronizing	**Ultimatums**–while necessary in certain circumstances, such forcing tactics can evoke a particularly negative reaction from Middle-Eastern cultures	**Issues of face**–for some cultures, appearing honourable and leaving the interaction with the respect of others is critical
Small talk–be cautious not to pre-judge somebody as rude or distance because they don't engage in small talk	**Story telling**–the more information the better, so remain patient and listen to the contextual storyteller	**Rational persuasion**–consider more collaborative interactions with high-context cultures	**Resistance**–be open minded as to why the interviewee is resisting an agreement (explore why don't try to force the solution)
Role differences–if appropriate, identify the role to take to provide a strategic advantage	**Empathizing**–avoid using with high-context cultures such as Middle Eastern and Far East, as it may lead them to become defensive	**Ultimatums**–use sparingly and, rather than repeat, seek an alternative solution from the interviewee	**Issues of face**–remember that solutions are not all about substantive exchanges/issues

(Left margin labels: "Communication features" for the top two rows; "Learning points" for the bottom two rows)

Figure 8.1 A summary of eight communication dynamics that often lead to misunderstanding during cross-cultural interaction.

problem-solving dialogue, which refers to efforts to develop a mutually acceptable solution to the problem at hand or involve a substantive exchange of interaction; and resolution dialogue, which focuses on resolving or concluding the interaction or a particular part of the interaction. These four aspects occur in many interpersonal encounters, including interviews and hostage negotiations (Donohue, Ramesh, Kaufmann, & Smith, 1991; Milne & Bull, 1999; Poole & Roth, 1989).

Orientation Dialogue

Orientation dialogue dominates (though is not exclusive to) early stages of interaction, and so it appears first within Figure 8.1. An orientation may be as short as a few sentences to initiate dialogue, such as may occur during an airport screening. Or it may take a longer period as parties define their relationship, such as may occur within a police interview. Two factors that often raise confusion during orientation are small talk and role differences. Small talk serves a number of purposes, which are often collectively described as 'ticking over' behaviours (e.g. staying in touch). In investigative contexts, the importance of small talk is likely to be around 'establishing that both parties inhabit the same social reality' (Donovan, 2008). However, there are cultural differences in the expectation for small talk. For example, when the children's book *A Bear Called Paddington* was translated for the German audience, entire sequences had to be omitted to accommodate the characteristic absence of small talk in this language (House, 2006). To those accustomed to small talk, such omissions can appear cold or even rude.

The role of an individual, including their status but also how they act towards the other party, can have a significant impact on the way an interaction unfolds. Although such role effects are relevant to the whole interaction (Donohue & Taylor, 2007), they are critical during orientation dialogue because roles are typically determined at this stage. In law enforcement settings, the dimension of role that is likely to dominate is authority. For example, many East Asian cultures (e.g. Chinese) value extensive hierarchies and positions and are likely to be respectful to an investigator who presents with authority (Hofstede, 2001). While this may appear as useful, it can often be detrimental to an interaction when the appropriate reaction to authority is to demonstrate deference by being silent (Jenkins, 2000). In contrast, many with Middle Eastern cultural backgrounds will respect but mistrust authority figures (Barker et al., 2008). This can manifest as aggressive or removed behaviour, which heightens tension and may inappropriately raise an investigator's suspicions.

A related influence of role concerns its influence on recall. Research suggests that people perceived as being in authority can influence what the perceiver remembers of an event. In particular, individuals are more likely to conform to a story presented to them by someone perceived as possessing a high-powered role (Skagerberg & Wright, 2008), and this effect is even more pronounced in stressful contexts (Whitson & Galinsky, 2008). This is perhaps why, in some cross-cultural interactions, investigators are confronted with agreements to everything that they mention; the interviewee's answers influenced by what she or he *thinks* the investigator wants to hear, resulting in a distorted recall of the event.

Relational Dialogue

Relational dialogue refers to interaction that is focused on issues such as personal reputation, identity and social belonging. It is critical to cross-cultural interactions because of the different ways in which cultures value social groups and personal face and how these values manifest in conversations. One example of this, which we refer to as 'storytelling', relates to differences in the way people convey experiences. This aspect of dialogue is a central component of police interviews because such stories are later recontextualized into evidential material (Alison, 2008). Native speakers of English typically produce stories that contain a short orienting introduction, with sufficient scene setting, that then continue with an account of the main events in the story. By contrast, other cultural groups engage in a far more participatory form of storytelling, in which listener feedback and interjections are expected and in which departures of the account to the background of actors and the wider context of the event form as much a part of the account as the description of the event itself (Delwiche & Genderson, 2013). This contextualization often overwhelms those accustomed to more fact-driven storytelling and leads to pejorative evaluations of stories as rambling and unfocussed and ultimately not credible (Cook-Gumperz & Gumperz, 2002).

A second area for misunderstanding in relational dialogue concerns empathizing. Investigators often act kindly towards, or empathize with, their interlocutor in an effort to gain their trust. This is typically achieved with messages that present a willingness to listen to someone and have sympathy for their situation or by indicating a commonality between the interviewee and self (Beune et al., 2010). When examined in interactions involving individuals from cultures that place high value on social group, such as China, Kurdistan, Morocco and Surinam, the reaction to empathy is surprising. Specifically, rather than improving dialogue, a frequent reaction by interviewees of these cultures is to react negatively (Beune et al., 2010; Giebels & Taylor, 2009). This may have to do with issues of face and honour, which are dominant concepts within these cultures. Empathizing in situations where empathy is not due may be seen as undermining personal face and therefore understood as a challenging behaviour.

Problem-Solving Dialogue

The third type of dialogue in Figure 8.1, problem-solving dialogue, typically emerges out of the earlier orientation and relational phases. The bulk of investigative interactions involve problem solving as it relates to exploring issues and resolving suspicions. This may comprise a sequence of questions and answers as investigators seek to gather information (e.g. airport check-in), or it may involve persuading an individual to provide information based on the presentation of evidence (e.g. police interview) (Hartwig, Granhag, Stromwell, & Kronkvist, 2006). To many from Western cultures, the typical way of eliciting such information is to engage in argument and persuasion (Beune et al., 2010). Identifying inconsistencies in a story, pointing out the absence of evidence and debating relative values are characteristics of a persuasion approach that is successful in cultures where communication focuses on message content (e.g. North American, Western European) (Ting-Toomey & Oetzel, 2001). However, this is not true of all cultures. Cultures such as those associated with the Middle East and Far East typically solve problems and resolve conflicts in ways that are less direct, where meaning is located in the social or physical context of the interaction rather than solely in its content. As might be expected, persuasion is less central to the interaction of such cultures, and individuals from these cultures often fail to reciprocate debate (Beune et al., 2010; Giebels & Taylor, 2009). This can appear avoidant and suspicious to somebody who expects debate to be central to the interaction. Each interactant attempts to move forwards in the way that he or she sees as appropriate, and the result is an interaction that 'goes around in circles'.

When an issue cannot be resolved (or objective achieved), either because of procedural issues or because of an impasse, it is sometimes necessary to lay down an ultimatum. This ultimatum may suggest, for example, that it is not possible to move forwards until a particular piece of evidence is available (e.g. 'there is little I can do until…'). It involves a somewhat forceful behaviour – often referred to as intimidation behaviour – that aims to provoke the interviewee into an action that they were reluctant to make (Deutsch & Krauss, 1962). While investigators know that it is generally best to avoid using ultimatums (Walton, 2003), some recent research of police interviews suggests that people from different cultures vary in their response to such behaviours. For example, Beune et al. (2010) examined the reactions of Dutch and Moroccan suspects to ultimatums. With the low-context Dutch suspects, the use of intimidation was found to be most effective when focused on personal issues. In contrast, with the high-context Moroccan suspects, intimidation was more effective when focused on friends and/or family. This finding again highlights the different values that cultures place on different forms of lying and suggests that there may also be variation in the techniques that can be used to uncover the truth.

Resolution Dialogue

The final aspect of communication that can give rise to cross-cultural misunderstanding is the closing stages of interaction, where decisions are made and resolutions reached. While the closure of interaction is often expected to emerge naturally out of problem-solving dialogue, evidence suggests that, in cross-cultural interactions, the conclusion that one party believes they are making does not always tally with the perception of the other party. For example, research suggests that many police detectives are unsure about what to do when a suspect shows signs of resistance and that they often interpret the resistance as an indication of guilt (Moston & Engelberg, 1993). Yet, suspects may show resistance for a number of reasons, even when they are not guilty. For example, they may not trust the police to recognize their innocence, or they may be concerned about incriminating themselves in the enquiry (Shepherd, 1993). This is why current interviewing in some countries (e.g. the United Kingdom) focuses less on how to obtain a confession and more on how to gather information about the person interviewed and the circumstances and actions surrounding the crime (Bull & Milne, 2004; Meissner, Redlich, Bhatt, & Brandon, 2012).

A second issue that is often prominent towards the end of interactions, though it is clearly important throughout, is 'face'. Face may be conceived broadly as an 'individual's claimed sense of positive image in the context of social interaction' (Oetzel, Ting-Toomey, Yokochi, Masumoto, & Takai, 2000, p. 398). For some cultures, 'face' is a paramount motivation during interaction. This is true to the extent that people will be willing to provide false information, or not reveal true information, if doing so 'saves personal face' or indeed the 'face' of the interlocutor (e.g. if the interviewer has made a mistake). A widely represented example in the literature is when business negotiations end in 'yes' but the deal falls through because this context, 'yes' was to not embarrass the businessman at the end of the meeting, not in reality to reflect a done deal. It is perhaps inevitable that such behaviour will be seen as deliberate evasion by some cultures, though the motivation behind the misdirection is more complex than may first appear.

One interesting consequence of examining cross-cultural interactions using the four aspects of dialogue in Figure 8.1 is that it becomes apparent how misunderstandings can emerge from interaction over time. Arguably, out of the four dialogues outlined in Figure 8.1, it is the orientation and relational dialogues that are most vulnerable to cultural misunderstanding. If interactants struggle over substantive (problem-solving) aspects of interaction, there is a good chance that such misunderstandings will surface in subsequent discussion, at which point they can be dealt with through careful re-discussion. In contrast, issues relating to relationship or role may be difficult to spot, and these first impressions can shape the direction in which an interaction unfolds.

CROSS-CULTURAL DIFFERENCES IN CUES TO DECEPTION

The focus of this chapter so far has been judgement of deception and how cultural differences in normative behaviour can lead to suspicion and accusations of deceit. In this section, we turn to a different question, namely, whether or not there are differences in the cues that differentiate liars and truth tellers of different cultures. Given what is known about cultural differences in self-construal and episodic memory, there is a basis for predicting that there will be differences. For example, research suggests that people with individualistic backgrounds tend to root their memories to objects and perceptual stimuli that are personally seen, felt and understood (Oyserman, 2002). By contrast, a collectivist's remembering is tied to group actions and outcomes and so may be expected to emphasize social interconnections and relationships among actors over perceptual details (Markus & Kitayama, 1991; Wang, 2009). This single difference has important implications for methods of deception detection that associate the inclusion of contextual details with a genuine account (e.g. criteria-based content analysis; Vrij, 2005). It suggests that collectivist liars may be differentiated by cues related to a description of the relationships among actors, which is quite distinct from the common association of contextual details with inclusion of perceptual and sensory details.

Non-Verbal Behaviour

Early explorations of cues to deception across cultures have tended, much like the literature on deception as a whole, to focus on non-verbal behaviour. In their analysis of simulated police–civilian encounters, Vrij and Winkel (1991) found that Black Surinam participants made more speech errors and trunk movements, showed greater gaze aversion and performed more self-manipulations and illustrations compared to Dutch participants. However, they did so regardless of whether or not they were lying, suggesting a difference in the magnitude of expression rather than a culture-bound differential in cues to deception. Similarly, Vrij, Semin, and Bull (1996) found no difference in the type of non-verbal behaviour shown by Dutch and British liars, despite the fact that British participants reported experience of significantly more cognitive load than the Dutch participants.

One explanation for both of these results is that the cultural difference between the participating groups is not significant. Arguably, Dutch and British liars are quite similar on many cultural dimensions, while the Surinam participants were both resident in the Netherlands and sufficiently engaged within the community to be willing to take part in a research study; thus, their social norms may well have Western influences. There are two available studies where the cultural differences might arguably be larger, although in neither study was this measured. Cheng and Broadhurst (2005) report a number of behavioural differences across Cantonese and English truth tellers and liars. For example, when telling the truth, Cantonese postgraduate students showed more gaze aversion and trunk movements compared to U.S. students, but when lying, they showed less gaze aversion and less trunk movements compared to U.S. students. The opposite was true for head movements and speech aversions. Similarly, in her comparison of Spanish and U.S. liars using computer-mediated communication, Lewis (2009) found commonalities across some indicators but not others. For the Spanish students, smiling and stronger swallowing were distinctive indicators of deception. Yet, both cultures exhibited excessive hand and leg movements, fidgeting, vocal tension, repetition, illogical sentence structure and brief replies while lying.

More recently, there have been several studies of differences in non-verbal behaviour that have monitored interpersonal coordination across cultures (Rotman, 2012; Taylor, 2013; Taylor, Miles, & Dixon, 2010; Van der Zee, 2013). The process of coordination may be defined as non-verbal movements by one person that coincide with the timing and rhythm of the movements of their interlocutor (Kendon, Harris, & Key, 1975). For example, behavioural coordination may take the form of discrete movements such as matched touching of the face (Stel, van Dijk, & Olivier, 2009) or more continuous patterns of behaviour such as mutual changes in posture (Cappella, 1990). Such mutual coordination of behaviour typically occurs unconsciously, and it is associated with increased cooperation and liking (Chartrand & Lakin, 2013). As a consequence, changes in the degree to which coordination occurs may reflect an unconscious response to a lack of cooperation or a great reliance on autonomic behaviour due to the cognitive load associated with lying (or both). In either case, a change in the extent of non-verbal coordination observed between interviewer and suspect may signify deception.

To capture behavioural coordination, Taylor et al. (2010) used wireless motion capture sensors that measured the similarity in interviewer and suspects' arm, head and torso movement over the course of an interview. In this interview, a student participant of either South Asian or White British ethnicity told the truth about a prior task that they had experienced (e.g. having a chat in a coffee shop) and a lie about a second task that they had not experienced. A confederate who was of the same or different ethnicity interviewed them using a set of standard questions. Taylor et al. found that White British interviewees increased their level of interpersonal coordination when lying during within-cultural interactions. This, they suggest, reflects the fact that behavioural coordination is an autonomic process that becomes more pronounced as interviewees' conscious efforts to control their behaviour (e.g. to gesture alongside verbal behaviour) are diminished by the cognitive load of lying. By contrast, however, they also found that South Asian interviewees did not show this change in non-verbal behaviour and, if anything, showed a decrease in the degree of their coordination. This reveals a critical cross-cultural difference in the way people naturally coordinate their behaviour, which may be responsible for suspicions about deception.

Verbal Behaviour

The data on differences in verbal behaviour across cultures is equally sparse, but what exists fits hypotheses that are based on social and cognitive norms. One of the earliest examples of such differences comes from unpublished pilot data presented here for the first time. In this study, 60 individuals who self-identified being from four cultural groups (Arabian, Pakistani, North African and White British) were asked to write one truthful and one deceptive statement about a personal experience. These statements were examined for a number of key language features, such as the amount of contextual details included in the statement and the extent to which individuals expressed their feelings within the statement. People are known to change their use of such language features when writing fictitious and genuine accounts, and a comparison of the 120 statements sought to determine if this was true of all cultures.

Table 8.1 gives a schematic representation of the results that emerged from this research. In Table 8.1, an upward-pointing arrow indicates that the feature of language being examined occurred significantly more often in deceptive statements compared to genuine statements. A downward-pointing arrow indicates the opposite. The weight of the arrow indicates the significance of the difference, with heavier arrows indicating much larger differences between truthful and deceptive statements.

The variation among arrows in Table 8.1 demonstrates the complex nature of language use across cultures. There are at least three important lessons in this table. First, some aspects of language use, such as positive affect, appear to be used consistently across all cultural groups (or at least those included in this study). When they are being deceptive, people typically compensate by using overly positive language compared to when they are telling the truth (Zhou, Burgoon, Nunamaker, & Twitchell, 2004). This is consistent with evidence

Table 8.1 Summary of differences in language use between genuine and deceptive statements across four cultural groups

Language indicator	Description of indicator	Cultural group			
		White British	Arabian[a]	North African	Pakistani
Positive affect	Language relating a positive affect towards person or object	↑	↑	↑	↑
Negations	Language that negates the main clause (e.g. denial)	--	↑	--	↑
Spatial information	Language describing the locations or the spatial arrangement of people or objects	↓	↓	↑	↑

↑, more in deceptive; ↓, more in genuine; --, no difference; arrow weight = significance.
[a]It was necessary to combine Iraqi and Yemen responses in this category because of the unavailability of participant and the related problem of not being able to ascertain cultural background until after the individual has begun the study. We use the category Arabian here simply to provide a brief label for that combination of participants.

suggesting that, for many cultures, the expression of socially engaged emotions (e.g. friendly) is a common way to avoid conflict and ensure group harmony (Ting-Toomey, 1988). It may also reflect the belief that appearing positive and happy will militate against the behaviours that may leak because of underlying feelings of anxiety (Frank & Ekman, 1997). Second, other aspects of language appear more critical to some cultures than to others. For example, the use of negations in a statement is indicative of deception for Arabian and Pakistani participants but less so for White British and North African populations. This kind of finding is more nuanced, but, if found to be a robust effect, it is likely to stem from culturally normative differences in the way that cultures use negations (Zanuttini, 1997).

Third, and perhaps most critical, some aspects of language appear to reflect different intentions in different cultures. In Table 8.1, the use of spatial information is more indicative of truth in Arabian and White British populations but more indicative of deception in North African and Pakistani populations. This difference reflects the cultural differences in people's sampling, processing and recall of experiences that were described previously. The spatial elements of an experience are central to the memory constructed by the relatively more individualistic

White British and Arabian participants, such that their genuine recall contains significantly more spatial detail than their lie (Oyserman, Coon, & Kemmelmeier, 2002). This difference is less apparent for the North African and Pakistani participants because spatial details were less central to the encoding that occurred when they experience the event, and so that kind of detail is less prominent in their genuine recall. This is a good example of why misunderstandings occur in cross-cultural interactions. If an investigator of White British culture has learned through experience that stories without spatial details should be treated with suspicion (i.e. what is often described as a story that sounds empty or lacking in texture), then there is a good chance that she or he will be mistaken when the interviewee is of North African or Pakistani culture.

Taylor, Tomblin, Conchie and Menacere (submitted) extended this initial work in a study that involved participants from local community centres who self-identified as coming from one of four cultural groups (North Africa, South Asian, White European and White British). Each participant was asked to write one truthful and one deceptive statement, either about a past experience (or fabricated experience) or an opinion (or 'fabricated' counter-opinion). They were incentivized to produce good lies through payment, which they believed they would receive only if another participant was unable to identify their genuine and fabricated statement correctly.

The results of this study mirror the findings of the pilot work. They found that the use of first person pronouns and contextual embedding in a statement decreased for lies and that this effect was moderated by the participants' degree of individualism–collectivism. Specifically, in line with previous research, White British participants reduced their use of first person pronouns and perceptual details when lying to the greatest extent. By contrast, the effect was weakest and in the opposite direction for North African participants (the most collectivist of the four groups; Oyserman, 2002). Instead, this group, and to a lesser extent the South Asian group, decreased their use of plural pronouns and inclusion of social details in their lies and compensated for this by using more first person pronouns and contextual details. Taylor et al. argue that this behaviour is in keeping with a collectivist norm of wishing to protect the social group rather than self, which drives the change in behaviour for the individualistic White British participants. Indeed, the fact that these linear trends increased in significance when the analyses focused purely on references to family (rather than to anybody in a social group) serves to strengthen this explanation. Finally, Taylor et al. found no cultural effect in the use of affective language. Across all groups, participants used more positive emotion language and less negative emotion language when lying compared to when telling the truth.

Interestingly, Taylor et al. showed that differences in language use were moderated by event type. Specifically, differences in pronoun use and contextual embedding emerged for fabricated statements about personal experiences, but not statements on counter-opinions. The opposite was true for affective language. Differences in the use of positive and negative affective words emerged in statements about opinion, but not statements about personal experiences. This finding is useful for investigators as it suggests that different factors (cognitive/affect) are implicated in different types of deceit. Efforts to identify interview questions that make lying difficult (e.g. Vrij et al., 2008) might focus on asking questions appropriate for the type of story being examined. If the event concerns one of personal experience, investigators may focus on how frequently the person makes reference to themselves versus those in their immediate social group. In this scenario, examining a person's use of emotive words is less likely to provide discriminatory evidence.

SUMMARY

The potential impacts of cross-cultural misunderstandings within security settings vary widely. As noted previously, one possibility is that investigators become frustrated by, and suspicious of, the behaviour of an interviewee, when in fact the interviewee's behaviour is the result of cultural norms (i.e. false alarms). A second is that investigators are unsure about how to interpret an interviewee's behaviour, choose not to risk offending them and give them the benefit of the doubt (i.e. misses). Both of these can have a significant impact within law enforcement and security settings. However, the latter arguably poses the greatest threat to law enforcement because it potentially overlooks a significant incident. This makes it particularly important for investigators to feel confident enough to make judgements during cross-cultural interactions and, of equal importance, for them to feel supported when they feel it is necessary to delay proceedings to resolve a suspicion.

The examples described previously serve to illustrate how misunderstanding across cultures can easily occur in a variety of situations. Common to all of these illustrations is the need to remember that one's own norms and expectations are not always applicable to other cultures. Communication with people whose cultural backgrounds are different to our own is frequently associated with feelings of anxiety and awkwardness because of communication obstacles (McGovern, 2002). It is important to take this into account when involved with such interactions. Feelings of awkwardness and anxiousness could easily be interpreted as deceptive or dishonest behaviour, but, as the examples in this chapter demonstrate, this is not necessarily the case.

As well as the potential for false alarms and misses, poor cross-cultural interactions may have a wider impact on public trust and satisfaction. This was made clear in a recent set of focus groups in which a culturally diverse set of attendees were encouraged to discuss their experiences with authorities (Tomblin, Taylor, & Menacere, 2008). One participant, describing his expectation of interacting with the police, highlighted the fact that misunderstandings emerge from both interviewer and interviewee. He noted, '... so in this case [it] is very important to speak and act properly and without, you know, providing any misunderstanding; but the other point is that 50% of this misunderstanding can come from the other person'. Similarly, some participants provided clues as to the potential limits of the effectiveness of particular intervention/questioning approaches. For example, one participant noted, 'I have been at conflict ... where torture or such things ... I see police, I [was] scared regardless of innocence or not, and here [in the UK] it is doubled because here I don't know the law plus I [am] scared of the police'. This participant's negative reaction to U.K. authorities suggests that it may be important to evaluate the suitability of approaches that rely on provoking anxiety or guilt. An individual who is already fearful of authorities is perhaps better interviewed under conditions that encourage trust rather than conditions that further add to their anxiety.

There is little doubt that cultural differences among interactants can lead to misunderstandings and that, under certain circumstances, these misunderstandings will have a detrimental effect on investigations. To avoid such misunderstandings, investigators need to tread a fine line between not judging behaviour through their own cultural lens and, at the same time, being confident enough to challenge individuals about their behaviour when it appears suspicious, regardless of their cultural background. Training in common misunderstandings and differences in deception across cultures will help investigators go a long way in achieving this goal (Castillo & Mallard, 2012). But, in order for that training to be effective, researchers need to derive a better understanding of cultural differences in cues to deceit.

There are arguably three broad questions that researchers must address to support investigative practice in this way. The first question concerns identifying the key individual difference dimensions that account for the variations in cues to deception observed across cultures. Current research in the field has only scratched the surface of this issue, which is, in effective, a question about the extent to which the field's studies of student can be generalized to populations beyond the university campuses on which they were conducted. However, addressing this question serves not only to reaffirm the validity of the current literature, but it also pushes the boundaries of that literature, since it requires existing cognitive and social accounts of lying to encompass known cultural differences in the processes that they assert impact a liar's behaviour. For example, anxiety-based accounts of why people change their behaviour when lying will need to be elaborated to encompass differences in the way cultures experience anxiety in social situations. The result of this elaboration is a set of new, nuanced hypotheses that enrich the field's theoretical understanding of the link between liar's experience and behaviour.

The second question that will need to be addressed concerns the extent to which interviewing practices that have been shown to improve investigators' abilities to detect lies also generalize across cultures. By interviewing practices, we refer to specific techniques that have been shown to make salient lie behaviours, such as asking for reverse-order recall (Vrij et al., 2008), asking a suspect to draw the critical location (Vrij, Mann, Leal, & Fisher, 2011) and using influence techniques to elicit information (Beune et al., 2010). These practices are rightly routed in the current literature, but this focus means that they also rely on some culturally specific assumptions about the nature of memory and social behaviour. For example, the reverse-order questioning practice is based on the notion that people construct and recall memories of their experiences in a linear form. In reality, however, the way in which people recall events that occurred in the past varies greatly across cultures (Boroditsky, Fuhrman, & McCormick, 2011; Casasanto & Boroditsky, 2008). Similarly, the practice of asking a suspect to draw the location is likely to work best with cultures whose memory emphasizes the encoding of spatial and perceptual details, which, as we have argued previously, is not true of all cultures.

The final question that will need to be addressed concerns how findings within the area can be translated into effective training. Castillo and Mallard's (2012) findings suggest that it may be possible to reduce the degree to which investigators rely on inappropriate norms. The extent to which this is possible and the extent to which some interviewing practices render this concern moot (i.e. because they work across all cultures) remain open questions. It is one thing to demonstrate a clear understanding of cultural variation in behaviour within an experimental context but quite another to implement that understanding within the field. Thus, the impact of research in this area will ultimately be determined by the degree to which the cultural differences in behaviour can be integrated into interviewing strategies in an utilizable way. It is difficult to speculate on how this will be achieved, but whatever the approach, the result is likely to shift our current understanding of deception and deception detection.

REFERENCES

Abu-Lughod, L. (1986). *Veiled sentiments: Honor and poetry in a Bedouin society*. Los Angeles, CA: University of California Press.

Alison, J. (2008). 'From where we're sat...': Negotiating narrative transformation through interaction in police interviews with suspects. *Talk & Text, 28*, 327–349.

Aune, R. K., & Waters, L. L. (1994). Cultural differences in deception: Motivations to deceive in Samoans and North Americans. *International Journal of Intercultural Relations, 18*, 159–172.

Barker, V., Giles, H., Hajek, C., Ota, H., Noels, K., Lim, T.-S., & Somera, L. (2008). Police-civilian interaction, compliance, accommodation, and trust in an intergroup context: International data. *Journal of International and Intercultural Communication, 1*, 93–112.

Baumeister, R. F., Vohs, K. D., & Funder, D. C. (2007). Psychology as the science of self-reports and finger movements: Whatever happened to actual behaviour? *Perspectives on Psychological Science, 2*, 396–403.

Beune, K., Giebels, E., & Taylor, P. J. (2010). Patterns of interaction in police interviews: The role of cultural dependency. *Criminal Justice and Behavior, 37*, 904–925.

Black, J. S., & Mendenhall, M. (1990). Cross-cultural training effectiveness: A review and a theoretical framework for future research. *Academy of Management Review, 15*, 113–136.

Bond, C. F., & Atoum, A. O. (2000). International deception. *Personality and Social Psychology Bulletin, 26*, 385–395.

Bond, C. F., & DePaulo, B. M. (1996). Accuracy of deception judgements. *Personality and Social Psychology Review, 10*, 214–234.

Bond, C. F., Omar, A., Mahmoud, A., & Bonser, R. N. (1990). Lie detection across cultures. *Journal of Nonverbal Behavior, 14*, 189–204.

Bond, C. F., Omar, A., Pitre, U., Lashley, B. R., Skaggs, L. M., & Kirk, C. T. (1992). Fishy looking liars: Deception judgment from expectancy violation. *Journal of Personality and Social Psychology, 63*, 969–977.

Boroditsky, L., Fuhrman, O., & McCormick, K. (2011). Do English and Mandarin speakers think differently about time? *Cognition, 118*, 123–129.

Bull, R., & Milne, R. (2004). Attempts to improve the police interviewing of suspects. In D. Lassiter (Ed.), *Interrogations, confessions, and entrapment* (pp. 182–195). New York, NY: Kluwer Academic.

Cappella, J. N. (1990). On defining conversational coordination and rapport. *Psychological Inquiry, 1*, 303–305.

Casasanto, D., & Boroditsky, L. (2008). Time in the mind: Using space to think about time. *Cognition, 106*, 579–593.

Castillo, P. A., & Mallard, D. (2012). Preventing cross-cultural bias in deception judgements: The role of expectancies about nonverbal behavior. *Journal of Cross-Cultural Psychology, 43*, 967–978.

Chartrand, T. L., & Lakin, J. L. (2013). The antecedents and consequences of human behavioural mimicry. *Annual Review of Psychology, 64*, 285–308.

Cheng, K. H. W., & Broadhurst, R. (2005). The detection of deception: The effects of first and second language on lie detection ability. *Psychiatry, Psychology and Law, 12*, 107–118.

Collett, P. (1971). Training Englishmen in the non-verbal behavior of Arabs. *International Journal of Psychology, 6*, 209–215.

Cook-Gumperz, J., & Gumperz, J. (2002). Narrative accounts in gatekeeping interviews: Intercultural differences or common misunderstandings? *Language and Intercultural Communication, 2*, 25–36.

Da Silva, C. S., & Leach, A-M. (2013). Detecting deception in second-language speakers. *Legal and Criminological Psychology, 18*, 115–127.

Delwiche, A., & Genderson, J. J. (2013). *The participatory cultures handbook*. Abingdon, UK: Routledge.

Deutsch, M., & Krauss, R. M. (1962). Studies of interpersonal bargaining. *Journal of Conflict Resolution, 6*, 52–76.

Donohue, W. A., Ramesh, C., Kaufmann, G., & Smith, R. (1991). Crisis bargaining in intense conflict situations. *International Journal of Group Tensions, 21*, 133–145.

Donohue, W. A., & Taylor, P. J. (2007). Role effects in negotiation: The one-down phenomenon. *Negotiation Journal, 23*, 307–331.

Donovan, J. M. (2008). *Legal anthropology: An introduction* (p. 244). London, UK: Rowman & Littlefield.

Eades, D. (1996). Legal recognition of cultural differences in communication: The case of Robyn Kina. *Language & Communication, 16*, 215–227.

Ekman, P., & Friesen, W. V. (1971). Constants across cultures in the face and emotion. *Journal of Personality and Social Psychology, 17*, 124–129.

Frank, M. G., & Ekman, P. (1997). The ability to detect deceit generalizes across different types of high-stakes lies. *Journal of Personality and Social Psychology, 72*, 1429–1439.

Fu, G., Lee, K., Cameron, C. A., & Xu, F. (2001). Chinese and Canadian adults' categorization and evaluation of lie- and truth-telling about proso-cial and antisocial behaviors. *Journal of Cross-Cultural Psychology, 32*, 720–727.

Giebels, E., & Taylor, P. J. (2009). Interaction patterns in crisis negotiations: Persuasive arguments and cultural differences. *Journal of Applied Psychology, 94*, 5–19.

Global Deception Research Team. (2006). A world of lies. *Journal of Cross-Cultural Psychology, 37*, 60–74.

Gould, L. A. (1997). Can an old dog be taught new tricks?: Teaching cultural diversity to police officers. *Policing: An International Journal of Police Strategies & Management, 20*, 339–356.

Grice, H. P. (1975). Logic and conversation. In P. Cole & J. L. Morgan (Eds.), *Syntax and semantics 3: Speech acts* (pp. 41–58). New York, NY: Academic Press.

Gudykunst, W. (1997). Cultural variability in communication. *Communication Research, 24*, 327–348.

Gumperz, J. (1982). *Discourse strategies*. Cambridge, UK: Cambridge University Press.

Hartwig, M., & Bond, C.F., Jr. (2011). Why do lie-catchers fail? A lens model meta-analysis of human lie judgments. *Psychological Bulletin, 137*, 643–659.

Hartwig, M., Granhag, P. A., Strömwall, L. A., & Kronkvist, O. (2006). Strategic use of evidence during police interviews: When training to detect deception works. *Law and Human Behavior, 30*, 603–619.

Hofstede, G. (2001). *Culture's consequences: Comparing values, behaviors, institutions and organizations across nations* (2nd ed.). London, UK: Sage.

House, J. (2006). Communicative styles in English and German. *European Journal of English Studies, 10*, 249–267.

Jenkins, S. (2000). Cultural and linguistic miscues: A case study of international teaching assistant and academic faculty miscommunication. *International Journal of Intercultural Relations, 24*, 477–501.

Jones, T., & Newburn, T. (2001). *Widening access: Improving police relations with hard to reach groups. Police Research Series, Paper 138*. London, UK: Home Office.

Kendon, A., Harris, R. M., & Key, R. M. (1975). *Organisation of behaviour in face-to-face interaction*. The Hague, the Netherlands: Mouton.

Lee, K., Xu, F., Fu, G., Cameron, C. A., & Chen, S. (2001). Taiwan and Mainland Chinese and Canadian children's categorization and evaluation of lie- and truth-telling: A modesty effect. *British Journal of Developmental Psychology, 19*, 525–542.

Lewis, C. C. (2009). *To catch a liar: A cross-cultural comparison of computer-mediated deceptive communication* (Unpublished doctoral dissertation). Florida State University, Tallahassee, FL.

Levine, T. R., Anders, L. N., Banas, J., Baum, K. L., Endo, K., Hu, A. D. S., & Wong, N. C. H. (2000). Norms, expectations, and deception: A norm violation model of veracity judgements. *Communication Monographs, 67*, 123–137.

Li, S., Triandis, H. C., &Yu, Y. (2006). Cultural orientation and corruption. *Ethics & Behavior, 16*, 199–215.

Markus, H., & Kitayama, S. (1991). Culture and the self: Implications for cognition, emotion, and motivation. *Psychological Review, 98*, 224–253.

Matsumoto, D., & Kudoh, T. (1993). American-Japanese cultural differences in attributions of personality based on smiles. *Journal of Nonverbal Behavior, 17*, 231–243.

McCornack, S. A., Levine, T. R., Soloqczuk, K. A., Torres, H. I., & Campbell, D. M. (1992). When the alternation of information is viewed as deception: An empirical test of information manipulation theory. *Communication Monographs, 59*, 17–29.

McGovern, T. (2002). Attitudes toward the culturally different: The role of intercultural communication barriers, affective responses, consensual stereotypes, and perceived threat. *International Journal of Intercultural Relations, 26*, 609–631.

Mealy, M., Stephan, W., & Urrutia, C. (2007). The acceptability of lies: A comparison of Ecuadorians and Euro-Americans. *International Journal of Intercultural Relations, 31*, 689–702.

Meissner, C. A., Redlich, A. D., Bhatt, S., & Brandon, S. (2012). *Interview and interrogation methods and their effects on true and false confessions. Campbell Systematic Reviews*. Oslo, Norway: The Campbell Collaboration.

Milne, R., & Bull, R. (1999). *Investigative interviewing: Psychology and practice*. Chichester, UK: Wiley.

Moston, S., & Engelberg, T. (1993). Police questioning techniques in tape recorded interviews with criminal suspects. *Policing and Society, 6*, 61–75.

Neuman, A., & Salinas-Serrano, D. (2006). Custodial interrogations: What we know, what we do, and what we can learn from law enforcement experiences. In R. Fein (Ed.), *Educing information* (pp. 141–234). Washington, DC: NDIC Press.

Ning, S. R., & Crossman, A. M. (2007). We believe in being honest: Examining subcultural differences in the acceptability of deception. *Journal of Applied Social Psychology, 37*, 2130–2155.

Nishiyama, S. (1995). Speaking English with a Japanese mind. *World Englishes, 14*, 27–36.

Oetzel, J. G., Ting-Toomey, S., Yokochi, Y., Masumoto, T., & Takai, J. (2000). A typology of facework behaviors in conflicts with best friends and relative strangers. *Communication Quarterly, 48*, 397–419.

Oyserman, D. (2002). Rethinking individualism and collectivism. *Psychological Bulletin, 128*, 3–72.

Oyserman, D., Coon, H. M., & Kemmelmeier, M. (2002). Rethinking individualism and collectivism: Evaluation of theoretical assumptions and meta-analysis. *Psychological Bulletin, 128*, 3–72.

Park, H. S., & Ahn, J. Y. (2007). Cultural differences in judgement of truthful and deceptive messages. *Western Journal of Communication, 71*, 294–315.

Poole, M. S., & Roth, J. (1989). Decision development in small groups IV: A typology of group decision paths. *Human Communication Research, 15*, 323–356.

Rosenquist, C. M., & Megargee, E. I. (1970). *Delinquency in three cultures.* Austin, TX: University of Texas Press.

Rotman, L. H. (2012). *How culture influences the telling and detection of lies: Differences between low- and high-context individuals* (Unpublished master's dissertation). Twente University, Enschede, the Netherlands.

Sagarin, B. J., Rhoads, K. V. L., & Cialdini, R. B. (1998). Deceiver's distrust: Denigration as a consequence of undiscovered deception. *Personality and Social Psychology Bulletin, 24*, 1167–1176.

Scherer, K. R., Banse, R., & Wallbott, H. G. (2001). Emotion inferences from vocal expression correlates across languages and cultures. *Journal of Cross-Cultural Psychology, 32*, 76–92.

Seiter, J. S., & Bruschke, J. (2007). Deception and emotion: The effects of motivation, relationship type, and sex on expected feelings of guilt and shame following acts of deception in United States and Chinese samples. *Communication Studies, 58*, 1–16.

Seiter, J. S., Bruschke, J., & Bai, B. (2002). The acceptability of deception as a function of perceiver's culture, deceiver's intention, and deceiver-deceived relationship. *Western Journal of Communication, 66*, 158–180.

Shepherd, E. (1993). Resistance in interviews: The contribution of police perceptions and behaviour. In E. Shepherd (Ed.), *Aspects of police interviewing.* Issues in Criminological and Legal Psychology. Leicester, UK: British Psychological Society.

Sims, R. L. (2002). Support for the use of deception within the work environment: A comparison of Israel and United States employees. *Journal of Business Ethics, 35*, 27–34.

Skagerberg, E. M., & Wright, D. B. (2008). Manipulating power can affect memory conformity. *Applied Cognitive Psychology, 22*, 207–216.

Stel, M., van Dijk, E., & Olivier, E. (2009). You want to know the truth? Then don't mimic! *Psychological Science, 20*, 693–699.

Tannen, D. (2006). Language and culture. In R. Fasold & J. Connor-Linton (Eds.), *An introduction to language and linguistics* (pp. 343–372). Cambridge, UK: Cambridge University Press.

Taylor, P. J. (2013, June). *How technology is revolutionizing our understanding of human cooperation (Inaugural lecture)*. Twente University Press. http://www.utwente.nl/academischeplechtigheden/oraties/archief/2013/Oratieboekje_Taylor.pdf. Accessed 7 June 2014.

Taylor, P. J., Miles, R., & Dixon, J. (2010, June). *Changes in nonverbal mimicry predict deception in cross-cultural interviews*. Presentation given at the Twentieth European Association of Psychology and Law conference. Gothenburg, Sweden.

Taylor, P. J., Tomblin, S., Conchie, S. M., & Menacere, T. (submitted). Evidence of cultural differences in linguistic indicators of deception.

Ting-Toomey, S. (1988). Intercultural conflict styles: A face negotiation theory. In Y. Y. Kim & W. Gudykunst (Eds.), *Theories in intercultural communication* (pp. 213–235). Newbury Park, CA: Sage.

Ting-Toomey, S., & Oetzel, J. G. (2001). *Managing intercultural conflict effectively*. Thousand Oaks, CA: Sage.

Tomblin, S., Taylor, P. J., & Menacere, T. (2008). *Supplementary report: Excerpts from focus groups* (Unpublished internal report). Lancaster, UK: Lancaster University.

Van der Zee, S. (2013). *The effect of cognitive load on nonverbal mimicry in interview settings* (Unpublished doctoral thesis). Lancaster, UK: Lancaster University.

Vrij, A. (2005). Criteria-based content analysis: A qualitative review of the first 37 studies. *Psychology, Public Policy, and Law, 11*, 3–41.

Vrij, A., Mann, S., Fisher, R., Leal, S., Milne, B., & Bull, R. (2008). Increasing cognitive load to facilitate lie detection: The benefit of recalling an event in reverse order. *Law and Human Behavior, 32*, 253–265.

Vrij, A., Mann, S., Leal, S., & Fisher, R. (2011). Is anyone there? Drawings as a tool to detect deceit in occupation interviews. *Psychology, Crime and Law, 18*, 377–388.

Vrij, A., Semin, G. R., & Bull, R. (1996). Insight into behaviour displayed during deception. *Human Communication Research, 22*, 544–562.

Vrij, A., & Winkel, F. W. (1991). Cultural patterns in Dutch and Surinam nonverbal behaviour: An analysis of simulated police/citizen encounters. *Journal of Nonverbal Behavior, 15*(3), 169–184.

Vrij, A., & Winkel, F. W. (1994). Perceptual distortions in cross-cultural interrogations: The impact of skin color, accent, speech style, and spoken fluency on impression formation. *Journal of Cross-Cultural Psychology, 25*, 284–295.

Walton, D. (2003). The interrogation as a type of dialogue. *Journal of Pragmatics, 35*, 1771–1802.

Wang, Q. (2009). Are Asians forgetful? Perception, retention, and recall in episodic remembering. *Cognition, 111*, 123–131.

Watson, O., & Graves, T. (1966). Quantitative research in proxemic behavior. *American Anthropologist, 68*, 971–985.

Whitson, J. A., & Galinsky, A. (2008). Lacking control increases illusory pattern perception. *Science, 322*, 115–117.

Yeung, L. N. T., Levine, T. R., & Nishiyama, K. (1999). Information manipulation theory and perceptions of deception in Hong Kong. *Communication Reports, 12*, 1–11.

Zanuttini, R. (1997). *Negation and clausal structure: A comparative study of romance languages.* New York, NY: Oxford University Press.

Zhou, L., Burgoon, J. K., Nunamaker, J. F., & Twitchell, D. (2004). Automated linguistics based cues for detecting deception in text-based asynchronous computer mediated communication: An empirical investigation. *Group Decision and Negotiation, 13*, 81–106.

Zhou, L., & Lutterbie, S. (2005). Deception across cultures: Bottom-up and top-down approaches. *Lecture Notes in Computer Science, 3495*, 465–470.

Section III

Improving Lie Detection: New Approaches

9

A Cognitive Approach to Lie Detection

ALDERT VRIJ

This chapter introduces a new cognitive approach to non-verbal and verbal lie detection. The starting point of this approach is that lying can be more mentally taxing than telling the truth. This starting point is far from new. It was acknowledged by Zuckerman, DePaulo, and Rosenthal (1981) in their seminal paper and has been included in most theories on deception and lie detection ever since (Vrij, 2008). The new aspect of the cognitive lie detection approach is that investigators can enhance the difference in cognitive load that liars and truth tellers experience through specific interventions. If successful, those interventions should result in liars displaying more diagnostic cues to deception and should facilitate lie detection. This chapter commences by summarizing the reasons *why* lying can be more difficult than truth telling and *when* this is the case, followed by empirical evidence that supports the notion that lying can be more cognitively demanding than truth telling. The cognitive lie detection approach has two elements, imposing cognitive load and asking unanticipated questions. The second section presents the underlying rationale of these two elements

Detecting Deception: Current Challenges and Cognitive Approaches, First Edition.
Edited by Pär Anders Granhag, Aldert Vrij, and Bruno Verschuere.

together with brief descriptions of numerous studies carried out in this area to date. This section shows that a cognitive lie detection approach (i) results in more cues to deceit and (ii) facilitates lie detection. The final section of this chapter presents some final thoughts about the cognitive lie detection approach, including ideas for future research.

LYING AND COGNITIVE LOAD

Why and When Liars Experience More Cognitive Load than Truth Tellers

Lying is a cognitive task that results in increased cognitive load. The term cognitive load can be defined as a multidimensional construct representing the load that performing a particular task imposes on the actor's cognitive system (Paas, Renkl, & Sweller, 2003; Paas, Tuovinen, Tabbers, & van Gerven, 2003; Paas & Van Merriënboer, 1994). There are many factors that contribute to a liar's cognitive load while being interviewed. First, formulating the lie itself is cognitively taxing. Liars need to make up their stories while monitoring their fabrications so that they are plausible and adhere to everything the observer knows or might find out. In addition, liars must remember their earlier statements and what they told to whom, so that they appear consistent when retelling their story. Liars should also avoid making slips of the tongue and should refrain from providing investigators with new leads (Vrij, 2008).

Second, liars are typically less likely than truth tellers to take their credibility for granted (DePaulo et al., 2003; Gilovich, Savitsky, & Medvec, 1998; Kassin, 2005; Kassin, Appleby, & Torkildson-Perillo, 2010; Kassin & Gudjonsson, 2004; Kassin & Norwick, 2004; Vrij, Mann, & Fisher, 2006b). There are at least two reasons for this. The stakes (i.e. negative consequences of getting caught and positive consequences of getting away with the lie) are sometimes higher for liars than for truth tellers. Smugglers are probably keener to make an honest impression on customs officers than non-smugglers, because the negative consequences for having to open their suitcases are much higher for smugglers than for non-smugglers. In addition, truth tellers typically assume that their innocence shines through (Granhag, Strömwall, & Hartwig, 2007; Kassin, 2005; Kassin & Gudjonsson, 2004; Kassin & Norwick, 2004; Vrij et al., 2006b), which could be explained by the *illusion of transparency* (Gilovich et al., 1998), the belief that 'one's inner feelings will manifest themselves on the outside', and the *belief in a just world* (Lerner, 1980), the belief that people 'will get what they deserve, and deserve what they get'. As such, liars will be more inclined than truth tellers to monitor and control their demeanour in order that they appear honest to the interviewer (DePaulo & Kirkendol, 1989). Monitoring and controlling behaviour is cognitively demanding (Baumeister, 1998). For example, a guilty suspect may experience powerful emotions (e.g. fear, remorse, anger or even excitement) which must be hidden or faked (Gambos, 2006; Mohamed et al., 2006; Porter & Ten Brinke, 2010; Richards, 2010). Consider a woman publicly pleading for the safe return of her partner who, in reality, she has murdered (see also Vrij & Mann, 2001). She must monitor her body language and emotional expressions while keeping the details of the story straight. A high level of cognitive load accompanies high-stakes deception.

Third, because liars do not take their credibility for granted, they may monitor the *interviewer's* reactions more carefully in order to assess whether they appear to be getting away with their lie (Buller & Burgoon, 1996; Schweitzer, Brodt, & Croson, 2002). Carefully monitoring the interviewer also requires cognitive resources. Fourth, liars may be preoccupied by the task of reminding themselves to act and role-play (DePaulo et al., 2003), which requires extra cognitive effort. Fifth, deception requires a justification, whereas truth telling does not (Levine, Kim, & Hamel, 2010). People typically lie for psychological or material reasons (DePaulo, Kashy, Kirkendol, Wyer, & Epstein, 1996). For example, they lie because they are too embarrassed to tell the truth (psychological reasons) or they lie to make money (material reason). Considering such justifications is mentally taxing. Sixth, liars have to suppress the truth while they are lying and this is also cognitively demanding (Spence & Kaylor-Hughes, 2008; Spence et al., 2001; Verschuere, Spruyt, Meijer, & Otgaar, 2011). Finally, while the truth often comes to mind automatically, activation of **a** lie is more intentional and deliberate and thus requires mental effort (Gilbert, 1991; Walczyk, Roper, Seemann, & Humphrey, 2003; Walczyk et al., 2005).

Obviously, lying is not always more cognitively demanding than truth telling (McCornack, 1997). Perhaps the seven reasons given as to *why* lying is more cognitively demanding could give us insight into *when* it is more cognitively demanding. That is, lying is more cognitively demanding to the degree that these seven principles are in effect. For at least some of these seven principles to be fulfilled, two elements are required. First, lying is likely to be more demanding than truth telling only *when interviewees are motivated to be believed*. Only under those circumstances can it be assumed that liars take their credibility less for granted than truth tellers and hence will be more inclined than truth tellers to monitor their own non-verbal and verbal behaviour and/or the interviewer's reactions. Second, for lying to be more cognitively demanding than truth telling, *liars must be able to retrieve their truthful activity easily and have a clear image of it.* Only when liars' knowledge of the truth is easily and clearly accessed will it be difficult for them to suppress the truth. On the other side of the equation, *truth tellers also need to have easy access to the truth* for their task of truthfully reporting an event to be relatively undemanding. If truth tellers have to think hard to remember the event in question (e.g. because it was not distinctive or it occurred long ago), their cognitive demands may exceed the cognitive demands that liars require for fabricating a story.

In forensic settings, we can reasonably assume that interviewees will be motivated to be believed, but we cannot assume that they will always be able to easily retrieve the target event from memory, as this will vary from one case to another. However, interviewers can check this. For example, at the beginning of the interview, they can tell an interviewee that they would like to discuss with her/him what she/he did last Tuesday night. They then can give the interviewee some time to think about it. Only when the interviewee says they remember what she/he did on that night can the cognitive lie detection approach be implemented.

Lying Is More Cognitively Demanding than Truth Telling: The Empirical Evidence

In experimental studies, researchers ensure that interviewees are motivated (typically by giving them a reward for making a credible impression) and that the target event is easily retrieved (typically by interviewing the suspects shortly after informing them about the target event). In those experiments, lying has been found to be more demanding than truth telling in various settings. Participants who have been asked after the interview about the cognitive load they experienced during it reported that lying is more cognitively demanding than telling the truth. This occurred when lengthy, elaborative responses were required (Granhag & Strömwall, 2002; Hartwig, Granhag, Strömwall, & Kronkvist, 2006; Strömwall, Hartwig, & Granhag, 2006; Vrij, Edward & Bull, 2001b; Vrij & Mann, 2006; Vrij, Mann, & Fisher, 2006a; White & Burgoon, 2001) but also when short responses were sufficient (Caso, Gnisci, Vrij, & Mann, 2005; Vrij et al., 2006b; Vrij, Semin, & Bull, 1996). In fMRI deception research, lying and truth telling are differentiated only by the act of pressing either a 'lie' or 'truth' button. Nevertheless, reviews of fMRI deception research (Christ, Van Essen, Watson, Brubaker, & McDermott, 2009; Langleben, 2008; Spence, 2008; Spence et al., 2004) reveal that deception generally activates the higher centres of the brain which are typically associated with cognitive demand.

Analyses of police interviews with real-life suspects suggest that lying is also often more cognitively demanding than truth telling in forensic settings. First, in those police interviews, lies were accompanied by increased pauses, decreased blinking and decreased hand and finger movements, all of which are signs of cognitive load (Mann, Vrij, & Bull, 2002; Vrij & Mann, 2003). Second, police officers who saw a selection of these police interviews (but did not know when the suspects were lying or truth telling) reported that the suspects appeared to be thinking harder when they lied than when they told the truth (Mann & Vrij, 2006). Finally, when police officers attempted to detect deceit explicitly ('Is the person lying?') or implicitly ('Is the person having to think hard?'), they were able to discriminate between liars and truth tellers, albeit only in the implicit condition where their attention was drawn towards the suspect's cognitive demands ('think hard') (Vrij, Edward, & Bull, 2001a). Moreover, only in the implicit condition did they pay attention to the cues that actually discriminated between the truth tellers and liars, such as a decrease in hand movements. In all, several findings converge on the claim that lying is more cognitively demanding than truth telling. Observers can recognize cues to cognitive demand without the use of sophisticated equipment (e.g. Vrij, Evans, Akehurst, & Mann, 2004).

Evidence has suggested that people engaged in cognitively complex tasks blink less (Bagely & Manelis, 1979), make more speech hesitations and speech errors, speak slower, pause more and wait longer before giving an answer (Goldman-Eisler, 1968). Cognitive complexity also leads to fewer hand and arm movements and to more gaze aversion (Ekman, 1997; Ekman & Friesen, 1972). This decrease in hand and arm movements occurs because cognitive demand results in a neglect of body language, reducing overall animation. For example, research examining truth tellers' and liars' brain activity showed that deception was related to increased activity in 'higher' areas of the brain (Spence et al., 2004), which, in turn, inhibits fidgety movements (Shallice & Burgess, 1994). Gaze aversion (usually to a motionless point) occurs because looking a conversation partner in the eye can be distracting (Doherty-Sneddon, Bruce, Bonner, Longbotham, & Doyle, 2002; Doherty-Sneddon & Phelps, 2005).

Cognitive load also affects speech. Increased cognitive load often leads to providing fewer details (Köhnken, 2004) and less plausible answers (Leal, Vrij, Warmelink, & Fisher, in press). It can also result in more contradictions and less overlap in answers both within

individuals (when different statements from one person are compared; Leins, Fisher, & Vrij, 2012) and between individuals (when
statements from different people are compared; Vrij et al., 2009).

Enhancing the Differences in Cognitive Load between Truth Tellers and Liars

Imposing Cognitive Load Imposing cognitive load refers to interventions
that investigators make that are aimed to make the interview setting
harder. Liars who require more cognitive resources than truth tellers
will have fewer cognitive resources left over. If cognitive demand is
further raised, which could be achieved by making additional requests,
liars may not be as good as truth tellers in coping with these additional
requests (Vrij, Granhag, Mann, & Leal, 2011; Vrij, Granhag, & Porter,
2010). One way to raise cognitive load is to ask interviewees during the
interview to carry out an additional task that is unrelated to giving
their story (e.g. press a button every 15 seconds). Carrying out two
tasks simultaneously (pressing a button and storytelling) is cognitively
more difficult than carrying out one task (i.e. just storytelling), because
in the former situation interviewees need to divide their attention
between the two tasks (Johnston, Greenberg, Fisher, & Martin, 1970;
Smith, 1969). This type of imposing cognitive load has not yet been
examined, but other ways to impose cognitive load have been tested,
including asking interviewees to recall a story in reverse order, asking
interviewees to maintain eye contact with the interviewer, introducing
a supportive interviewer and providing interviewees with an example
of a detailed answer.

Asking interviewees to tell their stories in reverse order is mentally
demanding, because (a) it opposes the natural forward-order coding
of sequentially occurring events (Gilbert & Fisher, 2006; Kahana,
1996) and (b) it disrupts the reconstructing of events from a schema
(Geiselman & Callot, 1990). In one experiment, half of the liars and
truth tellers were asked to recall their stories in reverse order, whereas
no instruction was given to the other half of participants (Vrij et al.,
2008). More cues to deceit emerged in this reverse-order condition (nine
cues, including fewer details, slower speech and more hesitations) than
in the control condition (one cue, a reduction in hand and finger movements). More importantly, observers who watched these videotaped
interviews could distinguish between truths and lies better in the
reverse-order condition than in the control condition. In the control condition, only 42% of the lies were correctly classified, well below the 54%
that is typically found in a lie detection experiment (Bond & DePaulo,
2006), suggesting that the lie detection task in this experiment was

particularly difficult. Yet, in the experimental condition, 60% of the lies were correctly classified, which is slightly more than typically found in lie detection research. The difference between the two deception conditions (18%) represents a medium effect size ($d = 0.40$).

The reverse-order technique is one of the components of the cognitive interview (Fisher & Geiselman, 1992). The cognitive interview is a sophisticated interview technique based on memory theory, social dynamics and communication. The cognitive interview results in truthful examinees providing a more detailed and more accurate recall of an experienced event (Fisher, 2010). Experimental deception studies in which the cognitive interview was compared with a 'standard' interview revealed that the cognitive interview resulted in more cues to deceit and facilitated lie detection (Colwell, Hiscock, & Memon, 2002; Hernandez-Fernaud & Alonso-Quecuty, 1997; Zimmerman, Veinott, Meissner, Fallon, & Mueller, 2010).

It has been noted that British police have generally not used the reverse-order instruction within the cognitive interview when interviewing cooperative witnesses (Kebbell, Milne, & Wagstaff, 1999). One reason for this reluctance is that asking to recall a story in reverse order is an unusual request and may therefore be perceived as odd. However, there are settings in which the reverse-order technique can be introduced in a natural way, for example, when interviewees describe travel routes. In Vrij, Leal, Mann, and Fisher (2012), participants (human intelligence personnel) carried out a mission and were asked to tell the truth about the route they took when interviewed by 'friendly' agents but to lie about the route they took when interviewed by 'hostile' agents. The participants were asked to describe these real and fabricated routes in chronological order ('Please describe in detail how you went from A to B?') and reverse order ('Visualize how you went from A to B; if I wanted to go from B to A using your route, how would I do that?'). Truths and lies were better distinguished (with computer software) in the reverse-order route transcriptions (87% accuracy) than in the chronological-order route descriptions (71% accuracy[1]). Importantly, when we asked about the technique in a post-mission questionnaire, none of the participants reported that they found the request to describe the route they took in reverse order odd, and many participants (48%) believed it to be an efficient way to detect deceit.

[1]Lie detection accuracy is typically obtained via one of two methods. First, observers watch videotapes or read transcripts and make veracity judgements. Second, truths and lies are classified via (often sophisticated) computer models. Computer-based accuracy rates are often higher than observer-based accuracy rates, as becomes evident in the quantitative analysis part of this chapter.

Another way to increase cognitive load is by instructing interviewees to maintain eye contact with the interviewer. This should increase cognitive load (Beattie, 1981). When people have to concentrate on telling their story, which is likely when they are asked to recall what has happened, they are inclined to look away from their conversation partner every now and then (typically to a motionless point), because maintaining eye contact with a conversation partner is distracting from the task at hand (Doherty-Sneddon et al., 2002; Doherty-Sneddon & Phelps, 2005; Glenberg, Schroeder, & Robertson, 1998). When interviewees are instructed to maintain eye contact continuously, their concentration on telling their stories is therefore likely to be compromised, and since lying is more mentally taxing than truth telling, this should impair the storytelling of liars more than of truth tellers. In an experiment, half of the liars and truth tellers were asked to maintain eye contact with the interviewer continuously throughout the interview, whereas no instruction was given to the other half of participants (Vrij, Mann, Leal, & Fisher, 2010). It was again found that more cues to deceit emerged in the eye contact condition (two cues, including fewer details) than in the control condition (no cue emerged) and that observers who watched these videotaped interviews could discriminate between truths and lies only in the eye contact condition.

An alternative method of imposing cognitive load on liars is to ensure that in a given interview setting, truth tellers will provide more information. Talkative truth tellers raise the standard for liars, who also need to become more talkative to match truth tellers. Liars may be reluctant to add more information out of fear that it will provide leads to investigators and, consequently, give their lies away. They may also find it too cognitively difficult to add as many details as truth tellers do. Alternatively, if liars do add a sufficient amount of detail, the additional information may be of lesser quality or may sound less plausible. We recently successfully tested two ways of increasing the amount of detail truth tellers generate: by introducing a second interviewer and by providing interviewees a model example. Regarding introducing a second interviewer, participants in an experiment told the truth or lied about their occupation. In the interview room, two interviewers were present, whereby the second interviewer remained silent throughout the interview but displayed different demeanours (Mann et al., 2013). In one condition, he was supportive throughout (e.g. nodding his head and smiling); in a second condition, he was neutral; and in a third condition, he was suspicious (e.g. frowning). Being supportive during an interview facilitates talking and encourages cooperative witnesses (e.g. truth tellers) to talk (Bull, 2010; Fisher, 2010; Memon, Meissner, & Fraser, 2010). Indeed, truth tellers provided the most detail in the supportive condition and only in that condition did they provide significantly more detail than liars (Mann et al., 2013).

In a modelling experiment, truth tellers had experienced an incident of theft, loss or damage in the recent past, whereas liars had not experienced anything but were asked to pretend they had. The interviewees were called about their 'insurance claim'. Half of the participants were asked before being interviewed about their alleged claim to listen to an audiotape in which someone gave a detailed account of an event unrelated to the participant's interview, a day at the motor racing (Leal et al., in press). Participants were informed that the purpose of the model audiotape was to give them an idea of what a detailed account actually entails. Interviewees have inadequate expectations about how much detail is expected from them (Fisher, 2010), and interviewees say less when they do not know the interviewer well (Fisher, 2010; Fisher, Milne, & Bull, 2011). Perhaps investigators can alter the participants' expectations about how much detail is required by providing them with a model answer. That is, if participants hear a model of a detailed answer, they are more likely to provide a more detailed answer themselves. Indeed, Leal et al. (in press) found that although truth tellers and liars did not differ from each other in the non-model condition, they did so in the model condition, whereby truth tellers gave more detailed answers that also sounded more plausible.

In sum, imposing cognitive load can be achieved in two different ways: first, by using interventions that increase the difficulty to recall information (e.g. reverse order and maintaining eye contact) and, second, by using interventions that make examinees more talkative. Both ways have shown to elicit cues to deceit and enhance lie detection.

Asking Unanticipated Questions

A consistent finding in deception literature is that liars prepare themselves for anticipated interviews. They do so by preparing possible answers to questions they feel they are likely to be asked (Granhag, Andersson, Strömwall, & Hartwig, 2004; Granhag, Strömwall, & Jonsson, 2003; Hartwig, Granhag, & Strömwall, 2007; Vrij et al., 2009). Planning makes lying easier, and planned lies typically contain fewer cues to deceit than spontaneous lies (DePaulo et al., 2003). The positive effects of planning will only emerge if liars correctly anticipate which questions will be asked. Investigators can exploit this limitation by asking questions that liars do not anticipate. Though liars can refuse to answer unanticipated questions, such as 'I don't know' or 'I can't remember', responses will create suspicion if the questions are about central (but unanticipated) aspects of the target event. A liar, therefore, has little option other than to fabricate a plausible answer on the spot, which is cognitively demanding. In other words, *expected* questions will *reduce* a liar's cognitive load and *unexpected* questions will *increase* a liar's cognitive load.

Questions can be unexpected in two different ways. First, the content of the question can be unexpected. For example, people do not expect spatial questions, temporal questions or questions about the planning phase of their activities. Neither do people expect 'devil's advocate' questions (requests to generate arguments that counteract their own opinion) or questions about their intentions. Second, the format in which the questions are asked can be unexpected. For example, people expect to give verbal responses in an interview, and the request to sketch a drawing often comes as a surprise.

Spatial Questions, Temporal Questions and Planning In an empirical test of the unanticipated question technique, liars and truth tellers were interviewed individually about having lunch together at a restaurant (Vrij et al., 2009). Although the pairs of truth tellers did not have lunch together, the liars were instructed to pretend that they had. All pairs were given the opportunity to prepare for the interview. The interviewer asked typical opening questions that the interviewees later said they had anticipated (e.g. 'What did you do in the restaurant?'), followed by questions about spatial details (e.g. 'In relation to the front door and where you sat, where were the closest diners?') and temporal details (e.g. 'Who finished their food first, you or your friend?') that the interviewees had not anticipated. Further, they were asked to draw the layout of the restaurant (unanticipated). On the basis of the overlap between individuals' responses to the anticipated opening questions, the liars and truth tellers could not be classified at a level above chance. However, on the basis of responses to the unanticipated questions, they could. A total of 72% could be classified on the basis of spatial questions (i.e. the answers were less alike for the pairs of liars than they were for the truth tellers). This demonstrates the potential of asking spatial questions for lie detection purposes, which was also noted by Soufan (2011), an experienced American FBI interrogator who has interrogated numerous al-Qaeda suspects. An even higher percentage of truth tellers and liars, 78%, could be correctly classified when assessing drawings (i.e. the drawings were less alike for the pairs of liars than they were for the truth tellers). In summary, asking unanticipated questions about central topics leads to identifiable betrayals among liars.

Comparing the answers to anticipated and unanticipated questions can also be used to detect deceit in individual liars, as recent experiments have demonstrated. The underlying rationale is that expected questions will decrease a liar's cognitive load, whereas unexpected questions will increase a liar's cognitive load. The difference liars experience in cognitive load while answering these two sets of questions may become visible. In contrast, truth tellers experience same levels of cognitive load while answering expected and unexpected questions.

Observers pay attention to detail, and the richer an account is perceived to be in detail, the more likely it is to be believed (Bell & Loftus, 1989). Liars are aware that interviewers pay attention to detail when making veracity judgements and are therefore keen to provide details in order to make an honest impression (Nahari, Vrij, & Fisher, 2012). As a result, liars may prepare a detailed alibi and report it as soon as the opportunity arises. This opportunity does arise when an expected question is asked. In contrast, liars will not have prepared answers for unexpected questions and may therefore struggle to generate detailed answers to them. As a result, liars will be more detailed when answering the expected questions than the unexpected questions. For truth tellers, the difference in detail between expected and unexpected questions should be less pronounced. When asked about an event they have experienced, truth tellers will search their memory for details about that event and there is no reason why those details are less accessible for unexpected than for expected questions, as long as the expected and unexpected questions are both about core aspects of the event. If liars' and truth tellers' answers to expected and unexpected questions are compared separately, the following pattern may emerge. Liars' prepared answers to expected questions may be *more* detailed than the answers truth tellers typically generate when searching their memory. In contrast, liars' answers to unexpected questions may be *less* detailed than the answers truth tellers typically generate when searching their memory. This hypothesis was experimentally tested and supported in three experiments.

In the first experiment, truth tellers and liars were interviewed about their alleged activities in a room (Lancaster, Vrij, Hope, & Waller, 2013). Expected questions (e.g. 'Tell me in as much detail as you can what you did in the room') were followed by unexpected spatial and temporal questions (e.g. 'Please describe exactly how you arranged the four objects you placed on the table at the centre of the room'). In a second experiment (Shaw, Vrij, Leal, & Mann, 2013), truth tellers and liars were interviewed about their alleged activities in a room, but this time they were interviewed by two interviewers (one speaking and one silent interviewer) of whom the silent interviewer displayed either a supportive or neutral demeanour. The aforementioned pattern of findings – that liars are more detailed than truth tellers when answering expected questions but less detailed when answering unexpected questions – emerged once again, particularly when the second interviewer was supportive. In that condition, the liars were particularly detailed when answering the expected question. Liars had in all likelihood prepared an answer for that question, and a supportive second interviewer may have encouraged them to provide more detail when answering this expected question.

In a third experiment, truth tellers and liars were interviewed about their alleged forthcoming trip (Warmelink, Vrij, Mann, Jundi, & Granhag, 2012). Expected questions about the purpose of the trip (e.g. 'What is the main purpose of your trip?') were followed by unexpected questions about transport (e.g. 'How are you going to travel to your destination?'), planning ('What part of the trip was easiest to plan?') and the core event ('Keep in mind an image of the most important thing you are going to do on this trip. Please describe this mental image in detail'.). In both experiments, compared to truth tellers, liars gave significantly more detail to the expected questions and significantly less detail to the unexpected questions. This indeed suggests that the expected question encouraged liars to recall their prepared stories, whereas liars subsequently struggled with answering the unexpected questions. Warmelink et al.'s (2012) experiment has real-life implications. Throughout the world, immigration officers mainly ask purpose questions when quizzing passengers at airport border controls. We can assume that they pay attention to the amount of detail the passengers give, with detailed answers being treated as honest answers. However, those questions are expected by potential wrongdoers. For example, they appear in the al-Qaeda 'Manchester Manual', a manual with guidelines for potential terrorists on how to avoid detection. Because they are expected, potential wrongdoers are able to answer such questions in detail and subsequently make an honest impression when doing so.

Drawings In other studies, the unexpected question approach has been used in a different way when assessing the veracity of individual interviewees. This time, rather than asking a mixture of expected and unexpected questions, the same unexpected question was asked twice albeit in different formats (a request to verbally recall an event vs. a request to sketch the event). When liars have not anticipated the question, they have to fabricate an answer on the spot. A liar's memory of this fabricated answer may be more unstable than a truth teller's actual memory of the event. Therefore, liars may contradict themselves more than truth tellers (Fisher, Vrij, & Leins, 2013). An experiment supported this hypothesis (Leins, Fisher, Vrij, Leal, & Mann, 2011). Truth tellers went to a restaurant for lunch. Liars did not but were asked to pretend they had. In the interview, they were asked to both verbally describe and sketch the layout of the restaurant. Truth tellers' verbal answers and drawings showed more overlap than did those of liars. There is evidence to suggest that the approach of asking the same question twice works best if different formats (e.g. verbal recall vs. sketching) are used. Truth tellers will have encoded the topic of investigation along more dimensions than will liars. As a result, compared with liars, truth tellers should be able to recall the event more flexibly (along more dimensions). In Leins et al.'s (2012) experiment, truthful participants had visited a room, whereas deceptive participants had not. In the interview however, all participants claimed to have visited the room. Participants were asked to verbally recall the layout of the room twice, to sketch it twice or to verbally recall it once and to sketch it once. Liars contradicted themselves more than truth tellers but only in the verbal recall – drawing condition. Truth tellers have encoded the topic of investigation along more dimensions than liars. They therefore find it easier than liars to recall the event more flexibly (along more dimensions).

Vrij et al. (2009) were the first researchers to use drawings as a lie detection tool. Their experiment, in which pairs of truth tellers and pairs of liars discussed visiting a restaurant to have lunch, has already been discussed previously. Three further experiments have demonstrated that drawings have potential as a lie detection tool. More than a verbal request, the request to sketch forces the interviewee to convey spatial information. That is, including an object within a drawing requires that object to be spatially located. By comparison, verbally describing an object in a room means that disclosing its spatial location can be avoided. If a liar has not experienced an item in a particular location, she/he may still verbally describe the object but may do so without referring to its location to avoid the risk of misplacing it. Such a 'masking strategy' is not possible when asked to sketch. As a result, a liar may instead decide that it is safest to avoid sketching the object. In a first experiment, truth tellers discussed their real occupation, whereas liars discussed an occupation they pretended to have. When asked to *verbally describe* the layout of their office, truth tellers' and liars' answers were equally detailed; however, when asked to *sketch* the layout of their office, liars' drawings were less detailed than truth tellers' drawings (Vrij, Mann, Leal, & Fisher, 2012).

In a second drawing experiment, 31 'agents' were sent on a mission during which they had to collect a decoder from another agent (Vrij, Leal et al., 2010). After delivering the decoder, they were asked to (i) *verbally describe* and later to (ii) *sketch* what they could see at the location where they had received the decoder. Half of the agents were requested to lie and half to tell the truth. The liars were asked to pretend to have been on a different mission and to pretend to have received the decoder at a different location. In other words, they had to pretend to have received the decoder at a location where the other agent was not present. Only 2 out of 16 (12.5%) liars included the alleged agent from whom they had allegedly received the decoder in their drawing, whereas 12 out of 15 truth tellers (80%) did sketch the agent from whom they had received the decoder. In their verbal descriptions, again 2 out of 16 (12.5%) liars mentioned the other alleged agent, whereas 8 out of 15 (53%) truth tellers mentioned the real agent. In other words, like the occupations experiment, truth tellers' and liars' drawings differed more from each other than did their verbal recalls. Liars may have been inclined to omit the alleged agent from the sketch and verbal description for at least two possible reasons: First, the alleged agent had not been present at the location they sketched/described, and so they forgot to include him/her. Second, liars may be reluctant to include people in their drawings/descriptions in case they trigger further questions (about clothing, appearance, etc.). Why did more truth tellers sketch the real agent (80%) than verbally describe the real agent (53%)? Perhaps after sketching the stable elements, the truth tellers may have noticed that the real agent was missing from the drawing. After narrating the stable elements of the location, however, truth tellers will have been less aware of this omission because of difficulties in building a mental picture of a location on the basis of narratives.

In a third drawing experiment, Roos af Hjelmsäter, Öhman, Granhag, and Vrij (2014) argued that for drawings to elicit diagnostic cues to deceit, the focus should be on salient aspects, as these are the aspects truth tellers are most likely to remember. In groups of three, adolescents (13–14 years old) experienced an encounter with a man near a statue (truth tellers) or imagined this event (liars). In the subsequent interview, in which the adolescents were interviewed individually, they were asked to give a general verbal description of the event (anticipated task) or to produce spatial information by marking on a sketch the position of fellow adolescents when they encountered the man and from which direction he had come (unanticipated task). Since the man was the focus of the event, the direction from which the man came could be considered as the salient aspect of the event, whereas the exact position of the fellow adolescents could be considered non-salient. The liars' and truth tellers' verbal responses showed similar overlap. In contrast, the liars' sketches showed less overlap than the truth tellers' sketches but only regarding the salient aspects of the event.

Odd Questions Liu et al. (2010) operationalized an unexpected question in yet another way. They examined the effect of asking 'odd' (e.g. impossible to answer) questions on the ability to detect deceit. In their experiment, they asked half of a group of children (10–12 years of age) to tell the truth about a self-experienced event and the other half to lie about such an event. The researchers found that lying children were more willing to answer odd questions (e.g. 'Can you remember what you had in your left pocket when being stung by the bee?') than were truth-telling children, whereas no difference was found in the willingness to answer standard questions. Hence, asking unanticipated questions elicited a cue to deception (e.g. increased willingness to answer the impossible questions). In this experiment, lying children had to *act* to appear honest, whereas truth-telling children did not have to do this. Liu et al. speculated that liars were afraid that an 'I don't know' answer would sound suspicious. Hence, attempting to act in an honest manner requires metacognitive knowledge about how truth tellers actually act. Obtaining metacognitive knowledge requires considerable cognitive skill (Flavell, 1979, 1987), and such knowledge is probably lacking in many liars. It may result in responses that are more rarely seen among truth tellers.

Devil's Advocate The devil's advocate lie detection tool was developed to detect truths and lies in expressing opinions (Leal, Vrij, Mann, & Fisher, 2010). Verbal lie detection often focuses on the ability to distinguish between truths and lies when people describe events that they claim to have experienced. In such instances, questions that appear to discriminate between truth tellers and liars, such as spatial questions, can be asked. However, people lie not only about their experiences but also about their opinions (e.g. 'What is your view about the war in Afghanistan?'). In such instances, spatial questions are inappropriate to ask. Determining the veracity of such conceptual representations may not be important in typical police suspect interviews because they are mainly concerned with detecting lies about transgressions. However, it can be important in many security settings, for example, when deciding whether an informant is (a) indeed as much anti-Taliban or against Muslim fundamentalism as he or she claims or (b) truly entering the United Kingdom or the United States solely for the purpose of university study. Incorrect veracity judgements can do irreparable harm in such situations, as was demonstrated by the loss of seven CIA agents in Afghanistan on 30 December 2009. The CIA agents were killed in a suicide attack by a man they thought was going to give them information about Taliban and al-Qaeda targets in Pakistan's tribal areas. The CIA agents had used polygraph tests to check the man's sincerity and were aware that he had posted extreme anti-American views on the Internet. However, it was decided that the views he had expressed were part of a good cover, and the possibility that they represented his real views had been discounted (Leal et al., 2010).

In the devil's advocate technique, interviewees are first asked an opinion-eliciting question that induces them to argue in favour of their personal view on a topic ('What are your reasons for supporting the Americans in the war in Afghanistan?'). This is followed by a question that asks participants to argue against their personal view ('Playing devil's advocate, is there anything you can say against the involvement of the Americans in Afghanistan?'). People normally think more deeply about, and hence are likely to be more able to generate, reasons that support rather than oppose their beliefs and opinions (Ajzen, 2001; Darley & Gross, 1983; Waenke & Bless, 2000). Therefore, truth tellers will be able to generate more information when thinking about the opinion-eliciting question than the devil's advocate question and are likely to provide more information in answer to the opinion-eliciting question than the devil's advocate question. Since they express their real attitude in answer to the opinion-eliciting question, they are probably also emotionally involved when answering that answer. For liars to sound like truth tellers in a devil's advocate questioning, interviewing requires considerable cognitive skill. They need to possess the metacognitive knowledge on how truth tellers will respond. They then should produce such responses, which is difficult because for them the devil's advocate question is more compatible with their beliefs than is the opinion-eliciting question. They will therefore have most information available when thinking about the devil's advocate question, and for them to succeed in a devil's advocate interview could involve fabricating some plausible reasons in answer to the opinion-eliciting question and suppressing some reasons readily available to them in answer to the devil's advocate question. And they also should show most emotional involvement when providing the reasons they do not believe in.

An experiment testing the devil's advocate approach showed that liars failed to respond like truth tellers. For truth tellers, their opinion-eliciting answers were longer than their devil's advocate answers, whereas liars' opinion-eliciting answers were shorter than their devil's advocate answers (Leal et al., 2010). Also, observers judged that the truth tellers' opinion-eliciting answers sounded more immediate and plausible and revealed more emotional involvement than did their devil's advocate answers. In contrast, no differences emerged in liars' answers to the two types of question. On the basis of these differences in speech content, 86% of truth tellers and 79% of liars were correctly classified.

CONCLUSIONS AND FINAL THOUGHTS

This chapter introduced the empirical findings to date about a new cognitive approach to non-verbal and verbal lie detection. Key of the approach is that investigators can use specific interventions that are particularly demanding for liars and therefore enhance the differences in cognitive load than liars and truth tellers experience. The findings in this chapter revealed that the cognitive load perspective results in more cues to deceit than standard conditions and in a more accurate classification of both truths and lies.

We finish this chapter with some final thoughts. First, we have demonstrated that a cognitive lie detection approach reveals more cues to deceit but have not mentioned what these cues actually are. Cues that have been associated with deception on more than one occasion are '(lack of) overlap in answers', 'difference in detail between expected and unexpected questions', 'lack of plausibility' and 'lack of detail'. All of these are cues of cognitive load. We do not rule out that cognitive load lie detection techniques also result in increased anxiety. Therefore, cues to anxiety may also emerge. In fact, they did emerge in one of the reverse-order experiments (Vrij et al., 2008). However, anxiety cues are a side effect, and when they arise, they are considered to be irrelevant and not to be relied upon. They are therefore ignored (Vrij & Granhag, 2012).

The cognitive lie detection technique not only elicits cues to deceit, but it also improves truth and lie detection accuracy. It is important to note that in none of the cognitive lie detection studies to date where observers made veracity judgements were the observers coached in which cues to pay attention to. In other words, it appears that observers pick up these cues naturally and a training programme in which cues to pay attention to does not seem to be required.

Some of the imposing cognitive load interventions such as asking interviewees to recall a story in reverse order or asking them to maintain eye contact may appear odd and therefore difficult to implement in real life. However, other imposing cognitive load methods, such as using a supportive second interviewer, can be implemented more easily. Research, and perhaps creativity among investigators, is needed to develop other imposing cognitive load techniques that are suited for use in real life. As mentioned previously, introducing a secondary task may be a fruitful way forwards.

Regarding the unanticipated question approach, the question arises of how to define an 'unanticipated question'. As discussed previously, it is possible to distinguish between two types of unanticipated questions. First, the content of the question can be unexpected. The experiments to date have shown that spatial questions are unexpected and so are temporal questions and questions about planning. No doubt, many more types of unexpected questions will emerge in future research. Second, the format of the question can be unexpected. A request to sketch a layout of a room is unexpected, whereas a question to verbally recall it is not. The difference between truth tellers and liars is not how unexpected the questions are. In fact, unexpected questions are unexpected for both truth tellers and liars. The difference emerges in how difficult they are for truth tellers and liars to answer. Truth tellers can rely on their memory when answering these questions and therefore will not find the questions too difficult to answer. In contrast, liars will not have ready-made answers prepared for these unanticipated questions and will therefore find them much more difficult to answer. The key for this technique to work is that truth tellers will know the answer to the expected and unexpected questions. It means that all questions should be about central rather than peripheral parts of the event. In that respect is the unanticipated question approach different from the 'strategic questioning' approach Levine and colleagues refer to (Levine, Shaw, & Shulman, 2010). In their experiment, some participants cheated on a test and had to deny this in a subsequent interview (liars), whereas other participants did not cheat. 'Strategic' questions about the cheating ('Did any cheating occur?') were compared with 'non-strategic' questions that were unrelated to cheating ('How much experience have you had with doing teamwork activities?'). Observers were better able to detect deceit in the strategic questioning condition. This is probably unsurprising as the non-strategic questions had nothing to do with cheating and were not about the core elements of the event. Please note that the question asked in the strategic questioning condition 'Did cheating occur?' is most likely anticipated by the interviewees and therefore perhaps not the best question to ask to distinguish between truth tellers and liars.

The lie detection techniques that we have discussed can be employed in various settings. The devil's advocate technique can be employed when examining the veracity of opinions. The other techniques can be employed to determine the veracity of statements about past activities and future activities (intentions). It has been shown that the unanticipated question technique can be employed to identify deceit in both individuals and groups of liars. Future research should examine whether the techniques are sensitive to countermeasures, that is, liars' attempts to fool investigators. The unanticipated question technique should be immune to this, as its method is to ask questions that a liar has not anticipated and therefore not prepared answers for. The number of unexpected questions that can be asked about core elements of the event is vast, which reduces the risk that the unexpected questions become expected after some time. Due to individual differences in people's responses, within-subject lie detection techniques are preferable because they control for such individual differences. The unanticipated question and devil's advocate techniques are within-subject techniques.

REFERENCES

Ajzen, I. (2001). Nature and operation of attitudes. *Annual Review of Psychology, 52*, 27–58.

Bageley, J., & Manelis, L. (1979). Effect of awareness on an indicator of cognitive load. *Perceptual and Motor Skills*, 49, 591–594.

Baumeister, R. F. (1998). The self. In D. T. Gilbert, S. T. Fiske, & G. Lindzey (Eds.), *Handbook of social psychology* (4th ed. pp. 680–740). Boston, MA: McGraw-Hill.

Beattie, G. W. (1981). A further investigation of the cognitive interference hypothesis of gaze patterns during conversation. *British Journal of Social Psychology, 20*, 243–248.

Bell, B. E., & Loftus, E. F. (1989). Trivial persuasion in the courtroom: The power of (a few) minor details. *Journal of Personality and Social Psychology, 56*, 669–679.

Bond, C. F., & DePaulo, B. M. (2006). Accuracy of deception judgements. *Personality and Social Psychology Review, 10*, 214–234.

Bull, R. (2010). The investigative interviewing of children and other vulnerable witnesses: Psychological research and working/professional practice. *Legal and Criminological Psychology, 15*, 5–24.

Buller, D. B., & Burgoon, J. K. (1996). Interpersonal deception theory. *Communication Theory, 6*, 203–242.

Caso, L., Gnisci, A., Vrij, A., & Mann, S. (2005). Processes underlying deception: An empirical analysis of truths and lies when manipulating the stakes. *Journal of Interviewing and Offender Profiling, 2*, 195–202.

Christ, S. E., Van Essen, D. C. Watson, J. M., Brubaker, L. E., & McDermott, K. B. (2009). The contributions of prefrontal cortex and executive control to deception: Evidence from activation likelihood estimate meta-analyses. *Cerebral Cortex, 19*, 1557–1566.

Colwell, K., Hiscock, C. K., & Memon, A. (2002). Interview techniques and the assessment of statement credibility. *Applied Cognitive Psychology, 16*, 287–300.

Darley, J. M., & Gross, P. H. (1983). A hypothesis-confirming bias in labelling effects. *Journal of Personality and Social Psychology, 44*, 20–33.

DePaulo, B. M., Kashy, D. A., Kirkendol, S. E., Wyer, M. M., & Epstein, J. A. (1996). Lying in everyday life. *Journal of Personality and Social Psychology, 70*, 979–995.

DePaulo, B. M., & Kirkendol, S. E. (1989). The motivational impairment effect in the communication of deception. In J. C. Yuille (Ed.), *Credibility assessment* (pp. 51–70). Dordrecht, the Netherlands: Kluwer.

DePaulo, B. M., Lindsay, J. L., Malone, B. E., Muhlenbruck, L., Charlton, K., & Cooper, H. (2003). Cues to deception. *Psychological Bulletin, 129,* 74–118.

Doherty-Sneddon, G., Bruce, V., Bonner, L., Longbotham, S., & Doyle, C. (2002). Development of gaze aversion as disengagement of visual information. *Developmental Psychology, 38,* 438–445.

Doherty-Sneddon, G., & Phelps, F. G. (2005). Gaze aversion: A response to cognitive or social difficulty? *Memory and Cognition, 33,* 727–733.

Ekman, P. (1997). Deception, lying, and demeanor. In D. F. Halpern & A. E. Voiskounsky (Eds.), *States of mind: American and post-Soviet perspectives on contemporary issues in psychology* (pp. 93–105). New York, NY: Oxford University Press.

Ekman, P., & Friesen, W. V. (1972). Hand movements. *Journal of Communication, 22,* 353–374.

Fisher, R. P. (2010). Interviewing cooperative witnesses. *Legal and Criminological Psychology, 15,* 25–38.

Fisher, R. P., & Geiselman, R. E. (1992). *Memory-enhancing techniques in investigative interviewing: The cognitive interview.* Springfield, IL: C.C. Thomas.

Fisher, R., Milne, R., & Bull, R. (2011). Interviewing cooperative witnesses. *Current Directions in Psychological Science, 20,* 16–19.

Fisher, R. P., Vrij, A., & Leins, D. A. (2013). Inconsistency as a predictor of memory inaccuracy and lying. In B. S. Cooper, D. Griesel, & M. Ternes (Eds.) *Applied issues in investigative interviewing, eyewitness memory, and credibility assessment.* New York, NY: Springer.

Flavell, J. H. (1979). Metacognition and cognitive monitoring: A new area of cognitive-developmental inquiry. *American Psychologist, 34,* 906–911.

Flavell, J. H. (1987). Speculations about the nature and development of metacognition. In F. E. Weinert & R. H. Kluwe (Eds.), *Metacognition, motivation and understanding* (pp. 21–29). Hillside, NJ: Lawrence Erlbaum.

Gambos, V. A. (2006). The cognition of deception: The role of executive processes in producing lies. *Genetic, Social, and General Psychology Monographs, 132,* 197–214.

Geiselman, R. E., & Callot, R. (1990). Reverse and forward order recall of script based text. *Applied Cognitive Psychology, 4,* 141–144.

Gilbert, D. T. (1991). How mental systems believe. *American Psychologist, 46,* 107–119.

Gilbert, J. A. E., & Fisher, R. P. (2006). The effects of varied retrieval cues on reminiscence in eyewitness memory. *Applied Cognitive Psychology, 20,* 723–739.

Gilovich, T., Savitsky, K., & Medvec, V. H. (1998). The illusion of transparency: Biased assessments of others' ability to read one's emotional states. *Journal of Personality and Social Psychology, 75,* 332–346.

Glenberg, A. M., Schroeder, J. L., & Robertson, D. A. (1998). Averting the gaze disengages the environment and facilitates remembering. *Memory & Cognition, 26,* 651–658.

Goldman-Eisler, F. (1968). *Psycholinguistics: Experiments in spontaneous speech.* New York, NY: Doubleday.

Granhag, P. A., Andersson, L. O., Strömwall, L. A., & Hartwig, M. (2004). Imprisoned knowledge: Criminals' beliefs about deception. *Legal and Criminological Psychology, 9,* 103–119.

Granhag, P. A., & Strömwall, L. A. (2002). Repeated interrogations: Verbal and nonverbal cues to deception. *Applied Cognitive Psychology, 16,* 243–257.

Granhag, P. A., Strömwall, L. A. & Hartwig, M. (2007, January). The SUE technique: The way to interview to detect deception. *Forensic Update, 88*, 25–29.

Granhag, P. A., Strömwall, L. A., & Jonsson, A. C. (2003). Partners in crime: How liars in collusion betray themselves. *Journal of Applied Social Psychology, 33*, 848–868.

Hartwig, M., Granhag, P. A., & Strömwall, L. (2007). Guilty and innocent suspects' strategies during interrogations. *Psychology, Crime, & Law, 13*, 213–227.

Hartwig, M., Granhag, P. A., Strömwall, L., & Kronkvist, O. (2006). Strategic use of evidence during police interrogations: When training to detect deception works. *Law and Human Behavior, 30*, 603–619.

Hernandez-Fernaud, E., & Alonso-Quecuty, M. (1997). The cognitive interview and lie detection: A new magnifying glass for Sherlock Holmes? *Applied Cognitive Psychology, 11*, 55–68.

Johnston, W. A., Greenberg, S. N., Fisher, R. P., & Martin, D. W. (1970). Divided attention: A vehicle for monitoring memory processes. *Journal of Experimental Psychology, 83*, 164–171.

Kahana, M. J. (1996). Associate retrieval processes in free recall. *Memory & Cognition, 24*, 103–109.

Kassin, S. M. (2005). On the psychology of confessions: Does innocence put innocents at risk? *American Psychologist, 60*, 215–228.

Kassin, S. M., Appleby, S. C., & Torkildson-Perillo, J. (2010). Interviewing suspects: Practice, science, and future directions. *Legal and Criminological Psychology* (Special issue 'What works in investigative psychology'), *15*, 39–56.

Kassin, S. M., & Gudjonsson, G. H. (2004). The psychology of confessions: A review of the literature and issues. *Psychological Science in the Public Interest, 5*, 33–67.

Kassin, S. M., & Norwick, R. J. (2004). Why people waive their Miranda rights: The power of innocence. *Law and Human Behavior, 28*, 211–221.

Kebbell, M. R., Milne, R., & Wagstaff, G. F. (1999). The cognitive interview: A survey of its forensic effectiveness. *Psychology, Crime, & Law, 5*, 101–115.

Köhnken, G. (2004). Statement validity analysis and the 'detection of the truth'. In P. A. Granhag & L. A. Strömwall (Eds.), *Deception detection in forensic contexts* (pp. 41–63). Cambridge, UK: Cambridge University Press.

Lancaster, G. L. J., Vrij, A., Hope, L., & Waller, B. (2013). Sorting the liars from the truth tellers: The benefits or asking unanticipated questions on lie detection. *Applied Cognitive Psychology, 27*(1), 107–114.

Langleben, D. D. (2008). Detection of deception with fMRI: Are we there yet? *Legal and Criminological Psychology, 13*, 1–10.

Leal, S., Vrij, A., Mann, S., & Fisher, R. (2010). Detecting true and false opinions: The Devil's Advocate approach as a lie detection aid. *Acta Psychologica, 134*, 323–329.

Leal, S., Vrij, A., Warmelink, L., Vernham, Z., & Fisher, R. (in press). You can't hide your telephone lies: Providing a model statement as an aid to detect deception in insurance telephone calls. *Legal and Criminological Psychology*.

Leins, D., Fisher, R., & Vrij, A. (2012). Drawing on liars' lack of cognitive flexibility: Detecting deception through varying report modes. *Applied Cognitive Psychology, 26*, 601–607.

Leins, D., Fisher, R. P., Vrij, A., Leal, S., & Mann, S. (2011). Using sketch-drawing to induce inconsistency in liars. *Legal and Criminological Psychology, 16*, 253–265.

Lerner, M. J. (1980). *The belief in a just world*. New York, NY: Plenum.

Levine, T. R., Kim, R. K., & Hamel, L. M. (2010a). People lie for a reason: Three experiments documenting the principle of veracity. *Communication Research Reports, 27*, 271–285.

Levine, T. R., Shaw, A., & Shulman, H. C. (2010b). Increasing deception detection accuracy with strategic questioning. *Human Communication Research, 36*, 216–231.

Liu, M., Granhag, P. A., Landström, S., Roos af Hjelmsäter, E., Strömwall, L. A., & Vrij, A. (2010). 'Can you remember what was in your pocket when you were stung by a bee?' – Eliciting cues to deception by asking the unanticipated. *Open Criminology Journal, 3*, 31–36.

Mann, S., & Vrij, A. (2006). Police officers' judgements of veracity, tenseness, cognitive load and attempted behavioural control in real life police interviews. *Psychology, Crime, & Law, 12*, 307–319.

Mann, S., Vrij, A., & Bull, R. (2002). Suspects, lies and videotape: An analysis of authentic high-stakes liars. *Law and Human Behavior, 26*, 365–376.

Mann, S., Vrij, A., Shaw, D., Leal, S., Ewens, S., Hillman, J., … Fisher, R. P. (2013). Two heads are better than one? How to effectively use two interviewers to elicit cues to deception. *Legal and Criminological Psychology, 18*, 324–340.

McCornack, S. A. (1997). The generation of deceptive messages: Laying the groundwork for a viable theory of interpersonal deception. In J. O. Greene (Ed.), *Message production: Advances in communication theory* (pp. 91–126). Mahwah, NJ: Lawrence Erlbaum.

Memon, A., Meissner, C. A., & Fraser, J. (2010). The cognitive interview: A meta-analytic review and study space analysis of the past 25 years. *Psychology, Public Policy, & Law, 16*, 340–372.

Mohamed, F. B., Faro, S. H., Gordon, N. J., Platek, S. M., Ahmad, H., & Williams, J. M. (2006). Brain mapping of deception and truth telling about an ecologically valid situation: Functional MR imaging and polygraph investigation – Initial experience. *Radiology, 238*, 679–688.

Nahari, G., Vrij, A., & Fisher, R. P. (2012). Does the truth come out in the writing? SCAN as a lie detection tool. *Law & Human Behavior, 36*, 68–76.

Paas, F., & van Merriënboer, J. J. G. (1994). Instructional control of cognitive load in the training of complex cognitive tasks. *Educational Psychology Review, 6*, 51–71.

Paas, F., Renkl, A., & Sweller, J. (2003a). Cognitive load theory and instructional design: Recent developments. *Educational Psychologist, 38*, 1–4.

Paas, F., Tuovinen, Tabbers, & van Gerven, P. W. M. (2003b). Cognitive load measurement as a means to advance cognitive load theory. *Educational Psychologist, 38*, 63–71.

Porter, S., & Ten Brinke, L. (2010). Truth about lies: What works in detecting high-stakes deception? *Legal and Criminological Psychology, 15*, 57–76.

Richards, J. M. (2010). The cognitive consequences of concealing feelings. *Current Directions in Cognitive Sciences, 13*, 131–134.

Roos af Hjelmsäter, E., Öhman, L., Granhag, P. A., & Vrij, A. (2014). Mapping' deception in adolescents: Eliciting cues to deceit through an unanticipated spatial drawing task. *Legal and Criminological Psychology, 19*, 179–188.

Schweitzer, M. E., Brodt, S. E., & Croson, R. T. A. (2002). Seeing and believing: Visual access and the strategic use of deception. *The International Journal of Conflict Management, 13*, 258–275.

Shallice, T., & Burgess, P. (1994). Supervisory control of action and thought selection. In L. Weiskrantz, A. Baddeley, & D. Alan (Eds.), *Attention: Selection, awareness and control: A tribute to Donald Broadbent* (pp. 171–187). New York, NY: Clarendon Press.

Shaw, D., Vrij, A., Leal, S., & Mann, S. (2013). Expect the unexpected? Variations in question type elicit cues to deception in joint interviewer contexts. *Applied Cognitive Psychology, 27*, 336–343.

Smith, M. C. (1969). Effect of varying channel capacity on stimulus detection and discrimination. *Journal of Experimental Psychology, 82*, 520–526.

Soufan, A. H. (2011). *The black banners: The inside story of 9/11 and the war against al-Qaeda*. New York, NY: W. W. Norton & Company.

Spence, S. (2008). Playing devil's advocate: The case against fMRI lie detection. *Legal and Criminological Psychology, 13*, 11–26.

Spence, S. A., Farrow, T. F. D., Herford, A. E., Wilkinson, I. D., Zheng, Y., & Woodruff, P. W. R. (2001). Behavioural and functional anatomical correlates of deception in humans. *Neuroreport: For Rapid Communication of Neuroscience Research, 12*, 2849–2853.

Spence, S. A., Hunter, M. D., Farrow, T. F. D., Green, R. D., Leung, D. H., & Hughes, C. J. (2004). A cognitive neurobiological account of deception: Evidence from functional neuroimaging. *Philosophical Transactions of the Royal Society of London, 359*, 1755–1762.

Spence, S. A., & Kaylor-Hughes, C. J. (2008). Looking for truths and finding lies: The prospects for a nascent neuroimaging of deception. *Neurocase, 14*, 68–81.

Strömwall, L. A., Hartwig, M., & Granhag, P. A. (2006). To act truthfully: Nonverbal behaviour and strategies during a police interrogation. *Psychology, Crime, & Law, 12*, 207–219.

Verschuere, B., Spruyt, A., Meijer, E. H., & Otgaar, H. (2011). The ease of lying. *Consciousness and Cognition, 20*, 908–911.

Vrij, A. (2008). *Detecting lies and deceit: Pitfalls and opportunities* (2nd ed.). Chichester, UK: John Wiley & Sons.

Vrij, A., Edward, K., & Bull, R. (2001a). Police officers' ability to detect deceit: The benefit of indirect deception detection measures. *Legal and Criminological Psychology, 6*, 2, 185–197.

Vrij, A., Edward, K., & Bull, R. (2001b). Stereotypical verbal and nonverbal responses while deceiving others. *Personality and Social Psychology Bulletin, 27*, 899–909.

Vrij, A., Evans, H., Akehurst, L., & Mann, S. (2004). Rapid judgements in assessing verbal and nonverbal cues: Their potential for deception researchers and lie detection. *Applied Cognitive Psychology, 18*, 283–296.

Vrij, A., & Granhag, P. A. (2012). Eliciting cues to deception and truth: What matters are the questions asked. *Journal of Applied Research in Memory and Cognition, 1*, 110–117.

Vrij, A., Granhag, P. A., Mann, S., & Leal, S. (2011a). Outsmarting the liars: Towards a cognitive lie detection approach. *Current Directions in Psychological Science, 20*, 28–32.

Vrij, A., Granhag, P. A., & Porter, S. B. (2010a). Pitfalls and opportunities in nonverbal and verbal lie detection. *Psychological Science in the Public Interest, 11*, 89–121.

Vrij, A., Leal, S., Granhag, P. A., Mann, S., Fisher, R. P., Hillman, J., & Sperry, K. (2009). Outsmarting the liars: The benefit of asking unanticipated questions. *Law and Human Behavior, 33*, 159–166.

Vrij, A., Leal, S., Mann, S., & Granhag, P. A. (2011b). A comparison between lying about intentions and past activities: Verbal cues and detection accuracy. *Applied Cognitive Psychology, 25*, 212–218.

Vrij, A., Leal, S., Mann, S., & Fisher, R. (2012a). Imposing cognitive load to elicit cues to deceit: Inducing the reverse order technique naturally. *Psychology, Crime, & Law, 18*, 579–594.

Vrij, A., Leal, S., Mann, S., Warmelink, L., Granhag, P. A., & Fisher, R. P. (2010b). Drawings as an innovative and successful lie detection tool. *Applied Cognitive Psychology, 4*, 587–594.

Vrij, A., & Mann, S. (2001). Who killed my relative? Police officers' ability to detect real-life high-stake lies. *Psychology, Crime, & Law, 7*, 119–132.

Vrij, A., & Mann, S. (2003). Deceptive responses and detecting deceit. In P. W. Halligan, C. Bass, & D. Oakley (Eds.), *Malingering and illness deception: Clinical and theoretical perspectives* (pp. 348–362). Oxford, UK: University Press.

Vrij, A., & Mann, S. (2006). Criteria-based content analysis: An empirical test of its underlying processes. *Psychology, Crime, & Law, 12*, 337–349.

Vrij, A., Mann, S., & Fisher, R. (2006a). An empirical test of the behaviour analysis interview. *Law and Human Behavior, 30*, 329–345.

Vrij, A., Mann, S., & Fisher, R. (2006b). Information-gathering vs accusatory interview style: Individual differences in respondents' experiences. *Personality and Individual Differences, 41*, 589–599.

Vrij, A., Mann, S., Fisher, R., Leal, S., Milne, B., & Bull, R. (2008). Increasing cognitive load to facilitate lie detection: The benefit of recalling an event in reverse order. *Law and Human Behavior, 32*, 253–265.

Vrij, A., Mann, S., Leal, S., & Fisher, R. (2010c). 'Look into my eyes': Can an instruction to maintain eye contact facilitate lie detection? *Psychology, Crime, & Law, 16*, 327–348.

Vrij, A., Mann, S., Leal, S., & Fisher, R. (2012b). Is anyone out there? Drawings as a tool to detect deception in occupations interviews. *Psychology, Crime, & Law, 18*, 377–388.

Vrij, A., Semin, G. R., & Bull, R. (1996). Insight in behavior displayed during deception. *Human Communication Research, 22*, 544–562.

Waenke, M., & Bless, H. (2000). The effects of subjective ease of retrieval on attitudinal judgements: The moderating role of processing motivation. In H. Bless & J. P. Forgas (Eds.), *The message within: The role of subjective experience in social cognition and behaviour* (pp. 143–161). Philadelphia, PA: Psychology Press.

Walczyk, J. J., Roper, K. S., Seemann, E., & Humphrey, A. M. (2003). Cognitive mechanisms underlying lying to questions: Response time as a cue to deception. *Applied Cognitive Psychology, 17*, 755–774.

Walczyk, J. J., Schwartz, J. P., Clifton, R., Adams, B., Wei, M., & Zha, P. (2005). Lying person-to-person about live events: A cognitive framework for lie detection. *Personnel Psychology, 58*, 141–170.

Warmelink, L., Vrij, A., Mann, S., Jundi, S., & Granhag, P. A. (2012). Have you been there before? The effect of experience and question expectedness on lying about intentions. *Acta Psychologica, 141*, 178–183.

White, C. H., & Burgoon, J. K. (2001). Adaptation and communicative design: Patterns of interaction in truthful and deceptive conversations. *Human Communication Research, 27*, 9–37.

Zimmerman, L. A., Veinott, E. S., Meissner, C. M., Fallon, C., & Mueller, S. T. (2010). *Field training and testing of interview and elicitation methods* (Final

Report prepared under Contract W91CRB-09-C-0082 for US ARMY REDCOM Acquisition Center, Aberdeen Proving Ground, MD). Fairborn, OH: Klein Associates Division of Applied Research Associates.

Zuckerman, M., DePaulo, B. M., & Rosenthal, R. (1981). Verbal and nonverbal communication of deception. In L. Berkowitz (Ed.), *Advances in experimental social psychology* (Vol. 14, pp. 1–57). New York, NY: Academic Press.

10

The Strategic Use of Evidence Technique: A Conceptual Overview

PÄR ANDERS GRANHAG AND MARIA HARTWIG

The past decade has seen a new wave of deception detection research focusing on strategic ways of interviewing in order to elicit cues to truth and deception (Vrij & Granhag, 2012). The Strategic Use of Evidence (SUE) technique pioneered this new line of research. The research programme on the SUE technique has been running for more than 10 years; and there are now more than 20 scientific papers that directly or indirectly relate to the technique. The SUE technique has proven successful in eliciting cues to deception in single suspects (Hartwig, Granhag, Strömwall, & Kronkvist, 2006) and small groups of suspects (Granhag, Rangmar, & Strömwall 2013); in adults (Hartwig et al., 2011) and children (Clemens et al., 2010), as well as for suspects lying about their past actions (Hartwig, Granhag, Strömwall, & Vrij, 2005) and suspects lying about their intentions (Clemens, Granhag, & Strömwall, 2011). For a recent review of the empirical findings on the SUE technique including the first meta-analysis of the technique, see Hartwig, Granhag, and Luke (2014).

In this chapter, we will present a current conceptualization of the SUE technique. As a point of departure, we will introduce the so-called

Detecting Deception: Current Challenges and Cognitive Approaches, First Edition.
Edited by Pär Anders Granhag, Aldert Vrij, and Bruno Verschuere.
© 2015 John Wiley & Sons, Ltd. Published 2015 by John Wiley & Sons, Ltd.

SUE model, making clear the different conceptual levels of the technique. Second, we will discuss the general principles on which the SUE technique rests. Specifically, we will (a) explicate four basic principles, (b) explain how these principles are related and (c) tie our reasoning to basic psychological theory. Third, we will elaborate on the different SUE tactics, offering examples of how these tactics can be implemented and the result that are likely to follow. Critically, we will provide empirical support for the psychological processes that are key to the SUE technique. Fourth, we will state the overall goals of the SUE technique.

There are several reasons for providing a conceptual overview of the SUE technique. The SUE technique is by now an empirically established interview technique (Hartwig et al., 2014). In a previous article, we discussed several basic theoretical principles related to the SUE technique (Granhag & Hartwig, 2008). However, the technique has developed substantially since the publication of that article, and consequently, a more comprehensive discussion of the principles of the SUE technique is warranted. Furthermore, during recent years we have given lectures on the SUE technique in many parts of the world (e.g. Canada, Sweden, Norway, the Netherlands, Japan, China, Russia, Wales, England, Scotland, Germany and the United States) and we have trained practitioners from a wide variety of domains in using the technique (e.g. police, military, migration boards, tax authorities, prosecutors, judges, customs and the intelligence and security services). Hence, it makes sense to explicate the general principles on which the SUE technique rests. We believe that a grasp of these general principles, and how they are related, will allow for a flexible use of the technique. Relatedly, like with any interview approach, a basic understanding of the general principles underpinning the technique will help to apply it in different contexts and to the individual case. Finally, research on deception detection remains outcome-oriented, typically focusing on observers' accuracy rates at the expense of the study of processes (Vrij & Granhag, 2012). The present chapter attempts to remedy for this by casting light on the underlying processes. Hence, viewed from a wider perspective, we believe the chapter may contribute to the research domain at large.

THE SUE MODEL

Granhag (2010) introduced the SUE model, which consists of a strategic level and a tactical level (see Figure 10.1). The *strategic level* is more abstract and consists of general, case-independent principles underlying

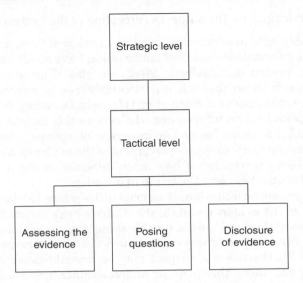

Figure 10.1   The SUE model.

the technique. These principles are at the core of the current chapter. The *tactical level* is more concrete, and contains a package of specific, case-dependent tactics. These tactics can be organized into three categories: tactics related to (1) the preinterview assessment of the background information (henceforth, evidence) (e.g. Granhag, 2010); (2) the questions posed (Hartwig et al., 2011) and (3) the disclosure of the evidence (Granhag, Strömwall, Willén, & Hartwig, 2013). The SUE tactics are relevant for planning, executing and analyzing interviews. Importantly, all tactics are derived from the general principles underlying the SUE technique (the strategic level).

THE GENERAL PRINCIPLES OF THE SUE TECHNIQUE

The strategic level of the SUE technique consists of four principles. Three of these principles are directly related to the suspect: (1) the suspect's perception of the evidence, (2) the suspect's counter-interrogation strategies and (3) the suspect's verbal responses. The fourth principle relates to the interviewer: (4) perspective-taking. In the following section, we will first describe each principle, after which we will explain how the four principles are related.

Principle 1 – The Suspect's Perception of the Evidence

It is probably safe to argue that most suspects will form a hypothesis about what information the investigator might have about them and the crime (e.g. Moston & Engelberg, 2012, see also Hilgendorf & Irving, 1981). Research shows that this is particularly true for suspects who are guilty of the crime under investigation (Hartwig, Granhag, & Strömwall, 2007). We posit that an interviewer who acts on this insight will be in a better position to reach his or her interview objectives (Soufan, 2011). Here, we use the term 'suspect's perception of the evidence' as shorthand for the suspect's perception of how much information the investigators might hold about them and the crime in question.

For the present discussion, it is crucial to relate (a) the suspects' perception of the evidence and (b) the interviewer's actual knowledge. If we consider these as marks on the same dimension, the suspect's perception can be more or less correct vis-á-vis the interviewer's actual knowledge. Furthermore, a suspect may be miscalibrated in different ways: he or she may either over- or underestimate how much information the interviewer holds. To understand this, consider Figure 10.2. This figure displays the general dimension on which suspects may differ: Simply put, they may believe that the interviewer holds only a little information, or they may believe that the interviewer holds a substantial amount of information (or anywhere in between). Further, the figure shows that a suspect's perception can be more or less well-calibrated (in Figure 10.2, the suspect underestimates the interviewer's knowledge). For our conceptualization, it suffices to relate (a) the suspect's perception of the totality of the interviewer's knowledge to (b) the total amount of information in fact held by the interviewer. However, for applied settings and with respect to many tactical considerations, it

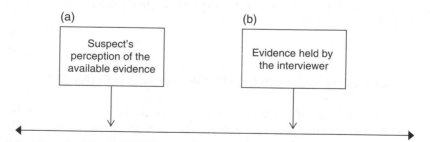

Figure 10.2 Suspects' perception of the evidence. The figure illustrates the general notion that a suspect will estimate the amount of information held by the interviewer on a scale ranging from low to high (the horizontal axis). In this particular example, the suspect is underestimating the amount of information held by the interviewer.

makes more sense to relate (a) and (b) for separate 'themes' (domains) of evidence (e.g. from the perspective of the suspect: 'Their knowledge about which people I know', 'Their knowledge about what I did last night'). The suspect's perception of the evidence may be influenced by a host of factors. Of particular importance for the current discussion is that a suspect's perception of the evidence can be changed as a function of *the tactics* employed by the interviewer (to be discussed subsequently).

Principle 2 – The Suspect's Counter-interrogation Strategies

A basic assumption of the SUE technique is that both liars and truth tellers attempt to convince the interviewer that they are innocent. These attempts are referred to as *counter-interrogation strategies* (Granhag & Hartwig, 2008). Research shows that counter-interrogation strategies can concern both verbal and non-verbal behaviour (Clemens, 2013). The SUE technique focuses solely on suspects' verbal strategies (for a systematic review of the empirical research on suspect's counter-interrogation strategies, see Chapter 13 in the present volume).

Another premise behind the SUE technique is that liars and truth tellers employ *different* strategies to convince the interviewer that they are telling the truth. In the research programme on the SUE technique, suspects' counter-interrogation strategies have been studied extensively, and several important findings have emerged from this research. First, since lying entails strategic decision-making, liars will report a plan or strategy before entering an interview (e.g. Hartwig et al., 2007). Second, we have found that liars (if given the opportunity) will avoid disclosing critical information (e.g. Hartwig, Granhag, Strömwall, & Doering, 2010). Third, if liars are deprived of the avoidance alternative, they will turn to escape responses (Hartwig et al., 2005). That is, faced with direct questions about incriminating information, their strategy will be to deny the critical information. Importantly, this pattern of strategies has been replicated for people with extensive experience of interrogation: In a study mapping criminals' counter-interrogation strategies, participants reported using aversive and avoidant strategies when deceiving (Granhag, Clemens, & Strömwall, 2009). As for truth tellers, psychological theory predicts that when they express specific strategies, these are primarily strategies of verbal forthcomingness (Kassin, 2005; Strömwall, Hartwig, & Granhag, 2006).

The Psychology of Counter-interrogation Strategies It is possible to connect suspects' counter-interrogation strategies to basic social cognitive theory. In particular, counter-interrogation strategies can be understood through the lens of self-regulation theory (Carver & Sheier, 2012). Self-regulation theory is a framework for understanding how people control their behaviour in order to direct themselves towards desired goals or away from undesirable outcomes. As such, self-regulation theory deals with motivated, goal-oriented behaviour (Carver & Sheier, 2002). For the current context, the desired goal for both liars and truth tellers is to convince an interviewer that their statement is true. Conversely, the undesirable outcome is that an interviewer will classify their statement as deceptive.

As described earlier, liars and truth tellers share the goal of being perceived as honest (for a theoretical discussion of this, see DePaulo, 1992; DePaulo et al., 2003). However, according to the SUE perspective, liars and truth tellers differ in at least one important way: A liar is per definition motivated to conceal certain information from the interviewer. The main threat for a liar is thus that the interviewer will come to know this information. In contrast, a truth-telling person does not possess information that he or she is motivated to conceal; thus, truth tellers have the very opposite problem – that the interviewer may *not* come to know the truth. Because of the crucial difference between liars and truth tellers in their motivation to conceal critical information, they can be expected to adopt different strategies with regard to what information to include in one's account. In other words, they will adopt different information management strategies (Hartwig et al., 2010).

Regarding liars, they need to balance several risks with regard to information. Obviously, they must conceal critical information to avoid the risk of incriminating themselves. Instead of offering the truth, they must provide an alternative account. Providing false information to conceal one's actual actions (e.g. asserting that one was at the shopping mall when one was in fact at the crime scene) entails a risk – if the interviewer holds information that the suspect indeed was at the crime scene, the suspect's credibility is in question. Striking the appropriate balance between concealing incriminating information and offering details in order to appear credible is a crucial consideration for liars. More generally speaking, liars need to engage in strategic decision-making regarding what information to avoid, deny and admit during an interview. As for the critical information, liars have two broad information management strategies at their disposal: A suspect could either choose an *avoidance strategy* (e.g. being vague about his or her whereabouts), or he could choose an *escape strategy* (e.g. denying being at the crime scene).

In contrast, truth tellers are in a different situation. More specifically, they are not facing the same information-management dilemma as liars. Since truth tellers (in most cases) have no critical information to conceal, we can expect them to employ rather simple strategies of forthcomingness – that is, to provide a complete and truthful account. It may appear as if we are proposing a self-evident prediction that truth tellers will primarily tell the truth, but we believe that the case is less trivial than this. What we suggest is that truth tellers have a strong, and perhaps motivated, belief that if they are forthcoming with information, they will achieve the goal of being believed. Bases for this prediction can be found in social psychological research. First, truth tellers may be influenced by the *belief in a just world* (Lerner, 1980). Just world theory states that people trust that the world is a fair place, and that they believe that one receives the outcomes one deserves (Hafer & Bègue, 2005). In essence, truth tellers may believe that if they are forthcoming, they will be believed simply because they deserve it (Feather, 1999). Second, the forthcomingness of truth tellers may be based on an *illusion of transparency* (Gilovich, Savitsky, & Medvec, 1998; Savitsky & Gilovich, 2003). This general tendency to overestimate the extent to which internal processes are evident in behaviour occurs in a number of contexts (e.g. Vorauer & Claude, 1998). Of particular relevance for this discussion, research on guilty and innocent crime suspects suggests that innocent people display an illusion of transparency. Kassin and Norwick (2004) found that innocent suspects were more prone to waive their Miranda rights than were guilty suspects. Innocent suspects frequently justified this behaviour by the argument that they had nothing to hide, and that if they could simply provide their story to the interrogator, he would 'see' that they were innocent. For an in-depth discussion of the psychological reasoning of innocent suspects, see Kassin (2005).

Principle 3 – The Suspect's Verbal Response

The suspect's verbal responses are the basis for (a) the cues to truth/deception and/or (b) the new case-relevant information elicited during the interview (to be discussed later). Hence, for the SUE technique to be effective, it is essential that the suspect's responses are documented in detail. As will be outlined later, different SUE tactics result in different cues to deception. However, two of these cues need to be introduced already at this point. The first cue is labelled *statement–evidence inconsistency* and reflects discrepancies or contradictions between the suspects' account and the critical background information (evidence) held by the interviewer. This cue is chief among the different cues to deception and truth that the SUE tactics might result in (Hartwig et al., 2014). The second cue is labelled *within-statement inconsistency*, which reflects that the suspect has continuously changed his statement in order to make it fit the evidence presented to him.

Recently, Granhag, Strömwall, et al. (2013) introduced the *Evidence Framing Matrix* (EFM) which is a tactical tool illuminating the different framing options that exist for one individual piece of evidence. This matrix is the result of orthogonally relating two independent dimensions: the *strength of the source of the evidence* (which can vary from weak to strong) and the *degree of precision (specificity) of the evidence* (which can vary from low to high). Consider a situation in which the interviewer has CCTV footage showing how the suspect buys a suitcase of the same model and colour as one later found containing bomb material. The source of the evidence can be framed as weak ('we have information telling us that...') or as strong ('we have CCTV footage showing us that...'). The specificity of the evidence can be framed as low ('... you visiting a luggage store') or as high ('... you buying a particular suitcase'). For this example, the EFM informs that the most *indirect* form of framing (the weak source/low specificity) is 'we have information telling us that you recently visited a luggage store' and that the *most direct* form of framing (the strong source/high specificity) is 'we have CCTV footage telling us that you recently bought a particular suitcase'. Simply put, the EFM offers guidance on how to reveal a single piece of evidence with increasing strength and precision. Recent studies support that using the EFM to reveal a piece of evidence in an incremental fashion (from the most general to the most precise framing) results in increased within-statement inconsistency for lying suspects (Granhag, Rangmar, & Strömwall, 2013; Granhag, Strömwall, et al., 2013).

Principle 4 – Perspective-Taking On Behalf of the Interviewer

Perspective-taking is the cognitive capacity to consider the world from another's viewpoint, which allows the anticipation of other people's behaviour and reactions (Galinsky, Maddux, Gilin, & White, 2008). Research shows that people typically use themselves as the point of reference (Davis, Conklin, Smith, & Luce, 1996), and that perspective-taking is a rather difficult skill to master (Idson et al., 2004). The ability to take the perspective of others is predictive of success in negotiations (Galinsky et al., 2008), and of importance for interrogators (e.g. Granhag & Hartwig, 2008; Justice et al., 2010; Soufan, 2011).

In the SUE framework, the interviewer's perspective-taking concerns the three principles discussed earlier; that is, an interviewer should attempt to (1) read the suspect's perception of the evidence, (2) predict the suspect's counter-interrogation strategies and (3) predict the verbal response that will follow. For example, the interviewer might find guidance in reading the suspect's perception of the evidence by considering how the suspect might group and label (if he is guilty) the incriminating information; 'what they definitely know', 'what they might know', and 'what they probably do not know', etc. In addition, perspective-taking facilitates the simulation of the alternative explanations that a suspect might offer to the evidence, and to prepare a line of questioning that will exhaust these alternative explanations. For the sake of completeness – and to further underscore the dynamic elements of a suspect interview – it should be acknowledged that suspects too may engage in perspective-taking, for example when trying to predict which tactics the interviewer will use.

THE RELATION BETWEEN SUE PRINCIPLES

The relation between the principles described earlier is at the very core of our conceptualization. In what follows, we will describe the two most fundamental relations.[1]

First, a guilty suspect's *perception of the interviewer's knowledge* will affect his choice of *counter-interrogation strategy*. In turn, the suspect's counter-interrogation strategy will affect his *verbal responses*. For example, if the suspect believes the interviewer to *not* be in possession of a certain piece of incriminating information [A], he will likely employ the strategy: 'I will not tell any information that might be incriminating'. Hence, he will avoid mentioning and/or deny holding A. In contrast, if the suspect believes the interviewer to know A, he might employ the strategy: 'It is meaningless to withhold what they already know'. The suspect might therefore volunteer A during the interview. For an illustration of the causal links between these three elements, see Figure 10.3.

Figure 10.3   Causal relations between three of the SUE principles. As the figure illustrates, suspects' perception of the evidence dictates their choice of counter-interrogation strategy, which in turn dictates their verbal response.

[1]Note that this discussion is primarily applicable to lying rather than truth-telling suspects. As we have described elsewhere in the chapter, the SUE technique posits that liars engage in strategic information management (the dynamics and consequences of which are discussed here), while truth tellers' strategy primarily involves verbal forthcomingness.

Second, we believe that an interviewer who (a) recognizes that the suspect is engaged in strategizing and (b) understands the dynamic of this strategizing will be in a better position to conduct an effective interview, compared to an interviewer who ignores these psychological elements. The reason is that the former interviewer is in a far better position to both predict and interpret the suspect's behaviour. More specifically, the interviewer's *perspective-taking* aims at reading the suspect's perception of the evidence, and to predict the suspect's counter-interrogation strategies and verbal responses. Expressed differently, perspective-taking will guide the interviewer's *implementation of the SUE tactics*. The SUE tactics can be viewed as means at the interviewer's disposal to reach his or her objectives. For example, let us assume that the interviewer – by means of perspective-taking – predicts that the suspect ascribes him to have information about A and B, but not about C. The interviewer will then predict the suspect to freely tell (or admit to) both A and B, but avoid/deny C. Hence, if the interviewer seeks to obtain statement–evidence inconsistency (indicating that the suspect might be lying), or statement–evidence consistency (indicating that the suspect might be telling the truth), then C is the information to focus on in a tactical manner.

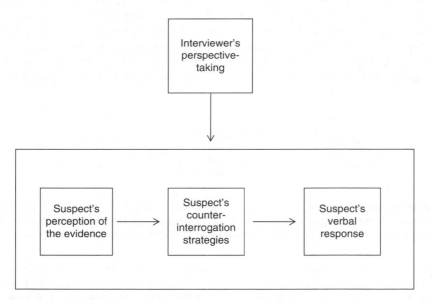

Figure 10.4 The relation between suspect-related principles and perspective-taking on behalf of the interviewer.

In sum, the general concepts of the SUE technique are related in the following manner: (a) the suspect forms a hypothesis on the evidence situation, (b) this hypothesis will influence the suspect's choice of counter-interrogation strategy, which in turn will be reflected in (c) the suspect's verbal behaviour during the interview. By means of (d) perspective-taking the interviewer can (for the individual case) use his or her insights about the overall causal processes to simulate the outcome of different scenarios. Depending on his or her objectives, the interviewer can employ the SUE tactics to alter the suspect's perception of the evidence in one or the other direction. For an illustration of this reasoning, see Figure 10.4.

EMPLOYING THE SUE TACTICS

So far we have discussed the general principles of the SUE technique and how these principles are related. In the following section, we will advance our conceptualization by making clear how different SUE tactics may result in different outcomes. Specifically, we will illustrate how different SUE tactics affect the suspect's perception differently and how this, in turn, affects the suspect's choice of counter-interrogation strategy and subsequent verbal responses. Our illustration revolves around four different phases, where each new phase rests on the previous phase(s). In addition, each phase introduces one (or several) new SUE tactic, and for each phase the tactics mentioned are to be employed sequentially. Importantly, although the four phases are linked, they are not to be viewed as fixed stages in a SUE interview protocol. The main reason for introducing phases is to illuminate how different SUE tactics may result in different outcomes. Importantly, the SUE technique is not limited to these four phases. The purpose of introducing these examples is to make conceptual arguments, and the examples are therefore stripped of the complexities characterizing real-life suspect interviews.

Phase 1
1) Suspect's perception of the evidence: 'They must have some information, but I am not sure how much and what'.
2) SUE tactics: Withhold the evidence; Ask for a free recall.
3) S's perception of the evidence: 'They do not mention any evidence; they might have less than I thought'.
4) S's counter-interrogation strategy: Avoid providing information that might be incriminating.
5) S's verbal responses will be coloured by *omissions*.

Importantly, there is solid empirical evidence showing that the SUE tactics specified at 2), result in guilty suspects employing avoidant counter-interrogation strategies, which in turn will result in statements characterized by omissions (e.g. Hartwig et al., 2005). Equally important, as predicted by the theoretical principles outlined earlier, innocent suspects tend to be forthcoming under these conditions (e.g. Hartwig et al., 2006).

Phase 2
6) S's perception of the evidence: 'Still not very clear how much and what information they hold'.
7) SUE tactics: Withhold the evidence; ask for a free recall; exhaust alternative explanations; ask specific questions.
8) S's perception of the evidence: 'They might have less information than I thought'.
9) S's counter-interrogation strategy: Deny any incriminating actions.
10) S's verbal response will be coloured by *statement–evidence inconsistency*.

The specific questions asked at 7) have two primary aims. First, they seek to exhaust alternative explanations to the evidence. Simply put, a guilty suspect should not be able to offer a plausible alternative explanation to a piece of evidence just disclosed to him. Hence, the interviewer must (a) foresee (simulate) which alternative explanations a guilty suspect might offer and (b) exhaust these prior to disclosing the evidence. That is, the interviewer should ask questions that will result in that (guilty) suspects' alternative escape routes are closed. For example, imagine a suspect denying having been close to the victim and having been at the scene of the crime. Further imagine that an analysis shows blood from the victim under the suspect's sneakers. If confronted with this evidence, the suspect may state that his many friends run in and out of his flat all the time, borrowing money, food, beer and clothes. Instead of having to disprove this, the interviewer should have exhausted this alternative explanation prior to disclosing the evidence: 'Do you live alone?'; 'Who has access to your flat?'; 'Are you careful with your belongings?'; 'Do you borrow stuff, food, clothes, etc. from your friends?'; 'Do they borrow stuff from you?', etc. Second, the questions posed should address the critical pieces of evidence, without revealing that the interviewer holds these particular pieces. There is considerable evidence that the SUE tactics specified at 7), will result in denial-oriented counter-interrogation strategies for guilty suspects, which in turn will result in statements characterized by statement–evidence inconsistencies (e.g. Hartwig et al., 2011). Equally important, for innocent suspects, their forthcomingness will lead to statements that are consistent with the evidence (e.g. Hartwig et al., 2005, 2006).

Phase 3
11) S's perception of the evidence: 'Still not very clear how much and what information they hold'.
12) SUE tactics: Withhold the evidence; ask for a free recall; exhaust alternative explanations; ask specific questions; disclosure according to the EFM.
13) S's perception of the evidence: 'They had more than I thought'.
14) S's counter-interrogation strategy: 'Need to alter my previous statement not to be inconsistent with the evidence presented to me'.
15) S's verbal response will be coloured by *within-statement inconsistency*.

Importantly, there is empirical support that the tactics specified at 12) will result in a portion of guilty suspects using counter-interrogation strategies aimed at 'repairing' the gap between what they had previously stated and the evidence as it is disclosed to them, which in turn will result in (c) a statement characterized by within-statement inconsistencies (e.g. Granhag, Strömwall, et al., 2013). Importantly, innocent suspects tend to present statements with zero-level of within-statement inconsistency (Granhag, Strömwall, et al., 2013).

Phase 4
16) SUE tactic: The suspect is confronted with within-statement and/or evidence–statement inconsistencies (this is repeated for two or more themes of evidence).
17) S's perception of the evidence: 'They have more than I thought, better start providing them with the information they already have, in order to avoid contradicting it'.
18) SUE tactics: Introducing a new theme; a theme for which the interviewer lacks critical information.
19) S's perception of the evidence: 'I am sure they hold more information on this theme than they pretend'.
20) S's counter-interrogation strategy: 'Need to avoid being confronted with more inconsistencies, better tell what they already know'.
21) The verbal response will be characterized by the suspect unintentionally telling information that is new to the interviewer.

The tactical reasoning described for Phase 4 demands access to several different themes of evidence, and that the investigator holds a certain amount of information on some of these. This is necessary to obtain the 'repeated inconsistencies' 16) needed to make the suspect overestimate the amount of knowledge held by interviewer on the critical theme (the theme where the interviewer seeks to obtain more information, see also Figure 10.2). That the SUE tactics can be used for eliciting new information (admissions) is backed up by both recent empirical research (Tekin, Granhag, Strömwall, Mac Giolla, Vrij, & Hartwig, 2014) and reports from interrogators sharing information on individual real life cases (Soufan, 2011).

Implications A number of important observations can be made from the aforementioned examples. The first is that each of the four phases contains the same general sequence: The SUE tactics affecting the (1) suspect's perception of the evidence, (2) moderating the choice of counter-interrogation strategy, which is mirrored in (3) the suspect's verbal responses (see Figure 10.3). The fact that the assumed causal process is structurally similar across all phases speaks of the systematic nature of the SUE technique. In essence, there are several SUE tactics and each tactic results in a different outcome, but the basic mechanism driving the different effects is the same across all phases.

Second, the different SUE tactics converge on the aim of *altering* the suspect's perception of the evidence. In essence, the tactics are used in order to make the suspect either underestimate how much knowledge the interviewer holds or overestimate how much information the interviewer holds. The earlier examples underscore what has already been stated in the chapter: that a suspect – forming a hypothesis about the evidence situation – might go wrong in one direction (with certain consequences), or wrong in another direction (with different consequences). But the examples also show what follows as soon as more than one theme (topic) of evidence is introduced (which is the more common situation for real cases). If a suspect – for the themes of evidence introduced early in an interview – *overestimates* how much information the interviewer holds, he runs the risk of volunteering incriminating information previously unknown to the investigators. On the other hand, if he – for the same themes – *underestimates* how much information the interviewer holds, he runs the risk of being confronted with statement–evidence inconsistencies (or within-statement inconsistencies). Similarly, if the suspect – for themes of evidence introduced at a later stage and on the basis of realizing having revealed too much information at an earlier stage – now *underestimates* how much information the interviewer holds, he runs the risk of being confronted with statement–evidence inconsistencies. On the other hand, if the suspect – for the same themes of evidence and on the basis of repeatedly having been confronted with statement–evidence inconsistencies – now *overestimates* how much information the interviewer holds, he runs the risk of volunteering incriminating information previously unknown to the investigators.

Introducing several themes of evidence, it stands clear that the act of forming perceptions about the evidence is a dynamic process. The perception formed before (or at the outset of) an interview is sensitive to different forms of influence and might change over the course of an interview (or over the course of repeated interviews). A proper use of the SUE tactics might force the suspect to continuously revise his perceptions of the evidence. Simply put, an interviewer may reach one sub-goal by using certain SUE tactics to affect the suspect's perception in one direction, and then reach a different subgoal by using other SUE tactics to affect the (same) suspect's perception of the evidence in a different direction. In essence, the aforementioned reasoning illuminates that the information management dilemma that the suspect needs to navigate in an SUE interview is indeed a difficult one.

Third, the examples given earlier show that in order to obtain the optimal effect of the more advanced SUE tactics (e.g. the EFM), it is necessary to employ a multiphased approach. That is, the more advanced SUE tactics rest on first properly having employed the more basic tactics (e.g. withhold the evidence; ask for a free recall; exhaust alternative explanations and ask specific questions which address the evidence).

Fourth, although all phases contained the very same sequence of general principles, each individual phase resulted in a different verbal response (omissions, statement–evidence inconsistency, within-statement inconsistency, new information). Critically, this shows that the SUE technique may be used both for eliciting different cues to deceit (the three former outcomes) and for eliciting new information of relevance for an investigation (the latter outcome).

THE OVERALL AIMS OF THE SUE TECHNIQUE

While one consequence of employing the SUE technique is the elicitation of one or several cues to deception that may guide an interviewer on whether the suspect is lying or not, we believe there is another critical goal of technique: The SUE technique can contribute to the prosecutor's case-construction (should the case result in an indictment), and in next instance, to the evidence presented in court. For example, the SUE tactics might result in that a guilty suspect will assert facts during the interview that subsequently, and in the light of the presented evidence, are unsustainable. Hence, we believe it is fair to argue that there is a judicial dimension to the SUE technique; a dimension that many other techniques for detecting deception lack.

Although the aim of this chapter is not to relate the SUE technique to other frameworks, we still consider it warranted to offer a few reflections on this note. Our view is that the SUE technique is fully compatible with already established and ethically sound frameworks for investigative interviewing, such as the *PEACE-model* (used in the United Kingdom), *The General Interviewing Strategy* (used in the Netherlands) and the *KREATIV-model* (used in Norway). Importantly, the SUE technique offers what these general frameworks lack: theoretically based and empirically supported guidelines (tactics) for how to optimize the value of the background information held by the interviewer.

THEMES OF EVIDENCE: A CHALLENGE FOR THE FUTURE

Although there has been extensive research on the SUE technique during the past 10 years, there are a number of aspects that await empirical attention. One such understudied aspect is how to approach 'themes (domains) of evidence'. Simply put, investigators may often have access to critical background information about the case that can be organized into different themes (Granhag, 2010), for example the list of contacts found in the suspect's cell phone, the envelope with cash found hidden in the suspect's summerhouse and CCTV footage showing how the suspect accepts a briefcase at the train station. Importantly, a theme can either be unrelated to other themes (i.e. it can be approached without the interviewer revealing that he also has information about other themes) or be related to other themes (i.e. if approached, the risk is that the suspect realizes that the interviewer must also know about X and Y). Furthermore, the interviewer may have more information about some themes and less information about others, and a particular theme may be more or less critical to the interviewer's objectives and the prosecutor's case-construction (e.g. Häkkinen, Ask, Kebbell, Alison, & Granhag, 2009). Examples of tactical considerations that arise are: (i) How should the relative potential of the different themes be assessed and (ii) in which order and (iii) how should the themes be introduced during the interview to achieve the optimal effects?

It is safe to say that using the very same tactical approach for all themes of evidence would be naive; that is, suspects tend to be quick learners, and tactics that are repeated mechanically may soon be rendered useless or counterproductive. To disclose the evidence in a drip-feeding/gradual manner (i.e. one piece of evidence at a time throughout the interview), a suggestion foreshadowed by Hartwig

(2005) and recently empirically addressed by Dando and Bull (2011) might, under certain circumstances, be an effective tactic. However, we do not subscribe to the view that drip-feeding by itself is an effective interview tactic. There are strong reasons to believe that whether the outcome of drip-feeding the evidence will be positive or not depends on a number of factors. First, the *prehistory* of drip-feeding the evidence will likely affect the outcome. For example, drip-feeding in itself might not be very effective if not first having exhausted alternative explanations for the evidence disclosed. Second, the *order* in which the different pieces of evidence are disclosed is likely to moderate efficacy. For example, many suspects may be quick learners, and pieces of evidence that are disclosed late in a sequence might be met with different (more effective) counter-interrogation tactics than pieces that are introduced early.

In connection to this, it should be acknowledged that *when* different pieces of evidence are disclosed should not be confused with *how* individual pieces of evidence are framed at the point of disclosure. Differently put, the *timing* of the disclosure is not the same as the *framing* of the evidence. If confounded, like in a recent study by Dando, Bull, Ormerod, and Sandham (2013), it is impossible to assess what is responsible for any observed effects.

Notably, research on the effects of drip-feeding the evidence is still in its infancy and much experimental work is needed before any clear advice can be offered with respect to the timing of disclosure. However, we believe that research aimed at predicting under which circumstances and why drip-feeding the evidence will be successful (or unsuccessful) could profit from the guidance offered by the general principles and the causal relations specified in this chapter.

LIMITATIONS

As described earlier, there is significant theoretical and empirical support for the SUE technique. However, as with any interview approach, there are limitations. One relates to its scope. The SUE technique is not a general framework of interviewing, designed to accomplish all the goals that interviewing may entail (e.g. establishment of rapport and facilitation of recall through the use of mnemonic techniques).

Also, there are some fairly obvious constraints as to when the SUE technique may be used. For example, the SUE technique will not work if the suspect decides to be silent. Furthermore, the principles of the SUE technique can only be employed if the investigator is in possession of some sort of case evidence/information. On a positive note, research shows that such information is available in the vast majority of criminal investigations (Wagenaar, van Koppen, & Crombag, 1993), which indicates that the SUE technique may be applicable in most cases.

Finally, there may be limitations related to the methodology underlying SUE research. Most of the research has been conducted in experimental settings, and there is a shortage of research on the technique in field settings (but see Hartwig et al., 2006; Luke, Hartwig, Joseph et al., 2014). We do not see a theoretical reason to expect that the fundamental mechanisms of the SUE technique (i.e. counter-interrogation strategies) will operate differently under high-stake circumstances. Still, we encourage future research to examine the SUE technique under settings of high ecological validity.

CONCLUSIONS

In the present chapter, we have presented the first conceptualization of the SUE technique. We have identified and described the general principles upon which the SUE technique rests, and we have presented a causal model making clear how these principles are related. In addition, we have offered an array of examples illustrating how different SUE tactics may result in different outcomes. We believe that the current conceptualization offers transparency with respect to the processes explaining the effects of the different SUE tactics. In brief, we have explained *why* the SUE technique works.

Drawing on past SUE research, we have been able to provide empirical support of our conceptual arguments. The conceptualization makes it clear that the SUE technique is an integrated system of principles; a system which may generate different outcomes, but which always draws on the very same set of general principles. Importantly, conceptual clarity will allow for a more flexible use of the SUE technique.

REFERENCES

Carver, C. S., & Scheier, M. F. (2002). Control processes and self-organization as complementary principles underlying behavior. *Personality and Social Psychology Review, 6*, 304–315.

Carver, C. S., & Scheier, M. F. (2012). A model of behavioral self-regulation. In P. M. Van Lange, A. W. Kruglanski, & E. Higgins (Eds.), *Handbook of theories of social psychology* (Vol. 1, pp. 505–525). Thousand Oaks, CA: Sage.

Clemens, F. (2013). *Detecting lies about past and future actions: The Strategic Use of Evidence (SUE) technique and suspects' strategies* (Doctoral dissertation). Department of Psychology, University of Gothenburg, Gothenburg, Sweden.

Clemens, F., Granhag, P. A., &Strömwall, L. A. (2011). Eliciting cues to false intent: A new application of strategic interviewing. *Law and Human Behavior, 35*, 512–522.

Clemens, F., Granhag, P. A., Strömwall, L. A. Vrij, A., Landström, S., Roos af Hjelmsäter, E., & Hartwig, M. (2010). Skulking around the dinosaur: Eliciting cues to children's deception via strategic disclosure of evidence. *Applied Cognitive Psychology, 24*, 925–940.

Dando, C. J., & Bull, R. (2011). Maximising opportunities to detect verbal deception: Training police officers to interview tactically. *Journal of Investigative Psychology & Offender Profiling, 8*, 189–202.

Dando, C. J., Bull, R., Ormerod, T. C., & Sandham, A. L. (2013). Helping to sort the liars from the truth-tellers: The gradual revelation of information during investigative interviews. *Legal and Criminological Psychology*. doi:10.1111/lcrp.12016.

Davis, M. H., Conklin, L., Smith, A., & Luce, C. (1996). Effect of perspective taking on the cognitive representation of persons: A merging of self and other. *Journal of Personality and Social Psychology, 70*, 713–726.

DePaulo, B. M. (1992). Nonverbal behavior and self-presentation. *Psychological Bulletin, 111*, 203–243.

DePaulo, B. M., Lindsay, J. J., Malone, B. E., Muhlenbruck, L., Charlton, K., & Cooper, H. (2003). Cues to deception. *Psychological Bulletin, 129*, 74–118.

Feather, N. T. (1999). Judgments of deservingness: Studies in the psychology of justice and achievement. *Personality and Social Psychology Review, 3*, 86–107.

Galinsky, A. D., Maddux, W. W., Gilin, D., & White, J.B. (2008). Why it pays to get inside the head of your opponent: The differential effects of perspective taking and empathy in negotiations. *Psychological Science, 19*, 378–384.

Gilovich, T., Savitsky, K., & Medvec, V. H. (1998). The illusion of transparency: Biased assessments of others' ability read one's emotional states. *Journal of Personality and Social Psychology, 75*, 332–346.

Granhag, P.A. (November 18–19, 2010). The Strategic Use of Evidence (SUE) technique: A scientific perspective. High Value Detainee Interrogation Group (HIG; FBI). HIG Research Symposium: Interrogation in the European Union, Washington, DC.

Granhag, P. A., Clemens, F., & Strömwall, L. A. (2009). The usual and the unusual suspects: Level of suspicion and counter-interrogation tactics. *Journal of Investigative Psychology and Offender Profiling, 6*, 129–137.

Granhag, P. A., & Hartwig, M. (2008). A new theoretical perspective on deception detection: On the psychology of instrumental mind reading. *Psychology, Crime & Law, 14*, 189–200.

Granhag, P. A., Mac Giolla, E., Strömwall, L. A., & Rangmar, J. (2013). Counter-interrogation strategies among small cells of suspects. *Psychiatry, Psychology & Law, 20*, 750–712.

Granhag, P. A., Rangmar, J., & Strömwall, L. A. (2013). Small cells of suspects: Eliciting cues to deception by strategic interviewing. *Journal of Investigative Psychology and Offender Profiling*. doi:10.1002/jip.1413.

Granhag, P. A., Strömwall, L. A., Willén, R., & Hartwig, M. (2013). Eliciting cues to deception by tactical disclosure of evidence: The first test of the Evidence Framing Matrix. *Legal and Criminological Psychology, 18*, 341–355.

Hafer, C. L., & Bègue, L. (2005). Experimental research on just-world theory: Problems, developments, and future challenges. *Psychological Bulletin, 131*, 128–167.

Häkkinen, H., Ask, K., Kebbell, M., Alison, L., & Granhag, P. A. (2009). Police officers' views of effective interview tactics with suspects: The effects of weight of case evidence and discomfort with ambiguity. *Applied Cognitive Psychology, 23*, 468–481.

Hartwig, M. (2005). *Interrogating to detect deception and truth: Effects of strategic use of evidence* (Doctoral dissertation). Department of Psychology, University of Gothenburg, Gothenburg, Sweden.

Hartwig, M., Granhag, P. A., & Luke, T. (2014). Strategic use of evidence during investigative interviews: The state of the science. In D. C. Raskin, C. R. Honts, & J. C. Kircher (Eds.), *Credibility assessment: Scientific research and applications* (pp. 1–36). Waltham, MA: Academic Press.

Hartwig, M., Granhag, P. A., & Strömwall, L. A. (2007). Guilty and innocent suspects' strategies during police interrogations. *Psychology, Crime & Law, 13*, 213–227.

Hartwig, M., Granhag, P. A., Strömwall, L. A., & Doering, N. (2010). Impression and information management: On the strategic self-regulation of innocent and guilty suspects. *Open Criminology Journal, 3*, 10–16.

Hartwig, M, Granhag, P. A., Strömwall, L. A., & Kronkvist, O. (2006). Strategic use of evidence during police interviews: When training to detect deception works. *Law and Human Behavior, 30*, 603–619.

Hartwig, M., Granhag, P. A., Strömwall, L. A., & Vrij, A. (2005). Detecting deception via strategic disclosure of evidence. *Law and Human Behavior, 29*, 469–484.

Hartwig, M., Granhag, P.A., Strömwall, L.A., Wolf, A., Vrij, A., Roos af Hjelmsäter, E. (2011). Detecting deception in suspects: Verbal cues as a function of interview strategy. *Psychology, Crime, & Law, 17*, 643–656.

Hilgendorf, E. L., & Irving, B. (1981). A decision-making model of confessions. In M. A. Lloyd-Bostock (Ed.), *Psychology in legal contexts: Applications and limitations* (pp. 67–84). London, UK: MacMillan.

Idson, L. C., Chugh, D., Bereby-Meyer, Y., Moran, S., Grosskopf, B., & Bazerman, M. (2004). Overcoming focusing failures in competitive environments. *Journal of Behavioral Decision Making, 17*, 159–172.

Justice, B. P., Bhatt, S., Brandon, S. E., & Kleinman, S. M. (2010). *Army field manual 2-22.3: Interrogation methods: A science-based review.* Washington, DC (Draft, September).

Kassin, S. M. (2005). On the psychology of confessions: Does innocence put innocent at risk? *American Psychologist, 60*, 215–228.

Kassin, S. M., & Norwick, R. J. (2004). Why people waive their Miranda rights: The power of innocence. *Law and Human Behavior, 28*, 211–221.

Lerner, M. J. (1980). *The belief in a just world.* New York, NY: Plenum.

Luke, T. J., Dawson, E., Hartwig, M., & Granhag, P. A. (in press). How awareness of possible evidence induces forthcoming counter-interrogation strategies. *Applied Cognitive Psychology*

Luke, T. J., Dawson, E., Hartwig, M. & Granhag, P. A. (2013). How awareness of evidence induces forthcoming counter-interrogation strategies. Manuscript under review.

Luke, T. J, Hartwig, M., Brimbal, L., Chan, G., Jordan, S., Joseph, E., ... Granhag, P. A. (2013b). Interviewing to elicit cues to deception: Improving strategic use of evidence with general-to-specific framing of evidence. *Journal of Police and Criminal Psychology, 28*, 54–62.

Luke, T. J., Hartwig, M., Joseph, E., Brimbal, L., Chan, G., Dawson, E., ... Granhag, P. A. (2014). *Training in the strategic use of evidence technique: Improving deception detection accuracy of American law enforcement officers,* Manuscript under review.

Moston, S., & Engelberg, T. (2012). The effects of evidence on the outcome of interviews with criminal suspects. *Journal of Police and Criminal Psychology, 12*, 518–526.

Savitsky, K., & Gilovich, T. (2003). The illusion of transparency and the alleviation of speech anxiety. *Journal of Experimental Social Psychology, 39*, 618–625.

Soufan, A. H. (2011). *The black banners: The inside story of 9/11 and the war against Al-Qaeda.* New York, NY: W.W. Norton & Company.

Strömwall, L. A., Hartwig, M., & Granhag, P. A. (2006). To act truthfully: Nonverbal behavior and strategies during a police interrogation. *Psychology, Crime & Law, 12*, 207–219.

Tekin, S., Granhag, P. A., Strömwall, L. A., Mac Giolla, E., Vrij, A., & Hartwig, M. (2014). Interviewing strategically to elicit admissions from guilty suspects. Manuscript submitted for publication.

Vorauer, J. D., & Claude, S.-D. (1998). Perceived versus actual transparency of goals in negotiation. *Personality and Social Psychology Bulletin, 24*, 371–385.

Vrij, A., & Granhag, P. A. (2012). Eliciting cues to deception and truth: What matters are the questions asked. [Invited target article]. *Journal of Applied Research in Memory & Cognition, 2*, 110–117.

Wagenaar, W. A., van Koppen, P. J., & Crombag, H. F. M. (1993). *Anchored narratives: The psychology of criminal evidence.* New York, NY: St. Martin's Press.

11

Investigating Deception and Deception Detection with Brain Stimulation Methods

GIORGIO GANIS

Neuroimaging (e.g. fMRI) and brain sensing (e.g. ERP) methods monitor neural activity associated with deceptive mental states in exquisite spatial and temporal detail, but they cannot reveal whether such activity is necessary for deceptive mental states. Even in the presence of a high correlation between a certain pattern of brain activity and a deceptive mental state, it is possible that such activity is only epiphenomenal, similar to the power LED on a laptop, which indicates that the laptop is on but does not contribute to the laptop's processing operations. This is not just a theoretical possibility because there are interesting cases in which findings from brain imaging and neurological patient studies are at odds with each other, consistent with the idea that some of the activations observed with neuroimaging methods may not be necessary for performing the task at hand. For example, some of the prefrontal brain areas in the right hemisphere that are often found in brain-imaging studies of language do not seem critical for language, according to data from patient studies with damage in these same areas (Sidtis, 2007).

Detecting Deception: Current Challenges and Cognitive Approaches, First Edition.
Edited by Pär Anders Granhag, Aldert Vrij, and Bruno Verschuere.
© 2015 John Wiley & Sons, Ltd. Published 2015 by John Wiley & Sons, Ltd.

The main way to assess causality between neural activation and performance is to produce targeted changes in neural activity and to observe if there are corresponding changes in task performance that are thought to depend on such activity. The principal methods that enable cognitive neuroscientists to address issues of causality of neural activation are neurostimulation ones, the focus of this chapter. Neuropharmacological methods are also relevant, but they will not be reviewed here (Farah, 2009). It is important to note that, on the one hand, the issue of causality per se is not central for neuroscience-based deception detection because one could have a perfectly accurate method to detect deception even if the brain activation that is being monitored is only correlated with (i.e. not causally related to) deceptive mental states. On the other hand, the issue of causality is potentially important for neuroscience-based deception detection because disrupting brain activation causally related to deceptive mental states with neurostimulation techniques could impair deception itself and/or result in deception signatures (e.g. more errors or longer response times during stimulation when lying than when telling the truth). Thus, learning more about which brain regions are causally related to deception could have practical implications for deception detection research.

Currently, there are two main non-invasive neurostimulation techniques that can be used in humans: transcranial magnetic stimulation (TMS) and transcranial direct current stimulation (TDCS). These techniques will be discussed in turn, together with the handful of published studies that have used them to investigate deception processes.

TMS BACKGROUND

Transcranial magnetic stimulation temporarily alters neural activity in a target brain region by means of magnetic pulses delivered using one or more special coils held against the scalp overlaying the target region (Rossini, Rossini, & Ferreri, 2010). Different types of TMS paradigms in cognitive neuroscience are defined by technical details such as the parameters of the stimulation and the kind of coil used for stimulation, as well as by the timing of task administration relative to stimulation. Single-pulse TMS delivers one pulse at a specific time during processing, causing disruption of neural activity that can last up to 40–60 ms (Amassian et al., 1989; Brasil-Neto, McShane, Fuhr, Hallett, & Cohen, 1992), which can be useful to measure the timing of processes very precisely. One problem with single-pulse TMS is that often a single pulse is not sufficient to induce observable changes in complex behaviour, probably because information is represented and processed in a highly redundant manner in our brain. To get around this limitation, repetitive TMS (rTMS) delivers rapid trains of pulses (Rossini et al., 2010), producing stronger and more sustained disruption of neural processing (likely due to temporal summation). However, given that rTMS is delivered over a relatively extended period of time, its temporal resolution is lower than that of single-pulse TMS. Thus, because of their complementary strength, single pulse and rTMS can be used in conjunction: rTMS can determine if a region is necessary for a certain task and, if so, subsequent single-pulse TMS studies can determine the time course of engagement of this region in the task. rTMS also comes in different forms, depending on the temporal pattern of pulse delivery. During low-frequency TMS, there is at least 1 s between successive pulses (Siebner et al., 1999), whereas during high-frequency TMS more than one pulse per second is delivered. Hybrid methods deliver short trains of pulses (e.g. repeating clusters of three pulses spaced 25 ms apart), so as to retain some of the advantages of both single-pulse and repetitive protocols (e.g. Schuhmann, Schiller, Goebel, & Sack, 2009).

TMS can be delivered during or before task performance. The potential problem with paradigms that deliver TMS during task performance is that TMS can be rather distracting for participants as the coil generates loud clicks and the stimulation produces a tapping sensation on the scalp overlaying the stimulated area. Furthermore, stimulation of muscles overlaying brain regions of interest (e.g. ventral parts of the prefrontal cortex) can produce unpleasant muscle twitches. To get around these problems, the effect of magnetic stimulation can be assessed on a task immediately, or soon after TMS delivery. These 'off-line' designs are only possible with TMS protocols that produce changes lasting several seconds after stimulation. For example, 1 Hz TMS stimulation (a form of low-frequency repetitive TMS) is thought to produce a decrease in the excitability of local networks, making it harder for neurons to fire for several minutes after stimulation (e.g. Boroojerdi, Prager, Muellbacher, & Cohen, 2000), and the rule of thumb is that the effect will last about half the duration period of the stimulation (Robertson, Theoret, & Pascual-Leone, 2003). Another example, is the recently developed TMS repetitive stimulation protocol, theta-burst stimulation (TBS), which involves the continuous delivery of triplets of pulses at 50 Hz with 200 ms between the pulse triplets (Huang, Edwards, Rounis, Bhatia, & Rothwell, 2005). One advantage of this protocol is that with very short applications times (e.g. 40 seconds), one can achieve inhibitory effects that last up to 30 minutes (Zafar, Paulus, & Sommer, 2008), leaving ample time to carry out experimental tasks.

There is also a more indirect way of using TMS in which magnetic pulses are employed to probe the state of the cortex, rather than to disrupt cortical neural activity (Sparing et al., 2002). For instance, using this method researchers can probe the excitability of the motor cortex (hand area) in the left or right hemisphere by delivering a TMS pulse and by determining the motor threshold, that is, the minimum stimulation strength (relative to maximum TMS stimulator output) required to elicit motor-evoked potentials (MEPs) measured from the corresponding hand 50% of the time. The effect of deception on motor cortex excitability can then be assessed by measuring changes in motor threshold. This method provides cortical excitability information that cannot be obtained easily from neuroimaging data and is functionally more related to the task at hand than neuroimaging data. The limitation of this method is that it can only be used to monitor the excitability of very few areas, including the motor cortex by measuring motor thresholds, and the early visual cortex by measuring phosphene thresholds (Sparing et al., 2002).

TMS FINDINGS

Only two TMS studies have tried to modulate deception performance (Karton & Bachmann, 2011; Verschuere, Schuhmann, & Sack, 2012), and no study to date has addressed the issue of whether the technique has any potential for reliably disrupting deception in single participants, which would be critical for any applications. Two additional studies used single-pulse TMS to probe motor cortex excitability during deception (Duzel et al., 2003; Kelly et al., 2009).

The first study used 1 Hz TMS to determine if it was possible to alter the proportion of honest or deceptive responses participants made when allowed to choose freely whether to lie or tell the truth about reporting the colour of a disk displayed on a computer monitor (Karton & Bachmann, 2011). Dorsolateral prefrontal cortex (DLPFC, BA 9) was stimulated on the left in one group of participants and on the right in a different group ($N=8$ in each group), just before performing the task. Furthermore, in each group, a parietal control region (BA 7) in the same hemisphere was also stimulated in a separate session. Results showed a small tendency for the left prefrontal cortex stimulation to decrease the probability that a participant would choose to lie, and for the right prefrontal cortex stimulation to increase such probability (relative to stimulation of the corresponding parietal control region in the same hemisphere). At face value, these results are partially consistent with the meta-analytic finding that anterior parts of BA 9 in the right hemisphere (but not the left) tend to be more engaged during deceptive than honest responses (Christ, Van Essen, Watson, Brubaker, & McDermott, 2009). Following this line of reasoning, 1 Hz stimulation of this region in the right hemisphere may reduce people's tendency to lie because it would make lying more effortful. However, stimulation of the left hemisphere should have no effect, rather than the opposite effect, as found here. More problematic for this interpretation of the data is that the largest difference among deception rates was not found between DLPFC stimulation in the two hemispheres, but rather between the control parietal regions in the left and right hemispheres. In fact, the deception rates resulting from stimulation of left and right DLPFC were virtually identical. This is especially puzzling because area BA 7 is typically not found in studies that compare deceptive and honest responses (Christ et al., 2009). The lack of one or more sham TMS conditions makes it even more difficult to interpret these results. Furthermore, methodological issues such as that the age of the participants in the left and right stimulation groups was quite different (23.75 vs. 30.75 years), may potentially account for the small differences found between conditions.

The second TMS study (Verschuere et al., 2012) used cTBS to stimulate the posterior portions of the right IFG (part of BA 44) during an adapted version of the Sheffield lie test, a differentiation of deception task in which people are asked to lie or tell the truth about factual statements about their daily activities (Spence et al., 2001). The cue telling participants ($N = 26$) whether to lie or to tell the truth was the colour of the response labels on the screen (these colours alternated between yellow and blue every six trials). In addition to real TMS, there was also a sham TMS condition during which everything was the same, but TMS was carried out with a sham coil that delivered no stimulation to the cortex. Results showed the typical pattern of behaviour in which performance was worse for deceptive than honest responses, but this effect was not modulated by rTMS. The main conclusion that can be drawn from this study is that the stimulated part of right BA 44 is not necessary for generating deceptive relative to honest responses in the task employed. However, on the one hand, this is not that surprising, because brain-imaging studies using the Sheffield test do not reliably report differential activation in this region for deceptive and honest responses (Spence et al., 2001). Specifically, the original neuroimaging study using the Sheffield lie test only found differential activation between deceptive and honest responses in ventrolateral prefrontal cortex bilaterally (BA 47) and in medial prefrontal cortex (BA 6). On the other hand, this study does not show that right BA 44 is not typically involved in deception because it is entirely possible that other areas, perhaps BA 44 in the left hemisphere, could be compensating for the temporary loss of function in right BA 44. In other words, null effects with single-site TMS are always ambiguous because of potential redundancy in the way the brain carries out its operations. This particular issue could be partially addressed by stimulating the same region in both hemispheres, so that one could at least show that the lack of a TMS effect on a task is not due to processes taking place in the contralateral region.

Finally, two studies employed single-pulse TMS to probe the excitability of primary motor cortex during deceptive behaviour (Kelly et al., 2009; Lo, Fook-Chong, & Tan, 2003) since a number of neuroimaging studies have reported stronger motor cortex activation (especially in the left hemisphere) to deceptive than honest responses (Ganis, Kosslyn, Stose, Thompson, & Yurgelun-Todd, 2003; Kozel et al., 2005; Langleben et al., 2002; Spence et al., 2001, 2004). In the first study (Lo et al., 2003), MEPs were recorded from the participants' left or right thumb in response to single TMS pulses delivered to the contralateral primary motor cortex (in different blocks). Simple and complex questions (a mix of neutral autobiographical and non-autobiographical questions) were presented, requiring a yes/no or a one-word free response, respectively. Participants had to respond honestly or deceptively to each question, in different blocks. The amplitude of the MEPs to a TMS pulse delivered immediately after each question was compared to that elicited by a TMS pulse delivered just before each question. Results showed an increase in excitability (larger MEPs) after stimulation of both left and right primary motor cortex in the deceptive conditions, suggesting that primary motor cortex is functionally involved in generating deceptive responses. A similar study focused on the laterality of primary motor cortex involvement and used emotionally stronger materials by asking people to tell the truth or lie about whether they liked items belonging to their favourite (vs. least favourite) sports team (Kelly et al., 2009). Results showed higher excitability for deceptive than honest responses in left motor cortex but a trend in the opposite direction in right motor cortex. One way of interpreting these results is that the motor cortex may be more excitable during deception because of the combined effect of motor representations engaged by potential deceptive and pre-potent honest responses.

TDCS BACKGROUND

Transcranial direct current stimulation (TDCS) is a non-invasive and inexpensive technique that delivers a weak, constant current to a target site on the head with an electrode (e.g. left DLPFC), affecting the underlying brain tissue. Effects of TDCS on numerous cognitive tasks have been documented in humans (Jacobson, Koslowsky, & Lavidor, 2012) and, although the mechanisms are not well-understood, TDCS is believed to produce excitability shifts by means of subthreshold neuronal membrane depolarization (Nitsche & Paulus, 2000; Nitsche et al., 2003; Priori, 2003). Anodal TDCS (+electrode over the stimulation site) is generally thought to increase cortical excitability, whereas cathodal TDCS (–electrode over the stimulation site) is thought to decrease it (Nitsche & Paulus, 2000; Nitsche et al., 2003; Priori, 2003). However, the results of a recent meta-analysis suggest that this pattern may only hold for simple motor processes that rely heavily on primary motor cortex (Jacobson et al., 2012). For more complex cognitive processes supported by networks of brain regions, cathodal stimulation does not usually lead to inhibition (as measured by decreased task performance), possibly because of compensatory processes (Jacobson et al., 2012). As for TMS, several parameters can be manipulated during a TDCS session, including the location of the reference electrode, the area of the electrode, and current intensity and duration: the reference electrode can be placed either on another part of the head (postulated to be not important for the task at hand), or on another part of the body; electrodes can vary in area, from few square centimeters to several tens of square centimeters; current intensity can vary as well, but usually is on the order of 1 mA, and stimulation duration can vary from less than a minute to tens of minutes (Jacobson et al., 2012).

Among the main differences between TDCS and TMS are (a) TDCS is less focal than TMS because of the complex electrical properties of the biological structures between the stimulating electrodes and the cortex, (b) TDCS is typically easier to administer than TMS, since the equipment required is less expensive and more portable, and (c) TDCS is methodologically superior to TMS for cognitive studies in some ways, because it is easier to deliver true sham stimulation without the knowledge of the participants, reducing potential placebo effects.

TDCS FINDINGS

To date, there have been only three TDCS studies of deception. The first study using this technique investigated the effects of bilateral DLPFC stimulation (1.5 mA for 10 minutes over sites F3 and F4, according to the 10–20 EEG international system, with reference electrode over the right deltoid muscle) on deception (Priori et al., 2008). Before (baseline) and after stimulation, participants ($N = 15$) lied or told the truth about which of 5 cards they had selected from a set of 10. Two types of lies were examined: lies about something that really took place (denying possession of a selected card) and lies about something that did not take place (falsely declaring possession of an unselected card). In addition to cathodal and anodal stimulation, a sham condition was also included during which TDCS stimulation was switched off after 10 seconds. The key result of this study was that anodal stimulation, relative to baseline, slowed down RTs for lies about selected cards, but not for lies about unselected cards, providing evidence that generating these two types of lies engages DLPFC differentially.

Another study by the same group (Mameli et al., 2010) also stimulated prefrontal F3 and F4 regions (2 mA for 15 minutes) using anodal and sham TDCS to investigate the effects on generating lies about personal information (e.g. 'Are you in Milan') versus general knowledge (e.g. 'Is an apple a fruit?'). Furthermore, a visual attention task (Posner, 1980) was also tested to determine whether any effects were due to disruption of visual attention processes. As in the previous study, all tasks were conducted before (baseline) and after TDCS. The main result of this study was that anodal TDCS reduced RTs for lies about general knowledge (relative to sham), but it did not affect lies about personal information. There were no effects of TDCS on the attentional task, indicating that the results on the deception task were not due to general disruption of the kind of attentional processes engaged by the control task. There is an obvious discrepancy between the results in this study and those in the previous study in that the effect of TDCS to the same brain regions was in opposite directions, making any generalizations difficult to draw. Given that both studies were aimed at studying the final stages of deception production, those that involve response inhibition of honest responses, it is puzzling that opposite effects were found in the two studies since both paradigms should involve such inhibitory processes (in both cases the RTs were slower for deceptive than honest responses during the baseline period). Two possible explanations for this discrepancy are (a) methodological differences, since TDCS intensity was 33% higher in the second than the first study (2 vs. 1.5 mA) and TDCS duration was 50% longer (15 vs. 10 minutes); this could have affected the set of regions stimulated by TDCS and, given that many cognitive functions engage overlapping parts of the prefrontal cortex (Poldrack, 2011), slight changes in stimulation parameters may have strong effects on behaviour. (b) One or both results are false positives, a possibility that can only be evaluated by replication of the results using the same paradigm and parameters, as discussed later.

A third TDCS study investigated the effect of stimulation of right anterior prefrontal cortex on deception (Karim et al., 2010). In the first experiment, cathodal TDCS was delivered to the right anterior prefrontal cortex (1 mA over right frontal site FP2, with reference electrode over left occipitoparietal cortex at PO3), while participants ($N = 22$) lied or told the truth regarding information about items they had acquired during a mock crime scenario. Unlike the other two studies, participants could choose whether to lie or tell the truth on each trial. The main results of this experiment were that RTs for lies were faster during cathodal than sham TDCS and that participants felt slightly less guilty about lying during cathodal than sham TDCS. The second experiment was identical to the first one, but the polarity of the stimulating electrodes was reversed so that anodal stimulation now was delivered to the anterior prefrontal cortex. Results showed no effect of TDCS on RTs or on feeling of guilt in this experiment. Finally, the third experiment tested the effect of cathodal TDCS on a Stroop task to determine whether the effects in the deception task were due to general modulation of prefrontal function. Results showed no effect of TDCS on the Stroop task. Overall, these results are at odds with the inconsistent findings about cathodal TDCS in cognitive studies (Jacobson et al., 2012): if anything, one would expect to observe effects of anodal TDCS on the task. Given that the reference electrode was placed on the head as well, one has to wonder whether any of the effects were caused by stimulation at that site instead. The authors interpret the faster RTs in the cathodal TDCS condition as a result of an impairment in moral cognitive processes and corresponding moral conflict, reflected in the lower guilt feelings. Unfortunately, this explanation is not entirely convincing for two reasons. First, it is unlikely that people really felt guilty about what happened during the mock crime scenario because they were simply following instructions in an experimental setting. Second, the difference in ratings of feeling of guilt were only marginally significant in the cathodal TDCS condition ($z = -1.986$, $p = 0.047$) and no direct comparisons were provided with the anodal TDCS condition. Regardless of the specific interpretation, the main conclusion of the study is that combined stimulation of the right anterior prefrontal and left occipitoparietal cortex seems to slightly affect deceptive responses in a non-generic way.

FUTURE DIRECTIONS

It should be evident from this short review of the sparse literature on the topic that the results are not very consistent: some studies find no effects of prefrontal stimulation on deception tasks, others find that performance increases, and yet others find that performance decreases.

The main conclusion from all these studies is rather weak and generic: some parts of the prefrontal cortex may be causally involved in producing deceptive responses. This section discusses some of the variables that probably contribute to this variability in the results, and provides some methodological guidelines that may be useful to move the field forward.

First, it is difficult to separate the signal from the noise in the existing data: some results are barely significant and they are in apparent contradiction with results from other laboratories. The lack of standardization of stimulation parameters makes it impossible to compare studies across laboratories, suggesting that the first step may need to be taken at the level of individual laboratories. Since most studies on the topic are conducted with normal participants, using a relatively inexpensive technique (unlike, for instance, fMRI) it should be required that individual laboratories replicate their results before publishing, especially when the effects are barely significant or when they are unexpected. This should provide a first important step towards determining which effects are real and worth pursuing further and which are false positives.

Second, to understand the role of the stimulated areas, suitable control tasks should always be administered, possibly in the same participants. Control tasks were employed in a few of the studies described earlier (Kumar et al., 2001; Mameli et al., 2010), but they were not well-matched to the deception tasks. These control tasks should be as similar as possible to the deception tasks, in terms of stimuli and timing, but without a deception component. For example, if one wants to determine whether attentional processes are affected by the stimulation, then one should devise an attention task using the same kind of stimuli and responses used during the deception task, not a completely different task. Note that this logic is not foolproof because many neuroimaging studies have shown that commonly activated regions during two tasks can nonetheless show distinct spatial patterns of activity for different conditions (Tong & Pratte, 2012). For example, stimulation of a cortical patch showing effects of both deception and working memory does not necessarily imply that deception and working memory recruit this piece of cortex in exactly the same manner. Disruption of the same brain regions may lead to performance impairment in two tasks even though these tasks are supported by different neural populations, for example if the two types of neural populations are interdigitated. Thus, inferences about specific processes may be harder to make than it may appear at first sight, and only convergent evidence can provide conclusive answers.

Third, studies should stimulate multiple brain regions simultaneously in order to increase the size of the effects and to be able to better interpret null effects. This is easier with TDCS (Mameli et al., 2010; Priori et al., 2008) than with TMS, mostly due to equipment cost and logistics. Disrupting neural activation in a single area may produce a null result on task performance not necessarily because this area is usually not engaged by the cognitive task of interest, but simply because the task is carried out by a network of regions that can compensate for a single malfunctioning node. Bilateral stimulation can at least show that the null result is not due to compensation by the contralateral cortical region.

Fourth, computer simulations of the pattern of current distribution should be conducted for the electrode configuration employed, especially for TDCS (Faria, Hallett, & Miranda, 2011; Im, Jung, Choi, Lee, & Jung, 2008; Oostendorp et al., 2008; Sadleir, Vannorsdall, Schretlen, & Gordon, 2010; Wagner et al., 2007), since currents can spread well beyond the stimulating electrodes (Kar & Krekelberg, 2012) and the overall pattern is very sensitive to electrode geometry.

Fifth, ideally, all studies should adopt a double-blind logic to avoid placebo and experimenter effects: if a subject knows the condition she is in (real vs. sham stimulation), then the effects could be due to expectation phenomena, rather than to the stimulation itself. Unfortunately, double-blind studies are nearly impossible to carry out with TMS, despite the use of specialized coils, and they are very difficult with TDCS as well. At minimum, all studies should ask participants whether they thought they were in the experimental or sham condition at the end of the study to determine whether expectation could have been a factor. One way to partially address this issue is to actually manipulate subject expectations by playing with the instructions. So, in one condition (or group) subjects may be told that stimulation typically produces an improvement in performance, whereas in another condition subjects may be told the opposite.

Sixth, given that deception is a complex cognitive phenomenon and is supported by a network of interacting brain areas, it makes sense to assume that neural oscillations reflecting such interactions play a key role, and that interfering with these oscillations may be a powerful way to affect deception processes. To explore this possibility, there should be studies using transcranial alternating current stimulation (TACS) or transcranial random noise stimulation (TRNS), since they are thought to interfere with brain oscillations (Kuo & Nitsche, 2012; Paulus, 2011). For instance, since there is evidence that alpha power decreases during deceptive, relative to honest responses (Seth, Iversen, & Edelman, 2006), it would be interesting to determine whether deception performance may be affected by interfering with oscillations in that alpha range (Schutter & Hortensius, 2011; Zaehle, Rach, & Herrmann, 2010).

Seventh, with regard to the specific issue of using brain stimulation to detect deception in single individuals, future papers should report accuracy rates, when appropriate. For instance, if TDCS slows down RTs for deceptive but not honest responses (Priori et al., 2008), it would be important to document whether this effect can be used to enhance deception detection in single individuals.

A NOTE ON ETHICS

Over the last decade, there has been growing discussion about neuro-ethics (Farah, 2002, 2009), that is, about the implications of using neuroscientific knowledge for practical applications such as detecting deception. There are ethical issues specifically associated with brain stimulation techniques. Such ethical issues are different, and probably more serious, than those posed by using neuroimaging to detect deception (Greely & Illes, 2007; Stoller & Wolpe, 2007), as they are more directly related to the key bioethical principle of individual autonomy (Abe et al., 2009). Indeed, brain stimulation methods do not just monitor neural activity, but they may be able to alter temporarily cognitive, affective, and social processes, including those related to self-perception and intention generation. For example, as discussed earlier, participants in the study by Karim and collaborators (2010) claimed they felt slightly less guilty about lying during cathodal TDCS than sham stimulation. In other words, if we take these results at face value, the prefrontal stimulation may have temporarily increased the tendency of participants towards a behaviour that normally participants would not engage in. Stronger forms of brain stimulation (e.g. some of the rTMS methods discussed earlier) could produce more pronounced effects. Although, to there has been no evidence that these methods can have applications for deception detection, it is clear that any potential use of these methods in the field needs to be closely monitored.

FINAL CONSIDERATIONS AND CONCLUSIONS

Despite the widespread use of brain stimulation methods over the last decade, there have been fewer than 10 published studies on deception. This is surprising because over 30 studies on deception have been carried out using much more expensive and laborious neuroimaging methods during the same period. The reasons for this dearth of studies is unknown, but one possibility is that many researchers may actually have tried using these techniques to study deception but failed to find any significant effects and so they did not report the results (Rosenthal, 1979). The weak and inconsistent results in the literature support this hypothesis, as they suggest that the effects are very small, at least with the methods and paradigms used so far.

Although these observations indicate that investigating deception processes using brain stimulation methods is quite complex, they should not be taken as evidence that such investigation is not possible in principle because the field is still young and only the surface has been scratched. We have discussed a few ideas that may help move the field forward, from the need of within-laboratory replication of findings to better standardization of methods, from the need of biophysical modelling of current distribution in the brain to the need of examining complementary aspects of brain function such as oscillatory phenomena.

REFERENCES

Abe, N., Fujii, T., Hirayama, K., Takeda, A., Hosokai, Y., Ishioka, T., ... Mori, E. (2009). Do Parkinsonian patients have trouble telling lies? The neurobiological basis of deceptive behaviour. *Brain, 132*(Pt 5), 1386–1395.

Amassian, V. E., Cracco, R. Q., Maccabee, P. J., Cracco, J. B., Rudell, A., & Eberle, L. (1989). Suppression of visual perception by magnetic coil stimulation of human occipital cortex. *Electroencephalography and Clinical Neurophysiology, 74*(6), 458–462.

Boroojerdi, B., Prager, A., Muellbacher, W., & Cohen, L. G. (2000). Reduction of human visual cortex excitability using 1-Hz transcranial magnetic stimulation. *Neurology, 54*(7), 1529–1531.

Brasil-Neto, J. P., McShane, L. M., Fuhr, P., Hallett, M., & Cohen, L. G. (1992). Topographic mapping of the human motor cortex with magnetic stimulation: Factors affecting accuracy and reproducibility. *Electroencephalography and Clinical Neurophysiology, 85*(1), 9–16.

Christ, S. E., Van Essen, D. C., Watson, J. M., Brubaker, L. E., & McDermott, K. B. (2009). The contributions of prefrontal cortex and executive control to deception: Evidence from activation likelihood estimate meta-analyses. *Cerebral Cortex, 19*(7), 1557–1566.

Duzel, E., Habib, R., Schott, B., Schoenfeld, A., Lobaugh, N., McIntosh, A. R., ... Heinze, H. J. (2003). A multivariate, spatiotemporal analysis of electromagnetic time-frequency data of recognition memory. *Neuroimage, 18*(2), 185–197.

Farah, M. J. (2002). Emerging ethical issues in neuroscience. *Nature Neuroscience, 5*(11), 1123–1129.

Farah, M. J. (2009). Neuroethics. *Annual Review of Psychology, 63,* 571–591.

Faria, P., Hallett, M., & Miranda, P. C. (2011). A finite element analysis of the effect of electrode area and inter-electrode distance on the spatial distribution of the current density in tDCS. *Journal of Neural Engineering, 8*(6), 066017.

Ganis, G., Kosslyn, S. M., Stose, S., Thompson, W. L., & Yurgelun-Todd, D. A. (2003). Neural correlates of different types of deception: An fMRI investigation. *Cerebral Cortex, 13*(8), 830–836.

Greely, H. T., & Illes, J. (2007). Neuroscience-based lie detection: The urgent need for regulation. *American Journal of Law & Medicine, 33*(2–3), 377–431.

Huang, Y. Z., Edwards, M. J., Rounis, E., Bhatia, K. P., & Rothwell, J. C. (2005). Theta burst stimulation of the human motor cortex. *Neuron, 45*(2), 201–206.

Im, C. H., Jung, H. H., Choi, J. D., Lee, S. Y., & Jung, K. Y. (2008). Determination of optimal electrode positions for transcranial direct current stimulation (tDCS). *Physics in Medicine and Biology, 53*(11), N219–N225.

Jacobson, L., Koslowsky, M., & Lavidor, M. (2012). tDCS polarity effects in motor and cognitive domains: A meta-analytical review. *Experimental Brain Research, 216*(1), 1–10.

Kar, K., & Krekelberg, B. (2012). Transcranial electrical stimulation over visual cortex evokes phosphenes with a retinal origin. *Journal of Neurophysiology, 108*(8), 2173–2178.

Karim, A. A., Schneider, M., Lotze, M., Veit, R., Sauseng, P., Braun, C., & Birbaumer, N. (2010). The truth about lying: Inhibition of the anterior prefrontal cortex improves deceptive behavior. *Cerebral Cortex, 20*(1), 205–213.

Karton, I., & Bachmann, T. (2011). Effect of prefrontal transcranial magnetic stimulation on spontaneous truth-telling. *Behavioural Brain Research, 225*(1), 209–214.

Kelly, K. J., Murray, E., Barrios, V., Gorman, J., Ganis, G., & Keenan, J. P. (2009). The effect of deception on motor cortex excitability. *Social Neuroscience, 4*(6), 570–574.

Kozel, F. A., Johnson, K. A., Mu, Q., Grenesko, E. L., Laken, S. J., & George, M. S. (2005). Detecting deception using functional magnetic resonance imaging. *Biological Psychiatry, 58*(8), 605–613.

Kumar, A. M., Fa, K., Vankawala, R., Vora, M., Kode, R. K., Pankewycz, O. G., ... Kumar, M. S. (2001). Simulect, calcineurin inhibitor, mycophenolate mofetil, and prednisone is more effective than OKT3, calcineurin inhibitor, hycophendate mofetil, and prednisone in African American kidney recipients in reducing acute rejections and prolonging graft survival. *Transplantation Proceedings, 33*(7–8), 3195–3196.

Kuo, M. F., & Nitsche, M. A. (2012). Effects of transcranial electrical stimulation on cognition. *Clinical EEG and Neuroscience, 43*(3), 192–199.

Langleben, D. D., Schroeder, L., Maldjian, J. A., Gur, R. C., McDonald, S., Ragland, J. D., ... Childress, A. R. (2002). Brain activity during simulated deception: An event-related functional magnetic resonance study. *Neuroimage, 15*(3), 727–732.

Lo, Y. L., Fook-Chong, S., & Tan, E. K. (2003). Increased cortical excitability in human deception. *Neuroreport, 14*(7), 1021–1024.

Mameli, F., Mrakic-Sposta, S., Vergari, M., Fumagalli, M., Macis, M., Ferrucci, R., ... Priori, A. (2010). Dorsolateral prefrontal cortex specifically processes general – But not personal – Knowledge deception: Multiple brain networks for lying. *Behavioural Brain Research, 211*(2), 164–168.

Nitsche, M. A., Fricke, K., Henschke, U., Schlitterlau, A., Liebetanz, D., Lang, N., ... Paulus, W. (2003). Pharmacological modulation of cortical excitability shifts induced by transcranial direct current stimulation in humans. *The Journal of Physiology, 553*(Pt 1), 293–301.

Nitsche, M. A., & Paulus, W. (2000). Excitability changes induced in the human motor cortex by weak transcranial direct current stimulation. *The Journal of Physiology, 527*(Pt 3), 633–639.

Oostendorp, T. F., Hengeveld, Y. A., Wolters, C. H., Stinstra, J., van Elswijk, G., & Stegeman, D. F. (2008). Modeling transcranial DC stimulation. *Conference proceedings : ... Annual International Conference of the IEEE Engineering in Medicine and Biology Society*. IEEE Engineering in Medicine and Biology Society, (pp. 4226–4229). Vancouver, British Columbia, Canada, August 20–24, 2008. doi: 10.1109/IEMBS.2008.4650142.

Paulus, W. (2011). Transcranial electrical stimulation (tES - tDCS; tRNS, tACS) methods. *Neuropsychological Rehabilitation, 21*(5), 602–617.

Poldrack, R. A. (2011). Inferring mental states from neuroimaging data: From reverse inference to large-scale decoding. *Neuron, 72*(5), 692–697.

Posner, M. I. (1980). Orienting of attention. *Quarterly Journal of Experimental Psychology, 32*(1), 3–25.

Priori, A. (2003). Brain polarization in humans: A reappraisal of an old tool for prolonged non-invasive modulation of brain excitability. *Clinical Neurophysiology, 114*(4), 589–595.

Priori, A., Mameli, F., Cogiamanian, F., Marceglia, S., Tiriticco, M., Mrakic-Sposta, S., ... Sartori, G. (2008). Lie-specific involvement of dorsolateral prefrontal cortex in deception. *Cerebral Cortex, 18*(2), 451–455.

Robertson, E. M., Theoret, H., & Pascual-Leone, A. (2003). Studies in cognition: The problems solved and created by transcranial magnetic stimulation. *Journal Cognirioc Neuroscience, 15*(7), 948–960.

Rosenthal, R. (1979). The file drawer problem and tolerance for null results. *Psychological Bulletin, 86*(3), 638–641.

Rossini, P. M., Rossini, L., & Ferreri, F. (2010). Brain-behavior relations: Transcranial magnetic stimulation: A review. *IEEE Engineering in Medicine and Biology Magazine, 29*(1), 84–95.

Sadleir, R. J., Vannorsdall, T. D., Schretlen, D. J., & Gordon, B. (2010). Transcranial direct current stimulation (tDCS) in a realistic head model. *Neuroimage, 51*(4), 1310–1318.

Schuhmann, T., Schiller, N. O., Goebel, R., & Sack, A. T. (2009). The temporal characteristics of functional activation in Broca's area during overt picture naming. *Cortex, 45*(9), 1111–1116.

Schutter, D. J., & Hortensius, R. (2011). Brain oscillations and frequency-dependent modulation of cortical excitability. *Brain Stimulation, 4*(2), 97–103.

Seth, A. K., Iversen, J. R., & Edelman, G. M. (2006). Single-trial discrimination of truthful from deceptive responses during a game of financial risk using alpha-band MEG signals. *Neuroimage, 32*(1), 465–476.

Sidtis, J. J. (2007). Some problems for representations of brain organization based on activation in functional imaging. *Brain and Language, 102*(2), 130–140.

Siebner, H. R., Tormos, J. M., Ceballos-Baumann, A. O., Auer, C., Catala, M. D., Conrad, B., & Pascual-Leone, A. (1999). Low-frequency repetitive transcranial magnetic stimulation of the motor cortex in writer's cramp. *Neurology, 52*(3), 529–537.

Sparing, R., Mottaghy, F. M., Ganis, G., Thompson, W. L., Topper, R., Kosslyn, S. M., & Pascual-Leone, A. (2002). Visual cortex excitability increases during visual mental imagery – A TMS study in healthy human subjects. *Brain Research, 938*(1–2), 92–97.

Spence, S. A., Farrow, T. F., Herford, A. E., Wilkinson, I. D., Zheng, Y., & Woodruff, P. W. (2001). Behavioural and functional anatomical correlates of deception in humans. *Neuroreport, 12*(13), 2849–2853.

Spence, S. A., Hunter, M. D., Farrow, T. F., Green, R. D., Leung, D. H., Hughes, C. J., & Ganesan, V. (2004). A cognitive neurobiological account of deception: Evidence from functional neuroimaging. *Philosophical Transactions of the Royal Society B: Biological Sciences, 359*(1451), 1755–1762.

Stoller, S. E., & Wolpe, P. R. (2007). Emerging neurotechnologies for lie detection and the fifth amendment. *American Journal of Law & Medicine, 33*(2–3), 359–375.

Tong, F., & Pratte, M. S. (2012). Decoding patterns of human brain activity. *Annual Review of Psychology, 63*, 483–509.

Verschuere, B., Schuhmann, T., & Sack, A. T. (2012). Does the inferior frontal sulcus play a functional role in deception? A neuronavigated theta-burst transcranial magnetic stimulation study. *Frontiers in Human Neuroscience, 6*, 284.

Wagner, T., Fregni, F., Fecteau, S., Grodzinsky, A., Zahn, M., & Pascual-Leone, A. (2007). Transcranial direct current stimulation: A computer-based human model study. *Neuroimage, 35*(3), 1113–1124.

Zaehle, T., Rach, S., & Herrmann, C. S. (2010). Transcranial alternating current stimulation enhances individual alpha activity in human EEG. *PLoS One, 5*(11), e13766.

Zafar, N., Paulus, W., & Sommer, M. (2008). Comparative assessment of best conventional with best theta burst repetitive transcranial magnetic stimulation protocols on human motor cortex excitability. *Clinical Neurophysiology, 119*(6), 1393–1399.

12

Detecting Deception Through Reaction Times

BRUNO VERSCHUERE, KRISTINA SUCHOTZKI AND EVELYNE DEBEY

INTRODUCTION

Reaction times (RTs) are amongst the most extensively studied behavioural measures in psychology. RTs are often used to reveal processes people may not consciously be aware of, or that may be biased when asked to subjectively report upon (De Houwer, Teige-Mocigemba, Spruyt, & Moors, 2009). The use of RTs is popular in social psychology to objectively assess people's attitudes about socially sensitive issues. In clinical psychology, RTs are used to assess how biased information processing may contribute to the aetiology and maintenance of mental disorders. Cognitive psychologists use RT to map the time needed to execute specific cognitive operations. Common across these disciplines is the use of RTs to gain insight into processes people are not willing or able to report upon. For the very same reasons, RTs may provide clues for deception. This possibility has intrigued researchers for a long time (Henke & Eddy, 1909; Jung, 1910; Marston, 1927). In the following section, we consider the conditions under which RTs may provide reliable cues for deception.

Detecting Deception: Current Challenges and Cognitive Approaches, First Edition.
Edited by Pär Anders Granhag, Aldert Vrij, and Bruno Verschuere.
© 2015 John Wiley & Sons, Ltd. Published 2015 by John Wiley & Sons, Ltd.

Conditions Under which RTS May Provide a Reliable Cue for Deception

With RT one usually refers to the time interval between the onset of a stimulus and a given response. In the context of deception detection: How much time does one need to start answering a question? This time interval will not only be influenced by the veracity of the answer, but also by many other factors. An analogue example may help to illustrate these other factors. Imagine you want to know how much time it takes to brake. In order to answer this question, one may invite participants to a drive simulator, and record the time in between the appearance of certain cues (e.g. a child crossing the street) and the hitting of the brakes. We will use this example to illustrate the necessary conditions for reliable RT measurement, and how these conditions apply to deception detection.

Clearly, the *measurement* needs to be *precise*. Human observers could be asked to estimate the time between the appearance of the object and the actual braking, but this estimate is unlikely to be very accurate. The use of a stopwatch could improve precision, yet a computerized estimate based upon synchronization of the visual input and the braking will have highest precision. Whereas stopwatches were used in initial work on deception (e.g. Marston, 1927), computerized measurement is now most common.

Furthermore, it is important to instruct participants to *respond as fast as possible* after the appearance of the stimulus. Such instruction allows the investigator to get an estimate of the minimum time people need to brake. Likewise, this instruction is required to estimate how much time people minimally need to initiate a truthful or deceptive response. Absent the instruction to respond as fast as possible, RT may not provide a meaningful cue for deception. Studies with a main focus on physiological activity do not always instruct their participants to respond immediately after stimulus appearance. For example, the polygraph study by Ambach, Dummel, Luer, and Vaitl (2011) required participants to answer the crime questions (e.g. 'Did you steal this cosmetic from the administration room?') after a delay of 4 seconds. Such delay allows ample time to process the stimuli, prepare the required response and strategically control task performance, diminishing the possibility to observe meaningful RT differences between lying and truth telling.

The reliable estimation of RTs requires averaging over *multiple observations*. Our example again clarifies this requirement. When lighting a cigarette, singing along with a radio tune or simple mind wandering, the RT of the driver may be atypically slow. Attention fluctuates over time, and RT will vary accordingly. Reliable RT measurement, therefore, requires averaging across a number of observations. There are no firm guidelines for the minimum number of measurements for RT, but as a rule of thumb, about 20 observations (in each condition) seems a minimum.[1] The validity of RT as a cue for deception has often been looked at in studies using an interrogation situation (Buller, Comstock, Aune, & Strzyzewski, 1989). Typically, the interview situation involves only a brief interaction between sender and receiver, with a very limited number of questions being asked. Given the limited number of observations, such interview designs are not suitable for the reliable estimation of reaction time differences between truthful and deceptive responses.

Multiple measurements also allow to *assess and exclude outliers*, observations that differ markedly from the remainder of the observations. In the drivers' example, one can easily see how sneezing or a cell phone tune can extensively delay responding. When most observations of braking time vary around 200ms, it becomes clear that a single braking time observation of over a second may blur the RT estimate, even when based upon multiple observations. Electrophysiological (e.g. Rosenfeld, Shue, & Singer, 2007) and neuroimaging (e.g. Ganis, Kosslyn, Stose, Thompson, & Yurgelun-Todd, 2003) studies of deception often neglected to trace and/or report outliers, thereby increasing unwanted variability in RTs and reducing the chance to observe reliable lie–truth differences in RTs.

In sum, precise computerized measurement, the instruction to react as fast as possible, multiple observations and tracing of outliers seem prerequisites for any meaningful RT measurement. The absence of these conditions in many deception studies, may explain why RTs failed to differentiate reliably between lying and truth telling in the meta-analysis by DePaulo et al. (2003). In the remainder of the chapter, we will argue that certain RT paradigms can reliably distinguish lie from truth, provided that the aforementioned four prerequisites are incorporated in the design.

RT-Based Paradigms for Deception Detection

Since the 1990s, several computerized tasks that meet the aforementioned minimum conditions for reliable RT measurement have been proposed for deception detection purposes. Most often, these paradigms originate from established RT paradigms in cognitive psychology that were modified in order to measure deception. Among those are the lexical decision task (Locker & Pratarelli, 1997), the Stroop task (Engelhard, Merckelbach, & van den Hout, 2003; Gronau, Ben-Shakhar, & Cohen, 2005), the dot probe task (Verschuere, Crombez, & Koster,

---

[1]The required number of items depends on the signal-to-noise ratio. Given the large effect sizes obtained in some deception paradigms, fewer than 20 observations may suffice. Psychometric work is needed to establish the minimum required number of items to obtain reliable lie–truth differences.

2004), the secondary RT task (Verschuere, Crombez, De Clercq, & Koster, 2004), the oddball task (Farwell & Donchin, 1991; Seymour, Seifert, Shafto, & Mosmann, 2000), and the Implicit Association Test (IAT) (Sartori, Agosta, Zogmaister, Ferrara, & Castiello, 2008). For most paradigms (dot probe, Stroop, secondary RT tasks, lexical decision), the research base is restricted to only a few studies. Moreover, analyses were mostly conducted at the group level only, and the observed differences in RT between lying and truth telling were very modest.

At present, there are two paradigms that have been tested in a series of studies, and seem to produce a more substantial RT difference between liars and truth tellers: The oddball task (Farwell & Donchin, 1991; Seymour et al., 2000), and the autobiographical Implicit Association Test (aIAT) (Sartori et al., 2008). The oddball task has been used for memory detection purposes (Lykken, 1959; Verschuere, Ben-Shakhar, & Meijer, 2011), and is therefore also known as the RT-based Concealed Information Test (RT-CIT).

The RT-CIT

The RT-CIT is a variant of the Concealed Information Test (CIT) that is used to assess recognition of critical information. The CIT presents the examinee with the critical information, embedded among appropriate control items, and examines whether the examinee reacts differently to the critical items. Thus, the CIT looks much like a multiple-choice test, with each question having one correct and several incorrect items. Say for instance, the examinee is suspected of stealing a white Mazda that was used in a bank robbery, and only the police and the culprits know about the car. In such a case, the examinee could be asked: What car was used in the robbery? Was it a … blue Chevrolet? … green Mercedes? … red Toyota? … grey Mustang? … white Mazda? An innocent suspect is expected to show similar responses to all items. A marked reaction to the critical item reveals knowledge of the critical crime details. The CIT is extensively tested during the last 60 years (for a review see Verschuere et al., 2011). The vast majority of these studies used physiological measures; originally autonomic nervous system measures, and later on also electrophysiological recordings and neuroimaging. As electrophysiological recordings require the presentation of hundreds of trials, researchers modified the Concealed Information Test polygraph protocol to assure participants were paying attention to the stimuli. Most importantly, they combined the CIT with the oddball task, and this paradigm is now also known as the RT-CIT.

Like the classic CIT, the RT-CIT (see Table 12.1) presents the examinee with critical details (called *probes*), embedded among a series

Table 12.1 Test structure of the RT-based Concealed Information Test (RT-CIT)

Stimuli	Stimulus type	Required response	Frequency	Expected response
Blue Chevrolet Green Mercedes Red Toyota White Mazda	Irrelevant	Press 'NO'	Frequent (4/6)	Fast and accurate
Yellow Peugeot	Target	Press 'YES'	Infrequent (1/6)	Slow and inaccurate
Grey Mustang	Probe	Press 'NO'	Infrequent (1/6)	Guilty: Slow and inaccurate Innocent: Fast and accurate

of equally plausible control items (called *irrelevants*). In order to assure attention to the stimuli, a third category of stimuli was introduced: *Targets*. The behavioural task is to press a unique (e.g. left) button as fast as possible for targets, and to press another (e.g. right) button for all other stimuli (probes and irrelevants). Targets (1/6) and probes (1/6) are rarely presented, whereas irrelevants are common (4/6), making the examinee to press the non-target button most of the time. Building on the aforementioned example, the examinee could be asked: 'In order to examine whether you recognize critical crime details, we will rapidly flash pictures of vehicles on the computer screen. The question is whether you recognize any of these vehicles. Your task is to press YES as fast as possible whenever you see a yellow Peugeot. For all other vehicles, you press the NO button as fast as possible'. The critical question is whether the NO response to the probes differs from that to the irrelevant items. Marked RT slowing to the probes reveals recognition of the critical information, see Figure 12.1.

With their main interest in central nervous activity, ERP researchers have not always statistically analysed (Rosenfeld et al., 2007) or even reported (e.g. Farwell & Smith, 2001; Rosenfeld et al., 1988) findings for RTs. Nonetheless, several ERP studies have reported that response latencies successfully reveal concealed information (Allen, Iacono, & Danielson, 1992; Allen & Movius, 2000; Farwell & Donchin, 1991; Gamer, Bauermann, Stoeter, & Vossel, 2007; Kubo & Nittono, 2009; Meijer, Smulders, Merckelbach, & Wolf, 2007; Rosenfeld, Soskins, Bosh, & Ryan, 2004; Rosenfeld et al., 2008; Verschuere, Rosenfeld, Winograd, Labkovsky, & Wiersema, 2009). In the study by Allen et al. (1992), for instance,

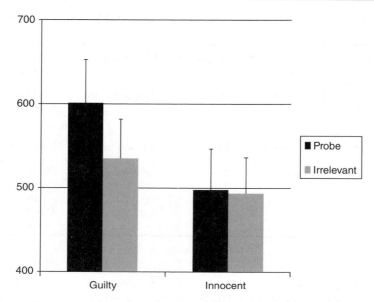

Figure 12.1 Expected response pattern in the RT-based Concealed Information Test (RT-CIT), as observed in Noordraven and Verschuere (2013).

participants were instructed to try to conceal recognition of a previously memorized list of words. RTs allowed detecting concealed information with near-perfect accuracy (sensitivity: 95–97.50%, specificity: 95–100%). These and other ERP studies point to the potential of the RT-CIT, yet may not necessarily generalize to an RT-CIT as a stand-alone test without concurrent ERP recordings. For instance, it is possible that participants may engage more effort in strategically controlling their behavioural responding when it becomes the prime measure of interest of the investigation. In three experiments, Seymour et al. (2000) examined whether the RT effects hold without the concurrent ERP measurement. Like Farwell and Donchin (1991), they had participants memorize a list of code words through a mock espionage, and embedded these probes among target and irrelevant items in an RT-CIT. The data from the three experiments confirmed the high validity of the RT-CIT as a stand-alone test. An important novel feature added by Seymour and colleagues is the inclusion of a response deadline to ensure fast responding (<1 second). Such response deadlines have been used in nearly all RT-CIT studies (i.e. Visu-Petra, Miclea, Bus, & Visu-Petra, 2014, being the only exception).

Table 12.2 summarizes accuracy rates of RT-CIT studies. We included all (a) published studies that (b) used the three-stimulus RT-CIT (c) as a stand-alone test, hence excluding studies that used additional

Table 12.2 Laboratory studies of the RT-based Concealed Information Test

Stimuli	Paradigm	Sensitivity (%)	Specificity (%)	Overall accuracy
Seymour et al. (2000), Experiment 1	Mock espionage	89	100	—
Seymour and Kerlin (2008)	Mock computer crime	88–91	96–97	ROC = 0.95–0.99
Seymour and Fraynt (2009)	Mock espionage	54–100	96.7	—
Verschuere, Crombez, et al. (2009)	Autobiographical	—	—	Cohen's d = 1.97
Visu-Petra et al. (2012)	Mock crime	—	—	Cohen's d = 1.92
				ROC = 0.92
Visu-Petra et al. (2014)	Mock crime	—	—	Cohen's d = 2.24
Noordraven and Verschuere (2013)	Planned mock crime	—	—	Cohen's d = 1.25
				ROC = 0.87
	Cutoff d = 0.2	81	85.7	
	Cutoff d = 0.5	47.6	100	
Hu et al. (2013) 'pure CIT'	Mock crime	—	—	ROC = 0.91
Visu-Petra et al. (2013)	Mock crime	64–68	—	ROC = 0.83–0.87
				Cohen's d = 1.39–1.71.

1. Some studies (e.g. Seymour et al., 2000) combined RTs with other behavioural indices (e.g. error rate or RT variability), but the results in this table reflect those based upon RT only.
2. Classification results for Experiments 2–3 of Seymour et al. (2000) were similar to those of Experiment 1, yet not reported upon in full. Therefore, we only report results for Experiment 1.
3. We only included RT-CIT studies that used the three-stimulus protocol; hence, the dot probe CIT in Hu et al. (2013) was not included in this table.

equipment for other measurements (e.g. fMRI, EEG/ERP, rTMS/tCDS). The table lists estimates for sensitivity (correctly detecting the presence of concealed information in knowledgeable individuals) and specificity (correctly assessing the absence of concealed information in unknowledgeable individuals). The final column provides an estimate of the overall accuracy of the RT-CIT. With the applied purpose of deception detection, several studies reported hit rates (in %). Hit rates have the downside of depending on an arbitrary cutoff, and other statistics are often provided instead. The Receiver Operating Characteristic or ROC curve provides an estimate of accuracy over all possible cutoff points. The area under the ROC curve varies from 0.50 (chance level) to 1 (perfect classification). Cohen's d provides an estimate of the effect size of the RT difference between probes and irrelevant items. The effect sizes can be considered as small, moderate or large from 0.2, 0.5 and 0.8 onward, respectively (Cohen, 1988). These data show that the false-positive rate can be kept at a very low level (0–4%), while still obtaining a reasonable sensitivity (54–100%) with the RT-CIT.

The studies reviewed thus far illustrate the capacity of the RT-CIT to reveal previously memorized words. This is a fairly specific situation that may have applied potential for instance in counterespionage. Further studies have demonstrated that the validity of the RT-CIT is not limited to this application. Seymour and Kerlin (2008) showed that the RT-CIT has similar high accuracy for previously memorized faces. This broadens the applicability of the RT-CIT, for instance to the identification of a crime accomplice. It also points to the possibility to assess recognition of pictorial scenes, for instance, of the crime scene itself or other objects that had a central position in a crime. Visu-Petra, Miclea, and Visu-Petra (2012) were the first to report the results of a classic mock crime procedure. Student participants were randomly allocated to either a guilty or an innocent group. Guilty participants committed exam fraud by stealing a CD with exam questions from a laptop bag, whereas innocent participants had no knowledge of the crime under investigation. During the RT-CIT, participants had to press the 'yes' button as fast as possible for a set of pictures they memorized just prior to the start of the test (i.e. the targets), and to press the 'no' button for all other pictures (including crime-related pictures such as a picture of the laptop bag that contained the CD). Unlike innocent participants, guilty participants reacted slower and erred more often to crime-related pictures, and the RT-CIT allowed to discriminate guilty from innocent participants with great accuracy (see also Hu, Evans, Wu, Lee, & Fu, 2013; Visu-Petra, Varga, Miclea, & Visu-Petra, 2013). Furthermore, the RT-CIT may help to reveal a suspect's true identity, as it is able to detect concealed autobiographical information.

Verschuere, Crombez, Degrootte, and Rosseel (2009) asked participants to feign complete amnesia and hide recognition of their autobiographical information (e.g. first name, last name, first name of the father, first name of the mother and birthday), promising a financial reward for being able to do so successfully. The autobiographical RT-CIT proved to have high validity, in fact as high as a CIT based upon autonomic nervous system measures.

In sum, the RT-CIT appears to be a promising test to assess recognition of concealed information. Its low false-positive rate – a feature common to the CIT procedure in general – is particularly attractive. Still, its applicability is restricted to situations where only the investigators and the guilty examinee are aware of the critical details. The aIAT has – at least in principle – a much broader applicability.

The Autobiographical Implicit Association Test (AIAT)

The IAT (Greenwald, McGhee, & Schwartz, 1998) was developed by social scientists as an indirect attitude measure. After all, when asking about socially sensitive information (e.g. one's opinion about homosexuality or ethnic minorities), self-report measures may be biased by social desirability. Rather than asking someone directly about the attitude in question, the IAT assesses the attitude indirectly. The IAT consists of a number of blocks that impose different rules on how to categorize words. When trying to assess one's attitude about Christians versus Muslims, for instance, words would need to be sorted into the categories GOOD/BAD, on the one hand, and the categories CHRISTIAN/MUSLIM, on the other hand.[2] The first block requires simple GOOD/BAD categorization (e.g. left key press to indicate that *Peace* goes with GOOD, right key press to indicate that *War* goes with BAD), and the second block simple CHRISTIAN/MUSLIM categorization (e.g. left key press to indicate that *Jesus* goes with CHRISTIAN, and right key press to indicate that *Mohammed* goes with MUSLIM). Critically, the categories are combined in the third and the fifth blocks, and words of the different categories are presented intermixed. In the third block, the left key press is needed for GOOD and CHRISTIAN, whereas the right key press is needed for BAD and MUSLIM. In the fourth block, the response buttons for CHRISTIAN/MUSLIM are switched such that one now needs to press the left button for words related to MUSLIM and the right button for words related to CHRISTIAN. Finally, the fifth block pairs GOOD with MUSLIM and BAD with

[2]Throughout the manuscript we put the aIAT category labels in CAPITAL and the items in *italic*.

CHRISTIAN. The key assumption of the IAT is that the ease of pairing provides an indication of the association strength of the categories. Faster responding in the third block, which pairs GOOD with CHRISTIAN and BAD with MUSLIM, as compared to the fifth block, which pairs GOOD with MUSLIM and BAD with CHRISTIAN, is taken as an indication of a relative preference for Christians over Muslims. There is a very large research base on the theory, reliability and validity of the IAT (see, for example, http://faculty.washington.edu/agg/).

Sartori and colleagues (2008) reasoned that the IAT may also have potential as a lie detection test. The crux of the aIAT is that one assesses the ease of pairing propositions with TRUE or FALSE. Sentences known to be TRUE (e.g. 'I am in front of a computer') or FALSE (e.g. 'I am in front of a TV') are used for the TRUE–FALSE dimension. The other dimension exists of two contrasting statements. Building on the robbery example given earlier, one could contrast I STOLE THE WHITE MAZDA with I DID NOT STEAL THE WHITE MAZDA, using sentences that correspond to either the guilty statement (e.g. *I took the keys of the white Mazda*) or the innocent statement (e.g. *I did not take the keys of the white Mazda*). Sentences are randomly presented one by one on the computer screen, and participants classify them as fast as possible. Easier pairing of guilty statements with TRUE (and the innocent statements with FALSE) is taken as an indication of the examinee's guilt, whereas greater ease in pairing the innocent statements with TRUE (and the guilty statements with FALSE) would provide an indication of the examinee's innocence (Table 12.3 and Figure 12.2).

Sartori et al. (2008) provided a series of six experiments to assess the validity of the aIAT in different subjects (e.g. students, community volunteers addicts) with different paradigms. In Experiment 2, participants were randomly assigned to either a guilty condition (stealing a CD) or to an innocent condition (reading a newspaper article on the mock CD theft). The main predictions of the aIAT were confirmed, and classification accuracy was impressively high (ROC = 0.96). Similarly, high accuracy was found in the other five experiments that were used to detect which card one had chosen (Experiment 1), which drug one had used (Experiment 3), where one spent the last holiday (Experiment 4), whether one's driving licence was suspended for drunk driving (Experiment 5), and which crime one had committed (Experiment 6; a study with two convicted murderers). Sensitivity in these initial studies was 88–100% and specificity was 87–88%, see Table 12.4.

The results of an independent replication of Sartori et al.'s (2008) Experiment 2 also indicated that the aIAT could discriminate liars from truth tellers, yet the classification accuracy was substantially lower, with sensitivity being 67–87% and specificity being 61% in naive participants

Table 12.3 Test structure of the autobiographical Implicit Association Test (aIAT). The combined blocks (Block 3 and Block5) are crucial as they pair the statements with TRUE versus FALSE. The dots (●) indicate the required button press (left versus right)

	Press left for	To be classified Sentences	Press right for
Block1. True-false	TRUE ●		FALSE
		I am in front of a computer	
		I am in front of a TV	●
Block2. Guilty-Innocent	I STOLE THE WHITE MAZDA ●		I WAS AT THE MOVIES ●
		I took the Mazda	
		I ate popcorn	
Block3. Guilty+True/ Innocent+False	I STOLE THE WHITE MAZDA		I WAS AT THE MOVIES
	TRUE ●		FALSE
		I am in front of a computer	
		I am in front of a TV	●
	●	*I took the Mazda*	
		I ate popcorn	●
Block4. Innocent-Guilty	I WAS AT THE MOVIES		I STOLE THE WHITE MAZDA
	●	*I took the Mazda*	●
		I ate popcorn	
Block5. Innocent+True/	I WAS AT THE MOVIES		I STOLE THE WHITE MAZDA
Guilty+False	TRUE ●		FALSE
		I am in front of a computer	
		I am in front of a TV	●
		I took the Mazda	●
	●	*I ate popcorn*	

The combined blocks (Blocks 3 and 5) are crucial as they pair the statements with TRUE versus FALSE. The dots (●) indicate the required button press (left vs. right).

(Verschuere, Prati, & De Houwer, 2009). One possibility is that the higher accuracy in the initial study is due to developer bias, referring to the observation that developers of a method typically find better results than others after them (Tully, Chou, & Browne, 2013). Another possibility is related to the phrasing of the contrasting statements.

Figure 12.2 Expected response pattern in the autobiographical IAT (aIAT), as observed in Verschuere Prati, et al. (2009) Experiment 1 (aIAT1, before receiving faking instructions).

Sartori et al. (2008) used two different test versions: The A/non-A format and the A/B format. The A/non-A format contrasts a proposition to its negation (I STOLE THE WHITE MAZDA vs. I DID NOT STEAL THE WHITE MAZDA). A great advantage of the A/non-A format is its ease of use and its level of standardization. After all, developing an A/non-A aIAT merely involves contrasting a statement with the negation of that statement. The A/B format contrasts a proposition to an alternative such as the alibi in a criminal investigation (I STOLE THE WHITE MAZDA vs. I WAS AT THE MOVIES). While initially using the A/B and the A/non-A test format interchangeably (Sartori et al., 2008), the developers of the aIAT later argued that the A/B format provides higher validity than the A/nonA format. When replicating two of their own experiments (Experiments 1 and 4 from Sartori et al., 2008) with the A/non-A format rather than the A/B format in the original paper, lower accuracy was indeed obtained (Agosta, Mega, & Sartori, 2011). Furthermore, a replication of their original Sartori et al. Experiment 2, now with A/B format, produced high validity. Although the authors did not provide a direct comparison between the A/B format and the A/non-A format, the data indicate that the A/B test format leads to more reliable results than the A/non-A format. Data obtained in the most recent studies seem to confirm the high validity of the aIAT with the A/B format. A series of four experiments by the Sartori lab using a holiday and card test scenario led to hit rates in the 71–100% range (Agosta, Ghirardi, Zogmaister, Castiello, & Sartori, 2011). Two mock crime studies from another group (Hu & Rosenfeld, 2012; Hu, Rosenfeld, &

Table 12.4 Laboratory studies of the Autobiographical Implicit Association Test (aIAT)

Stimuli	Event	Contrast category	Sensitivity (%)	Specificity (%)	Overall accuracy
Sartori et al. (2008)					
Experiment 1	Chosen card	A/B	95	—	ROC = 0.98
Experiment 2	Mock crime	A/non-A	100	87	ROC = 0.96
Experiment 3	Addiction	A/non-A	93	—	—
Experiment 4	Holiday	A/B	90	—	ROC = 0.91
Experiment 5	Drunk driving	A/non-A	88	88	—
Experiment 6	Real crime	A/non-A	100	—	—
Verschuere, Prati, et al. (2009)					
Experiment 1	Mock crime	A/non-A	67	61	Cohen's $d = 0.86$
Experiment 3	Mock crime	A/non-A	76 (control)	—	—
			86 (speeded)		
Agosta, Mega et al. (2011)					
Experiment 1	Card test	A/non-A	100	—	57%
Experiment 2	Holiday	A/non-A	100	7.5	52%
Experiment 3	Mock crime	A/B	—	—	95%
Agosta, Ghiradi et al. (2011)					
Experiment 1	Holiday	A/B	100	—	—
Experiment 2	Holiday	A/B	83	—	—
Experiment 3	Card test	A/B	100	—	—
Experiment 4	Card test	A/B	71	—	—
Agosta, Castiello et al. (2011)					
Experiment 1	Intentions	A/B	100	—	—

(*Continued*)

Table 12.4 (Cont'd)

Stimuli	Event	Contrast category	Sensitivity (%)	Specificity (%)	Overall accuracy
Experiment 3	Intentions	A/B	72	—	—
Hu and Rosenfeld (2012)	Mock crime	A/B	—	—	ROC=0.90 (immediate) ROC=0.79 (delay)
Hu et al. (2012)	Mock crime	A/B	—	—	ROC's>0.90
Lanciano, Curci, Mastandrea, and Sartori (2013)					
Experiment 1	Flashbulb memories	A/non-A			D-measure=3.87
Experiment 2	True memory of words	A/non-A			D-measure=1.48
Marini et al. (2012)	True memory of words	A/non-A	—	—	D-measure=0.98
	False memories of words	A/non-A	—	—	D-measure=0.86
Takarangi et al. (2013)	Actions				
	Contrasted with non-performed actions	A/non-A		—	D-measure=0.59
	Contrasted with non-performed, yet imagined actions	A/non-A	97.5 (collapsed)	—	D-measure=0.58
Agosta et al. (2013)	White lies	A/B	100	—	—
	Motives	A/B	95–100	—	—

Study	Condition	Format			Effect size
		[A/B] and A/non-A			
Vargo and Petroczi (2013)	Cocaine use	Collapsed [A/B]	78	39%	Cohen's $d = 0.39$
	Heroin use	Collapsed [A/B]	—	—	Cohen's $d = 0.27$
Freng and Kehn (2013) Experiment 1	Crime witness Central details	A/non-A			D-measure = 0.50
	Peripheral details	A/non-A			D-measure = 0.42
Experiment2	Control.	A/non-A			D-measure = 0.67
	Misinformed	A/non-A			D-measure = 0.95

1. Data for naive guilty only (no faking instructions). Note that data from what Agosta, Ghiradi, et al. (2011) called 'naive fakers' are included, as no actual faking instructions or coaching was given to participants in this condition. The data of Verschuere et al. and Hu et al. are those of the first administration of the aIATs.

2. The D-measure refers to a particular way of calculating the standardized mean difference score that is common in the IAT literature (Greenwald et al., 2003), and it is roughly comparable to Cohen's d.

3. We classified all aIATs that contrasted the target category with its negation as A/non-A, including the aIATs contrasting 'real' with 'unreal' (Lanciano et al., 2013), 'present' with 'absent' (Lanciano et al., 2012; Marini et al., 2012), and 'guilty' with 'innocent' (as it referred to 'performed' vs. 'not performed' actions; Takarangi et al., 2013). Following the logic, the AS IF YOU WERE COCAINE USER vs. AS IF YOU ABSTAIN FROM COCAIN USE aIAT of Vargo and Petroczi (2013) might be better labelled A/non-A than A/B. In the table, we mark this ambiguity by putting the format between brackets: [A/B]

Bodenhausen, 2012) also showed very high accuracy. Vargo and Petroczi (2013) were the first to provide a direct comparison of the two test formats. An aIAT to detect cocaine use was administered in recreational cocaine users and non-users, following either the A/non-A format (AS IF YOU WERE A COCAINE USER vs. AS IF YOU WERE NOT A COCAINE USER) or the A/B format (AS IF YOU WERE A COCAINE USER vs. AS IF YOU ABSTAIN FROM COCAINE USE). IAT scores did not differ with format. Given that neither aIAT format proved valid, and that the methodology differed substantially from previous studies (i.e. responding through a touch screen; and only 1/3 of the normal amount of trials), the data are not conclusive. Moreover, the two formats were not clearly separated from each other (see point 3 in Table 12.4). The A/B format used in this study contrasts A (cocaine user) with its negation (non-A; that is, no cocaine user) as is typical for the A/non-A format. A clear example of the A/B format would have been AS IF YOU WERE A COCAINE USER vs. AS IF YOU WERE A HEROINE USER. Overall, it seems that the A/B format may have higher validity than the A/non-A format, yet this conclusion requires studies that directly compare the two formats under standard conditions.

It should be noted that developing an aIAT along the A/B format requires more consideration than the A/B format as the alternatives need to be mutually exclusive. The aIAT will not be valid when the alternatives are both correct (e.g. a suspect stole the Mazda after going to the movies). Furthermore, the A/B format needs to be tailored to the individual (e.g. one crime suspect's alibi may involve going to the movies, whereas another suspect may claim to been sleeping), whereas the same A/non-A could be administered in all suspects.

A great advantage of the aIAT is its flexibility, providing the aIAT with very broad applicability. In principle, the veracity of any statement can be tested with the aIAT. The aIAT may be used not only to find out what someone did (e.g. I PLACED THE BOSTON BOMB; or I SET FIRE AT STARBUCKS), but also what someone planned or intended to do (e.g. I INTENDED TO PARTICIPATE IN THE 9/11 ATTACKS) and even the motives for doing so (e.g. I WAS ANGRY AT HER; or THE UNITED STATES HAS NO RIGHT TO INTERFERE IN AFGHANISTAN). Agosta, Castiello, Rigoni, Lionetti, and Sartori (2011) from the Sartori lab asked neuropsychology students where they intended to spend the night, and about their career plans. Separate aIATs were conducted for the short-term and the long-term intentions, and 100% accuracy was obtained. Furthermore, the Sartori lab (Agosta, Pezzoli, & Sartori, 2013) showed that the aIAT can be used to assess someone's motives. Participants were asked to reveal real-life lies, and the reasons for telling those lies. The aIAT allowed not only to detect the lies, but also uncovered the reasons for telling these lies. These studies confirm the broad applicability of the aIAT to assess the veracity of propositions related to past actions, and the motives of those actions and future intentions.

BOUNDARY CONDITIONS AND NEW DIRECTIONS

There is no published research available on how the aIAT and the RT-CIT perform under real-life conditions. As diagnostic tests typically perform worse under field circumstances compared to controlled laboratory conditions (National Research Council, 2003), the accuracy levels obtained thus far should probably be regarded as the upper limit of the validity in real-life circumstances.

Apart from external validity, it is important to address threats to internal validity: Are there variables other than deception that could produce the same outcome? As for any deception detection test, the control items are crucial. In the RT-CIT, it is imperative that the probe and irrelevant items are equivalent. If the probe is inherently more salient than the irrelevant items, the RT difference between probes and irrelevant items may not only be due to deception, but also to the difference in salience. Pretesting in a sample of innocent examinees can assure equivalence of the items (Doob & Kirschenbaum, 1973). Equivalence is also of importance in the aIAT, as differences in saliency may affect the test outcome. The IAT assesses the similarity of two concepts, with the aIAT intending to assess similarity in veracity. The ease in pairing is assumed to only vary with the veracity of the contrasting statements. Similarity on dimensions other than veracity such as valence, however, also affects the ease of pairing the two concepts (Rothermund & Wentura, 2004). The guilty statements are typically more negative than the innocent statements. Because FALSE is also more negative than TRUE, the pairing of the guilty statements with FALSE and the innocent statements with TRUE may be facilitated due to similarity in valence, which may lead to false-negative outcomes. It is imperative to assess to what extent similarity on dimensions other than veracity affects the aIAT.

Furthermore, memory biases may threaten the validity of both RT paradigms. Simple forgetting may account for divergence between memory and reality. The critical information may only evoke a distinguished response in the RT-CIT when explicitly recognized (on the possibility of the CIT as an implicit memory test see J. J. B. Allen (2011)), and the correct autobiographical statement will only be regarded

TRUE when fitting with memory. False memories are a more blatant case of memory biases, and may distort the outcome of both paradigms. False memories are often investigated with the Deese/Roediger-McDermott (DRM) paradigm (Roediger & Mcdermott, 1995). In the DRM, lists of semantically related words (e.g. *alive, coffin, corpse, grave, black*) are memorized in a study phase. During the subsequent test phase, the participant's task is to determine whether or not certain words were presented during the study phase. Critically, the test phase includes 'lures' (e.g. *dead*) – words that are thematically associated with the words from a memorized list, but were not actually presented in the study phase. Research with the DRM paradigm indicates that neither the RT-CIT (Allen & Mertens, 2009) nor the aIAT (Marini, Agosta, Mazzoni, Dalla Barba, & Sartori, 2012) can differentiate true from false memories.

As with other lie detection tests, a matter of concern is vulnerability to faking. With RT itself being under voluntary control, several researchers have expressed the concern that RTs may be too easily manipulated (e.g. Farwell & Donchin, 1991). Seymour et al. found that the high accuracy of the RT-CIT was preserved even when participants were warned not to respond differently and/or when the participant was informed about the expected pattern of results. Specific faking instructions on how to fake the CIT (e.g. pressing a finger or wiggling a toe when confronted with the irrelevant items), however, does allow to beat the test: The accuracy of the RT-CIT dropped from 91 to 45% (Rosenfeld et al., 2004). Likewise, providing participants with specific information on how the aIAT works and how it can be beaten (i.e. deliberately slowing down when the guilty statements are paired with TRUE) made accuracy drop from 67–86% to 22–61% (Verschuere, Prati, et al., 2009).

There are two ways to cope with the issue of faking (Verschuere & Meijer, 2014): Faking prevention and faking detection. Faking prevention concerns any strategy of the examiner that aims at reducing successful faking. For instance, researchers typically apply a response deadline in the RT-CIT, which obliges the participant to respond very fast (e.g. <800 ms). There is, however, no empirical research on whether such a response deadline efficiently reduces faking success in the RT-CIT. At least for the aIAT, such response deadline failed to prevent faking (Verschuere, Prati, et al., 2009). Although faking detection has not always been successful (Fiedler & Bluemke, 2005; Kim, 2003; Steffens, 2004; Verschuere, Prati, et al., 2009), two research groups showed that novel algorithms allowed to identify three out of four fakers in the aIAT (Agosta, Ghirardi, et al., 2011; Cvencek, Greenwald,

Brown, Gray, & Snowden, 2010). The algorithm developed by Cvencek et al. has the disadvantage that it requires data from an unfaked IAT, which may not always be available. The Agosta et al. algorithm is easier to apply as it does not require such data. Substantial slowing in the combined blocks compared to the simple blocks is taken as an indication of faking. In sum, both the aIAT and the RT-CIT appear vulnerable to faking. To date, no successful faking prevention strategy has been developed, yet some promising ways to detect faking have been proposed.

SUMMARY

RT-based tests have great potential as they can be administered quickly (10–15 minutes) and potentially remotely (through the Internet), require only a single laptop computer and the test outcome can be obtained quickly (automated analyses and feedback). In recent years, several RT-based lie detection tests have been developed, with two paradigms showing most promise: The RT-CIT and the aIAT. The RT-CIT is a memory detection method and aims to assess recognition of critical (e.g. crime) details. The RT-CIT has the advantage of having high specificity (i.e. few false positives), but its applicability is confined to specific situations of memory recognition. The aIAT is a deception detection method, and has very broad applicability as it aims to assess not only past actions, but also intentions, and the motives for those (intended) actions. However, subtle differences (e.g. A/B vs. A/non-A test format) seem to heavily impact on aIAT validity, calling for more research on the optimal test format and other aspects (e.g. similarity between statements on dimensions other than veracity) that may affect the aIATs validity. Apart from internal validity threats, both tests await research assessing how they perform under more externally valid circumstances. Given their ease of application, and initial indications that they can produce high internal validity, it seems worthwhile to start this endeavour.

ACKNOWLEDGEMENT

The authors wish to thank Bram Van Bockstaele for his constructive comments on an earlier draft of this chapter.

REFERENCES

Agosta, S., Castiello, U., Rigoni, D., Lionetti, S., & Sartori, G. (2011a). The detection and the neural correlates of behavioral (prior) intentions. *Journal of Cognitive Neuroscience, 23*(12), 3888–3902.

Agosta, S., Ghirardi, V., Zogmaister, C., Castiello, U., & Sartori, G. (2011b). Detecting fakers of the autobiographical IAT. *Applied Cognitive Psychology, 25*(2), 299–306. doi:10.1002/Acp.1691

Agosta, S., Mega, A., & Sartori, G. (2011c). Detrimental effects of using negative sentences in the autobiographical IAT. *Acta Psychologica, 136*(3), 269–275. doi:10.1016/j.actpsy.2010.05.011.

Agosta, S., Pezzoli, P., & Sartori, G. (2013). How to detect deception in everyday life and the reasons underlying it. *Applied Cognitive Psychology, 27*(2), 256–262. doi:10.1002/Acp.2902

Allen, J., Iacono, W. G., & Danielson, K. D. (1992). The identification of concealed memories using the event-related potential and implicit behavioral measures – A methodology for prediction in the face of individual-differences. *Psychophysiology, 29*(5), 504–522.

Allen, J., & Movius, H. L. (2000). The objective assessment of amnesia in dissociative identity disorder using event-related potentials. *International Journal of Psychophysiology, 38*(1), 21–41.

Allen, J. J. B. (2011). Clinical applications of the Concealed Information Test. In B. Verschuere, G. Ben-Shakhar, & E. Meijer (Eds.), *Memory detection: Theory and application of the Concealed Information Test* (pp. 231–252). Cambridge, UK: Cambridge University Press.

Allen, J. J. B., & Mertens, R. (2009). Limitations to the detection of deception: True and false recollections are poorly distinguished using an event-related potential procedure. *Social Neuroscience, 4*, 473–490.

Ambach, W., Dummel, S., Luer, T., & Vaitl, D. (2011). Physiological responses in a Concealed Information Test are determined interactively by encoding procedure and questioning format. *International Journal of Psychophysiology, 81*(3), 275–282. doi:10.1016/j.ijpsycho.2011.07.010

Buller, D. B., Comstock, J., Aune, R. K., & Strzyzewski, K. D. (1989). The effect of probing on deceivers and truthtellers. *Journal of Nonverbal Behavior, 13*(3), 155–170. doi:10.1007/Bf00987047

Cohen, J. (1988). *Statistical power analysis for the behavioural sciences.* Hillsdale, MI: Lawrence Erlbaum.

Cvencek, D., Greenwald, A. G., Brown, A. S., Gray, N. S., & Snowden, R. J. (2010). Faking of the Implicit Association Test is statistically detectable and partly correctable. *Basic and Applied Social Psychology, 32*(4), 302–314. doi:10.108 0/01973533.2010.519236

De Houwer, J., Teige-Mocigemba, S., Spruyt, A., & Moors, A. (2009). Implicit measures: A normative analysis and review. *Psychological Bulletin, 135*(3), 347–368. doi:10.1037/A0014211

DePaulo, B. M., Lindsay, J. J., Malone, B. E., Muhlenbruck, L., Charlton, K., & Cooper, H. (2003). Cues to deception. *Psychological Bulletin, 129*(1), 74–118.

Doob, A. N., & Kirschenbaum, H. M. (1973). Bias in police lineups – Partial remembering. *Journal of Police Science and Administration, 1*, 187–293.

Engelhard, I. M., Merckelbach, H., & van den Hout, M. A. (2003). The guilty knowledge test and the modified Stroop task in detection of deception: An exploratory study. *Psychological Reports, 92*, 683–691.

Farwell, L. A., & Donchin, E. (1991). The truth will out: Interrogative polygraphy (lie detection) with event-related brain potentials. *Psychophysiology, 28*, 531–547.

Farwell, L. A., & Smith, S. S. (2001). Using brain MERMER testing to detect knowledge despite efforts to conceal. *Journal of Forensic Sciences, 46*, 135–143.

Fiedler, K., & Bluemke, M. (2005). Faking the IAT: Aided and unaided response control on the Implicit Association Tests. *Basic and Applied Social Psychology, 27*(4), 307–316.

Freng, S., & Kehn, A. (2013). Determining true and false witnessed events: Can an eyewitness-Implicit Association Test distinguish between the seen and unseen? *Psychiatry Psychology and Law, 20*(5), 761–780. doi:10.1080/132187 19.2012.735885

Gamer, M., Bauermann, T., Stoeter, P., & Vossel, G. (2007). Covariations among fMRI, skin conductance and behavioral data during processing of concealed information. *Human Brain Mapping, 28*, 1287–1301.

Ganis, G., Kosslyn, S. M., Stose, S., Thompson, W. L., & Yurgelun-Todd, D. A. (2003). Neural correlates of different types of deception: An fMRI investigation. *Cerebral Cortex, 13*(8), 830–836.

Greenwald, A. G., McGhee, D. E., & Schwartz, J. L. K. (1998). Measuring individual differences in implicit cognition: The implicit association test. *Journal of Personality and Social Psychology, 74*(6), 1464–1480.

Greenwald, A. G., Nosek, B. A., & Banaji, M. R. (2003). Understanding and using the implicit association test: I. An improved scoring algorithm. *Journal of Personality and Social Psychology, 85*, 197–216.

Gronau, N., Ben-Shakhar, G., & Cohen, A. (2005). Behavioral and physiological measures in the detection of concealed information. *Journal of Applied Psychology, 90*(1), 147–158.

Henke, F., & Eddy, M. W. (1909). Mental diagnosis by the association reaction method. *Psychological Review, 16*, 399–409.

Hu, X. Q., Evans, A., Wu, H. Y., Lee, K., & Fu, G. Y. (2013). An interfering dot-probe task facilitates the detection of mock crime memory in a reaction time (RT)-based concealed information test. *Acta Psychologica, 142*(2), 278–285. doi:10.1016/j.actpsy.2012.12.006

Hu, X. Q., & Rosenfeld, J. P. (2012). Combining the P300-complex trial-based Concealed Information Test and the reaction time-based autobiographical Implicit Association Test in concealed memory detection. *Psychophysiology, 49*(8), 1090–1100. doi:10.1111/j.1469-8986.2012.01389.x

Hu, X. Q., Rosenfeld, J. P., & Bodenhausen, G. V. (2012). Combating automatic autobiographical associations: The effect of instruction and training in strategically concealing information in the autobiographical Implicit Association Test. *Psychological Science, 23*(10), 1079–1085. doi:10.1177/0956797612443834

Jung, C. G. (1910). The association reaction method. *American Journal of Psychology, 21*, 219–240.

Kim, D. Y. (2003). Voluntary controllability of the implicit association test (IAT). *Social Psychology Quarterly, 66*(1), 83–96.

Kubo, K., & Nittono, H. (2009). The role of intention to conceal in the P300-based concealed information test. *Applied Psychophysiology and Biofeedback, 34*(3), 227–235.

Lanciano, T., Curci, A., Mastandrea, S., & Sartori, G. (2013). Do automatic mental associations detect a flashbulb memory? *Memory, 21*(4), 482–493. doi:10.1080/09658211.2012.740050

Locker, L., & Pratarelli, M. E. (1997). Lexical decision and the detection of concealed information. *The Journal of Credibility Assessment and Witness Psychology, 1*, 33–43.

Lykken, D. T. (1959). The GSR in the detection of guilt. *Journal of Applied Psychology, 43*, 385–388.

Marini, M., Agosta, S., Mazzoni, G., Dalla Barba, G., & Sartori, G. (2012). True and false DRM memories: Differences detected with an implicit task. *Frontiers in Psychology, 3*, 310.

Marston, W. M. (1927). Reaction-time symptoms of deception. *Journal of Experimental Psychology, 3*, 72–87.

Meijer, E. H., Smulders, F. T. Y., Merckelbach, H. L. G. J., & Wolf, A. G. (2007). The P300 is sensitive to concealed face recognition. *International Journal of Psychophysiology, 66*, 231–237.

National Research Council. (2003). *The polygraph and lie detection. Committee to review the scientific evidence on the polygraph.* Washington, DC: The National Academies Press.

Noordraven., E., & Verschuere, B. (2013). Predicting the sensitivity of the Reaction Time-based Concealed Information Test. *Applied Cognitive Psychology, 27*, 328–335.

Roediger, H. L., & Mcdermott, K. B. (1995). Creating false memories – Remembering words not presented in lists. *Journal of Experimental Psychology-Learning Memory and Cognition, 21*(4), 803–814. doi:10.1037/0278-7393.21.4.803

Rosenfeld, J. P., Cantwell, B., Nasman, V. T., Wojdac, V., Ivanov, S., & Mazzeri, L. (1988). A modified, event-related potential-based guilty knowledge test. *International Journal of Neuroscience, 42*(1–2), 157–161.

Rosenfeld, J. P., Labkovsky, E., Winograd, M., Lui, M. A., Vandenboom, C., & Chedid, E. (2008). The Complex Trial Protocol (CTP): A new, countermeasure-resistant, accurate P300-based method for detection of concealed information. *Psychophysiology, 45*, 906–919.

Rosenfeld, J. P., Shue, E., & Singer, E. (2007). Single versus multiple probe blocks of P300-based concealed information tests for self-referring versus incidentally obtained information. *Biological Psychology, 74*(3), 396–404.

Rosenfeld, J. P., Soskins, M., Bosh, G., & Ryan, A. (2004). Simple, effective countermeasures to P300-based tests of detection of concealed information. *Psychophysiology, 41*, 205–219.

Rothermund, K., & Wentura, D. (2004). Underlying processes in the implicit association test: Dissociating salience from associations. *Journal of Experimental Psychology-General, 133*(2), 139–165. doi:10.1037/0096-3445.133.2.139

Sartori, G., Agosta, S., Zogmaister, C., Ferrara, S. D., & Castiello, U. (2008). How to accurately detect autobiographical events. *Psychological Science, 19*(8), 772–780. doi:10.1111/j.1467-9280.2008.02156.x

Seymour, T. L., & Fraynt, B. R. (2009). Time and encoding effects in the concealed knowledge test. *Applied Psychophysiology and Biofeedback, 34*(3), 177–187.

Seymour, T. L., & Kerlin, J. R. (2008). Successful detection of verbal and visual concealed knowledge using an RT-based paradigm. *Applied Cognitive Psychology, 22*(4), 475–490.

Seymour, T. L., Seifert, C. M., Shafto, M. G., & Mosmann, A. L. (2000). Using response time measures to assess 'guilty knowledge'. *Journal of Applied Psychology, 85*(1), 30–37.

Steffens, M. C. (2004). Is the implicit association test immune to faking? *Experimental Psychology*, *51*(3), 165–179.

Takarangi, M. K., Strange, D., Shortland, A. E., & James, H. E. (2013). Source confusion influences the effectiveness of the autobiographical IAT. *Psychonomic Bulletin Review*, *20*, 1232–1238.

Tully, R. J., Chou, S. N., & Browne, K. D. (2013). A systematic review on the effectiveness of sex offender risk assessment tools in predicting sexual recidivism of adult male sex offenders. *Clinical Psychology Review*, *33*(2), 287–316. doi:10.1016/j.cpr.2012.12.002

Vargo, E. J., & Petroczi, A. (2013). Detecting cocaine use? The autobiographical implicit association test (aIAT) produces false positives in a real-world setting. *Substance Abuse Treatment Prevention and Policy*, *8*, 22.

Verschuere, B., Ben-Shakhar, G., & Meijer, E. (Eds.). (2011). *Memory detection: Theory and application of the Concealed Information Test*. Cambridge, UK: Cambridge University Press.

Verschuere, B., Crombez, G., De Clercq, A., & Koster, E. (2004). Autonomic and behavioural responding to concealed information: differentiating orienting and defensive responses. *Psychophysiology*, *41*(3), 461–466.

Verschuere, B., Crombez, G., Degrootte, T., & Rosseel, Y. (2009). Detecting concealed information with reaction times: Validity and comparison with the polygraph. *Applied Cognitive Psychology*, *23*, 1–11.

Verschuere, B., Crombez, G., & Koster, E. (2004). Orienting to guilty knowledge. *Cognition & Emotion*, *18*, 265–279.

Verschuere, B., & Meijer, E. (2014). What's on your mind? Recent advances in memory detection using the Concealed Information Test. *European Psychologist*. doi: 10.1027/1016-9040/a000194.

Verschuere, B., Prati, V., & De Houwer, J. (2009). Cheating the lie detector: Faking in the autobiographical IAT. *Psychological Science*, *20*, 410–413.

Verschuere, B., Rosenfeld, J. P., Winograd, M., Labkovsky, E., & Wiersema, J. R. (2009c). The role of deception in the P300 memory detection. *Legal and Criminological Psychology*, *14*, 253–262.

Visu-Petra, G., Miclea, M., Bus, I., & Visu-Petra, L. (2014). Detection concealed information: The role of individual differences in executive functions and social desirability. *Psychology, Crime, & Law*, *20*, 20–36. doi: 10.1080/1068316X.2012.736509.

Visu-Petra, G., Miclea, M., & Visu-Petra, L. (2012). Reaction time-based detection of concealed information in relation to individual differences in executive functioning. *Applied Cognitive Psychology*, *26*(3), 342–351. doi:10.1002/Acp.1827

Visu-Petra, G., Varga, M., Miclea, M., & Visu-Petra, L. (2013). When interference helps: Increasing executive load to facilitate deception detection in the concealed information test. *Frontiers in Cognitive Psychology*, *4*, 146.

13

Suspects' Verbal Counter-Interrogation Strategies: Towards an Integrative Model

PÄR ANDERS GRANHAG, MARIA HARTWIG, ERIK MAC
GIOLLA AND FRANZISKA CLEMENS

INTRODUCTION AND BACKGROUND

The best ... anti-interrogation technique is to understand the techniques as practiced by police forces.

These words open the section on interrogation strategies of the IRA training manual – the *Green Book*. What is striking is the similarity between this statement and the idea that drives the research discussed in this chapter, where we focus on suspects' counter-interrogation strategies. Put briefly, we believe *the best approach to an interrogation is to understand the counter-interrogation techniques as practiced by suspects.*

Compelling anecdotal evidence for this approach can be gained by examining the proficient WW2 interrogator Hanns Scharff (Toliver, 1997). Scharff was a master at eliciting information from prisoners of war (POWS). He began by a detailed analysis of prisoners' interview strategies. His interview methods were in turn tailored to the observed prisoner strategies. For example, Scharff observed that a common strategy

Detecting Deception: Current Challenges and Cognitive Approaches, First Edition.
Edited by Pär Anders Granhag, Aldert Vrij, and Bruno Verschuere.
© 2015 John Wiley & Sons, Ltd. Published 2015 by John Wiley & Sons, Ltd.

of POWs was *it is meaningless to deny what the interviewer already knows*. Scharff played on this strategy by opening interviews with long and detailed stories, emphasizing how much he already knew. This *illusion of knowing it all* allowed POWs to validate and reveal information unknowingly, since they simply thought they were providing already known information. Scharff's approach allowed for a sophisticated, non-coercive, and most importantly, successful interview technique (Toliver, 1997; for empirical support of Scharff's techniques see Granhag, Cancino Montecinos, & Oleszkiewicz, 2013; Oleszkiewicz, Granhag, & Cancino Montecinos, 2014).

Of course, Scharff's aim was primarily to elicit information from his prisoners. It is, however, reasonable to assume that a similar analysis of suspects' strategies can inform on how best to interview for deceit. As discussed elsewhere in this volume, strategic interviewing is a promising tool in the elusive task of deception detection (see Chapter 9 this volume). We argue that central to strategic interviewing is an understanding of how truth tellers and liars approach an interview, what strategies they use to appear as truthful, and whether such strategies differ depending on whether the suspect is lying or telling the truth. Possible discrepancies in counter-interrogation strategies between truth tellers and liars could then be exploited in an interview context in an attempt to elicit cues to deceit. Indeed, strategic interviewing methods that explicitly build on such discrepancies have already been developed (e.g. the Strategic Use of Evidence technique, see Chapter 10 this volume).

Knowledge about suspects' counter-interrogation strategies can therefore help develop new interview protocols, as well as refine those already existing. Importantly, without empirical examination, such knowledge will at best be guided by theoretical assumptions and at worst be guided by mere speculation. At this point, the empirical literature on this topic is still relatively sparse. Our aim in this chapter is to review and organize the scientific literature that exists on suspects' counter-interrogation strategies, and highlight directions for future research.

We define *counter-interrogation strategies* in a broad sense, and let the term denote all attempts made by a suspect to successfully withstand an interrogation (Clemens, 2013), or expressed differently, to successfully appear as truthful. Here it should also be clarified that the chapter is on the counter-interrogation strategies that influence suspects' verbal responses. Hence, we do not review so-called countermeasures used to influence the outcome of polygraph tests (these are discussed in Chapter 4, see also Ben-Shahkar, 2011; Honts & Amato, 2002), and we do not review suspects' nonverbal strategies.

The chapter is structured in the following manner. First, we will briefly introduce the concept of self-regulatory strategies (control strategies) and the psychology of guilt and innocence as a theoretical backdrop for the empirical research to be discussed in the latter part of the chapter. Second, we will review empirical findings acknowledging some very basic differences in the mindset of guilty and innocent suspects. Third, we will introduce a model used for illustrating the causal processes at play, as well as for organizing the empirical research published so far on suspects' counter-interrogation strategies. Finally, we will provide a few thoughts on possible future directions.

THEORETICAL BACKDROP

During the last decades, researchers have extensively mapped the behaviours of liars and truth tellers. A large part of this research has been driven by the search for reliable cues to deception – that is verbal and/or nonverbal patterns of behaviour that differ in frequency or duration when people tell lies compared to when they are telling the truth. In the most comprehensive synthesis of the research to date, DePaulo and colleagues (2003) conducted a meta-analysis of 1,338 estimates of 158 possible behavioural cues to deception. For the present discussion, it is important to point out that this vast literature has focused almost exclusively on overt behavioural differences: Researchers have mapped in painstaking detail the quantity and types of details included in true and false statements; the frequency and nature of paralinguistic behaviours such as speech errors; and the frequency and duration of both global and minute elements of non-verbal behaviours (for a comprehensive list of the behavioural cues studied in deception research see DePaulo et al., 2003 and Sporer & Schwandt, 2007).

However, until recently, there has been no systematic attempt to map the underlying psychological processes that may distinguish liars from truth tellers. Researchers have of course theorized amply about such psychological processes (for a recent overview of theories of deception, see Chapter 2, this volume). The point we wish to stress is that despite this, the empirical study of the psychological processes of liars and truth tellers remains a neglected area of research. Put in simple terms, while there is a massive body of data on how liars and truth tellers behave, the empirical data on how they think, reason and strategize is much less developed. There is a simple reason for this; it is a relatively easy task to keep track of and describe the observable outcome (e.g. verbal behaviour), whereas it is a very challenging task to map the internal cognitive processes explaining the outcome.

Most of the recent work mapping the mindsets of liars and truth tellers has done so under the heading of *counter-interrogation strategies*

(Granhag & Hartwig, 2008). This label may suggest that the strategies of interest are solely those that are active in relation to formal questioning. However, the study of counter-interrogation strategies is broader than this: It aims to shed light on (a) similarities and differences in liars' and truth tellers' reasoning and strategies about how to convince an interviewer of their innocence and (b) how differences in liars' and truth tellers' reasoning may translate into overt cues to deception.

Basic Psychological Principles

The theoretical starting point for the work on counter-interrogation strategies is that both liars and truth tellers are motivated to be perceived as credible. This point of departure is partly derived from the self-presentational perspective on deception introduced by DePaulo and colleagues (2003, see also DePaulo, 1992). This perspective emphasizes the motivated and goal-oriented nature of both lying and truth telling. In the self-presentational view, attempts at creating a credible impression are efforts of self-control, and can thus be understood, at least in part, through the lens of self-regulation theory (Carver & Sheier, 2011; Forgas, Baumeister, & Tice, 2009).

Self-regulation theory is a social cognitive framework for understanding how people manage their behaviour to move away from undesired outcomes and to reach desired goals. As mentioned earlier, in the present context, the desired goal for both liars and truth tellers is to convince another (e.g. an interviewer) that their statement is truthful. In order to reach this goal, truth tellers as well as liars, may employ self-regulatory strategies (Carver & Scheier, 2011; Fiske & Taylor, 2008; for a discussion about the self-regulatory failure labeled ego depletion in the context of interrogation, see Davis & Leo, 2012). Psychological research has shown that self-regulatory behaviours are evoked by conditions of threat (Fiske & Taylor, 2008). This finding has significance in the context of investigative interviewing, since being judged as deceptive may have significant negative consequences (Granhag & Hartwig, 2008).

Differences in Liars' and Truth Tellers' Counter-Interrogation Strategies

Innocent and guilty suspects share a motivation to be believed. However, liars and truth tellers differ in at least one critical way: the information they hold. Hartwig, Granhag, Strömwall, and Doering (2010) argued that liars per definition are motivated to conceal certain information. For example, they may conceal information about their involvement in a crime, or information about other people's identities and actions. A primary threat for a liar is that the interviewer will come to know this information. In contrast, a truth telling person does not possess information that they are motivated to conceal. Thus, truth tellers have the very opposite problem: that the interviewer may *not* come to know the truth. In sum, both liars and truth tellers may plausibly perceive an interview as an event that activates goals; therefore, they will employ self-regulatory strategies to reach their goals. Critically, because liars and truth tellers differ in the extent to which they are (a) in possession of critical information and (b) motivated to conceal this information, the principal difference in liars' and truth tellers' counter-interrogation strategies will concern information management – what information to include in one's statement. In the following section, we will first focus on the information management strategies of liars and then provide an overview of the principles underlying truth tellers' strategies.

Liars' and Truth Tellers' Information Management Strategies

As discussed earlier, the primary threat for liars is that the interviewer will come to know the information they are attempting to conceal. In order to avoid this outcome, liars will have to deal with multiple risks. Clearly, they must suppress the critical information (not doing so would amount to an admission). However, unless a liar decides to not provide a statement at all – which may appear suspicious – they will have to offer false information to conceal the critical information (e.g. a liar might claim that they went to the mall on a given day, when in fact they participated in a crime in another part of town). Offering false information to conceal a criminal act entails a risk (e.g. if the interviewer knows that the suspect visited the part of town where the crime was committed, the plausibility of the suspects account is in jeopardy). Generally speaking, liars must typically strike a balance between (a) concealing incriminating information and (b) offering details in order to appear credible.

Granhag and Hartwig (2008) argued that liars who aim to conceal critical information have two general strategies at their disposal. First, they can attempt *avoidance* strategies (e.g. being vague about one's whereabouts when asked to provide a free narrative). If this option is not available – which would be the case if an interviewer asks direct questions about the suspect's whereabouts – liars may have to resort to *escape* (i.e. denial) strategies. Interestingly, psychological research shows that avoidance and escape strategies are fundamental responses to threatening stimuli, displayed by both humans and animals (Carlson, Buskist, & Martin, 2000; see also Caïn & LeDoux, 2008, for a discussion of the underlying neuropsychological mechanisms).

As mentioned earlier, truth tellers may instead fear that the interviewer will *not* come to know what they know. Therefore, it stands to

reason that truth tellers' strategies regarding information management will typically be to volunteer the information they hold – to 'tell
the truth like it happened' (Hartwig, Granhag, & Strömwall, 2007).
This strategy of forthcomingness can be predicted on the basis of at
least two major findings in the social psychological literature. First,
people have a fundamental and possibly motivated belief in the fairness of the world (the *belief in a just world*; Lerner, 1980). That is, people
believe that the world is a fair place, in which people get the outcomes
they deserve. Innocent suspects may thus be forthcoming with information because they reason that if they provide a truthful account, the
interviewer will believe them simply because they deserve to be
believed. Another finding, the so-called *illusion of transparency*, demonstrates that people overestimate the extent to which internal states
are apparent to observers (Savitsky & Gilovich, 2003). In other words,
truth tellers may believe that their innocence 'shines through', and if
they simply provide a complete account, the interviewer will 'see' that
they are innocent (e.g. Kassin & Norwick, 2004; for an in-depth discussion of the phenomenology of innocence, see Kassin, 2005).

SUSPECTS' COUNTER-INTERROGATION STRATEGIES: BASIC FINDINGS

There have been a series of studies examining the principles outlined
in the earlier section. The purpose of these studies is generally to
empirically examine commonalities and differences in liars' and truth
tellers' counter-interrogation strategies. The typical method employed
to study these strategies is to randomly assign participants to be guilty
or innocent of a mock transgression (e.g. Strömwall, Hartwig, &
Granhag, 2006; but see Gozna, Sully, & Teicher, 2005, for an exception
using field data). All participants are accused of the transgression, and
are asked to deny involvement in the crime (some truthfully, others
deceptively). In relation to the interview, participants are asked (a)
whether they had a strategy to convince the interviewer that they were
not involved in the crime and (b) if yes, what this strategy was.

Based on the psychological principles described earlier, we can predict
a number of patterns regarding the responses of guilty and innocent
suspects. First, because lying entails more complicated strategic reasoning, liars will more frequently report a plan or strategy compared to
truth tellers. Second, in terms of specific strategies, liars will express
strategies revolving around information management. That is, they will
report being conservative with information, and/or avoiding or denying

information that may be incriminating. Third, in line with the reasoning regarding the psychology of innocent suspects, we can predict that they will primarily report strategies of forthcomingness and openness.

The analyses of suspects' self-reported counter-interrogation strategies support these predictions. First, the data shows that liars are more likely than truth tellers to report having a strategy prior to an interview. For example, in the study by Hartwig et al. (2007), 60.50% liars reported having devised a strategy prior to being interviewed, compared to only 37.50% of truth tellers. Similar results were reported by Hines et al. (2010) and Vrij, Mann, Leal, and Granhag (2010). Second, liars' strategies were dominated by information management concerns, such as providing a simple and streamlined story, and avoiding, or outright denying, incriminating details (Hartwig et al., 2010). While some liars report strategies of partial admissions (e.g. 'avoid lying'), possibly in order to avoid contradicting known facts, such strategies are not common (11% of liars in Hartwig et al., 2007). A recent study by Leins, Fisher, and Ross (2013), which examined guilty suspects' strategies when free to choose the topic of their reports, generated similar results (see also Colwell, Hiscock-Anisman, Memon, Woods, & Michlik, 2006; Hines et al., 2010). Third, although truth tellers' do not report a strategy as often as liars, when they do, the strategies tend to be forthcoming (e.g. to 'to keep it real', expressed by 50% of truth tellers but only 13% of liars, see Strömwall et al., 2006).

Another approach to the topic is to infer suspects' counter-interrogation strategies by analysing their verbal behaviour during interviews (for a comprehensive review of such work see Hartwig, Granhag, & Luke, 2014). This research further supports the theoretical principles discussed in the earlier section. That is, liars are much more prone to employ avoidant-strategies: if they are given the opportunity, they typically avoid disclosing incriminating information (e.g. Hartwig, Granhag, Strömwall, & Vrij, 2005). Furthermore, if this option is not available (such as when they are asked direct questions about incriminating information), they tend to resort to denial responses. Analyses of truth tellers' verbal behaviour support the prediction that they are forthcoming, and that they tend to volunteer even potentially incriminating information such as being at the crime scene (e.g. Hartwig et al., 2005).

TOWARDS A CAUSAL MODEL

Figure 13.1 illustrates a basic causal model centering on suspects' counter-interrogation strategies, stating that (a) there are different categories that may influence which counter-interrogation strategy a

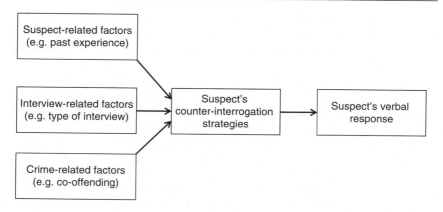

Figure 13.1   A causal model of suspects' counter-interrogation strategies.

suspect will adopt and (b) a suspect's counter-interrogation strategy will affect his or her verbal response. We have identified three categories of factors that may influence a suspect's choice of counter-interrogation strategy: (1) *suspect-related factors*; (2) *interview-related factors*; and (3) *crime-related factors*. Each category contains a number of specific influencing factors. In the following section, we will discuss each category, review some of the influencing factors found within each category and pinpoint how these factors may moderate the suspect's choice of counter-interrogation strategy. While there is a need for future research directly testing the causal mechanisms in our proposed model, we will review tentative support provided by previous research.

Before we proceed, two issues need to be addressed. First, we do not claim that these three categories capture all possible factors that may influence a suspect's choice of counter-interrogation strategy. What we offer is the first steps towards a more comprehensive model. Second, most interactions involving humans are dynamic and complex, and the 'interrogator-suspect' situation is no exception. For example, the style of interview might very well affect the suspect's perception of the evidence, which, in turn, will affect his or her counter-interrogation strategy. Additionally, a suspect's verbal response may influence the interviewer's choice of interview tactic, which again may affect the suspect's choice of counter-interrogation strategy. In other words, a specific factor may exert influence directly and/or indirectly, by influencing some other factor(s). However, the fact that an interrogation represents a complex and dynamic interaction is a poor excuse for not attempting to model some of the more basic processes taking place.

1. Suspect-related factors
The suspect's perception of the evidence. Suspects typically form a hypothesis about how much information investigators hold about them and the crime under investigation. Furthermore, many experienced interrogators agree that making inferences about (and affecting) suspects' perception of the evidence is key to a successful interrogation (e.g. Nilsson, 2010; Soufan, 2011). It is also important to acknowledge that a number of factors can potentially influence a suspect's perception of evidence. These factors can be sorted into two different categories. The first category contains factors exerting influence prior to the actual interrogation (e.g. the suspect's experience), and the second category contains factors that are tied to the interrogation per se (e.g. the general interrogation style). The focus here, however, will not be on what and how to influence a suspect's perception of the evidence, but rather how perception of the evidence may moderate the choice of interrogation strategy.

A suspect reflecting on an upcoming interrogation may reach a hypothesis with respect to the evidence by his own mental operations (e.g. 'Since they have searched my house, they have probably found...') or through some other source (e.g. legal advice that may be offered to the suspect, Cape, 1999). Importantly, either source of influence may result in specific hypotheses ('They probably know about my meeting with X yesterday') or a more general perception of the total evidence situation ('They cannot have much pointing in my direction').

A recent study by Luke, Dawson, Hartwig, and Granhag (2014) manipulated suspects' awareness of the existence of evidence before the actual interrogation, and inferred counter-interrogation strategies by observing the suspects' verbal behaviour in an interview. The study showed that innocent suspects adopted highly forthcoming verbal strategies, and did this independently of whether they were aware that there might be evidence against them or not. In contrast, guilty suspects' verbal strategies were highly influenced by the awareness manipulation: When informed about the possibility of evidence against them, guilty suspects were much more likely to employ a forthcoming verbal strategy. In sum, the awareness of possible evidence affected guilty suspects' counter-interrogation strategies more than it affected innocent suspects' strategies. These results are corroborated by a study examining the effectiveness of techniques for eliciting human intelligence (Oleszkiewicz et al., 2014). Results showed a significant positive correlation between perceived interviewer knowledge and the amount of new information reported during the interview. That is, the more information the source (correctly or incorrectly) believed the interviewer to hold, the more information he or she provided during the interaction. Taken together, these results lead to an interesting possibility: If interviewers can manipulate a suspect's perception of the evidence, they can influence his or her counter-interrogation strategies.

The suspect's experience. It is reasonable to assume that suspects who have experienced many previous interrogations, and/or who have received interrogation resistance training may use different counter-interrogation strategies than more naïve suspects. Experienced suspects may know how the legal system works and may hence be aware about the possible risks of providing self-incriminating information in an investigative interview (Leo, 1996).

Although there are few studies on the topic, the existing studies appear to point in the same direction: The more experienced the suspect, the more withholding and uncooperative he or she will be. For instance, in an early study by Softley (1980), it was shown that experienced suspects were more likely to make use of their right to remain silent. This result was supported in a later study by Leo (1996). In a similar vein, Strömwall and Willén (2011), who examined the strategies used by liars with a criminal history, found *not giving away any information* to be a common strategy. Interestingly, their participants reported a great diversity of other strategies, most of which related to issues of information management (e.g. *stay close to the truth*; *keep it simple*; *rich in detail*).

Explicit training may also influence suspect strategies. Terrorist training manuals, such as *The Green Book* and *The Manchester Manual*, both contain sections devoted to counter-interrogation strategies. Both manuals emphasize the use of avoidant (e.g. *say nothing*) and escape (e.g. *deny involvement*) strategies. A recent study demonstrates that such training manuals are likely to have an influence on counter-interrogation strategies (Alison et al., 2014). In this study, counter-interrogation strategies of Al Qaeda, Northern Irish Paramilitary and right wing terrorists were inferred from observations of suspects' behaviour in real life interviews. Barring some exceptions, the core of the results point to the use of withholding strategies akin to those emphasized in the training manuals. For instance, common strategies included staying silent, providing monosyllabic responses, answering 'no comment' and claiming a lack of memory. Interestingly, there was a difference in preferred strategy depending on which terrorist group suspects belonged to. For instance, compared to the other groups, Northern Irish Paramilitary terrorists used a 'no comment' strategy more often; Al Qaeda inspired terrorists used more 'retraction strategies' (i.e. denying a previously uttered statement) while right wing groups were more likely than others to claim a lack of memory or use monosyllabic responses. Such findings further highlight how experience may influence suspect strategies. When taken together, the research on suspects' experience implies that the more seasoned the criminal, the less they will say, and the more difficult the interview will be.

2. Interview-related factors

Degree of suspicion. A key interview-related factor is the degree of suspicion that is directed towards a suspect. Granhag, Clemens, and Strömwall (2009) conducted a study where they examined how suspects' counter-interrogation strategies were influenced by both *degree of suspicion* and *criminal experience*. Half of the participants were undergraduates who had never been interviewed by the police before (naïve suspects) and the other half were former criminals who all had experience of lying to the police in interviews (experienced suspects). All participants were exposed to a detailed crime vignette (a theft in a store), and they were asked to imagine being guilty of the theft. Furthermore, they were asked to imagine that they were called in by the police for an interview, during which they should deny their guilt. Half of the suspects were informed that they just *appeared for questioning* (low degree of suspicion) and the other half were informed that they were *reasonably suspected* (high degree of suspicion). The results showed that naïve suspects volunteered more self-incriminating information in the initial free recall phase compared to experienced suspects. When asked crime-specific questions, naïve suspects admitted to more actions fitting with the crime under investigation. Furthermore, naïve suspects in the high-suspicion condition were more willing to report information than naïve suspects in the low-suspicion condition. In contrast, experienced suspects' willingness to report information was not affected by the degree of suspicion.

That naïve suspects disclosed more information when they were under a high degree of suspicion (vs. low degree of suspicion) suggests that they perceived that it was their duty to actively convince the interviewer of their innocence. Experienced suspects, however, disclosed overall very little possibly self-incriminating information – demonstrating insight with respect to the fact that it is the police that need to find evidence that proves them guilty. The results of these studies point in the same direction, namely, that the experienced suspects know that it is not their task to convince the investigator of their innocence – rather it is up to the police to find evidence that proves them guilty. More generally speaking, the results demonstrate how the factors discussed throughout this chapter are unlikely to work in isolation, but rather have a differing influence dependent on the population and contextual factors at hand.

Type of interview. For some decades, there has been an ongoing debate in the research field between accusatorial and information gathering interview styles (e.g. Hartwig et al., 2005; Moston & Engelberg, 1993).

Common criticisms of the sterner accusatorial style are that it is more likely to lead to false confessions (e.g. Kassin & Kiechel, 1996; Russano, Meissner, Narchet, & Kassin, 2005) and less effective at eliciting information compared to information gathering (Evans et al., 2013) and rapport-focused approaches (Alison, Alison, Noone, Elntib, & Christiansen, 2013). A related criticism, of particular importance for this chapter, is that accusatorial interviewing styles may result in fewer cues to deceit than information gathering styles.

Indirect support for this claim is provided, for example, in a study by Vrij, Mann, Kristen, and Fisher (2007). In this study, truth telling and lying suspects were interviewed either by accusatorial, information gathering, or behaviour analysis-styled interviews. Although interview type had no influence on truth tellers' statements, liars' produced significantly shorter statements in the accusatorial interview condition. Vrij et al. suggested that this was evident of liars adopting escape strategies, such as denials, when confronted with an accusatorial interview. In addition, the shorter statements obtained in the accusatorial interviews produced comparatively fewer cues to deceit when availing of content analysis deception techniques.

Issues of interrogation style need of course not be limited to accusatorial vs. information gathering. Beune, Giebels, and Sanders (2009) examined how *being kind* and *rational persuasion* (i.e. arguments of logic and rationality) influenced suspects guilty of a mock theft from *low-context* cultures (i.e. western cultures, where meaning is attached explicitly in the message) and *high-context* cultures (i.e. non-western cultures, where a great deal of the meaning of a message is derived from the context). Their results showed that being kind led to more admissions, but particularly for high-context cultures. In contrast, rational arguments led to more admissions, but particularly for low-context cultures. Again, however, as with the study by Vrij et al., counter-interrogation strategies were not directly measured, and can only be inferred from other dependent variables such as admissions of guilt. Taking this liberty, the results indicate (a) how the type of interrogation can influence suspects' strategies and (b) how this influence can be moderated by suspects' experience, such as cultural background.

Repeated investigative interviews. In real-life situations there is a high likelihood that a suspect will be interrogated on numerous occasions (e.g. Miller & Stiff, 1993). ·On this note, Granhag and Strömwall (2002) examined strategies of truth tellers and liars in the context of repeated interrogations. The participants saw a staged event that they were subsequently asked to lie about (liars) or to truthfully recapitulate (truth tellers). All participants were given extensive time to plan their statements and they were informed that they would be interviewed on three occasions during the following days. In the first interview, interviewers were instructed to actively listen and encourage the suspect to tell as much as possible, but not to ask him/her any questions. In the second interview, which took place 4 days later, each interviewer (not the same as in the first interview) received background information about the event and was informed that the person he or she was going to interview could either be truthful or deceptive. For the second interview, the interviewer received written instructions regarding the questions he or she was supposed to ask, and the order in which to ask them. One week after the second interview, the suspects were asked to return to be interviewed a final time. The third interview was almost identical to the second, with the exception that the interviewers were now additionally allowed to ask questions of their own. After the final interview, suspects were asked about their counter-interrogation strategies. The most common verbal strategy among liars was *to not give a too detailed testimony*. Truth tellers reported strategies like to *talk spontaneously* and to *only tell things they were very confident in*.

Abstracting the discussion somewhat, Granhag and Strömwall (1999) have also proposed the 'repeat versus reconstruct hypothesis'. This holds that liars, in an explicit attempt to reduce inconsistencies, will repeat their statements across interviews. Truth tellers in contrast, will reconstruct their statements from memory, allowing for the natural errors associated with this process (e.g. errors of omission and commission). These differing strategies can result in comparable levels of between-statement consistency for truth tellers and liars. This proposal has found direct support with results showing that truthful and deceptive statements are capable of being equally consistent over repeated interviews (Granhag & Strömwall, 2002) and indirect support from research on counter-interrogation strategies. For instance, truth tellers' strategies such as to *talk spontaneously* (Granhag & Strömwall, 2002) or *tell the truth like it happened* (Hartwig et al., 2007) are indicative of typical reconstructive memory processes. In contrast, liars' strategies such as *stick to the cover story* (Clemens, Granhag, & Strömwall, 2013) or *be consistent* (Granhag et al., 2013) are indicative of a repeat strategy.

3. Crime-Related Factors

Crimes are not uniform acts. They can vary on a host of dimensions. For instance, crimes can be white-collar or blue-collar; they can be committed by individuals or groups; they can be planned (premeditated) or can happen in the 'heat of the moment'; they can be once off or repeated acts. This list highlights just a handful of ways in which crimes can differ, which may alter how both interviewers and suspects approach an interview. In this section, we will examine suspects' strategies when (a) crimes are committed by groups rather than individuals and (b) crimes that are planned but not yet performed – intended crimes.

Groups of suspects. The study by Vrij et al. (2010) was one of the first to examine counter-interrogation strategies of pairs of liars and truth tellers. The interview concerned their whereabouts during a certain period of time. The pairs of truth tellers had lunch together in a restaurant and were subsequently confronted with the suspicion of having committed a crime (the theft of money from a purse) and informed about an upcoming interview in which they had to convince the interviewer of their innocence. They were given 10 minutes to prepare for the interview. Next, they were asked to individually fill out a pre-interview questionnaire in which they were asked whether they had developed an interview strategy, and if so, what strategy they had chosen. If they had not developed a strategy, they were asked to explain why. Subsequently, the pairs of truth tellers were interviewed individually.

The pairs of liars actually stole money from a purse and were subsequently asked to construct a 'joint lunch' alibi to mask this illegal action. Their task was to convince the interviewer of their innocence and the truthfulness of their alibi. The pre-interview questionnaire and interview procedure were similar to those employed for truth tellers. Vrij and colleagues (2010) found that more liars than truth tellers had prepared a strategy for the interview (which is in line with previous findings in this field, e.g. Clemens et al., 2010; Hartwig et al., 2007; Strömwall et al., 2006). Truth tellers' main reason for not developing a joint interview strategy was that it was not needed. Liars' main reason for not doing so was that they were not certain which questions would be asked during the interview. Differences between truth tellers' and liars' strategies were found for the verbal but not the nonverbal strategies. Whereas pairs of truth tellers' main verbal strategy was to *tell the truth*, pairs of liars prepared their statements more thoroughly by *thinking of details that they would incorporate in their stories* and *creating a high degree of conformity between their statements*. In addition, pairs of liars aimed for restricted statements – *not giving too much detail to the interviewer*.

The pattern of truth tellers employing forthcoming strategies and liars employing evasive strategies was also found in a recent study by Granhag, Mac Giolla, Strömwall, and Rangmar (2013). However, they examined the counter-interrogation strategies of suspects that acted in groups of three. Truth-telling suspects' main strategy was to *be honest*, which can reasonably be viewed as a forthcoming strategy. Liars' most common strategy was to *be restrictive*, which is not forthcoming at all. The previously mentioned finding that liars tend to control the content of their statements was corroborated in this study, as the second most common strategy of liars was to *be consistent*.

Future crimes. Clemens et al. (2013) conducted a study examining mock suspects' counter-interrogation strategies in interviews in which they anticipated questions on their intentions. Since planning is an inherent part of many intentions, mock suspects were asked, in addition to questions about their intentions, a set of questions which pertained to the planning phase in which they formed their intentions. The latter set of questions was expected to be more unanticipated than the questions asked about their intentions. As liars depend on pre-interview preparation and correct anticipation of interview questions more than truth tellers (who can fall back on their memory), it was expected that it would be more difficult for liars (vs. truth tellers) to answer the unanticipated questions in a satisfying way (see Chapter 9 in this volume).

The experiment started with the planning phase in which all participants were given 10 minutes to plan either a non-criminal (truth tellers) or a criminal (liars) activity. Liars were additionally instructed to prepare a cover story, since they would need to mask their criminal intention if they were stopped and questioned during their mission. The experiment was designed in such a way that liars and truth tellers had to perform the same planning activities but for different reasons (truth tellers had non-criminal reasons, liars had criminal ones). All participants were intercepted before executing their planned actions and had to deny their guilt during the subsequent interview. In a post-interview questionnaire, suspects were asked to write down their principal strategy for being perceived as truthful. The most common strategy for truth-telling suspects was to *be honest*. For lying suspects, the most common verbal strategies were *stick to the cover story* and *avoid lying*.

In another recent study conducted by Mac Giolla and Granhag (2014), the factors *groups of suspects* and *future crimes* were combined. The participants had planned, but not yet committed, either a mock crime (liars) or a non-criminal activity (truth tellers) in a group of three. The results largely replicated those of Clemens et al. (2013) and Granhag et al. (2013). Truth tellers' most common strategy was to *be honest*, while liars commonly reported the strategy to *stick to the cover story*.

FUTURE DIRECTIONS

The study of suspect counter-interrogation strategies is still in its infancy. For this reason, it is no exaggeration to say that all of the categories of the model discussed earlier would benefit from more research at both the theoretical and empirical level. For instance, consider crime-related factors. Thus far, studies have primarily focused on situations when suspects deny their engagement in a specific behaviour: truth tellers' denials are honest, while liars' are not. There are many situations, however, when it is the intentionality of the act, and not the act per se, that is the focus of an investigative interview. This would include many white-collar or economic crimes. Consider the politician who used a government credit card to buy personal items. Here the issue is unlikely to be whether the purchase was made or not, but rather whether the use of the government credit card was intentional or an unfortunate mistake. Such a focus will likely affect, either directly or indirectly, the type of counter-interrogation strategies employed.

A further issue regards advancing the methodological approaches to the topic. To examine suspect strategies, studies have so far relied either on self-reports (e.g. Clemens et al., 2013) or inferred strategies by observing a suspect's behaviour in an interview (e.g. Alison et al., 2014). Future studies may benefit by combining these two measures. Such an approach may illuminate not only which strategies suspects employ, but also how effective they are at doing so (see Granhag et al., 2013). Furthermore, such research may shed light on the extent to which there are discrepancies between how people plan to behave during an interrogation and how they·actually behave (for a related example, see Diekmann, Tenbrunsel, & Galinsky, 2003). Practical difficulties notwithstanding, it may also be of value to attempt some form of 'online' measure (e.g. through a modified think aloud protocol; van Someren, Barnard, & Sandberg, 1994). Such an approach could provide data about which – and how many – strategies suspects' use throughout an interview; whether they choose to change their strategy at any stage in the interview, and if so why they choose to change. Progressions of this kind would strengthen the goal of this research program, which ultimately can aid in the development of strategic interviewing techniques.

CONCLUSIONS

At the outset of this chapter, we argued for the importance of knowledge of counter-interrogation strategies, while highlighting that research on the topic is meager. In recent years, some efforts have been made to add knowledge to this small body of research. Based on the summary of the existing literature on suspects' counter-interrogation strategies provided in the current chapter, the following main conclusions can be drawn.

First, the empirical studies reviewed here generally support the theoretical reasoning on suspects' counter-interrogation strategies outlined earlier. That is, research largely supports the idea that guilty suspects tend to apply avoidance strategies, such as withholding information (*avoid giving a too detailed testimony; keep the story simple*), whereas innocent suspects tend to apply more forthcoming strategies (*talk spontaneously; keep it real*) (e.g. Granhag & Strömwall, 2002; Strömwall et al., 2006). When liars employ forthcoming strategies, this is usually due to strategic self-presentational reasons and their mission to imitate truth tellers (see Kassin & Norwick, 2004).

Second, if given the chance to prepare for an interview, liars' will be more likely to make use of it than truth tellers (e.g. Clemens et al., 2010; Hartwig et al., 2007, 2010). Furthermore, liars report the use of counter-interrogation strategies more·often than truth tellers. These strategies broadly concern two tasks. On the one hand, based on their stereotypical beliefs about cues to truthfulness, liars' may try to imitate the behaviour of an innocent person. To *be consistent*, to *make the statement sound unrehearsed*, and to *act calm* are examples of strategies that liars may use to attempt to emulate truthful statements. On the other hand, liars also apply strategies that facilitate the otherwise taxing task of lying (for a more detailed account, see Vrij, Fisher, Mann, & Leal, 2009). To *avoid lying whenever it is possible*' and to *keep the story simple* are two examples from the reviewed literature of how liars' attempt to decrease their cognitive load.

Third, the reviewed literature illustrates that liars' strategies are strongly affected by the suspect-specific and context-specific factors discussed in the chapter. In contrast, the strategies reported by truth-telling suspects (e.g. *tell the truth like it happened; keep it real; be honest*) tend to be consistent across conditions. Put simply, they trust in their honesty to prevail if they just share their knowledge with the interviewer, and this strategy is for the most part independent of external conditions. If truth tellers do report strategies other than simply telling the truth (e.g. *be cooperative, answer spontaneously*), like liars' they tend to be strategies designed to emphasize their honesty based on stereotypical beliefs.

We began this chapter with a quote from a terrorist manual that emphasized just how sophisticated a suspect's reasoning about an interview can be. Interrogation techniques and counter-interrogation strategies can therefore be seen as an ongoing game of cat and mouse, between interviewer and suspect. An empirically driven approach to this game may give practitioners an important edge in the interview room.

REFERENCES

Alison, L., Alison, E., Noone, G., Elntib, S., & Christiansen, P. (2013). Why tough tactics fail and rapport gets results: Observing rapport-based interpersonal techniques (ORBIT) to generate useful information from terrorists. *Psychology, Public Policy, and Law, 19*, 411–431. doi: 10.1037/a0034564.

Alison, L., Alison, E., Noone, G., Elntib, S., Waring, S., & Christiansen, P. (2014). *Whatever you say, say nothing: Individual differences in counter interrogation tactics amongst a field sample of right wing, AQ inspired and paramilitary terrorists*. Unpublished manuscript.

Ben-Shakhar, G. (2011). Countermeasures. In: B. Verschuere, G. Ben-Shakhar, & E. Meijer (Eds.), *Memory detection: Theory and application of the Concealed Information Test* (pp. , 200-214). Cambridge: Cambridge University Press.

Beune, K., Giebels, E., & Sanders, K. (2009). Are you talking to me? Influencing behaviour and culture in police interviews. *Psychology, Crime and Law, 15*, 597–617. doi:10.1080/10683160802442835

Cain, C. K., & LeDoux, J. E. (2008). Emotional processing and motivation: In search of brain mechanisms. In A. J. Elliot (Ed.), *Handbook of approach and avoidance motivation* (pp. 17–34). New York, NY: Psychology Press.

Cape, E. (1999). *Defending suspects at police stations. The practitioners' guide to advice and representation*. London, UK. Legal Action Group.

Carlson, N. R., Buskist, W., & Martin, G. N. (2000). *Psychology: The science of behavior*. Harlow, UK: Allyn & Bacon.

Carver, C. S., & Scheier, M. F. (2011). Self-regulation of action and affect. In K. D. Vohs & R. F. Baumeister (Eds.), *Handbook of self-regulation: Research, theory and applications* (2nd ed., pp. 3–21). New York, NY: Guilford.

Clemens, F. (2013). *Detecting lies about past and future actions: The strategic use of evidence (SUE) technique and suspects' strategies* (Unpublished doctoral dissertation). University of Gothenburg, Sweden.

Clemens, F., Granhag, P. A., & Strömwall, L. A. (2013). Counter-interrogation strategies when anticipating questions on intentions. *Journal of Investigative Psychology and Offender Profiling, 10*, 125–138. doi:10.1002/jip.1387

Clemens, F., Granhag, P. A., Strömwall, L. A., Vrij, A., Landström, S., Roos af Hjelmsäter, E., & Hartwig, M. (2010). Skulking around the dinosaur: Eliciting cues to children's deception via strategic disclosure of evidence. *Applied Cognitive Psychology, 24*, 925–940. doi:10.1002/acp.1597

Colwell, K., Hiscock-Anisman, C., Memon, A., Woods, D., & Michlik, P. M. (2006). Strategies of impression management among deceivers and truth-tellers: How liars attempt to convince. *American Journal of Forensic Psychology, 24*, 31–38.

Davis, D., & Leo, R. A. (2012). Interrogation-related regulatory decline: Ego depletion, failures of self-regulation, and the decision to confess. *Psychology, Public Policy, and Law, 18*, 673–704. doi:10.1037/a0027367

DePaulo, B. M. (1992). Nonverbal behavior and self-presentation. *Psychological Bulletin, 111*, 203–243. doi:10.1037/0033-2909.111.2.203

DePaulo, B. M., Lindsay, J. J., Malone, B. E., Muhlenbruck, L., Charlton, K., & Cooper, H. (2003). Cues to deception. *Psychological Bulletin, 129*, 74–118. doi:10.1037/0033-2909.129.1.74

Diekmann, K. A., Tenbrunsel, A. E., & Galinsky, A. D. (2003). From self-prediction to self-defeat: Behavioral forecasting, self-fulfilling prophecies, and the effect of competitive expectations. *Journal of Personality and Social Psychology, 85,* 672–683. doi:10.1037/0022-3514.85.4.672

Evans, J. R., Meissner, C. A., Ross, A. B., Houston, K. A., Russano, M. B., & Horgan, A. J. (2013). Obtaining guilty knowledge in human intelligence interrogations: Comparing accusatorial and information-gathering approaches with a novel experimental paradigm. *Journal of Applied Research in Memory and Cognition, 2,* 83–88.

Fiske, S. T., & Taylor, S. E. (2008). *Social cognition: From brains to culture.* Boston, MA: McGraw-Hill.

Forgas, J. P., Baumeister, R. F., & Tice, D. M. (Eds.). (2009). *Psychology of self-regulation: Cognitive, affective, and motivational processes.* New York, NY: Psychology Press.

Gozna, L. F., Sully, L., & Teicher, S. (2005). *It weren't me Gov, honest! Observations of the suspect tactics in real life police interviews.* Paper Presented at the 8th International Investigative Psychology Conference, London, UK.

Granhag, P. A., Cancino Montecinos, S., & Oleszkiewicz, S. (2013a). Eliciting intelligence from sources: The·first scientific test of the Scharff-technique. *Legal and Criminological Psychology.* Advance online publication. doi:10.1111/lcrp.12015.

Granhag, P. A., Clemens, F., & Strömwall, L. A. (2009). The usual and the unusual suspects: Level of suspicion and counter-interrogation tactics. *Journal of Investigative Psychology and Offender Profiling, 6,* 129–137. doi:10.1002/jip.101

Granhag, P. A., & Hartwig, M. (2008). A new theoretical perspective on deception detection: On the psychology of instrumental mind reading. *Psychology, Crime and Law, 14,* 189–200. doi:10.1080/10683160701645181

Granhag, P. A., Mac Giolla, E., Strömwall, L. A., & Rangmar, J. (2013b). Counter-interrogation strategies among small cells of suspects. *Psychiatry, Psychology and Law, 20,* 705–712. Available online. doi:10.1080/13218719.2012.729021

Granhag, P. A., & Strömwall, L. A. (1999). Repeated interrogations–stretching the deception detection paradigm. *Expert Evidence, 7,* 163–174. doi:10.1023/A:1008993326434.

Granhag, P. A., & Strömwall, L. A. (2002). Repeated interrogations: Verbal and non-verbal cues to deception. *Applied Cognitive Psychology, 16,* 243–257. doi:10.1002/acp.784

Hartwig, M., Granhag,·P. A., & Strömwall, L. A. (2007). Guilty and innocent suspects' strategies during police interrogations. *Psychology, Crime and Law, 13,* 213–227. doi:10.1080/10683160600750264

Hartwig, M., Granhag, P. A., & Luke, T. (2014). Strategic use of evidence during investigative interviews: The state of the science. In D. C. Raskin, C. R. Honts, & J. C. Kircher (Eds.), *Credibility assessment: Scientific research an applications* (pp. 1–36). Oxford, UK: Academic Press.

Hartwig, M., Granhag, P. A., Strömwall, L. A., & Doering, N. (2010). Impression and information management: On the strategic self-regulation of innocent and guilty suspects. *Open Criminology Journal, 3,* 10–16. doi:10.2174/1874917801003020010

Hartwig, M., Granhag, P. A., Strömwall, L. A., & Vrij, A. (2005). Detecting deception via strategic disclosure of evidence. *Law and Human Behavior, 29,* 469–484. doi:10.1007/s10979-005-5521-x

Hines, A., Colwell, K., Hiscock-Anisman, C., Garrett, E., Ansarra, R., & Montalvo, L. (2010). Impression management strategies of deceivers and honest reporters in an investigative interview. *The European Journal of Psychology Applied to Legal Context, 2*, 73–90.

Honts, C. R., & Amato, S. L. (2002). Countermeasures. In M. Kleiner (Ed.), *Handbook of polygraph testing* (pp. 251–264). San Diego, CA: Academic Press.

Kassin, S. M. (2005). On the psychology of confessions: Does innocence put innocents at risk? *American Psychologist, 60*, 215. doi:10.1037/0003-066X.60.3.215

Kassin, S. M., & Kiechel, K. L. (1996). The social psychology of false confessions: Compliance, internalization, and confabulation. *Psychological Science, 7*, 125–128. doi:10.1111/j.1467-9280.1996.tb00344.x

Kassin, S. M., & Norwick, R. J. (2004). Why people waive their Miranda rights: The power of innocence. *Law and Human Behavior, 28*, 211–221. doi:10.1023/B:LAHU.0000022323.74584.f5

Leins, D. A., Fisher, R. P., & Ross, S. J. (2013). Exploring liars' strategies for creating deceptive reports. *Legal and Criminological Psychology, 18*, 141–151. doi:10.1111/j.2044-8333.2011.02041.x

Leo, R. A. (1996). Inside the interrogation room. *Journal of Criminal Law and Criminology, 86*, 266–303. doi:10.2307/1144028

Lerner, M. J. (1980). *The belief in a just world*. New York, NY: Plenum Press.

Luke, T. J., Dawson, E., Hartwig, M., & Granhag, P. A. (2014). How awareness of possible evidence induces forthcoming counter-interrogation strategies. *Applied Cognitive Psychology*. doi: 10.1002/acp.3019.

Mac Giolla, E., & Granhag, P. A. (2014). *Small cells of suspects interviewed about their planned future actions: An analysis of their counter-interrogation strategies*. Manuscript in preparation.

Miller, G. R., & Stiff, J. B. (1993). *Deceptive communication, Sage series in interpersonal communication*. Newbury Park, CA: Sage.

Moston, S., & Engelberg, T. (1993). Police questioning techniques in tape recorded interviews with criminal suspects. *Policing and Society: An International Journal, 3*(3), 223–237.

Nilsson, R. (2010). *How to use the evidence when interrogating suspects*. High Value Detainee Interrogation Group (HIG, FBI). HIG Research Symposium: Interrogation in the European Union, Washington, DC.

Oleszkiewicz, S., Granhag, P. A., & Cancino Montecinos, S. (2014). The scharff-technique: Eliciting intelligence from human sources. *Law and Human Behavior*. Advance online publication. doi: 10.1037/lhb0000085.

Russano, M. B., Meissner, C. A., Narchet, F. M., & Kassin, S. M. (2005). Investigating true and false confessions within a novel experimental paradigm. *Psychological Science, 16*, 481–486. doi:10.1111/j.0956-7976.2005.01560.x

Savitsky, K., & Gilovich, T. (2003). The illusion of transparency and the alleviation of speech anxiety. *Journal of Experimental Social Psychology, 39*, 618–625. doi:10.1016/S0022-1031(03)00056-8

Softley, P. (1980). *Police interrogation: An observational study in four police stations*. London, UK: Home Office Research Study, Royal Commission on Criminal Procedure Research Study.

Soufan, A. H. (2011). *The black banners: The inside story of 9/11 and the war against Al-Qaeda*. New York, NY: W. W. Norton & Company.

Sporer, S. L., & Schwandt, B. (2007). Moderators of nonverbal indicators of deception: A meta-analytic synthesis. *Psychology, Public Policy, and Law, 13*, 1–34. doi:10.1037/1076-8971.13.1.1

Strömwall, L. A., Hartwig, M., & Granhag, P. A. (2006). To act truthfully: Nonverbal behaviour and strategies during a police interrogation. *Psychology, Crime and Law, 12*, 207–219. doi:10.1080/10683160512331331328

Strömwall, L. A., & Willén, R. M. (2011). Inside criminal minds: Offenders' strategies when lying. *Journal of Investigative Psychology and Offender Profiling, 8*, 271–281. doi:10.1002/jip.148

Toliver, R. F. (1997). *The interrogator: The story of Hanns Joachim Scharff master interrogator of the Luftwaffe.* Atglen, PA: Schiffer Publishing Ltd.

Van Someren, M. W., Barnard, Y. F., & Sandberg, J. A. (1994). *The think aloud method: A practical guide to modelling cognitive processes.* London, UK: Academic Press.

Vrij, A., Fisher, R. P., Mann, S., & Leal, S. (2009). Increasing cognitive load in interviews to detect deceit (Invited chapter). In B. Milne, S. Savage, & T. Williamson (Eds.), *International developments in investigative interviewing* (pp. 176–189). Uffculme, UK: Willan Publishing.

Vrij, A., Mann, S., Kristen, S., & Fisher, R. P. (2007). Cues to deception and ability to detect lies as a function of police interview styles. *Law and Human Behavior, 31*, 499–518. doi:10.1007/s10979-006-9066-4

Vrij, A., Mann, S., Leal, S., & Granhag, P. A. (2010). Getting into the minds of pairs of liars and truth tellers: An examination of their strategies. *Open Criminology Journal, 3*, 17–22. doi:10.2174/1874917801003010017

14

Covert Detection of Deception

EITAN ELAAD

Having remote methods/measures for rapid detection of deception, thereby discriminating between individuals involved in an illegal activity and innocent suspects, is very appealing. Most appealing is the use of covert methods/measures without the awareness of the suspects that they are being interrogated. Such capabilities provide clear advantages to the operator who may gather valuable information without hooking the suspect to a machine. The information may be gathered from a distance (e.g. telephone, microphone, camera, microwaves and Internet) without a physical contact with the interrogated person. Information may also be gathered from covert transducers hidden in the chair on which the examinee is sitting. Collecting information about suspects without their awareness may be welcomed by security personnel, law enforcement officers, politicians, private investigators, lawyers and many others as they can be useful in a variety of anti-terrorism, law enforcement, intelligent, commercial, political and other applications that are based on information gathering from humans. The use of covert measures may also enrich the interrogation tactics

Detecting Deception: Current Challenges and Cognitive Approaches, First Edition.
Edited by Pär Anders Granhag, Aldert Vrij, and Bruno Verschuere.
© 2015 John Wiley & Sons, Ltd. Published 2015 by John Wiley & Sons, Ltd.

and questioning methods. On the other hand, the use of covert measures may raise ethical and legal questions. The question of privacy may be raised as well as the issue of pre-examination consent that is currently required from polygraph examinees. Therefore, one should think of ways to limit and control the use of covert methods/measures. I will describe the main theoretical accounts underlying lie detection, methods of gathering information from a distance that are based on these theories and several covert measures that were developed for this matter. I will discuss their accuracy and limitations and conclude with the ethical concerns about their use.

UNDERLYING THEORETICAL APPROACHES TO DETECTING DECEPTION

Lying is believed to be associated with emotions such as fear, guilt and delight (Ekman, 2001). The emotional approach suggests that liars experience stronger emotions than truth-tellers and the emotional experience trigger cues to deception, mostly nervousness-related cues. However, experiencing emotions is not limited to liars, and truth-tellers who fail to convince may be equally nervous. Therefore, one cannot rely on manifested nervousness to distinguish between truthful and deceptive individuals (Vrij, Mann, & Leal, 2013). Another approach to detecting deception associates lying to heightened cognitive load. It is claimed that lying is more mentally demanding than telling the truth and the extra cognitive load surrender lies. Vrij et al. (2013) summarized that liars have to formulate a plausible story that adheres to everything that the target person knows or might find out. Liars must remember what they have said and to whom it was said, to maintain their consistency. They have to monitor their demeanour to impress the other person of their honesty. All these are cognitively demanding. Furthermore, liars have to invest cognitive resources to carefully monitor the other person's reactions to assess whether they are getting away with their lies. Further, people are inclined to tell the truth which happens automatically, while for telling lies, liars have to deliberately suppress the truth and this requires extra cognitive effort. However, cues of cognitive load are not necessarily indications of deception and telling the truth may sometimes be equally loaded and requires mental effort.

Several unobtrusive lie detection methods are based on either the emotional or the cognitive load approach. A noticeable example of the emotional approach is the analysis of micro-expressions in the targets face.

COVERT DETECTION OF MICRO-EXPRESSIONS IN THE FACE

The most forthcoming attempt to unravel deception without the awareness of the target is to look at the behaviour of that individual and figure
out whether or not that person is lying. However, most people including
professionals such as police investigators often fail in their attempt to
catch liars. Bond and DePaulo (2006) conducted a meta-analysis about
the ability of people to detect lies and truths and reported an average
accuracy rate of 54% where chance expectancy is 50%. There are several
explanations for this failure: Cues to deception are often faint and unreliable (DePaulo et al., 2003); people have incorrect beliefs about non-
verbal indicators of deception; police investigators never know whether
the suspect they decided to release is indeed guilty or innocent
(Stromwall & Granhag, 2003) due to lack of on-the-job feedback about
whether a previous judgment was correct or incorrect (Vrij, 2008). There
seems to be, however, an exception to this rule. Ekman (2001) suggested
seeking micro-expressions of emotions in the face of the target person.
Such micro-expressions are spontaneous emotional expressions that
appear for a short period of time before they fade away. Strong felt emotions activate almost automatically the muscles in the face. If a person
denies the emotional state that he or she experiences, these automatic
facial expressions must be suppressed. People have experience in controlling their facial expressions and are able to avoid showing emotions
that they don't want other people to see. However, from time to time
involuntary expressions are released and are shown in the face. They
are quickly suppressed within 1/25th of a second after their appearance.
Lay people usually miss these micro-expressions but trained observers
may notice them. Running a video footage of the target person in slow
motion may surrender these micro-expressions as well. When these
micro-expressions contrast the feelings that the individual tries to convey, they may reveal valuable information, including deception.

However, the application of micro-expressions in the face as indicators of deception is controversial (Porter & Ten Brinke, 2008). A more
recent account, published in *Nature* (Weinberger, 2010), indicated that
scientists were not persuaded by the data that Ekman provided and
failed to replicate Ekman's findings.

PSYCHOPHYSIOLOGICAL DETECTION OF DECEPTION

To help people detect deception, various tools and methods were developed, of which the psychophysiological test of lie detection (polygraph)
is the prominent one. The most commonly used psychophysiological

test of lie detection is the Comparison Question Test (CQT). It is widely used in criminal cases, security screening and in civil proceedings and therefore deserves attention. There are many variation of the CQT, for example the modified general questions test (MGQT), Backster zone of comparison test (ZCT), Utah directed lie test (DLT) (see Raskin & Honts, 2002, for a review). However, in all these tests, there are basically three types of questions: relevant questions which refer to the crime under investigation in the 'did you do it?' form, such as: 'Did you take $100 from Mr. Smith last Saturday?' Relevant questions are typically answered 'no' claiming innocence. Another type of questions is the comparison questions (or probable lie questions), which deal with undesirable acts in the past and pertain to matters similar to the crime being investigated but with a larger scope (the DLT uses a known lie instead of a probable lie.as a comparison question). An example of a comparison question might be, 'between the ages of 12 and 16 did you ever steal anything valuable?' The comparison questions are formulated during the pretest interview with the intention that the examinee will have some doubt about the veracity of his 'no' answer. The third group of questions consists of irrelevant questions, which correspond to a neutral issue to which the affirmative answer is a known truth. For example, 'are you sitting on a chair?'

The assumption is that stronger responses to the relevant, relative to the comparison questions, can be interpreted as indicating guilt. In the case of stronger responses to the comparison than to the relevant questions, an innocent decision is made. The assumption is based on the view that comparison questions serve to determine whether the suspect is more concerned or less concerned about the relevant questions.

The more concerned guilty suspects are expected to react more strongly to relevant questions which deal with the specific issue under investigation, than to the more general comparison questions. The less concerned innocent suspects, who answer the relevant questions truthfully, are deceptive or are unsure that they answer truthfully to the comparison questions. Hence, they are expected to react more strongly to comparison questions than to relevant questions (for a detailed description of CQT, see Chapter 4).

A more researched and less applied psychophysiological interrogation format is the Concealed Information Test (CIT). The CIT (known also as the guilty knowledge test) is designed to detect information that an individual tries to conceal (Lykken, 1974, 1998). Normally, suspects are presented with a series of multiple-choice questions, each having one correct alternative (e.g. a feature of the crime under investigation) and several incorrect (control) alternatives, chosen so that an innocent person would not be able to discriminate them from the correct alternative (Lykken, 1998). It is assumed that a guilty person knows the details of the crime, and therefore will respond to the correct alternative more than to the incorrect alternatives. An innocent suspect, for whom all stimuli are neutral, is expected to respond unsystematically to all stimuli (for more details on CIT, see Chapter 4). Either the CQT or the CIT were used to examine unobtrusive methods/measures designed to detect liars and truth tellers.

VOICE STRESS ANALYSIS

An early attempt to introduce covert measures for emotional detection of deception took place in the early seventies when a commercial lie detector employing voice analysis, the Psychological Stress Evaluator (PSE), was distributed. The PSE was welcomed by users from law enforcement agencies as well as from the private sector. It was treated as a reliable instrument and was employed in actual criminal interrogations. The PSE is based on the notion that the human voice produces inaudible frequency changes or microtremors in the 8–12 Hz range that disappear under stress. It was claimed that the pattern of these changes provide a measure of psychophysiological arousal, which can be detected from voice recordings. While such microtremors were found in skeletal muscles (Lippold, 1971), their direct effect was never systematically examined and found in the muscles involved in speech production. Therefore, there is no scientific evidence to support the idea that microtremors in the 8–12 Hz range are present in the voice muscles (Eriksson & Lacerda, 2007) and that the PSE measures the alleged changes.

As to the validity of the PSE, research did not support it in the CIT context. The few attempts to study the PSE using the CIT format failed to demonstrate any significant accuracy rates beyond chance level (e.g. Brenner, Branscomb, & Schwartz, 1979; Horvath, 1978,1979). In 1990s, a computerized version of the voice analyser was developed (CVSA – computer voice stress analyzer). The underlying theory for the computer analyser remained the same, namely, it was promised that the CVSA detects physiological microtremors in the voice path. This version of the PSE was examined with the CIT by the U.S. Department of Defense Polygraph Institute – DoDPI (Cestaro & Dollins, 1994). Cestaro and Dollins reported that the CVSA detection rate was not different from chance level. A more recent attempt to examine the validity of the CVSA (Hollien, Harnsberger, Matin, & Hollien, 2008) was equally disappointing. Note that the Hollien et al. study did not use the CIT, but their results are still relevant to the detection of concealed information. Another marketing wave of voice stress analysers appeared after 9/11 with the increasing concern about terrorism and the search to enhance security. The analysers were offered under new names (e.g. TrusterPro, Vericator, Layered Voice Analysis-LVA). Unlike the PSE, there was no attempt to link these voice stress analyses performance to any existing theory. Instead, it is based on trial and error. Still the LVA and similar devices were proved invalid (e.g. Harnsberger, Hollien, Martin, & Hollien, 2009; Sommers, Brown, Senter, & Ryan, 2002).

The question about the use of voice stress analysis was brought before the National Research Council (NRC) (2003). The councils' report summarized that: 'there is little or no scientific basis for the use of the computer voice stress analyzer or similar voice measurement instruments as an alternative to the polygraph for the detection of deception' (p. 168).

To date, voice stress analysis remains a controversial lie detection technology and for the time being it is not recommended as a detection of deception device.

EYE-TRACKING TECHNOLOGIES

The eye-tracking technology is a premise of the heightened cognitive load theory about detecting deception. The underlying assumption is that lying, or the additional cognitive load that accompany lying, is associated with pupil dilation, longer fixation on a target and decreased blinking. Usually eye-tracking is measured by cameras from a distant, which makes them relevant to this review.

Pupillary Size

Kahneman (1973) already argued that pupillary size can be used as an index of processing load or increased attention. This was the theoretical basis on which early studies on pupillary size as an indicator of deception were initiated. These studies reported a relationship between pupil dilation and deception (e.g. Bradley & Janisse, 1979; Heilveil, 1976; Janisse & Bradley, 1980). Other studies (Bradley & Janisse, 1981a; Lubow & Fein, 1996, and more recently Seymour, Baker, & Gaunt, 2013) used the CIT format and concluded that pupil dilation can be a valid index of the possession of crime-related information. Note, however, that pupil dilation is also related to arousal and emotional states. This may explain the results that Bradley and Janisse (1981b) reported with respect to the CQT. They found that when applying the CQT, the pupil size index is effective in discriminating between guilty and innocent examinees. More recent research on the association between pupil size increase and deception supports these results (e.g. Dionisio, Granfolm, Hillix, & Ferrine, 2001; Heaver & Hutton, 2011). Pupil dilation is a reliable physiological index of increased cognitive processing load and therefore can aid in discriminating between truth and deception. Most important, pupil size values can be recorded without the suspect's awareness (Lubow & Fein, 1996).

Fixation Duration

Another facet of eye tracking is eye fixation. Fixation duration reveals face recognition (e.g. Hannula et al., 2010; Ryan, Hannula, & Cohen, 2007). Schwedes and Wentura (2012) extended these results to the CIT in a laboratory study and reported longer fixation duration for concealed faces as compared to neutral faces. Applying a predetermined cutoff point, they correctly detected 64.9% of the guilty participants with 8.1% of the innocents being falsely accused. This study replicates earlier reports on fixation duration and lying conducted for the DoD polygraph institute (Baker, Goldsmith, & Stern, 1992). Again, eye fixation can be recorded from a distance without the awareness of the suspect. To date, there are no reports in the scientific literature about field studies supporting the application of eye fixation measure as a reliable and valid procedure to differentiate between guilty and innocent suspects in actual settings; however, this field of research seems promising.

Blinking

Another measure of eye tracking that can be used unobtrusively with a remote camera is eye blinking rate. Research indicated that eye blinks decrease when the cognitive load increases (e.g. Goldstein, Bauer, & Stern, 1992). Leal and Vrij (2008) extended this to lying situations, indicating that when liars experience cognitive load, a decrease in eye blinking occurs followed by a compensatory effect of an increase in eye blinking when the load ceases after the lie. The study conducted by Leal and Vrij is a low-stakes laboratory study and therefore may have a limited value when it is applied to more stressing situations. However, Mann, Vrij, and Bull (2002) already showed a decrease in eye blinking while lying when they examined real suspects in actual police interviews.

Current Attempts to Apply Eye-Tracking and Similar Devices

Recently, researchers from the University of Utah led by Kircher, Hacker and Raskin have developed a technology that can detect deception through eye-tracking and have commercialized it. The device records a number of measurements while the examinee is answering a series of true and false questions on a computer. Measurements include pupil dilation, longer response time, longer reading time and more errors. These are indications of mental load. The premise is that this technology does not require any contact with the person being tested.

The FAST (Future Attribute Screening Technology) is a U.S. Department of Homeland Security program designed to remotely determine if a person has the intent to cause harm and therefore is a security risk. The FAST measures a variety of physiological indicators (e.g. eye movement, body language and facial expression), all based on non-contact sensors and does not depend on active questioning of the examined person. To date, there are no convincing laboratory and field studies reported in the scientific literature to support the validity of the program. Furthermore, the EPRODD (European Consortium of Psychological Research on Deception Detection) recommended that the emphasis of deception research should shift from technological to behavioural sciences (Meijer et al., 2009). There are no indications that the FAST adopted this recommendation.

THERMAL IMAGING

Another measure that can be carried out unobtrusively is thermal imaging or thermography. Thermal imaging is a technique whereby changes in facial temperature, which are related to changes in the blood flow, are detected by a special camera. The notion is that liars, while being interviewed, would increase the blood flow in their faces more than truth-tellers and thus be detected. It was proposed that such a tool may provide capabilities in remote and rapid screening of people who are unaware of the procedure (Pavlidis, Eberhardt, & Levine, 2002). Pavlidis et al. (2002) published a paper in *Nature* where they reported a study that used the comparison question testing format. They claimed that thermal imaging is a valid method for detecting both guilty and innocent participants, and blood flow in the face and more specifically around the eyes may be a valid cue for deception. The National Research Council (2003) related to thermal imaging and indicated that the published paper is based on a larger research project conducted by investigators at the U.S. DoDPI (Pollina & Ryan,

2002). Thirty trainees at a nearby army camp were enrolled in a mock crime scenario, 5 were dropped out and of the remaining 25, 12 were assigned to be guilty and 13 to be innocent. The report of Pavlidis et al. (2002) used a subset of the original examinees without indicating the selection criteria. The NRC conclusion was that the Pavlidis et al. (2002) report is a flawed evaluation of the thermal imaging procedure and does not provide scientific-based evidence to support the use of facial thermography in detecting deception (p. 157). Another DoDPI mock crime study on the association between facial skin surface temperature (SST) and CIT detection (Pollina et al., 2006) found significant facial SST differences between deceptive and non-deceptive participants. They further reported that the right and left side of the face can produce different SST responses. Recently, Warmelink et al. (2011) tested the efficiency of thermal imaging as a lie detection tool on passengers in an international airport. They instructed passengers to tell the truth or lie about their forthcoming trip and then asked them questions. The questions enhanced mental demands in liars but not in truth-tellers. Liars contradicted themselves more often than truth-tellers and their stories were less plausible than those of the latter. It was reported that liars' skin temperature rose significantly during the interview whereas truth-tellers' skin temperature remained constant. However, thermal imaging accuracy in detecting liars and truth-tellers was lower than the accuracy of the interviewers. The authors stressed the importance of the interview in detecting deception because prior to being interviewed, thermal imaging did not indicate differences between liars and truth-tellers. Finally, even during the interview, not enough liars and truth-tellers were correctly classified. The authors warned against relying on thermal imaging in airports interviews because of the expected high false-positive error rates as most of the passengers are likely to be truthful. It seems that much additional work is needed to determine whether facial temperature changes may be used to detect deception.

COVERT RESPIRATION MEASURES IN PHYSIOLOGICAL DETECTION OF CONCEALED INFORMATION

The CIT is usually conducted using obtrusive physiological measures (e.g. skin conductance, respiration changes and cardiovascular activity) and suspects are well aware that they undergo an interrogation and that their physiological responses are being monitored. Guilty examinees who are attached to the polygraph sensors may attempt to distort their physiological responses. Previous results show that the CIT is vulnerable to such countermeasures attempts (e.g. Ben-Shakhar & Dolev, 1996; Elaad & Ben-Shakhar, 1991; Honts, Devitt, Winbush, & Kircher, 1996). In addition, such awareness might impair the detection of overexcited guilty examinees due to the extra noise involved in testing these examinees.

The use of covert physiological measures (i.e. methods of measuring physiological responses without the awareness of the examinee) may provide a partial solution for these difficulties. Guilty suspects may shift attention from unfamiliar physiological reactions to the more familiar verbal responses and facial expressions (Ekman, 2001) and therefore avoid attempting countermeasures. Nevertheless, they are still under interrogation and they are still concerned that their lies might be detected. Therefore, their physiological responses to the correct alternative are expected to remain larger than those to the incorrect alternatives. Covert measures may also serve to reduce excitement of anxious guilty examinees while experiencing the stress of the test. Detaching these examinees from the transducers may enhance detection accuracy.

Two covert respiration measures which used respiratory effort transducers hidden in the seat and in the back support of a polygraph examination chair were introduced by Elaad and Ben-Shakhar (2008). The transducers recorded changes in the pressure that inhaling and exhaling put on the seat and back support. Responses were defined on the basis of the total respiration line length (RLL) during the 15 seconds interval following stimulus onset (for a detailed description of RLL definition and measurement see Elaad, Ginton, & Jungman, 1992).

Elaad and Ben-Shakhar (2008) assessed the efficiency of the two covert respiration measures in detecting concealed information and compared them with three standard measures typically used for the detection of concealed information (electrodermal, overt respiration and finger pulse measures). For this end, participants were randomly allocated into 'guilty' and 'innocent' roles. Participants simulating the guilty conducted a mock crime while those simulating the innocent were ignorant of the critical information. Both guilty and innocent participants were examined in two sessions. In each, either an 'unobtrusive' or a 'standard polygraph' test was employed. In the unobtrusive condition, the participants were told that their task was to cope with a professional lie catcher who will detect their lies from their behaviour and therefore they will not be attached to the polygraph. However, during the unobtrusive session, participants' respiration traces were monitored with the two covert measures. In the standard polygraph condition, participants were attached, in addition to the two covert respiration measures, to three non-covert, standard polygraph measures: respiration, skin conductance response and finger pulse volume.

Results revealed that under the unobtrusive condition, the covert respiration measures produced better than chance discrimination between 'guilty' participants who were aware of the critical items and 'innocent' participants unaware of the critical information. To make detection rates easier to understand, an arbitrary false-positive error rate (4.2%) was selected. Giving this error rate, the covert seat measure was able to detect 44% of the guilty participants and the covert back measure 30%. Finally, a combined measure of the two covert measures was created. It was defined as the average Z score of the two measures and it displayed 49% detection of guilty participants. Results indicate that the covert measures can be used as independent measures of CIT detection.

Under the polygraph condition, results showed once again that the covert measures' detection efficiency was significantly better than chance. Given the 4.2% false-positive error rate, it was observed that the covert back measure was successful in detecting 44% of the guilty suspects. However, the seat measure produced much lower efficiency (18%). The polygraph condition allows a comparison of the covert measures with the standard polygraph measures. The detection rates computed for the non-covert respiration measure, finger pulse volume and skin conductance response amplitude were 27, 51 and 62%, respectively. Finally, the combined measure of the two covert measures displayed a 51% detection rate of guilty participants. In comparison, the measure that combined the three non-covert measures displayed 67% correct detection. To conclude, the two covert measures and their combination can be used as an addition to the existing measures in the standard CIT test.

Although respiration is the key element in the two covert measures, they seem to record different aspects of respiration. The respiration patterns show that the tracings of the covert back measure and those of the standard respiration measure in the polygraph condition are very similar for guilty participants. In contrast, the covert seat measure looks different. For about half of the participants, the pressure that inhaling put on the respiration belt and the back support increases, whereas the pressure on the seat decreases and vice versa, exhaling produces pressure on the seat while the pressure on both the respiration belt and the back support decreases (see Figure 14.1).

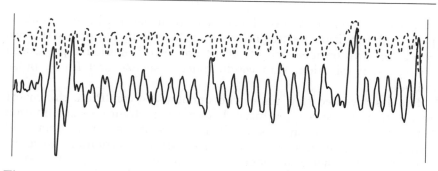

Figure 14.1 Recordings of covert back and seat respiration responses. Upper graph – covert back respiration recordings. Lower graph – covert seat respiration recordings.

Would Covert Respiration Measures Protect Against Countermeasure Attempts?

Studies conducted in laboratory settings have indicated that the CIT is a highly valid method for differentiating between guilty and innocent participants (see Ben-Shakhar & Elaad, 2003 for a review). However, several studies (e.g. Ben-Shakhar & Dolev, 1996; Elaad & Ben-Shakhar, 1991; Honts et al., 1996) demonstrated that the CIT is vulnerable to physical (such as biting the tongue) as well as mental countermeasures (such as silently counting numbers). Such countermeasures may increase false negative outcomes and impair the validity of the CIT. However, it may be expected that only examinees who are connected to the transducers and therefore aware of being tested with the polygraph would deliberately attempt to distort their responses. Examinees that are not connected to the polygraph have no reason to make such attempts. Therefore, the use of covert respiration measures may be part of a solution to the countermeasure problem.

A first attempt to examine the covert measures when the participants actually exercised countermeasures was made by Elaad and Ben-Shakhar (2009). More specifically, Elaad and Ben-Shakhar examined whether the respiration covert measures can protect the CIT against the use of physical and mental countermeasures.

In Elaad and Ben-Shakhars' experiment, participants were tested in two sessions. In the first, a standard CIT polygraph test was employed in which participants were attached to the standard polygraph measures: respiration, electrodermal and finger pulse volume. In addition, the two covert respiration measures were used. In the second session, participants were detached from the polygraph devices and were told that their task was to cope with a professional lie catcher who will detect their lies from their behaviour. To deal with the moral and legal concerns, all participants in this study were informed in advance that their physiological responses would be monitored throughout the entire test and participants were required to give a statement that they understood the instructions and agree to be examined with the polygraph under these conditions. It was hypothesized that when the participants were not connected to the polygraph, they should stop using countermeasures and consequently no increase in false-negative outcomes will be observed.

To examine the hypothesis, 64 college students were randomly allocated into three 'guilty' countermeasure conditions (physical – press their toes against the floor; mental – count silently backward by sevens from a number larger than 200; and no countermeasure) and one 'innocent' condition. Participants in the three guilty conditions were instructed to commit a mock theft. Participants in the innocent condition were instructed to wait outside the office for 5 minutes. Guilty examinees were instructed to apply their countermeasures selectively to two of the six items in each series. They were cautioned not to use countermeasures in response to critical items or to the first item.

Countermeasure examinees were instructed to begin their countermeasure attempts as soon as they recognized a chosen item, to stop for a while to answer 'no', and then continue the countermeasure until the next item is presented. Then, a training session began. Participants were asked to practice their countermeasures in this training session. The participants were further cautioned to perform the countermeasures unobtrusively so that the polygraph operator will not detect them.

Results revealed that both the seat and the back measures were resistant to physical (but not to the mental) countermeasures during the polygraph phase of the experiment. It is possible that pressing the toes against the floor activates muscles that press the seat (and to a lower extent the back), which results in an enlarged rather than reduced waveform length. Hence, physical countermeasures create larger line lengths for the selected foils, which enhance the salience of the responses to the other items, including the critical item. In that case, the likelihood for a correct detection of the guilty participants increases. In summary, it was demonstrated that the covert measures can be useful when participants are connected to the polygraph and apply physical countermeasures. In the two countermeasure conditions and in the no-countermeasures condition, the two covert measures performed much like the overt respiration measure.

In the video phase, deliberate countermeasures were unnecessary. During this phase, the covert seat respiration measure discriminated between guilty and innocent participants under the no-countermeasures and the mental countermeasures conditions but not under the physical countermeasure condition. It seems that when participants stopped pressing the toes against the floor, the increased respiration line lengths for the two selected foils disappeared with the advantage of the seat measure. The question is: why the seat measure does not perform just as well as it does under the no-countermeasure condition? A carry-over effect may answer this question. It is possible that participants, who were engaged in active physical countermeasure attempts in the polygraph phase, adopted a rather passive attitude in the video phase, which interfered with the attention they paid to the critical items. The covert back measure was entirely ineffective in the video phase.

To conclude, the use of countermeasures is a major obstacle to a successful application of the CIT and therefore it is essential to provide solutions to the problem. It was demonstrated that using covert respiration measures may be part of a solution as both covert measures were resistant to physical countermeasures in the polygraph phase and the covert seat measure was resistant to mental countermeasures when the transducers were removed.

Are Covert Respiration Measures Effective in Testing Anxious Examinees?

The polygraph and video conditions were used again to examine whether the two covert respiration measures, hidden in the seat and back of the examination chair, were effective in detecting concealed information held by anxious and less anxious examinees (Elaad & Cohenca, 2013). It was assumed that the polygraph examination is a stressful and unpleasant experience and some examinees are unable to calm down during the test. The stress interferes with the detection of physiological responses to critical information and impairs the CIT results.

Giesen and Rollison (1980) were the first to examine the relationship between trait anxiety and detection in the CIT when only electrodermal measures were used. They divided their participants into high- and low-anxiety groups and reported that the more anxious guilty participants were better detected than the less anxious guilty participants. Iacono, Boisvenu, and Fleming (1984) examined the relationship between state and trait anxiety and electrodermal detection in the CIT and found no significant correlation. Gudjonsson (1982) found positive relations between reported tension during a card test experiment and interference with the electrodermal detection. Additional research is necessary to answer the question whether and to what extent the electrodermal measures are vulnerable to anxiety effects.

The notion that anxiety interferes with respiration responses is well known and early attempts to study how anxiety affects breathing (Cristie, 1935) were followed by more recent ones (e.g. Barlow, 1988; Bass & Gardner, 1985). Cristie observed that anxious patients complained on 'inability to get enough air into the lungs' and 'a sense of oppression or suffocation'. These subjective experiences were accompanied by respiration response patterns such as hyperventilation (Bass & Gardner, 1985). Hyperventilation is a physiological state and refers to increased breathing that is in excess of metabolic requirements. Furthermore, variations in stress-related respiratory responses are associated with stress-related cardiovascular responses (Grossman, 1983). For example, it was observed that high trait-worry people exposed to stress, exhibited increased HR following certain stressors (Knepp & Friedman, 2008). Since CIT detection is based on respiratory and cardiovascular inhibition rather than activation, the arousal involved in the examination of anxious examinees may impair detection of guilty examinees that would show no consistent responses to both critical and neutral items. In that case, anxious guilty examinees might increase false-negative outcomes and escape detection.

The use of covert respiration measures may be part of a solution if the detachment of anxious examinees from the polygraph would result in more distinctive responses to critical items by informed (but not by ignorant) guilty examinees.

Elaad and Cohenca (2013) examined this question. Seventy-four Israeli college students were asked to answer a questionnaire designed to examine state anxiety – The A-state scale of the STAI (Spielberger, 1975). According to their scores, participants were divided into high ($N=24$), intermediate ($N=25$) and low ($N=25$) state anxiety groups. Then, participants were instructed to commit a mock theft and were invited to the examination room for a polygraph test. Participants were informed that their task in the experiment was to evade detection of their knowledge of any crime-related information and were promised a monetary reward for successful performance on the task. At this stage, the examinees were attached to the standard polygraph transducers and eight CIT questions were presented to them. Participants were aware of four critical items presented in these questions and were not aware of the remaining four items. After the completion of the test, examinees were detached from the transducers, a video camera was turned on in front of their face and they were told that an expert lie catcher will watch the film and will base his decision on their verbal and non-verbal behaviour. The eight CIT questions were presented to the examinees again while only the covert respiration measures were running. It was assumed that at the video phase, participants act in a familiar domain and therefore will feel more secure.

The electrodermal measure (SCR) emerged as the most effective measure in discriminating between known and unknown critical items in the polygraph phase. However, SCR is also more sensitive to anxiety effects than other measure (finger pulse volume and respiration).

The manipulation check reveled that participants were motivated to conceal information in the polygraph phase more than in the video phase, and were more concerned about the outcome of the test than in the video phase. While low and intermediate state anxiety scorers felt more involved in the polygraph phase than in the video phase, high state anxiety scorers felt no difference in involvement. For the less anxious participants (low and intermediate groups), both covert measures tended to be more accurate in the video phase than in the polygraph phase. For the more anxious participants, the two hidden measures were not at all effective in detecting concealed information in the video phase.

It seems that stress interferes with the inhibition of respiration responses. Such inhibition corresponds to enhanced attention to critical stimuli and to stronger responses to more significant items than to less significant items. It may be suggested that less stressful conditions are necessary for respiration measures to be effective in the CIT. Unfortunately, the video phase was unable to provide the optimal conditions for the examination of high state anxiety participants. It should be remembered that the present participants were all guilty and were aware of being interrogated. Under true covert conditions where examinees are unaware of the interrogation, the detachment of the polygraph transducers may be more effective in discriminating between actual knowledge and unknown information. Additional research is necessary to clarify this point.

COVERT RESPIRATION MEASURES IN THE GROUP CONCEALED INFORMATION TEST (GCIT): A PROMISE FOR THE FUTURE

Another form of the CIT is the searching CIT. Here, the guilty suspect is already identified and the interrogator suspects that this individual withholds information. A list of possible crime-related items of information is presented to the guilty suspect and the interrogator learns new facts about the crime from the suspects' physiological responses. Here, guilt is the known feature and new unknown information has to be detected and gathered. Anecdotal reports on the use of the searching CIT is occasionally published (e.g. MacLaren, 2001; Osugi, 2011).

However, there might be situations in which both the perpetrator is unknown and the critical information is lacking. Assuming that some people in a community (a group) know something about a future plot (e.g. security threat, terrorist attack, criminal felony and prisoners planning to escape) that might or might not be executed, and that different people may have different segmental knowledge of the event, it may be possible to use the searching CIT on a large group of people whose involvement in the plot is unknown. The task is to collect and combine these fragments of knowledge to a more complete picture of who, when, and what means will be used in the intended threatening activity.

Some experimental attempts have already been made in this direction under the name the 'Group Concealed Information Test' (GCIT). One study by Meijer, Smulders, and Merckelbach (2010) designed a mock terrorist scenario in which 12 participants were aware of three critical items of information. Using skin resistance responses as the sole physiological measure, they reported that all three critical items were detected. They concluded that with the CIT one can extract critical information about an upcoming terrorist attack. However, as the authors noted, their study was performed under ideal conditions where all the participants possessed the entire concealed information.

Another study conducted by Bradely and Barefoot (2010) used participants working in groups of 3–8 who witnessed either a person who made tea, a person who prepared a bomb or no staged event. Using field polygraph equipment, it was possible to identify the bomb-making information in four out of five bomb groups and the tea making information in three out of four tea groups. Again, in this study, the bomb groups were exposed to all the crime-related information, although they only remembered about half of the critical items.

Using the ERP-based CIT, Meixner and Rosenfeld (2011) designed a mock terrorist attack where participants planned an attack that they have not yet carried out. Twelve guilty participants choose the location, date and method of the planned attack and were fully aware of the critical information. Twelve innocent participants were ignorant of the crime-related details. It appeared that all 12 guilty participants were correctly identified and no false positive was observed among the 12 innocent participants. However, the more useful result corresponds to the elicitation of unknown information. As indicated, authorities may not know the nature of the critical information and might want to test a suspect for this information. Thus, Meixner and Rosenfeld (2011) conducted a test in which the item that produced the largest P300 response was assumed to be the critical item. It was then compared with the next largest response in the block of items. Results showed that 21 out of 36 critical details were successfully identified.

A recent study (Elaad, 2013) continued this line of research. A mock crime (prisoners planning to escape) procedure was used in which 52 undergraduate students were randomly, but not equally, allocated into 15 independent groups. In each group, participants possessed knowledge about 2 out of 6 critical items such that all possible combinations of the two known items were equally represented. Six series of questions were presented to the examinees while their physiological responses were recorded. Using skin conductance response amplitude, 3 out of 6 critical items were identified (elicited the largest responses). With the covert back respiration line length and finger pulse waveform length, 4 out of 6 critical items were identified. The combined measure, defined as the mean of the three individual measures, identified 5 out of 6 critical items. This is the first time that the capability of the covert back respiration measure to extract segmental information possessed by some members of a group was demonstrated.

It is necessary to continue this line of research to develop capabilities for gathering accurate information before a plot (e.g. security threat, criminal activity, commercial leakage and plan to escape) initiated by certain people may strike. This is most relevant in situations where not everyone is aware of the critical information and most examinees are not involved in the plot but possess some partial information that is accessible to them as they are part of a certain culture. For example, a drug culture where users are not highly criminal but are aware of dealers and suppliers of drugs; or villagers in occupied areas (e.g. Afghanistan) who may have some information about intended terrorist operations, which they are reluctant to share with the troops (Bradley & Barefoot, 2010); or a prison population that may share knowledge about drugs, hidden weapons and escape plans, which they conceal from the prison authorities.

The population from which the information is gathered is expected to be rather sensitive because of cultural barriers, divided loyalty and perceived danger (Bradley & Barefoot, 2010). Therefore, many would be reluctant to share the information with the authorities (police interrogators, prison authority and troops). The solution is properly conducted questionings which are not threatening. The use of covert physiological measures in general and covert respiration indices in particular may help in this respect. To date, a comprehensive research on unobtrusive GCIT testing was not yet initiated and its application in actual testing remains a promise for the future.

COUNTER-COUNTERMEASURES IN THE COMPARISON QUESTION TEST (CQT) USING COVERT RESPIRATION MEASURES

The CQT may face the problem of specific point (SP) countermeasures. SP countermeasures are designed to beat the test by affecting the differential responding to relevant and comparison questions. However, for the SP countermeasures to be effective, training and knowledge of how to use the countermeasures is essential. Honts and his colleagues conducted series of mock crime studies on countermeasures in the CQT. Participants in these studies were fully informed about the nature of the CQT and about its rationale. They were specifically told how and when to use the countermeasures and were coached in using them unobtrusively. Using physical countermeasures (either biting their tongue and/or pressing their toes to the floor) during comparison questions' presentation yielded a false-negative rate of 47% among the countermeasure-trained examinees (Honts, Hodes, & Raskin, 1985). In a follow up study, the mock crime situation was replicated in a stronger motivational context (Honts, Raskin, & Kircher, 1987). The false-negative error rate increased to 70%. In another study (Honts, Raskin, & Kircher, 1994), participants were asked to use mental countermeasures (pick a number larger than 200 and then count silently backwards by sevens each time a control question is asked). The mental countermeasure produced a significant effect but not as strong as the effect that the physical countermeasures produced.

As in the case of the CIT, it may be possible to combat countermeasures by using covert respiration measures. It is expected that CQT examinees, not yet connected to the polygraph, have no reason to employ countermeasure attempts. Therefore, the CQT may start with an interim session in which the questions are asked while the examinee is not connected to the polygraph but covert respiration responses are being recorded. This unexpected session can be introduced as a provisional session that is designed to help the suspect get used to the test. At least in Israel, respiration responses are regarded as the most useful indices in the CQT and receive most of the examiners' attention. It will be easy for a skillful examiner to see the difference between the respiration responses to relevant and comparison questions in the interim session and those in the test sessions. A conclusion whether or not countermeasures were attempted can be easily reached. However, comprehensive research should precede the introduction of the covert respiration test.

A covert respiration test is more promising than the old means for detecting countermeasures attempts in the CQT. For example, the Silent Answer Test (SAT) in which the examinee is advised to listen to the questions but not answer them verbally. Thus, the examinee remains silent throughout the entire session. The guilty examinee is in no need to lie and is assumed to stop the countermeasures attempts to the relevant questions. Still, the examinees are attached to the polygraph transducers and are well aware that their physiological responses are being monitored.

ETHICAL CONSIDERATIONS

The use of covert measures may raise moral, legal and ethical concerns. One major concern relates to pre-examination consent that is currently required from polygraph examinees. Another concern corresponds to the question of privacy· that may be. violated by the unobtrusive measures. One way to deal with these concerns is to apply the unobtrusive measurement within the context of a polygraph test. In this case, it is important to receive a written consent of the examinee to be examined with the polygraph. Furthermore, examinees are entitled to be warned in advance that their responses, physiological and/or vocal, would be monitored throughout the entire test. In that case, examinees should sign a statement that they received and understood the warning and that they agree to be examined under these conditions. Such a pretest warning may satisfy the ethical considerations of properly informing the examinee about the test and, at the same time, make it possible to use covert measures. Obviously, this limits the applicability of the covert measures and stands in contrast to the wishes of some law enforcement and security personnel to be able to detect deception from a distance without informing the suspect of the procedure.

CONCLUDING REMARKS

In principle, it is possible to collect information about suspects without their awareness of being interrogated. Promising procedures may involve covert respiration measures, eye-tracking technologies such as changes in pupillary size, fixation duration and blinking rate as well as thermal imaging. Even the more controversial procedures such as the search for micro-expressions in the face and the use of voice stress analysers should not be abounded. Yet, additional work is needed to determine whether these procedures are effective covert measures. Furthermore, there must be additional thinking of how to use covert measures in correspondence with basic ethical requirements.

REFERENCES

Baker, L., Goldstein, R., & Stern, J. A. (1992). *The gaze control system and the detection of deception* (Final Report No. #90-F131400). Retrieved from ORD/ SRD, http://www.dtic/tr/fulltext/u2/a304658.pdf. Accessed 11 July 2014.

Barlow, D. H. (1988). *Anxiety and its disorders*. New York, NY: Guilford Press.

Bass, C., & Gardner, W. N. (1985). Respiratory and psychiatric abnormalities in chronic symptomatic hyperventilation. *British Medical Journal, 290*(6479), 1387–1390.

Ben-Shakhar, G., & Dolev, K. (1996). Psychophysiological detection through the guilty knowledge technique: Effects of mental countermeasures. *Journal of Applied Psychology, 81*(3), 273–281.

Ben-Shakhar G., & Elaad, E. (2003). The validity of psychophysiological detection of information with the guilty knowledge test: A meta-analytic review. *Journal of Applied Psychology, 88*(1),131–151.

Bond, C. F., Jr., & DePaulo, B. M. (2006). Accuracy of deception judgments. *Personality and Social Psychology Review, 10*(3), 214–234.

Bradley, M. T., & Barefoot, C. A. (2010). Eliciting information from groups: Social information and the CIT. *Canadian Journal of Behavioral Sciences, 42*(2), 109–115.

Bradley, M. T., & Janisse, M. P. (1979). Pupil size and lie detection: The effect of certainty on detection. *Psychology, 4*(1), 33–39.

Bradley, M. T., & Janisse, M. P. (1981a). Accuracy demonstration, threat, and the detection of deception: Cardiovascular, electrodermal, and pupillary measures. *Psychophysiology, 18*(3), 307–315.

Bradley, M. T., & Janisse, M. P. (1981b). Extraversion and the detection of deception. *Personality and Individual Differences, 2*(2), 99–103.

Brenner, M., Branscomb, H. H., & Schwartz, G. E. (1979). Psychological stress evaluator – Two test of a vocal measure. *Psychophysiology, 16*(4), 351–357.

Cestaro, V. L., & Dollins, A. B. (1994). *An analysis of voice responses for the detection of deception* (Report No. DoDPI94-R-0001). Ft. McClellan, AL: Department of Defense Polygraph Institute.

Cristie, R. V. (1935). Some types of respiration in the neuroses. *Quarterly Journal of Medicine, 28*, 427–432.

DePaulo, B. M., Lindsay, J. J., Malone, B. E., Muhlenbruck, L., Charlton, K., & Cooper, H. (2003). Cues to deception. *Psychological Bulletin, 129*(1), 74–118.

Dionisio, D. P., Granfolm, E., Hillix, W. A., & Pertine, W. F. (2001). Differentiation of deception using pupillary responses as an index of cognitive processing. *Psychophysiology, 38*(2), 205–211.

Ekman, P. (2001). *Telling lies. Clues to deceit in the marketplace, politics, and marriage*. New York, NY: Norton.

Elaad, E. (2013). Extracting critical information from segmental knowledge of groups using the concealed information test. *Psychophysiology, 50*, S42.

Elaad, E., & Ben-Shakhar, G. (1991). Effects of mental countermeasures on psychophysiological detection in the guilty knowledge test. *International Journal of Psychophysiology, 11*(2), 99–108.

Elaad, E., & Ben-Shakhar, G. (2008). Covert respiration measures for the detection of concealed information. *Biological Psychology, 77*(3), 284–291.

Elaad, E., & Ben-Shakhar, G. (2009). Countering countermeasures in the concealed information test using covert respiration measures. *Applied Psychophysiology and Biofeedback, 34*(3), 197–208.

Elaad, E., & Cohenca, D. (2014). *Reducing anxiety of anxious and less anxious examinees in the concealed information test using unobtrusive respiration measures.* Unpublished manuscript.

Elaad, E., Ginton, A., & Jungman, N., (1992). Detection measures in real-life criminal guilty knowledge tests. *Journal of Applied Psychology, 77*(5), 757–767.

Eriksson, A., & Lacerda, F. (2007). Charlatanry if forensic speech science: A problem to be taken seriously. *Journal of Speech, Language and the Law, 14*(2), 169–193.

Giesen, M., & Rollison, M. A. (1980). Guilty knowledge versus innocent associations: Effects of trait anxiety and stimulus context on skin conductance. *Journal of Research in Personality, 14*(1), 1–11.

Goldstein, R., Bauer, L. O., & Stern, J. A. (1992). Effects of task difficulty and interstimulus interval on blink parameters. *International Journal of Psychophysiology, 13*(2), 111–118.

Grossman, P. (1983). Respiration, stress and cardiovascular function. *Psychophysiology, 20*(3), 284–300.

Gudjonsson, G. H. (1982). Some psychological determinants of electrodermal responses to deception. *Personality and Individual Differences, 3*(4), 381–391.

Hannula, D. E., Althoff, R. R., warren, D. E., Riggs, L., Cohen, N. J., & Ryan, J. D. (2010). Worth a glance: Using eye movements to investigate the cognitive neuroscience of memory. *Frontiers in Neuroscience, 4*, 166.

Harnsberger, J. D., Hollien, H., Martin, C. A., & Hollien, K. A. (2009). Stress and deception in speech: Evaluating layered voice analysis. *Journal of Forensic Sciences, 53*(1), 183–193.

Heaver, B., & Hutton, S. M. (2011). Keeping an eye on the truth? Pupil size changes associated with recognition memory. *Memory, 19*(4), 398–405.

Heilveil, I. (1976). Deception and pupil size. *Journal of Clinical Psychology, 32*(3), 675–676.

Hollien, H., Harnsberger, J. D., Martin, C. A., & Hollien, K. A. (2008). Evaluation of the NITV CVSA. *Journal of Forensic Sciences, 53*(1), 183–193.

Honts, C. R., Devitt, M. K., Winbush, M., & Kircher, J. C. (1996). Mental and physical countermeasures reduce the accuracy of the concealed knowledge test. *Psychophysiology, 33*(1), 84–92.

Honts, C. R., Hodes, R. L., & Raskin, D. C. (1985). Effects of physical countermeasures on the physiological detection of deception. *Journal of Applied Psychology, 70*(1), 177–187.

Honts, C. R., Raskin, D. C., & Kircher, J. C. (1987). Effects of physical countermeasures and their electromyographic detection during polygraph tests for deception. *Journal of Psychophysiology, 1*(3), 241–247.

Honts, C. R., Raskin, D. C., & Kircher, J. C. (1994). Mental and physical countermeasures reduce the accuracy of polygraph tests. *Journal of Applied Psychology, 79*(2), 252–259.

Horvath, F. (1978). An experimental comparison of the psychological stress evaluator and the galvanic skin response in detection of deception. *Journal of Applied Psychology, 63*(3), 338–344.

Horvath, F. (1979). Effect of different motivational instructions on detection of deception with the psychological stress evaluator and the galvanic skin response. *Journal of Applied Psychology, 64*(3), 323–330.

Iacono, W. G., Boisvenu, G. A., & Fleming, J. A. E. (1984). Effects of diazepam and methylphenidate on the electrodermal detection of guilty knowledge. *Journal of Applied Psychology, 69*(2), 289–299.

Janisse, M. P., & Bradley, M. T. (1980). Deception, information and the pupillary response. *Perceptual and Motor Skills, 50*(3), 748–750.

Kahneman, D. (1973). *Attention and effort*. Englewood Cliffs, NJ: Prentice-Hall.

Knepp, M. M., & Friedman, B. H. (2008). Cardiac reactivity in high and low trait worry woman. *Psychophysiology, 45*, S11 (abstract).

Leal, S., & Vrij, A. (2008). Blinking during and after lying. *Journal of Nonverbal Behavior, 32*(4), 187–194.

Lippold, O. C. (1971). Physiological tremor. *Scientific American, 224*(3), 65–73.

Lubow, R. E., & Fein, O. (1996). Pupillary size in response to a visual guilty knowledge test: New technology for the detection of deception. *Journal of Experimental Psychology: Applied, 2*(2), 164–177.

Lykken, D. T. (1974). Psychology and the lie detection industry. *American Psychologist, 29*(10), 225–239.

Lykken, D. T. (1998). *A tremor in the blood. Uses and abuses of the lie detector* (2nd ed.). New York, NY: Plenum Trade.

MacLaren, V. V. (2001). A quantitative review of the guilty knowledge test. *Journal of Applied Psychology, 86*(4), 674–683.

Mann, S., Vrij, A., & Bull, R. (2002). Suspects, lies and videotape: An analysis of authentic high-stakes liars. *Law and Human Behavior, 26*(3), 365–376.

Meijer, E. H., Smulders, F. T. Y., & Merckelbach, H. L. G. J. (2010). Extracting concealed information from groups. *Journal of Forensic Sciences, 55*(6), 1607–1609.

Meijer, E. H., Verschuere, B., Vrij, A., Merckelbach, H., Smulders, F., Leal, S., ... Gronau, N. (2009). A call for evidence-based security tools. *Open Access Journal of Forensic Psychology, 1*, 1–4.

Meixner, J. B., & Rosenfeld, P. J. (2011). A mock terrorism application of the p300-based concealed information test. *Psychophysiology, 48*(2), 149–154.

National Research Council. (2003). *The polygraph and lie detection*. Committee to Review the Scientific Evidence on the Polygraph. Division of Behavioral and Social Sciences and Education. Washington, DC: The National Academies Press.

Osugi, A. (2011). Daily application of the concealed information test: Japan. In B. Verschuere, G. Ben-Shakhar, and E. Meijer (Eds.), *Memory detection: Theory and application of the concealed information test* (pp. 253–275). Cambridge, UK: Cambridge University Press.

Pavlidis, I., Eberhardt, N. L., & Levin, J. A. (2002). Seeing through the face of deception: Thermal imaging offers a promising hands-off approach to mass security screening. *Nature, 415*, 35.

Pollina, D. A., Dollins, A. B., Senter, S. M., Brown, T. E., Pavlidis, I., Levine, J. A., & Ryan, A. H. (2006). Facial skin surface temperature changes during a 'Concealed Information' test. *Journal of Biomedical Engineering, 34*(7), 1182–1189.

Pollina, D. A., & Ryan, A. (2002). The relationship between facial skin surface temperature reactivity and traditional polygraph measures used in the psychophysiological detection of deception: A preliminary investigation. Ft. Jackson, SC: U.S. Department of Defense Polygraph Institute.

Porter, S., & Ten Brinke, L. (2008). Reading between the lies: How do facial expressions reveal concealed and fabricated emotions? *Psychological Science, 19*(5), 508–514. doi:10.1111/j.1467-9280.2008.02116.x

Raskin, D. C., & Honts, C. R. (2002). The comparison question test. In M. Kleiner (Ed.), *Handbook of polygraph testing* (pp. 1–48). San Diego, CA: Academic Press.

Ryan, J. D., Hannula, D. E., & Cohen, N. J. (2007). The obligatory effects of memory on eye movements. *Memory, 15*(5), 508–525.

Schwedes, C., & Wentura, D. (2012). The revealing glance: Eye gaze behavior to concealed information. *Memory and Cognition, 40*(4), 642–651.

Seymour, T. L., Baker, C. A., & Gaunt, J. T. (2013). Combining blink, pupil, and response time measures in a concealed knowledge test. *Frontiers in Psychology, 3,* 614. Published online February 4. doi:10.3389/fpsyg.2012.00614.

Sommers, M. S., Brown, T. E, Senter, S. M., & Ryan, A. H., Jr. (2002). Evaluating the reliability and validity of Vericator as a voice-based measure of deception. *International Journal of Psychophysiology, 45*, 28 (abstract).

Spielberger, C. S. (1975). The measurement of state and trait anxiety: Conceptual and methodological issues. In L. Levi (Ed.), *Emotions – Their parameters and measurement* (pp. 713–725). New York, NY: The Raven Press.

Stromwall, L. A., & Granhag, P. A. (2003). How to detect deception? Arresting the beliefs of police officers, prosecutors and judges. *Psychology, Crime, and law, 9*(1), 19–36.

Vrij, A. (2008). *Detecting lies and deceit: Pitfalls and opportunities* (2nd ed.). Chichester, UK: Wiley.

Vrij, A., Mann, S., & Leal, S. (2013). Deception traits in psychological interviewing. *Journal of Police and Criminal Psychology, 28*, 115. Published online 12 June 2013. doi:10.1007/s11896-013-9125-y

Warmelink, L., Vrij, A., Mann, S., Leal, S., Forrester, D., & Fisher, R. P. (2011). Thermal imaging as a lie detection tool at airports. *Law and Human Behavior, 35*(1), 40–48.

Weinberger, S. (2010). Airport security: Intent to deceive? *Nature, 465*(7297), 412–415.

Index

Detecting Deception: Current Challenges and Cognitive Approaches, First Edition.
Edited by Pär Anders Granhag, Aldert Vrij, and Bruno Verschuere.
© 2015 John Wiley & Sons, Ltd. Published 2015 by John Wiley & Sons, Ltd.